DATE DUE

DEMCO 38-296

THE CLINICAL USE
AND INTERPRETATION OF
THE WECHSLER INTELLIGENCE SCALE
FOR CHILDREN®—THIRD EDITION

ABOUT THE AUTHOR

Shawn Cooper has a Ph.D. in Clinical Psychology from the University of Massachusetts at Amherst, and an M.P.H. degree from the Harvard School of Public Health. He is an Associate Psychologist at the Mental Health Service at Harvard University in Cambridge, Massachusetts, and in private practice in Providence, Rhode Island.

THE CLINICAL USE AND INTERPRETATION OF THE WECHSLER INTELLIGENCE SCALE FOR CHILDREN®–THIRD EDITION

By

SHAWN COOPER, PH.D., M.P.H.

CHARLES C THOMAS • PUBLISHER

Springfield • Illinois • U.S.A.

Published and Distributed Throughout the World by

CHARLES C THOMAS • PUBLISHER
2600 South First Street
Springfield, Illinois 62794-9265

© *1995 by* CHARLES C THOMAS • PUBLISHER

ISBN 0-398-06523-3   (cloth)
ISBN 0-398-06524-1   (paper)

Library of Congress Catalog Card Number: 95-14202

With THOMAS BOOKS *careful attention is given to all details of manufacturing
and design. It is the Publisher's desire to present books that are satisfactory as to their
physical qualities and artistic possibilities and appropriate for their particular use.*
THOMAS BOOKS *will be true to those laws of quality that assure a good name
and good will.*

Printed in the United States of America
SC-R-3

Library of Congress Cataloging-in-Publication Data

Cooper, Shawn.
   The clinical use and interpretation of the Wechsler intelligence
scale for children—revised / by Shawn Cooper.—3rd ed.
      p.   cm.
   Includes bibliographical references and index.
   ISBN 0-398-06523-03 (cloth). —ISBN 0-398-06524-1 (pbk.)
   1. Wechsler Intelligence Scale for Children.   I. Title.
   [DNLM: 1. Wechsler Scales.   BF 432.5.W42 C778c 1995]
BF432.5.W42C66   1995
155.4'1393—dc20
DNLM/DLC
for Library of Congress   95-14202
                                                                        CIP

To Lesley
And to Jessica and Liza

PREFACE

I was born in New York City, the second of two brothers in an intact family. I grew up in a basically middle-class neighborhood in upper Manhattan, attended public schools throughout my elementary, secondary, and college educations, and thus was exposed to all the different kinds of people and experiences the city has to offer.

I attended the High School of Music & Art, planning to become an illustrator. After an uphill freshman year at Pratt Institute and in dealing with my own family issues, I decided to become a psychologist. I wound up working days while attending Hunter College of the City University of New York at night, then in the daytime, and upon graduation was accepted at the University of Massachusetts at Amherst where I obtained a Master's Degree and later my Doctorate in Clinical Psychology.

I came to Rhode Island for an internship in Clinical Psychology at a freestanding Children's Psychiatric Hospital and continued there for a number of years after my internship, as Chief Psychologist of the Out-Patient Clinic, and then as a part-time Staff Psychologist dealing with children, adolescents, and families, until the mid-late 1980s when I left that facility. During these years, I began my own private practice in Clinical Psychology, dealing with the assessment and treatment of children, adolescents, adults and families as well as with the provision of various kinds of school and agency consultation. Although my early training was in psycho-analytically oriented approaches to treatment, in the late 1960s, I became more interested in behavioral strategies in therapy, and over the years I have ordinarily integrated these two approaches as well as systems theory in my clinical work.

Along the way, I married, which I still am, and helped in the parenting of two daughters who are now in their early adulthoods.

In the mid 1980s, I obtained a Master of Public Health Degree at the Harvard School of Public Health, and for the past several years I have worked half-time at the Mental Health Service at Harvard University in Cambridge, Massachusetts while maintaining a private practice in Providence, Rhode Island.

It is my intent to make this book one that emphasizes conceptual approaches and original perspectives on using the WISC–III in the context of research that has been carried out with the Wechsler scales and the WISC–III. It is also my hope that the book will contain ideas about, and ways of looking at, the testing situation that may enable the reader to shift her or his paradigm for thinking about the clinical situation in general. I hope the ideas contained in the book are valuable enough that even clinicians who never use the WISC–III or who do not even believe in testing will find some of it worth reading. Lastly, I know that books have half lives, periods of time during which they are relevant and then cease to be consulted. It is my hope that this book will present ideas that will give the book a very long half life and make it meaningful to any clinician as he or she develops through, and at any point during, her or his professional career.

S.C.

INTRODUCTION

The present author believes that clinical interactions with clients or patients, analogous to life itself, involve a number of alternative pathways. Basically, the author believes that life is comprised of a series of choice points which individuals confront constantly. At each of these choice points, individuals select one pathway or another, or at times have the path chosen for them. Once the path has been selected, the individual proceeds down the chosen path toward, into, and through some particular experience or set of experiences. The individual's selection of a path, if he or she is the one to choose, and the behaviors she or he displays may reflect biological predisposition or necessity, past learning or the response to some immediately felt impulse.

A second relevant perspective on human behavior is the concept of context. It is the author's view that things in life occur within a particular context that provides the occurrence with meaning. The context of life events helps to define them, permits the individuals involved to make sense of their experience, and provides a structure that facilitates memory of what has occurred. Hence the author believes it is important to consider the context or multiple contexts within which life events occur.

A third important view of human behavior involves the concept of belief. It is the present author's conviction that aside from psychoanalytic constructs which propose unconscious motivation for human action (e.g., Freud, 1966), individuals' behavior follows from their belief systems. This view is represented by current cognitive and cognitive-behavioral formulations, which suggest that cognitions and thoughts underlie the way people interpret life events, how they feel and what behavior they engage in (Kendall, Vitousek, & Kane, 1991). It is the present author's view that the way individuals approach and process information, attempt to organize their life experience, and the decisions they make reflect their underlying belief systems.

The author thus conceptualizes psychological assessment from within such perspectives as path, context and belief. The encounter between a psychologist and an examinee reflects the intersection of two life paths with whatever set of historical antecedents exist in the backgrounds of the two participants. The context or multiple contexts for an assessment—for example,

ix

the setting of the evaluation, the reason or purpose for the evaluation, and the characteristics of the participants—provide an overall structure within which the evaluation occurs. And the set of beliefs held by the examiner will dictate her or his approach to the test situation, the interpretation of the resulting data, and the form in which the findings are reported.

Similarly, the particular way in which a psychologist conceptualizes the assessment process itself involves a choice among paths. It is the present author's intention to describe a number of alternative paths for the examiner to consider in his or her thinking about the intellectual assessment of children and adolescents. The author intends also to provide a number of potential frameworks, or contexts, and ways of thinking about or conceptualizing assessment that will transcend intellectual assessment itself. Lastly, this volume may provide data or perspectives that will either reinforce the reader's already held beliefs, or perhaps change some of those beliefs about the testing process.

Hopefully, the ideas presented in this volume will be of value to any clinician engaging in clinical work, whether it is the specific intellectual assessment of a child or adolescent, whether it is a more comprehensive assessment of a person's intellectual functioning and personality organization, or whether it is in some other form of clinical activity.

A GENERAL VIEW REGARDING INTELLECTUAL ASSESSMENT

The present author makes the assumption that the individual child is a psychobiological organism that progresses through a developmental trajectory which is determined by both genetic/biological as well as experiential factors (Plomin, 1989; Weinberg, 1989). The child's development and behavior occur within the context of a number of intrapersonal, interpersonal and extrapersonal systems, all of which contribute to and shape the functioning of the child at any point in time.

The present author also believes that intelligence is intertwined with aspects of personality and overall adaptive style. Although a child's performance on an intelligence test may not provide definitive information about the child's personality, the examiner assessing a child's intellectual functioning should remember that the child's intelligence is an integral part of the child as a total person. Thus, intellectual assessment provides information regarding the child's cognitive ability as it appears within the context of the child's personal style of being in the world (Zimmerman & Woo-Sam, 1985).

The present author also believes it is never wise, nor really possible, to draw definitive conclusions about an individual based on any one sample of behavior or functioning. In the assessment of any child, it is most reasonable to utilize a battery of assessment instruments including formal tests, interviewing, reports of significant others in the child's life, and possibly behavioral observations (Goldstein & Hersen, 1990).

These multiple sources of information will be likely to provide the most meaningful set of data from which to draw inferences and conclusions about the child and her or his adaptation, and to make recommendations for any intervention regarding the child and the systems within which he or she functions. It is important for the examiner to realize that both the examiner and the child who is evaluated exist within multiple systems (Fine, 1992; see discussion of systems theory below), and these must be considered during the course of the assessment and the interpretation of the data obtained. However, despite these caveats, this book will focus on the use of the WISC–III itself as an instrument for the intellectual assessment of children and adolescents.

ACKNOWLEDGMENTS

I would like to express my thanks to several individuals whose support and assistance in the writing of this book deserve extra mention. First, I would like to thank Mrs. Sylvia Gerhard of the John Peabody Monks Library at The Harvard University Health Services for her assistance in the initial literature search and in obtaining some of the materials which were used in writing this book. Her kindness is very much appreciated.

I would also like to express my special thanks to Bruce A. Bracken, Ph.D., for his good wishes in addition to his permission to reprint materials he authored or which appeared in the *Journal of Psychoeducational Assessment*. Similarly, I would like to offer many thanks to Jack A. Naglieri, Ph.D., for his kind wishes in addition to his permission to reprint materials he authored.

I would also like to thank Aurelio Prifitera, Ph.D., of The Psychological Corporation® for his good wishes and his permission to reprint materials which appeared in an article he authored with Jeffrey Dersh.

I would also like to thank Thomas H. Harrell, Ph.D., of Psychologistics, Inc.; Mr. Richard Grimord of Psychological Assessment Resources, Inc.; and Hugh Poyner, Ph.D., of The Psychological Corporation®, for their responses to my questionnaire regarding computerized-interpretive programs for the WISC–III offered by their respective organizations.

I would also like to express my appreciation to Williams & Wilkins/Waverly for their permission to include selected quotes from David Wechsler's book, *The Measurement and Appraisal of Adult Intelligence Fourth Edition* (Wechsler, 1958).

Last but most important to me, I would like to express my special gratitude to Lesley Cooper, my wife and best friend, for her inspiration and loving support in the writing of this book and in all my other life endeavors.

CONTENTS

PART III: FOUNDATIONS OF TESTING WITH THE WISC-III

PART V: THE PSYCHOLOGICAL REPORT

PART VI: SPECIAL TOPICS

PART VII: CONCLUDING COMMENT

FIGURES

TABLES

THE CLINICAL USE
AND INTERPRETATION OF
THE WECHSLER INTELLIGENCE SCALE
FOR CHILDREN®—THIRD EDITION

Part I
BACKGROUND ISSUES

Chapter One

THE FUTURE OF INTELLIGENCE TESTING

One of the major concepts dealt with in this volume is that of context. And one of the contexts within which psychology and all of us exist is the evolutionary (and sometimes revolutionary) changes that occur in society with the passage of time. One of the major activities of clinical and school psychologists throughout their professional histories has been that of testing (e.g., Wade & Baker, 1977). Intelligence tests have been among the most frequently administered of all tests given by clinical psychologists (Archer, Maruish, Imhof & Piotrowski, 1991; Korchin, 1976), and school psychologists administer intelligence tests more frequently than they do any other category of tests (Goh, Teslow, & Fuller, 1981). Hence as the end of the twentieth century and the beginning of the twenty-first century approach, it is reasonable to ask what the future of intellectual assessment will involve.

In regard to this issue, Matarazzo (1992) states that for the types of currently established individually- and group-administered tests of intelligence, he predicts few radical changes in either the types of tests or the kinds of test items that will be utilized in the assessment of individual differences in mental ability. Matarazzo (1992) bases his conclusion on the fact that in the early development of his scale, Binet (Binet & Simon, 1916) had discovered the kinds of items that reflect what Spearman (1904) identified as general intelligence. Because these kinds of items have good face validity as well as both concurrent and predictive validity, Matarazzo (1992) predicts that tests such as the Binet, Wechsler and Scholastic Aptitude Test, comprised of these items, will continue to be in wide use for the next several decades, although they will likely also be administered in languages other than English.

Matarazzo (1992), Kaufman (1990), and Sattler (1990) cite accumulating laboratory evidence that individuals' scores on a variety of biological measures correlate significantly with their scores on traditional measures of general intelligence. These biological measures include such things as: (a) individual differences in average evoked potential obtained from electroencephalographic recordings (Hendrickson, 1982); (b) individual differences in the length of both simple and more complex reaction times (Jensen,

---

*Note: "WISC-III" and "Wechsler Intelligence Scale for Children" and the "WISC-III logo" are registered trademarks of The Psychological Corporation. Their use herein does in no way indicate endorsement of this product by The Psychological Corporation.

1982, 1985; Vernon, 1987, 1990; Vernon & Kantor, 1986; Vernon & Mori, 1992); (c) visual stimulus inspection times (Sattler, 1990); (d) the trial-to-trial variability in individuals' specific reaction times and physiological measures (Hendrickson, 1982); and (e) significant correlations between the rate at which glucose is utilized by the brain and traditional IQ measures (Haier, Siegel, Nuechterlein, Hazlet, Wu, Paek, Browning, & Buchsbaum, 1988).

Therefore, in addition to the continued use of currently standard IQ measures, Matarazzo (1992) anticipates that in the near future, there will be advances in the development and use of techniques that evaluate intelligence by brain-imaging methods, such as positron emission tomography, and by strategies that measure the neurophysiological and neurochemical aspects of cortical functioning.

Although stating that the basic features of such tests as the Binet and Wechsler will remain fundamentally unchanged, Matarazzo (1992) does note his anticipation that the specific test items included on such tests will be refined based on the knowledge derived from cognitive psychology, information processing theories, and new concepts of developmental psychology (e.g., Sternberg, 1985b). Furthermore, based on research in cognition, there may not only be new test items but forms of individually administered intelligence tests comprised of entirely new types of verbal and performance items, such as those proposed by Naglieri and Das (1990).

Lastly, Matarazzo (1992) predicts that in the future there will be significant advances in both the technology and validation studies which will permit the administration and interpretation of a number of computerized versions of intellectual tests, with this allowing computerized assessment to become both practical and socially responsive (Azar, 1994). Such computer capability will enable clinicians to combine multiple data sources into an integrated "psychological-behavioral profile" of the individual (Matarazzo, 1992, p. 1016). Other psychologists express much greater enthusiasm than Matarazzo regarding the role computers will play in the psychological assessment as well as the treatment of individuals in the near future (e.g., see Schlosser & Moreland, 1993).

In the next decade, then, both continuity and change will characterize psychological assessment. It appears that there will be continued use of the traditional individually administered psychological test such as the WISC–III. In addition, however, based on continuing theoretical developments, there will be a wide variety of newly devised item forms and tests that will more precisely assess the thinking and reasoning capacities of children and adults. Further, there will be an increasing utilization of technologies that measure biological characteristics of individuals—including such qualities as brain size, nerve transmission velocity, and brain glucose metabolism—as highly sophisticated strategies for assessing individual variation in what we conceive of as intelligence.

Chapter Two

ETHICS AND THE WISC-III

In recent years ethics have become a critical focus in all of psychological practice (Koocher, 1976; Pope, 1991). Therefore any discussion of the clinical use of a test instrument such as the WISC–III needs to include a consideration of the ethical issues involved in testing.

If the reader of this volume has never read or has not recently read the most current version of the *Ethical Principles of Psychologists and Code of Conduct* of the American Psychological Association (American Psychological Association, 1992), or the *Principles for Professional Ethics* of the National Association of School Psychologists (National Association of School Psychologists, 1992), reading of one or both of these documents is highly recommended. Insofar as these Ethical Standards provide a framework from within which all clinical and/or school psychological practice should be carried out, reading and understanding of these Standards is a necessity as part of one's functioning as a psychologist, whether one is involved in providing psychological assessment, providing counseling or therapy, or offering consultation to the public.

Although the Principles in either of the above-noted documents are relevant in their entirety to the psychologist providing psychological assessment services, the most germane sections of the American Psychological Association Principles are those included in the "Preamble" (*American Psychologist,* 1992, p. 1599), "General Principles" (*American Psychologist,* 1992, pp. 1599–1600) and those in Section 2, "Evaluation, Assessment, or Intervention" (*American Psychologist,* 1992, pp. 1603–1604).

Section 2, "Evaluation, Assessment, or Intervention" excerpted from the American Psychological Association *Ethical Principles of Psychologists and Code of Conduct (American Psychologist,* 1992, pp. 1603–1604) appears in Table 1 for the reader's information.

The most relevant sections of the National Association of School Psychologists Principles are those in Section II, "Professional Competency" (National Association of School Psychologists, 1992, p. 6), Section III, "Professional Relationships and Responsibilities" (National Association of School Psychologists, 1992, pp. 6–10), and Section IV, "Professional Practices—Public and Private Settings" (National Association of School Psychologists, 1992, pp. 10–12).

Table 1

EXCERPT FROM THE AMERICAN PSYCHOLOGICAL ASSOCIATION
ETHICAL PRINCIPLES OF PSYCHOLOGISTS AND CODE OF CONDUCT

2. Evaluation, Assessment, or Intervention

2.01 Evaluation, Diagnosis, and Interventions in Professional Context

    (a) Psychologists perform evaluations, diagnostic services, or interventions only within the context of a defined professional relationship.

    (b) Psychologists' assessments, recommendations, reports, and psychological diagnostic or evaluative statements are based on information and techniques (including personal interviews of the individual when appropriate) sufficient to provide appropriate substantiation for their findings.

2.02 Competence and Appropriate Use of Assessments and Interventions

    (a) Psychologists who develop, administer, score, interpret, or use psychological assessment techniques, interviews, tests, or instruments do so in a manner and for purposes that are appropriate in light of the research on or evidence of the usefulness and proper application of the techniques.

    (b) Psychologists refrain from misuse of assessment techniques, interventions, results and interpretations and take reasonable steps to prevent others from misusing the information these techniques provide. This includes refraining from releasing raw test results or raw data to persons, other than to patients or clients as appropriate, who are not qualified to use such information.

2.03 Test Construction

Psychologists who develop and conduct research with tests and other assessment techniques use scientific procedures and current professional knowledge for test design, standardization, validation, reduction or elimination of bias, and recommendations for use.

2.04 Use of Assessment in General and With Special Populations

    (a) Psychologists who perform interventions or administer, score, interpret, or use assessment techniques are familiar with the reliability, validation and related standardization or outcome studies of, and proper applications and uses of, the techniques they use.

    (b) Psychologists recognize limits to the certainty with which diagnoses, judgments, or predictions can be made about individuals.

    (c) Psychologists attempt to identify situations in which particular interventions or assessment techniques or norms may not be applicable or may require readjustment in administration or interpretation because of factors such as individuals' gender, age, race, ethnicity, national origin, religion, sexual orientation, disability, language or socioeconomic status.

2.05 Interpreting Assessment Results

When interpreting assessment results, including automated interpretations, psychologists take into account the various test factors and characteristics of the person being assessed that might affect psychologists' judgments or reduce the accuracy of their interpretations. They indicate any significant reservations they have about the accuracy or limitations of their interpretations.

2.06 Unqualified Persons

Psychologists do not promote the use of psychological assessment techniques by unqualified persons.

2.07 Obsolete Tests and Outdated Test Results

(a) Psychologists do not base their assessment or intervention decisions or recommendations on data or test results that are outdated for the current purpose.

(b) Similarly, psychologists do not base such decisions or recommendations on tests and measures that are obsolete and not useful for the current purpose.

2.08 Test Scoring and Interpretation Services

(a) Psychologists who offer assessment or scoring procedures to other professionals accurately describe the purpose, norms, validity, reliability, and applications of the procedures and any special qualifications applicable to their use.

(b) Psychologists select scoring and interpretation services (including automated services) on the basis of evidence of the validity of the program and procedures as well as on other appropriate considerations.

(c) Psychologists retain appropriate responsibility for the appropriate application, interpretation, and use of assessment instruments, whether they score and interpret such tests themselves or use automated or other services.

2.09 Explaining Assessment Results

Unless the nature of the relationship is clearly explained to the person being assessed in advance and precludes provision of an explanation of results (such as in some organizational consulting, preemployment or security screening, and forensic evaluations), psychologists ensure that an explanation of the results is provided using language that is reasonably understandable to the person assessed or to another legally authorized person on behalf of the client. Regardless of whether the scoring and interpretation are done by the psychologist, by assistants, or by automated or other outside services, psychologists take reasonable steps to ensure that appropriate explanations of results are given.

2.10 Maintaining Test Security

Psychologists make reasonable efforts to maintain the integrity and security of tests and other assessment techniques consistent with law, contractual obligations, and in a manner that permits compliance with the requirements of this Ethics Code.

The most relevant sections of the National Association of School Psychologists Principles are those in Section II, "Professional Competency" (National Association of School Psychologists, 1992, p. 6), Section III, "Professional Relationships and Responsibilities" (National Association of School Psychologists, 1992, pp. 6–10), and Section IV, "Professional Practices—Public and Private Settings" (National Association of School Psychologists, 1992, pp. 10–12).

Section IV, "Professional Practices—Public and Private Settings," excerpted from the National Association of School Psychologists *Principles for Professional Ethics* (National Association of School Psychologists, 1992, pp. 10–12) appears in Table 2 for the reader's information.

RELEVANCE OF THE ETHICAL PRINCIPLES TO THE WISC-III

There are several basic similarities in the APA and NASP Ethical codes related to use of the WISC–III. Both Ethical codes emphasize the fact that the examiner must view testing or assessment as occurring in a professional relationship and that a primary concern of the examiner must be the rights, welfare and personal integrity of the particular individual being evaluated.

In terms of the WISC–III, this means that the psychologist should consider the specific purpose of testing any child and also determine if the WISC–III is the appropriate instrument to utilize. In addition, the psychologist providing an intellectual assessment with the WISC–III should view the testing interaction as one involving a professional relationship between the examiner and the child being evaluated, and one in which the personal integrity and rights of the child being assessed must be advocated for and be considered paramount.

Both the NASP and APA Ethical codes also stress the fact that psychologists who administer and score tests do so in a way which respects and reflects research-based conclusions about the test and its use, and both sets of Principles indicate that assessment techniques are utilized in a manner consistent with their design, intent, and established norms. In terms of the WISC–III, this means that the WISC–III is used for the evaluation of an individual's intellectual functioning rather than other constructs for which it was not intended; and that interpretation of the test should be carried out in relation to the published norms (Wechsler, 1991), and in relation to research investigations on the test that appear in the professional psychological and educational literature.

Both the APA and NASP Ethical codes note that psychologists who administer and score tests are familiar with the reliability, validity, and

Table 2

**EXCERPT FROM THE NATIONAL ASSOCIATION OF SCHOOL
PSYCHOLOGISTS** *PRINCIPLES FOR PROFESSIONAL ETHICS*

IV. PROFESSIONAL PRACTICES: PUBLIC AND PRIVATE SETTINGS

A) ADVOCACY

1. School psychologists consider the students or clients to be their primary responsibility, acting as advocates of their rights and welfare. When choosing a course of action, school psychologists take into account the rights of each individual involved and the duties of the school personnel.

2. School psychologists' concerns for protecting the rights and welfare of students is communicated to the school administration and staff and is the top priority in determining services.

B) ASSESSMENT AND INTERVENTION

1. School psychologists will maintain the highest standard for educational and psychological assessment.

    a) In conducting psychological, educational, or behavioral evaluation, or in providing therapy, counseling, or consultation services, due consideration will be given to individual integrity and individual differences.

    b) School psychologists respect differences in age, gender, socioeconomic, cultural, and ethnic backgrounds. They select and use appropriate assessment or treatment procedures, techniques, and strategies.

2. School psychologists collect relevant data using valid and reliable instruments and techniques that are applicable and appropriate for the benefit of the student or client.

3. School psychologists combine observations, background information, and information from other disciplines in order to reach comprehensive conclusions.

4. School psychologists use assessment techniques, counseling and therapy procedures, consultation techniques, and other direct service methods that the profession considers to be responsible, research-based practice.

5. School psychologists do not condone the use of psychological or educational assessment techniques by unqualified persons in any way, including teaching, sponsorship, or supervision.

6. School psychologists develop interventions which are appropriate to the presenting problems and are consistent with data collected. They modify or terminate the treatment plan when the data indicate the plan is not achieving the desired goals.

Source: National Association of School Psychologists *Principles for Professional Ethics* (National Association of School Psychologists, 1992, pp. 10–12). Copyright 1992 by the National Association of School Psychologists. Reprinted by permission of the publisher.

---

related standardization data on the technique being utilized. Psychologists also realize that particular individuals may differ in a variety of ways from the population on which the test was standardized, and this must be taken into consideration in interpreting the test or in making decisions about an individual based on the test findings.

C) USE OF MATERIALS AND TECHNOLOGY

1. School psychologists maintain test security, preventing the release of underlying principles and specific content that would undermine the use of the device.

2. School psychologists uphold copyright laws. Permission is obtained from authors to reproduce non-copyrighted published instruments.

3. School psychologists will obtain written prior consent or else remove identifying data presented in public lectures or publications.

4. When producing materials for consultation, treatment, teaching, public lectures, or publication, school psychologists acknowledge sources and assign credit to those whose ideas are reflected in the product. Recognition is given in proportion to the contribution. Plagiarism of ideas or product is a violation of professional ethics.

5. School psychologists do not promote or encourage inappropriate use of computer-generated test analyses or reports. For example, a school psychologist would not offer an unedited computer report as one's own writing, nor use a computer scoring system for tests in which one has no training.

6. School psychologists maintain full responsibility for any technological services used. All ethical and legal principles regarding confidentiality, privacy, and responsibility for decisions apply to the school psychologist and cannot be transferred to equipment, software companies, or data processing departments.

7. Technological devices should be used to improve the quality of client services. School psychologists will resist applications of technology that ultimately reduce the quality of service.

D) RESEARCH AND EVALUATION

1. In performing research, school psychologists accept responsibility for selection of topics, research methodology, subject selection, data gathering, analysis and reporting.

2. In publishing reports of their research, school psychologists provide discussion of limitations of their data and acknowledge existence of disconfirming data, as well as alternate hypotheses and explanations of their findings.

E) REPORTING DATA AND CONFERENCE RESULTS

1. School psychologists ascertain that student or client information reaches only authorized persons.

    a) The information is adequately interpreted so that the recipient can better help the student or client.

    b) The school psychologist assists agency recipients to establish procedures to properly safeguard the confidential material.

2. School psychologists communicate findings and recommendations in language readily understood by the intended recipient. These communications describe potential consequences associated with the proposals.

3. School psychologists prepare written reports in such form and style that the recipient of the report will be able to assist the student or client. Reports should emphasize recommendations and interpretations; reports which present only test scores or brief narratives describing a test are seldom useful. Reports should include an appraisal of the degree of confidence which could be assigned to the information.

4. School psychologists review all of their written documents for accuracy, signing them only when correct.

5. School psychologists comply with all laws, regulations and policies pertaining to the adequate storage and disposal of records to maintain appropriate confidentiality of information.

In terms of the WISC–III, this means that the psychologist must be familiar with the psychometric characteristics of the test as discussed in the manual (Wechsler, 1991) and as reviewed in other sources (e.g., Kamphaus, 1993; Sattler, 1992). In addition, the psychologist must realize that any particular individual tested with the WISC–III may differ from the standardization population in terms of such factors as race/ethnicity, physical handicap, or psychological state, and this must be considered when interpreting the test data or when making recommendations based on the data.

Both the NASP and APA guidelines also note the need to recognize limits as to the certainty with which diagnoses, judgments, or predictions can be made about individuals. That is, even with some degree of knowledge about the psychometric properties of the test and the test's normative population, it must be remembered that any test involves the sampling of a subset of behavior from a universe of behavior. No test or sample of human behavior allows for perfect characterization of the universe of behavior from which the sample was drawn.

In terms of the WISC–III, this means that the test provides a sample of a child's intellectual functioning, but the examiner must realize that any test involves an error of measurement and that a child's intellectual functioning may change over time. In addition, the examiner may be dealing with a child who varies from the standardization population in some significant way—e.g., by virtue of ethnic background or physical or emotional handicap. Hence, the examiner must take into consideration the nature of measurement error and the specific qualities or characteristics of the child being evaluated and therefore exercise due caution in drawing conclusions about a child's intellectual ability.

Both the APA and NASP Ethics codes point out that psychologists maintain the security of test instruments, do not promote the misuse of psychological assessment techniques, or allow assessment techniques to be used by individuals who are unqualified by virtue of education or training. In terms of the WISC–III, this means that psychologists do not reveal test content that might compromise the reliability or validity of the WISC–III should the child be retested with this instrument in the future.

Further, psychologists do not allow the test to be used to make decisions for which it is not appropriate, for example, using the WISC–III in isolation for diagnosis of psychological or emotional disorders. Finally, psychologists make reasonable efforts to prevent individuals with inadequate knowledge or training in the use of the test from administering or interpreting the WISC–III.

Both the NASP and APA Ethics codes note that psychologists do not employ assessment techniques which are outdated or where the test provides information that is irrelevant to the current purpose. This means that it is no longer appropriate to use the WISC–R for testing a child in the age range of 6 years through 16 years, 11 months now that the WISC–III has been published.

Although both the APA and NASP Ethics codes emphasize the importance of respecting the rights and dignity of the examinee, the APA standards specifically state that unless the circumstances of testing preclude this, psychologists ensure that results of testing are provided in language that is reasonably understandable to the person assessed or to another legally authorized person on behalf of the client. In terms of the WISC–III, this means that the psychologist should determine a specific plan for sharing the results of the testing with the child who has been tested and/or with the child's parent(s) or guardian. The model for assessment described in the present volume addresses this specific issue.

Although both the NASP and APA Ethics codes deal with protection of the rights of the client and any records generated, the APA standards specifically address the issue of maintenance of records, noting that psychologists maintain appropriate confidentiality in creating, storing, accessing, and disposing of records under their control. In terms of the WISC–III, this means that the psychologist using this instrument should be aware of the protocol generated, where it is stored, who has access to it, and how it is ultimately disposed of. Similarly, if any computerized records are generated or maintained, the psychologist should help to control these records in a responsible and ethical fashion.

Lastly, both the APA and NASP Ethics codes indicate that the psychologist maintains full responsibility for any technological services, such as computer scoring or interpretation, that may be utilized in the administration or interpretation of assessment instruments. In terms of the WISC–III, this means that the examiner takes responsibility for the accuracy, reliability, and validity of the findings she or he reports on an assessment; this responsibility cannot be shifted to a computer or technilogical device which has been used in the scoring or interpretation of a child's WISC–III test protocol.

GENERAL ISSUES REGARDING ETHICS IN PSYCHOLOGICAL PRACTICE

Morris (1993) notes that ethical issues arise in the practice of psychology when a psychologist engages in behavior that is inconsistent with the values and attitudes of the society in which the psychologist works, and the behavior is considered by the psychologist's own professional organization to be outside the boundaries of acceptable practice. Pope (1991), who has written extensively about ethical issues in psychological practice (e.g., Pope, 1989, 1990; Pope, Tabachnick, & Keith-Spiegel, 1987), notes that ethical standards have been conceptualized in a variety of frameworks.

The American Psychological Association, for example, focuses on a number of topic areas (e.g., General Standards; Privacy and Confidentiality) in its formulation of an ethics code (American Psychological Association, 1992), while Redlich and Pope (1980) suggest seven basic principles which should govern professional practice (e.g., avoiding harm, competence, and respect).

Essentially, an ethical code may be viewed as a set of guidelines that, although not defined by law, reflect the values or attitudes of a society as well as ideal standards for human conduct. These concepts are integrated with a set of practice statements set forth by one's professional organization to create an "ethical community" (Morris, 1993, p. 10) whose purpose is to promote the integrity of a given profession, structure the behavior of members of that profession, and to protect and promote the welfare of the consumer.

As noted above regarding the multiple contexts of assessment, the Ethical Standards of the psychologist's own professional organization should provide a broad context for his or her overall behavior as a professional. Within this context, the psychologist must develop and articulate a philosophy of testing or assessment. This philsophy should attempt to integrate the psychologist's personal beliefs about the value and appropriate function of testing with a code of ethics that reflects the psychologist's understanding of his or her role in society and in providing assessment services to a specific individual.

Although ethical codes represent frameworks which should guide and place limits on psychologists' behavior, there is ample evidence (e.g., Pope, Tabachnick, & Keith-Spiegel, 1987) that psychologists violate ethical standards at relatively high rates. This means that although one might ideally want to consider psychologists as behaving in a highly ethical fashion, this is an unfounded assumption.

It thus may be overly naive to assume that psychologists as a group are capable of displaying ethical behavior to any greater extent than any other group of human beings. Nonetheless, the present author would make the case for the reader to attempt a realistic application of these ethical principles to guide her or his activities as a psychologist. It may help the psychologist reflecting on the relevance of ethics in his or her practice to realize that the maintenance of high ethical standards is even more important when using the WISC–III since this test is designed for use with individuals who are under the age of majority and who, therefore, require additional consideration of their vulnerability as consumers of psychological services.

MAJOR AREAS OF ETHICAL CONCERN IN THE ASSESSMENT OF CHILDREN AND ADOLESCENTS

Morris (1993), in discussing ethical issues in the assessment of children and adolescents, focuses on four relevant issues: confidentiality, consent for assessment, dual relationships, and valid and reliable assessment procedures, and these will be reviewed below.

Confidentiality between a client and his or her therapist has been considered a vital part of the therapy relationship (Denkowski & Denkowski, 1982; Friedlander, 1982). Assessment of children and adolescents, however, is unique in that it is ordinarily the parent and not the child or adolescent who seeks the professional consultation. This then raises the question of how the clinician is to handle the responsibility of confidentiality when dealing with a child or adolescent client.

While the legal aspect of this issue is determined by statute (DeKraai & Sales, 1991a, 1991b), the ethical question is more difficult to resolve. The issue of confidentiality may be even more complicated when one is evaluating children or adolescents since the psychologist's objective is to obtain information about aspects and sources of the child's or adolescent's functioning that need to be shared with others in order to have a beneficial effect on the child's life.

One concept that facilitates the child's participation in the assessment and the examiner's handling of the issue of confidentiality is that of informed consent; and to satisfy the pertinent legal doctrine regarding this concept, consent by the individual must be voluntary, knowing, and competent (Brakal, Parry, & Weiner, 1985). From within the framework of informed consent, the psychologist should attempt to ensure that both the parent(s) or guardian and any child or adolescent who is to be evaluated are provided an explanation of the procedures which will be involved in the assessment as well as being informed what will happen to the information the child reveals during the assessment.

Morris (1993) suggests that whatever position a therapist takes on the issue of informed consent, this should be stated in writing, then signed and dated by the therapist, the child and the child's parents. The present author believes that in the case of testing, which often occurs at a child's school, the examiner may have no direct relationship with a child's parent, and hence Morris's (1993) suggestion may be unfeasible. However, before proceeding with testing of a child, the examiner should routinely check to determine that a child's parent or guardian has given appropriate consent for the child to be evaluated. Further, the examiner should review the consent form that is utilized to determine its appropriateness.

The present author recommends that the issue of confidentiality be handled within the context of consent for assessment. This means that a psychologist may only proceed with assessment of a child or adolescent under the age of 18 if: "(1) the psychologist has obtained written consent from the minor person's parent or legal guardian, or (2) that such psychological services have been ordered by the court, or (3) that the minor has been committed to an institution or is in a *bona fide* crisis or emergency situation" (Morris, 1993, p. 11).

When devising or designing a written consent form regarding the assessment of a child, the following elements should be considered for inclusion: the purpose of the psychological services to be provided; the type of assessment that will be provided; potential risks or negative consequences for the minor and/or his/her family that may result from the services; a confidentiality statement; and what will happen with the results of the assessment.

If the examiner intends to utilize the model discussed in this volume, which includes possible discussion of test results with the child evaluated, this should also be included in the consent form signed by the parent. In addition, the concepts of confidentiality and informed consent may be discussed with the child or adolescent at the beginning of the assessment.

Morris (1993) also discusses the ethics of dual relationships, noting that such relationships with clients may be considered to be unprofessional. Hence, the psychologist should carefully examine the nature of any relationship with a minor client that might be construed by the client, the client's parent(s) or the professional community as involving a dual relationship, one where the psychologist may function in more than one role in relation to the client, where the psychologist may have conflicting motives in her or his relationship to the client, or where the psychologist's knowledge of the client might be used to harm the client.

Consideration of this issue requires that the psychologist decide whether information gained in a psychological assessment of a child might be used by the psychologist in any other relationship with the child or the child's family in other settings than the professional relationship, or if the information obtained in such an assessment would be for the benefit of someone other than the child him- or herself.

Potential dual relationships which should be avoided would include, for example, the psychological assessment of children of the psychologist's own employees, colleagues, friends or associates; children or adolescents the psychologist is familiar with in other settings; or children or adolescents whose parents the psychologist interacts with frequently in either social or business relationships.

Although ideally, the psychologist should attempt to avoid all such dual relationships, in practice this may not be feasible, for example, if one is the only psychologist in a given community. If circumstances arise which appear to involve such dual relationships, it is reasonable for the psychologist to at least seek consultation from another psychologist, a State Psychological Board or the American Psychological Association to determine the most appropriate solution to the problem.

The present author's perspective on dual relationships with a child would emphasize the conflict an examiner may experience by being an employee of a school system with a set of significant interpersonal or financial relationships with that system, and yet having to provide an unbiased evaluation of a child's needs which might challenge the school system. It is this situation which could involve subtle or direct pressures on the examiner which might compromise his or her efforts to determine what services may be in the best interests of the child.

The last issue Morris (1993) deals with is that of valid and reliable assessment procedures. Ethical standards require that psychological assessment of individuals, whether adults or children, be conducted with reliable and valid test instruments. To this end, psychologists must determine that whatever test they are administering is utilized in a fashion consistent with the procedures used during standardization of the test; that the test has adequately established reliability and validity; and that the basic variables on which the test was normed apply to the particular individual who is being tested with the instrument.

If the conditions of an assessment do not meet the basic standards that applied during the standardization of the test instrument, the specific limitations of the findings, or any reservations the examiner has about the conclusions, should be stated clearly in the report which is generated regarding the assessment. Related to the issue of reliable and valid testing procedures is the requirement that the examiner has undergone appropriate training in the administration of individual tests in general and the specific test used in particular.

Thus, as noted above, the present author views psychological assessment in general, and intellectual assessment in particular, as occurring within a set of contexts or frameworks that define and guide the clinical process. The concept of ethical standards provides one such context for the psychologist providing an intellectual evaluation of a child with the WISC–III, and these guidelines should be kept in mind by the psychologist as he or she initiates, participates in, and concludes the testing of a particular child or adolescent.

Part II
DEVELOPMENT AND NATURE
OF THE WISC-III

Chapter Three

HISTORY OF THE WISC-III

The Wechsler Intelligence Scale for Children-Third Edition had its origin in the 1930s, when David Wechsler developed the first of his scales to measure the construct of intelligence (Wechsler, 1939). Wechsler put together a battery of tests that was comprised of subtests that had been developed by Binet (Binet & Simon, 1916) and World War I psychologists. Wechsler used tasks that others had devised for non-clinical purposes to create his battery, which he conceived of as a clinical instrument.

While others viewed intelligence tests as able to subdivide retarded individuals into various subgroups, Wechsler conceived of an intelligence test as a tool able to provide a variety of kinds of clinical information about the person tested. Many psychologists of his day did not see the value of utilizing nonverbal tasks with English-speaking populations. But Wechsler felt that verbal *and* performance items were equally important in assessing an individual's intellectual functioning.

The test Wechsler developed, the *Wechsler-Bellevue Intelligence Scale* (Wechsler, 1939), involved a standard battery of subtests which included both verbal and performance scales which were equally weighted in their contribution to the measurement of the individual's functioning. A major advantage of the test was that it provided a differentiated assessment of the examinee's intellectual functioning in that it yielded separate measures of the person's verbal, performance and overall abilities.

Additional features of Wechsler's original scale included the fact that the test yielded summary scores or IQs which were in the form of standard scores and hence had the same distributional characteristics across all ages of examinees; the same subtests were administered to all subjects; and each subtest contributed equally to the IQ scores at a given age. Each Wechsler Intelligence Scale devised since then has maintained these characteristics (e.g., Wechsler, 1949, 1955, 1967, 1974).

During the Second World War, Wechsler developed the *Wechsler-Bellevue Intelligence Scale Form II* (Wechsler, 1946) for use by the United States Army. The test was essentially considered an alternate form of the original Wechsler-Bellevue, and this test was extended downward to result in the *Wechsler Intelligence Scale for Children* (1949), for which the Wechsler-Bellevue provided most subtests and items. The *Wechsler Intelligence Scale for Children* later gave rise to the *Wechsler Preschool and Primary Scale of Intelligence* (1967), which was itself later revised and published as the *Wechsler Preschool and Primary Scale of Intelligence-Revised* (Wechsler, 1989), and the *Wechsler Intelligence Scale for Children* was revised to yield the *Wechsler Intelligence Scale for Children-Revised* (1974) which was itself revised to result in the *Wechsler Intelligence Scale for Children-Third Edition* (1991).

Wechsler (1991) notes that many of the test items which were prepared for the *Wechsler-Bellevue Intelligence Scale* have remained current and are also included in the WISC–III. While there has thus been some degree of specific item continuity in the Wechsler Scales for more than 50 years, the most essential similarity across all of the Wechsler scales is in terms of the domains assessed, the structure of the scales and the method used to obtain IQ scores.

WECHSLER'S CONCEPTION OF INTELLIGENCE

David Wechsler, the originator of the Wechsler Intelligence Scales, believed that intelligence was apparent not in any single way but instead it was evident in many different forms. He thus conceived of and defined intelligence not as a particular or specific ability but instead as "the aggregate and global capacity of the individual to act purposefully, to think rationally and to deal effectively with (sic) his environment" (Wechsler, 1958, p. 7).

Wechsler felt that intelligence was aggregate or global because it is comprised of elements or abilities which, although not completely independent of one another, are nonetheless qualitatively differentiable. Intelligence may also be considered global because it is a characteristic of the person's behavior as a whole (Zachary, 1990). Consistent with such a definition of intelligence, the subtests of the WISC–III were selected to assess a number of different cognitive abilities, which were felt overall to measure the examinee's general intellectual competence.

From within this perspective, no single subtest of the scale is assumed to reflect *all* facets of the examinee's intelligent behavior. Thus one subtest of the WISC–III may require the child or adolescent to utilize primarily verbal reasoning but not motor skill while another task may necessitate the examinee's utilization of visual motor coordination but not abstract reasoning. Hence, from within Wechsler's framework, it is not vital that a specific set of tasks always be used to measure an individual's intelligence; instead, an intelligence test must sample broadly from the full array of an individual's cognitive skills and thereby reflect the multifaceted nature of intelligence (Zachary, 1990).

Wechsler's view of intelligence as a unitary construct that must be measured by investigating a number of multifaceted abilities has several implications. First, the particular tasks one uses to assess intelligence may not be critical although they must vary and meet basic psychometric requirements. Second, no assumption is made about the relative value of the different abilities included in the measurement of intelligence; the different skills are weighted equally. Third, Wechsler believed that intelligence cannot be measured in an absolute sense; rather, one can only assess an individual's relative placement on a continuum of ability as compared to a referent group, ordinarily the examinee's peers of the same age (Zachary, 1990).

Based on this reasoning, it is assumed that the various tasks included in the current WISC–III do not necessarily cover all possible aspects of a person's intelligence. Rather, they provide a sample of the kinds of tasks that reflect an examinee's intelligent functioning. Certainly, other authors (e.g., Das, Naglieri, & Kirby, 1994; Kaufman & Kaufman, 1983; Naglieri & Das, 1990) have devised different approaches to the definition and assessment of the construct of intelligence.

The present scale, consistent with Wechsler's conceptualization (Wechsler, 1958), also posits that while the intellectual abilities present in the scale may be basic precursors of intelligent behavior, there are other determinants of an individual's intelligent functioning. These other "non-intellective" characteristics may involve traits, attitudes or personality features such as the capacity to use foresight, the individual's impulsivity-reflectivity (e.g., Brannigan & Ash, 1977), or the degree and kind of his or her psychological disturbance. These characteristics of the individual are not directly assessed by a test instrument and yet they may significantly influence an examinee's performance on such a test and may also impact on the person's adaptation to the real world.

Matarazzo (1972, 1990) also has addressed this issue and has noted that the clinician must be aware of, and take into consideration, the impact of non-intellective variables on an examinee's functioning. Hence, the clinician must always keep in mind the potential impact of the subject's life history, linguistic and cultural background when evaluating the examinee's performance on an intelligence test and when making recommendations for the examinee based on her or his intellectual test performance.

Chapter Four

DESIGN AND ORGANIZATION OF THE WISC-III

The manual of the WISC–III (Wechsler, 1991) is the most extensive of the three versions of the Wechsler Intelligence Scale for Children that have been published (Wechsler, 1949; Wechsler, 1974; Wechsler, 1991). The manual describes the test as "an individually administered clinical instrument for assessing the intellectual ability of children aged 6 years through 16 years, 11 months" (Wechsler, 1991, p. 1).

While retaining the essential features of the two earlier versions of the test, the WISC–III provides current normative data and revised or newly devised test materials, item content and administration procedures. As with its predecessors, the WISC–III consists of a number of subtests with each providing a measure of a different facet of the examinee's intellectual performance. As with past versions of the Wechsler Scales for Children, the current scale yields three composite scores, the Verbal, Performance and Full Scale IQs, which provide estimates of the examinee's verbal, performance and overall level of intellectual functioning. In addition, the WISC–III permits the calculation of four factor-based index scores to allow the examiner to obtain a more specific delineation of the child or adolescent's intellectual performance.

DEVELOPMENT OF THE WISC-III

It has been noted that the norms for intelligence tests become outdated over time (e.g., Flynn, 1984, 1987; Kaufman, 1990). It has been observed that average performance by individuals on intelligence tests has been increasing during the past several decades with greater changes evident in the performance sphere as opposed to the verbal sphere (Wechsler, 1991). Although there have been different theories proposed to explain these changes (Flynn, 1987), none have been determined to be *the* cause.

Regardless of the particular reason for this change in intelligence test performance, it is assumed that variation in intelligence and an underlying normal distribution of intelligence within the population still hold. In order for intelligence tests to function adequately in accurately reflecting and assessing the attribute of intellectual ability in the population, the development of new and current norms was the principal goal of the present revision of the Wechsler Intelligence Scale. However, Wechsler (1991) wanted to maintain the basic structure, organization and content of the WISC–R.

Past investigations of the Wechsler Scales (e.g., Kaufman, 1979a; Kaufman, Harrison, & Ittenbach, 1990) have provided support for the reporting of separate IQ scores that reflect verbal and performance abilities. Results of numerous investigations have found two major factors, one verbal and one reflecting perceptual organization, emerging from factor analysis of the Wechsler Scales (Cohen, 1957, 1959; Kaufman, 1979a, 1990). However, other studies (Kaufman, 1975) also revealed a smaller third factor, often labelled Freedom from Distractibility, which included the Coding, Arithmetic and Digit Span subtests. A second major goal of the development of the WISC–III was thus to further investigate and enhance the factorial structure of this test instrument. In order to better distinguish this third factor, the developers of the WISC–III added a new subtest, Symbol Search (Wechsler, 1991), but discovered that this resulted in the emergence of four factors in the analysis of the test.

A third major goal of the WISC–III development was the improvement of subtest content, as well as enhancement of administration and scoring rules. Based on inquiries, comments and structured questionnaire survey of users of the WISC–R as well as review of the WISC–R literature, the test developers constructed lists of potential improvements which were utilized to guide the revision process.

One focus of subtest revision was the minimization of bias in content of subtest items. Using a variety of methods (e.g., Wright & Stone, 1979), the test developers examined item-bias statistics for gender, ethnic and regional bias. The few items which were identified as having differential item effects were found primarily in the Information, Vocabulary and Comprehension subtests. The test developers replaced these items, and item-bias analyses were repeated with the WISC–III tryout data.

In addition to analyzing item bias statistically, a variety of reviewers also examined test items for bias. Psychologists familiar with ethnic-bias studies as well as staff members of The Psychological Corporation reviewed and evaluated all WISC–R items and the items which had been proposed for the WISC–III in terms of potential bias. Based on these reviews, the content of all subtests, particularly Picture Completion, Information, Similarities, Picture Arrangement, Arithmetic, Vocabulary, and Comprehension, was revised to result in a balance in terms of references to males and females as well as to a wide variety of ethnically identifiable persons and topics.

Another focus of subtest change was in the refinement and updating of pictorial items. Many of the stimulus materials were made larger and, after reviewing the literature which indicated that color in artwork would heighten the examinee's attentiveness and perception of realism in the material, color artwork was added to several of the Performance subtests. Feedback obtained from both examinees and examiners during pilot testing indicated that examinees responded positively to the presence of color in the test materials (Wechsler, 1991).

Still another improvement in the WISC–III dealt with the observation by WISC–R reviewers that the norms for certain WISC–R subtests tended to "bottom out" at age six and "top out" at age 16. Thus, for example, on the Similarities subtest, a raw score of 2 for a six-year-old examinee results in a scaled score of 7, and on the Arithmetic subtest at age 16, the maximum scaled score that can be achieved is 16. In order to permit more accurate measurement of intelligence at the extremes of the ability distribution, new items were developed.

In the revision procedure, items from the WPPSI–R were examined and used as a guide for the development of simpler items for the WISC–III Similarities subtest. In revising the Arithmetic subtest, new items were developed that were simpler and involved pictures; in addition, items of greater difficulty and multi-step word problem items were also devised. Both the Picture Arrangement and Block Design subtests were made longer by adding easier and more difficult items. Another complex maze was added to the Mazes subtest, and alterations in other subtests were also introduced.

Other improvements involved some changes in test administration. For example, the WISC–III begins with the Picture Completion subtest since it was felt that the Information subtest, which was the first subtest on the WISC–R, might remind the examinee of school and thus interfere with rapport. The new subtest sequence is presumably less threatening and makes less demand of the child or adolescent to respond verbally at the beginning of the test experience. In addition, those items which were felt to be technically unsuitable or outdated were revised or deleted. The order of items within the WISC–R was modified where indicated to accommodate new items or the difficulty of items, and the bonus-point structures of several Performance subtests were revised based on the new standardization data. Lastly, the newly developed Symbol Search subtest was added to the test to increase its diagnostic usefulness.

ORGANIZATION OF THE WISC-III

The WISC–III includes the 12 subtests which have been retained from the WISC–R as well as a newly developed subtest, Symbol Search. As with the WISC–R, the WISC–III subtests are organized into two groups, verbal and performance subtests, with the recommended sequence of subtest administration involving an alternation between verbal and performance tasks. The subtests, in their recommended order of administration, are as follows (a V or P in parentheses next to each subtest indicates whether that subtest is on the Verbal or Performance scale): Picture Completion (P), Information (V), Coding (P), Similarities (V), Picture Arrangement (P), Arithmetic (V), Block Design (P), Vocabulary (V), Object Assembly (P), Comprehension (V), and the supplementary subtests, Symbol Search [P], Digit Span [V], and Mazes [P].

The examinee's performance on a subset of 10 of these subtests, excluding the supplementary subtests, results in three scores. The sum of scaled scores on the Verbal subtests yields a Verbal IQ, the sum of the scaled scores on the Performance subtests yields a Performance IQ and the scaled scores on the Verbal and Performance subtests, when combined, result in a Full Scale IQ score.

The subtests of Digit Span and Mazes are supplementary subtests and were not used to develop norms for the Verbal and Performance IQ scores. These supplementary subtests are not needed to calculate the individual's IQ scores, although they may be administered if the examiner wishes to obtain additional information about the examinee's intellectual functioning.

The Digit Span subtest may be used to substitute for *any* verbal subtest and Mazes may be used as a substitute for *any* performance subtest in those instances where one of the standard subtests has been invalidated or cannot be administered. Wechsler (1991) reports that in those cases where a supplementary subtest score was substituted for each of the other subtest scores in its respective scale, verbal or performance, the mean scaled score remains stable, varying by only 0.1–0.3 points.

If either or both of these supplementary subtests is substituted for one of the standard subtests, the supplementary score is included in the IQ score computations. However, if either or both of these supplementary subtests is administered *in addition* to the standard subtests, their scores are not used in calculating the examinee's IQs. The examiner should note that the Symbol Search subtest can substitute only for the Coding subtest in determining the examinee's IQ scores. Furthermore, in order to calculate all of the factor-based index scores, the Digit Span and Symbol Search subtests must both be administered.

In addition to the three IQ scores which can be computed, it is possible to calculate four factor-based index scores with the WISC–III: Verbal Comprehension, or VCI; Perceptual Organization, or POI; Freedom from Distractibility, or FDI; and Processing Speed, or PSI. These factor-based scales, parallelling the IQ scales, have a mean of 100 and a standard deviation of 15. Table 3 presents the composition of each factor-based scale.

Table 3
SCALES DERIVED FROM FACTOR ANALYSES
OF THE WISC-III SUBTESTS

Factor I	Factor II	Factor III	Factor IV
Verbal Comprehension	Perceptual Organization	Freedom from Distractibility	Processing Speed
Information Similarities Vocabulary Comprehension	Picture Completion Picture Arrangement Block Design Object Assembly	Arithmetic Digit Span	Coding Symbol Search

Note. From D. Wechsler, *Manual for the Wechsler Intelligence Scale for Children — Third Edition,* 1991, p. 7. San Antonio, Tx: The Psychological Corporation. Wechsler Intelligence Scale for Children — Third Edition. Copyright © 1991 by the Psychological Corporation. Reproduced by permission. All rights reserved. "WISC–III" and "Wechsler Intelligence Scale for Children" and the "WISC–III logo" are registered trademarks of The Psychological Corporation. Their use herein does in no way indicate endorsement of this product by The Psychological Corporation.

CHANGES IN THE VERBAL SUBTESTS

Information

Content: On the WISC–III, this subtest has 30 items, 21 unchanged or slightly modified and two substantially modified from the WISC–R as well as seven new items. There are 30 items in the subtest, the same as in the WISC–R.

Administration and Scoring: There are four starting points on the WISC–III as there were on the WISC–R. The administration and scoring procedures are the same as on the WISC–R. The instructions for administering items in reverse sequence are the same, although the starting-point item is now counted in the reverse sequence.

Design: The subtest is now the second to be administered instead of the first and the space allotted to the examinee's response is more than twice the amount on the WISC–R. More instructions are included on the test form than on the WISC–R.

Similarities

Content: The WISC–III retains 13 of the 17 WISC–R items with 11 unchanged, two slightly modified and with six new items resulting in a total of 19 items, two more than on the WISC–R. A sample item has been added to demonstrate the appropriate response set for the examinee.

Administration and Scoring: Administration directions for the WISC–III are the same as for the WISC–R. However, the discontinue rule was changed from three to four consecutive failures. The sample responses and scoring criteria are included as part of the subtest directions rather than in a separate appendix and there are more sample responses to assist the examiner with scoring.

Design: The subtest is now fourth to be administered instead of third as on the WISC–R. There is twice as much space allotted on the WISC–III to record examinee responses as there was on the WISC–R. There are more subtest-relevant instructions on the test form than on the WISC–R.

Arithmetic

Content: Of the 18 items on the WISC–R, 14 have been retained for the WISC–III; the majority were reworded to reflect more contemporary subjects and prices. The WISC–III includes 10 new items which were added to extend both the lower and upper limits of the subtest.

Administration and Scoring: The WISC–III retains the four starting points of the WISC–R. The procedure for administration of items in reverse sequence differs from the WISC–R. On the WISC–III the starting-point item is counted in the reverse sequence and the *exception* to the reverse-sequence rule was dropped.

Design: The subtest is the fourth to be administered instead of fifth as on the WISC–R. A clock symbol indicates this is a timed subtest. Because the subtest is longer than on the WISC–R, much more space is allotted to the subtest but there is less room to record the examinee's actual response. The visual organization of the subtest can be confusing for the examiner to visually track where she or he is, and having to record Completion Time, skip over the Correct Response column and record the examinee's response may be inconvenient for the examiner. Instructions on the test form pertain to the reverse-sequence procedure for examinees ages 7–16.

Vocabulary

Content: Of the 32 items on the WISC–R, 13 items were dropped because they were either outdated or technically unsuitable. The WISC–III retains 19 items from the WISC–R and includes 11 new items for a total of 30 items, which is two less than the WISC–R.

Administration and Scoring: The WISC–III has four starting points as did the WISC–R. The instructions for administering items in reverse sequence remains essentially the same as on the WISC–R but the discontinue rule was changed from five to four consecutive failures. Sample responses and scoring criteria are included as part of the subtest administration directions rather than in a separate appendix.

Design: The subtest is eighth to be administered instead of seventh as on the WISC–R. The subtest now spans two pages of the test booklet. The prompts at the beginning of the subtest are not included at the top of the second page, an inconvenience for examiners who fold the test booklet. Slightly more space is allotted to each response on the WISC–III than on the WISC–R. Sample responses and scoring criteria are included with the subtest instructions in the manual rather than in an appendix, and more sample responses are provided. There are more instructions on the WISC–III test form than on the WISC–R.

Comprehension

Content: Of the 17 items on the WISC–R, five items were dropped because they were outdated or technically unsuitable; 12 items were retained, either unchanged or with minor rewording. Six new items were added to result in a total of 18 items, which is one more than the WISC–R.

Administration and Scoring: Eight WISC–III items require two responses from the examinee; the item prompts remain the same as on the WISC–R. The discontinue rule was reduced from four to three failures. Sample responses and scoring criteria are included with the subtest administration instructions rather than in a separate appendix and there are more sample responses to facilitate scoring.

Design: The subtest is tenth to be administered instead of ninth as on the WISC–R. There is much more space allotted to the subtest than on the WISC–R; the subtest spans two pages but the discontinue prompts do not appear on the second page, making it inconvenient for examiners who fold the test booklet.

Digit Span

Content: The WISC–III retains all seven of the Digit Span Forward and Backward items from the WISC–R. A two-digit item was added at the beginning of Digits Forward to extend the subtest downward.

Administration and Scoring: Administration and scoring of the WISC–III Digit Span subtest is the same as on the WISC–R.

Design: The subtest is the twelfth administered on the WISC–III instead of eleventh as on the WISC–R. The visual design is unchanged but more subtest instructions are included on the test form on the WISC–III.

CHANGES IN THE PERFORMANCE SUBTESTS

Picture Completion

Content: All of the stimulus pictures on the WISC–III are larger than on the WISC–R and they are now in color. Of the 26 items on the WISC–R, nine items were dropped, 16 have been retained either unchanged or slightly modified, one item was significantly modified and 13 new items were added to increase the total number of items from 26 to 30. The WISC–III includes a sample item to familiarize examinees with the subtest.

Administration and Scoring: The subtest includes four starting points instead of the two starting points on the WISC–R. These additional starting points allow older examinees to begin with later items, thus shortening administration time. The discontinue rule was increased from four to five consecutive failures.

Design: The subtest is the first administered on the WISC–III instead of second as on the WISC–R. This permits the examinee to begin the WISC–III with a less obviously school-related task, which should be less threatening to the examinee. The subtest is allotted more space for recording the examinee's item responses than on the WISC–R. The subtest is marked with a clock to indicate that it is timed and there are more subtest instructions on the test form than on the WISC–R.

Coding

Content: On the WISC–III, this subtest retains the two-level structure from the WISC–R Coding subtest, Coding A and Coding B; the age ranges of the two levels remain the same as on the WISC–R; the 120-second time limit remains the same; and the shape-symbol and number-symbol pairs remain the same as on the WISC–R. The total number of items was increased from 45 to 59 on Coding A and from 93 to 119 on Coding B, which results in additional rows of items on the subtest.

Administration and Scoring: Subtest instructions are the same as on the WISC–R except that the examinee is not required to use a red-lead pencil.

Design: The subtest is administered third on the WISC–III instead of tenth as on the WISC–R. The subtest is now printed on opposite sides of a single perforated sheet which is included in, and removed from, the test booklet instead of being in a separate booklet with the Mazes subtest as on the WISC–R. The symbols on the subtest are larger than on the WISC–R and there is more space between the key and stimulus items than on the WISC–R. There is no place on the subtest for the date or the examinee's name, which is problematic if the subtest becomes separated from the rest of the test booklet. The subtest is marked with a clock to indicate this is a timed subtest.

Picture Arrangement

Content: Of the 12 items on the WISC–R, five items were dropped and the Sample item was redrawn in view of the potentially negative content of those items. Seven items retained from the WISC–R were either unchanged or slightly modified, although a number of items were redrawn for the WISC–III. The total number of items on the subtest was increased from 12 to 14.

Administration and Scoring: The code for the correct response sequence and the name of the item were made identical to facilitate administration and recording. The WISC–III retains two starting points as on the WISC–R. Only the first two items have two trials, instead of the first four items as on the WISC–R. Only two WISC–III items permit alternative arrangements that receive credit, and the bonus-point structure was changed.

Design: The subtest is administered fifth on the WISC–III instead of fourth as on the WISC–R. The WISC–III form allots approximately the same space for the subtest as on the WISC–R. All of the picture cards are in color on the WISC–III as opposed to the black and white cards used on the WISC–R. There are more instructions on the WISC–III test form than on the WISC–R and the test form includes a clock symbol to indicate this is a timed subtest.

Block Design

Content: Of the 11 items of the WISC–R, 10 have been retained that are unchanged or slightly modified. One two-block design and one nine-block design have been added to the WISC–III and the number of designs on the subtest has been increased from 11 to 12. The new two-block design offers an easier item for younger children, while a fairly easy nine-block design on the WISC–R was replaced by a newly added nine-block design for the WISC–III.

Administration and Scoring: In the WISC–III, the examiner demonstrates Designs 1 and 2, using the illustrations that appear in the manual instead of those in the Stimulus Booklet as in the WISC–R. In both the WISC–R and the WISC–III, the first three designs have two trials each, but with the addition of the new Design 1, only two, rather than three, four-block designs are allowed two trials. The bonus-point structure was also revised.

Design: The subtest is administered seventh instead of sixth as on the WISC–R. Much more space is allotted to the subtest on the WISC–III than on the WISC–R. Pictures of each item appear on the test form and space is provided to record the examinee's item solution. Additional instructions are provided on the WISC–III test form and a clock indicates that it is a timed subtest.

Object Assembly

Content: Although the WISC–III retains the four Object Assembly items and the Sample item from the WISC–R, the WISC–III also includes a new item, Ball. Hence there are five subtest items on the WISC–III rather than four. The retained items and the Sample item were redrawn and all items are printed in brighter-colored material. The laminated material comprising the WISC–III items is thinner than the material on the WISC–R items. The number of junctures on three of the four retained items and the Sample item remain the same, but another juncture was added to the Face item.

Administration and Scoring: The Layout Shield for use with this subtest is now freestanding with diagrams of the items on the examiner side of the shield. The bonus-point structure was also revised.

Design: The space allotted to the subtest is essentially the same on the WISC–III as on the WISC–R. The subtest is administered ninth on the WISC–III instead of eighth as on the WISC–R. There is a clock on the form to indicate this is a timed subtest.

Symbol Search

Content: Symbol Search is a newly developed, optional subtest with two levels, A and B. Both levels are included in a booklet that is separate from the Record Form with each level comprised of 45 items. For each item, the examinee is required to visually scan a target and then a search group, and indicate whether the target symbol does or does not appear in the search group by checking a yes or no box to the right of the symbols.

Administration and Scoring: The time limit for the Symbol Search subtest is 120 seconds. An examinee's score is the total number of correct responses made during the allowed time minus the total number of incorrect responses. The subtest is scored with a scoring template.

Design: This subtest is administered 11th in the WISC–III. The subtest is in a separate booklet with sample and practice items for parts A and B on the front. Although the symbols might be considered letter-like, they also appear to resemble hieroglyphics. A left-handed examinee might cover the target and search groups with his or her hand, which might complicate the task somewhat.

Mazes

Content: The WISC–III retains all nine of the mazes from the WISC–R and also includes one new maze, resulting in ten instead of nine mazes, with the additional maze (Maze 9) being added as a difficult maze.

Administration and Scoring: The number of starting points on the subtest is the same as on the WISC–R. The maximum number of errors permitted for each maze was changed to reflect the data from the new standardization sample. Finally, the examinee no longer is required to use a red-lead pencil for the subtest.

Design: Although the overall design of the mazes is the same on the WISC–III as on the WISC–R, each maze is slightly larger and the Mazes subtest is contained in its own separate booklet. The Mazes subtest is administered 13th on the WISC–III instead of 12th as it was on the WISC–R. There is a clock on the form to indicate this is a timed subtest, and the discontinue criteria are printed on the WISC–III test booklet.

The WISC–III also included alterations in the test materials and administrative procedures which were intended to make the testing experience more interesting to examinees. These changes included printing many of the pictorial materials in color and changing the recommended sequence of subtest administration to make the examinee's entry into the test situation more gradual. Items that were outdated were replaced by newly constructed items; additional items were added at the lower or upper limits of particular subtests; and where analyses indicated particular items were unfair to some subject groups, these items were also replaced.

APPLICATIONS OF THE WISC–III

Wechsler (1991) notes that the WISC–III is useful and an appropriate assessment instrument for a number of purposes: psychoeducational assessment; diagnosis of exceptionality among school-aged children; clinical and neuropsychological assessment; and research.

In discussing the fact that there may be times when an examinee must be re-evaluated, Wechsler (1991) points out that the examiner must be aware of the effect of prior testing on subsequent test performance, i.e., "practice effects." It is known that such practice effects tend to be most significant with brief test-retest intervals; that they fade as the test-retest interval increases (Juliano, Haddad, & Carroll, 1988); and that performance subtests are more significantly affected by practice than are verbal subtests.

These observations essentially mean that: the examiner should allow as much time between testing and retesting as possible when retesting is to be required; that the examiner should be sensitive to the possibility that a given child or adolescent's current performance may reflect her or his recently having taken the test; and that if the examiner is aware of this occurrence with a given examinee that test results be interpreted cautiously.

USER QUALIFICATIONS FOR THE WISC–III

In view of the complex nature of the administration and interpretation of the WISC–III, examiners who use the test should have training as well as supervised experience in the administration and interpretation of standardized clinical instruments. Examiners should have knowledge of the statistical and psychometric properties of the test, as well as an understanding of the multiple complexities involved in relating to, establishing rapport with, and understanding children across the developmental span of childhood and adolescence. Finally, examiners should be able to appreciate the impact of differentness and variation, intellectually, culturally, racially, linguistically and psychologically (e.g., Canino & Spurlock, 1994), on the performance of a given examinee on a set of tasks such as those comprising the WISC–III.

Although typically, anyone administering the WISC–III will have had some formal graduate-level training in psychological assessment methods and strategies, there are instances and settings where the test may be administered and/or scored by a technician. However, the results of the test should always be interpreted by an individual who has had appropriate graduate or professional training and supervision in psychological assessment and who is familiar with the Standards for Educational and Psychological Testing (American Psychological Association, 1985).

It is also the user's responsibility to maintain the security of the test materials and protocols and to be certain that the handling of the information obtained about the examinee is dealt with in a professionally responsible and ethical manner. While discussion of the test findings with the examinee or his or her parents or guardians is proper clinical practice, such a discussion should not involve disclosure of any aspects of test materials which might compromise the validity or value of the test materials for future use.

Chapter Five

THE WISC-III STANDARDIZATION AND SCALED SCORE, IQ, AND INDEX SCORE DEVELOPMENT

THE SAMPLE

The norms presented in the WISC–III manual were derived from a standardization sample that was representative of the United States population of children according to the 1988 census (Wechsler, 1991). The test developers utilized a stratified random sampling plan so that representative proportions of children from each demographic group would be included in the standardization sample.

An analysis of the data gathered in 1988 by the U.S. Bureau of the Census resulted in stratification of the standardization sample according to the variables of: age, gender, race/ethnicity, geographic region, and parent education, which referred to parent(s) or guardian(s). The following provides a description of each of the above-noted characteristics of the standardization sample (Wechsler, 1991).

Age: The sample of 2200 children in the standardization group included 200 examinees at each of 11 ages from 6 through 16 years, with the median age for each group being the sixth month of that age group (e.g., 6 years, 6 months).

Gender: The sample consisted of 100 male and 100 female subjects at each of the 11 ages.

Race/Ethnicity: For each age group in the sample, the proportions of Whites, Blacks, Hispanics, and other racial/ethnic groups were based on the racial/ethnic group proportions of children between 6 and 16 in the national population as reflected in the 1988 Census. Each individual in the sample was categorized by her or his parent(s) as belonging to one of a number of racial/ethnic groups: White, Black, Native American, Eskimo, Aleut, Asian, Pacific Islander or Other, and the parent(s) also indicated whether or not the child included was of Hispanic origin. If the parent(s) indicated that the subject was of Hispanic origin, then the individual was assigned to the Hispanic category no matter how the parent(s) had responded to the other racial/ethnic group question. For sampling purposes, several categories (e.g., Native American, Eskimo, Aleut) groupings were combined with the

Other category. The racial/ethnic proportions based on the 1988 census were maintained within each age level, gender category, geographic region and parent education level.

Geographic Region: The United States was divided into four geographic regions as specified in the 1988 Census: Northeast, North Central, South, and West (Wechsler, 1991) and subjects were selected for the standardization sample according to the proportion of children living in each of the four regions.

Parent Education: The sample was stratified in terms of the following categories of parent education: (1) 8th grade or less; (2) 9th grade through 11th grade; (3) high school graduate or equivalent; (4) 1 through 3 years of college or technical school; (5) 4 or more years of college.

Knowledge regarding the parent(s)' educational level was obtained from parent responses to a question that asked the highest grade completed by each parent living in the household. If both parents lived with the subject, the average of the two educational levels was used. If only one parent lived with the subject, that person's educational level was used. A matrix of five parent educational levels by subject race/ethnicity for each combination of age group, gender, and geographic region was used as an organization for the sampling plan.

SELECTING AND TESTING THE SAMPLE

Invitations to participate in the standardization of the WISC–III were sent to school districts across the United States with invited districts being selected on the basis of urban-rural classification, socioeconomic status and race/ethnic composition.

Seventy-five school districts and several other sites across the United States were chosen for participation. Computer-scannable parent consent forms were distributed through school districts; these consent forms asked for the subject's age, gender, race/ethnicity and the occupation and educational level of the parent(s).

Following this step, a data base containing demographic information for all children available for participation in the study was completed and a stratified random sampling approach was utilized to choose subjects representative of the child population with only one child per family being included in the sample. Each subject to be tested was assigned to an examiner who was experienced in using individually administered psychological tests and who had demonstrated competence in administering the WISC–III. However, the manual provides no specific data on the age, gender or racial/ethnic composition of the pool of examiners.

The standardization sample was obtained from both private and public schools and included students who were receiving special services in schools. Thus, 7 percent of the sample consisted of subjects who were classified as learning disabled, speech or language impaired, emotionally disturbed, physically impaired or who were in Chapter 1 programs. However, the manual does not mention any inclusion in the sample of children who were not in school, for example, children in hospitals, residential treatment centers, children on home tutoring or children who were being educated by their parent(s). In addition to the students receiving special services for various handicapping conditions, 5 percent of the sample consisted of subjects in programs for the gifted and talented.

Wechsler (1991) concludes that the data on the demographic characteristics of the WISC–III standardization sample closely approximated the demographic composition of the United States population as reflected in the 1988 U. S. Census (for specific information on the WISC–III standardization sample, see Wechsler, 1991).

QUALITY CONTROL METHODS

The objective of the quality control procedures used in the WISC–III standardization was to ensure that the tests were properly administered and that test responses were scored accurately and reliably. First, examiners with extensive testing experience were selected to administer the WISC–III to the standardization sample. Before being chosen to participate in the WISC–III norming, examiners completed a detailed questionnaire about their education, professional experience, experience administering the WISC–R, and their certification and/or licensing status.

Wechsler (1991) notes that those selected were quite familiar with individual testing and with the administration of the WISC–R. However, the manual does not provide any detailed information on the characteristics of the examiners and no mention is made of their age, gender or race/ethnic characteristics. This would be relevant in terms of the potential impact any of these variables might have on examiner-examinee rapport during testing and consequently on examinee test performance.

While the overall test format of the WISC–III is quite similar to that of the WISC–R, the test developers felt there were a number of changes in the WISC–III that could affect proper test administration. Hence examiners submitted a practice protocol for review prior to their approval for testing subjects for the WISC–III standardization. The practice protocols were evaluated according to a set of guidelines which focused on thoroughness of test administration and accuracy of scoring, and examiners were given detailed feedback on their administration and test scoring. In addition, a newsletter entitled *Standardization Notes* was periodically sent to all examiners to inform them of problematic areas regarding the development of the test.

A series of three scoring studies were carried out and reported in the manual (Wechsler, 1991). These studies were conducted with approximately 500 subjects in the standardization sample and included 50% male and 50% female, 67% White and 33% minorities, with this sample including subjects across the age span from 6 to 16.

The studies focused on scoring criteria and procedures for the subtests of Picture Completion, Information, Arithmetic, Mazes, Similarities, Vocabulary and Comprehension. After the studies had been completed, the results were incorporated into the final scoring rules in the manual, and the effectiveness of training of the examiners was evaluated by comparing scorers' pre-training and post-training scoring performances.

SCALED–SCORE DERIVATION

In order to develop the scaled scores for the WISC–III, for each of the 13 subtests, the distribution of the raw scores for each age group was transformed into a uniform scale which had a mean of 10 and a standard deviation of 3. This was accomplished by preparing a cumulative frequency distribution of the raw scores for each age group, then normalizing this distribution, and then calculating an appropriate scaled score for each raw score with minor irregularities in the progression of scaled scores within each of the age groups being eliminated.

Table A.1. in the WISC–III manual (Wechsler, 1991, pp. 217–249) presents the scaled-score equivalents of the raw scores for each of the 13 subtests. These equivalent scores are listed in four-month intervals for children ranging in age from 6 years, 0 months, 0 days to 16 years, 11 months, 30 days with the scaled scores for each subtest ranging from 1 to 19 and providing 3 standard deviations above and below the mean.

IQ AND INDEX SCORE TABLES

The sums of scaled scores for the Verbal Scale, the Performance Scale, and the Full Scale were determined by summing each examinee's scaled scores on each of the relevant subtests in that scale, excluding the supplementary subtests. For each age group, the means and standard deviations of the distributions of the three sums of scaled scores was determined. Analyses of the data indicated that there was no significant variation by age in the mean scores for each scale and the standard deviations did not differ significantly by age. Hence the 11 age groups were combined based on the total sample of 2200 subjects and the tables of IQ score equivalents of sums of scaled scores was constructed. These tables, "IQ Equivalents of Sums of Scaled Scores: Verbal Scale"; "IQ Equivalents of Sums of Scaled Scores: Performance Scale"; and "IQ Equivalents of Sums of Scaled Scores: Full Scale," appear as Tables A.2.–A.4. in the WISC–III manual (Wechsler, 1991, pp. 251–254).

For each of the three scales (Verbal, Performance and Full Scale), the distribution of the sums of scaled scores was transformed into a scale with a mean of 100 and a standard deviation of 15. The test developers accomplished this by preparing a cumulative frequency distribution of the sums of scaled scores for each of the three scales; these distributions were then smoothed and normalized; and then the appropriate IQ score equivalents for each sum of scaled scores was calculated.

The manual provides little description of the four Index scale distributions. However, Wechsler (1991) notes that the tables for the four Index scores followed the same general procedures as were utilized in constructing the tables for the IQ scores. Tables A.5.–A.7. in the WISC–III manual present the "Index Score Equivalents of Sums of Scaled Scores" (Wechsler, 1991, pp. 255–257).

INTERPRETING IQ AND INDEX SCORES

Each of the distributions of the Verbal, Performance and Full Scale IQ scores has a mean of 100 and a standard deviation of 15. Thus a score of 100 on any of these three scales defines the performance of the average examinee of a particular age on that scale (see Table 4, "Relation of IQ and Index Scores to Standard Deviations from the Mean and Percentile Rank Equivalents"). The score one standard deviation below the mean is 85, the score two standard deviations below the mean is 70, and the score three standard deviations below the mean is 55. Similarly, a score of 115 is one standard deviation above the mean while a score of 130 is two standard deviations above the mean, and a score of 145 is three standard deviations above the mean.

Approximately two-thirds of all children in the standardization sample obtain scores between 85 and 115 while about 95% of subjects obtain scores within the 70–130 range. Virtually all children obtain scores between 55 and 145, which represent three standard deviations above and below the mean of 100.

Examiners using the WISC–III typically describe an examinee's performance in terms of the examinee's numerical IQ score within the above-noted framework as well as providing a qualitative or verbal label for the category within which the examinee's IQ score falls. Table 5, "Qualitative Descriptions of WISC–III Full Scale IQ Scores," presents specific IQ ranges, their

Table 4
RELATION OF IQ AND INDEX SCORES TO STANDARD DEVIATIONS FROM THE MEAN AND PERCENTILE RANK EQUIVALENTS

IQ/Index Score	Number of SDS from the Mean	Percentile Rank Equivalent[a]
145	$+3$	99.9
140	$+2^{2}/_{3}$	99.6
135	$+2^{1}/_{3}$	99
130	$+2$	98
125	$+1^{2}/_{3}$	95
120	$+1^{1}/_{3}$	91
115	$+1$	84
110	$+^{2}/_{3}$	75
105	$+^{1}/_{3}$	63
100	0 (Mean)	50
95	$-^{1}/_{3}$	37
90	$-^{2}/_{3}$	2
85	-1	16
80	$-1^{1}/_{3}$	9
75	$-1^{2}/_{3}$	5
70	-2	2
65	$-2^{1}/_{3}$	1
60	$-2^{2}/_{3}$	0.4
55	-3	0.1

[a]The percentile ranks are theoretical values for a normal distribution.

Note. From D. Wechsler, *Manual for the Wechsler Intelligence Scale for Children — Third Edition*, 1991, p. 32. San Antonio, TX: The Psychological Corporation. Wechsler Intelligence Scale for Children—Third Edition. Copyright © 1991 by The Psychological Corporation. Reproduced by permission. All rights reserved. "WISC–III" and "Wechsler Intelligence Scale for Children" and the "WISC–III logo" are registered trademarks of The Psychological Corporation. Their use herein does in no way indicate endorsement of this product by The Psychological Corporation.

corresponding qualitative descriptions, as well as the percents of these IQ ranges that would be expected based on the theoretical normal curve, and the percent actually obtained in the WISC–III standardization sample.

Wechsler (1991) notes that the percentages obtained in the actual sample are based on the Full Scale IQ for the total standardization sample of 2200, and the percentages obtained for the Verbal and Performance IQ are very similar. Wechsler (1991, p. 32) also points out that in place of the term *mentally retarded* which was used for the WISC–R IQ score of 69 and below, the WISC–III uses the term *intellectually deficient* to avoid the implication

Table 5

QUALITATIVE DESCRIPTIONS OF WISC-III FULL SCALE IQ SCORES

| | | Percent Included | |
		Theoretical Normal Curve	Actual Sample[a]
IQ	Classification		
130 and above	Very Superior	2.2	2.1
120–129	Superior	6.7	8.3
110–119	High Average	16.1	16.1
90–109	Average	50.0	50.3
80–89	Low Average	16.1	14.8
70–79	Borderline	6.7	6.5
69 and below	Intellectually Deficient[b]	2.2	1.9

[a]The percentages shown are for the Full Scale IQ and are based on the total standardization sample (N = 2200). The percentages obtained for the Verbal IQ and Performance IQ are very similar.
[b]In place of the term mentally retarded used in the WISC–R, the WISC–III uses the term *intellectually deficient*. This practice avoids the implication that a very low IQ is sufficient evidence for the classification of "mental" retardation. The term *intellectually deficient* is descriptive and refers only to low intellectual functioning. The usage is consistent with the standards recommended by the American Association of Mental Deficiency (Grossman, 1983) and the American Psychiatric Association (1987).

Note. From D. Wechsler, *Manual for the Wechsler Intelligence Scale for Children — Third Edition,* 1991, p. 32. San Antonio, TX: The Psychological Corporation. Wechsler Intelligence Scale for Children — Third Edition. Copyright © 1991 by The Psychological Corporation. Reproduced by permission. All rights reserved. "WISC–III" and "Wechsler Intelligence Scale for Children" and the "WISC–III logo" are registered trademarks of The Psychological Corporation. Their use herein does in no way indicate endorsement of this product by The Psychological Corporation.

that a very low IQ score is sufficient to diagnose an examinee as mentally retarded (see section on using the WISC–III with referral questions regarding the level of an individual's intellectual functioning).

Wechsler (1991) also notes that whenever the WISC–III is being interpreted, whether one is using a qualitative or a quantitative framework, the examiner should remember that test scores consist of both true and error variance. When the examiner is using the statistical or qualitative descriptions of the standardization sample to interpret WISC–III test results for a particular examinee, it is always important to remember this caveat: any test score is only an estimate of the underlying value it seeks to measure.

Chapter Six

RELIABILITY AND VALIDITY OF THE WISC–III

The psychometric properties of the WISC–III must be considered by the examiner since these features of the instrument provide the basis for analyzing and interpreting the examinee's performance on the test. The following two chapters discuss the basic psychometric and statistical characteristics of the WISC–III, on which the clinical use and interpretation of the test relies. (For the complete discussion of the statistical properties of the WISC–III, see Wechsler, 1991, Chapter 5, pp. 165–178.)

RELIABILITY OF THE WISC–III

The reliability of a test refers to the precision and consistency with which the test measures whatever it measures, and to the stability of the test's scores over time (Anastasi, 1988). Statistics useful in describing a test's reliability include reliability coefficients and standard errors of measurement for various aspects of the test, and the size of confidence intervals surrounding test scores.

Verbal, Performance and Full Scale Reliabilities

Each of the Verbal, Performance and Full Scale IQs has an internal reliability coefficient of .89 or above over the entire age span covered by the test. The reliability coefficients for the Verbal IQ range from .92 to .96 across the 11 age groups in the standardization sample, with an average reliability coefficient of .95. The reliability coefficients for the Performance IQ range from .89 to .94 across the 11 age groups, with an average reliability coefficient of .91. The reliability coefficients for the Full Scale IQ range from .94 to .97 across the 11 age groups, with an average reliability coefficient of .96. These reliability coefficients thus indicate that the WISC–III displays a very high degree of internal consistency across the age range for which the test was designed for use.

Subtest Reliabilities

The internal reliability for each subtest except Coding and Symbol Search was estimated by dividing the items on that subtest into two approximately parallel forms, correlating the two parallel forms and then correcting the resulting coefficient by the Spearman-Brown formula (Golden, Sawicki & Franzen, 1990). For the Coding and Symbol Search subtests, stability coefficients from a test-retest study of these subtests were used to estimate subtest reliability since ordinary measures of internal consistency are inappropriate for speeded tests. The average internal reliability coefficients for the entire sample range from .69 for the Object Assembly subtest to .87 for the Vocabulary and Block Design subtests.

Index Score Reliabilities

In terms of the four Index scores, the reliability coefficients of the Verbal Comprehension Index range from .91 to .95 across the 11 groups, with an average reliability coefficient of .94. The reliability coefficients of the Perceptual Organization Index range from .89 to .93 across the 11 groups, with an average reliability coefficient of .90.

The reliability coefficients of the Freedom from Distractibility Index range from .83 to .91 across the 11 groups, with an average reliability coefficient of .87. The reliability coefficients of the Processing Speed Index range from .80 to .91 across the 11 groups, with an average reliability coefficient of .85. As with the IQ scores, the Index scores typically have higher reliabilities than do the individual subtests since the IQ and Index scores are based on a larger sample of items than are the individual subtest scores.

Standard Errors of Measurement and Confidence Intervals

A second index of the reliability or consistency of the WISC–III is the standard error of measurement (SE_M), which provides an estimate of the amount of error present in an individual's observed test score. The SE_M is inversely related to the reliability coefficient in that the higher the reliability coefficient, the lower the SE_M and the greater confidence one may have in the accuracy of the obtained test score.

The average standard error of measurement in IQ points is 3.53 for the Verbal Scale, 4.54 for the Performance Scale and 3.20 for the Full Scale, indicating that there is the least measurement error on the Full Scale IQ score as compared to either the Verbal or Performance Scale IQ score and that the examiner may have the most confidence in the Full Scale IQ score as an accurate measure of the examinee's intellectual functioning.

The SE_Ms of the Index scores are typically larger than those of the Verbal, Performance and Full Scale IQs indicating that there is less consistency or certainty in these scores, and the examiner may have less confidence in these Index scores than in the WISC–III IQ scores.

The SE_Ms of the individual subtest scores are numerically smaller than those of the IQ and Index scores; this reflects the fact that the standard deviation of the subtest scaled scores is 3 while the standard deviation of the IQ and Index scores is 15 and the respective SE_Ms reflect these different standard deviations. The average standard errors of measurement for the subtests, in scaled score points, range from 1.08 (Vocabulary) to 1.45 (Comprehension) on the Verbal Scale and from 1.11 (Block Design) to 1.67 (Object Assembly) on the Performance Scale.

Confidence intervals are another indication of the precision of test scores. The confidence interval of a test score provides a range of scores which, with a given degree of certainty, is presumed to contain an examinee's true test score. The inclusion of confidence intervals when reporting the results of testing reflects the fact that any measurement contains some degree of error and the realization that an examinee's obtained IQ score or scores on the WISC–III are not perfectly accurate measures of the examinee's true abilities.

Although confidence intervals for test scores are often established based on SE_M values that center around the examinee's obtained score, confidence intervals for the WISC–III norms tables (Wechsler, 1991, pp. 251–257) were developed with a technically more precise methodology based on the standard error of estimation (SE_E) rather than the standard error of measurement (SE_M).

This approach results in an asymmetrical confidence interval around the obtained score with the reason being that the estimated score is closer to the mean of the scale (i.e., 100) than is the obtained score. A confidence interval based on the SE_E corrects for this regression toward the mean of the true score. However, when the reliability of a score is high, as is the case for the WISC–III IQ and Index scores, then confidence intervals centered around either the obtained score *or* the true score will be close to one another.

The IQ and Index score norms tables in the WISC–III manual (Wechsler, 1991, pp. 251–257) provide confidence intervals at the 90 and 95 percent confidence levels for each IQ and Index score value utilizing the SE_E method. The interpretation of these table entries is as follows. For an examinee who obtains a sum of scaled scores of 66 on the Verbal Scale, his or her Verbal IQ would be 119. There is a 90% probability, or the chances are 90 out of 100, that the examinee's true Verbal IQ score falls in the range from

113 to 123. There is a 95% probability, or the chances are 95 out of 100, that the examinee's true Verbal IQ score falls in the range from 112–124.

If one wishes to use the SE_M method to determine the 95% confidence interval for a WISC–III IQ or Index score, the entries for an examinee at a given age may be obtained from Table 5.2. in the manual (Wechsler, 1991, p. 168). Multiplying the SE_M for a given age by 1.96 and adding this to, and subtracting it from, the obtained score will result in the confidence interval based on the examinee's obtained score.

Sattler (1992) presents information on both kinds of confidence intervals and states that although confidence intervals can be used for every score obtained by the examinee, he recommends that they be used primarily for the Full Scale IQ since this is the score usually used to make diagnostic or classification decisions regarding the examinee. This appears to be a reasonable recommendation. However, the present author would point out that the clinician should always be aware of the setting in which his or her test results will be utilized and the report of test results should include what information the examiner believes is relevant to the use of the test findings on behalf of the examinee in that particular setting.

Test-Retest Stability

The stability of scores on the WISC–III over time was assessed in a study of 353 children who were tested on two occasions, with the sample of subjects for this study being drawn from among six age groups in the standardization sample: 6, 7, 10, 11, 14 and 15. For the calculation of test-retest reliabilities, the subjects were grouped into three age groups: 6–7, 10–11 and 14–15. The sample of subjects consisted of 52% males and 48% females and included 69% Whites, 15% Blacks, 13% Hispanics and 3% children of other racial/ethnic backgrounds. The interval between the two occasions of testing ranged from 12 to 63 days (median interval = 23 days).

Tables 5.3., 5.4., and 5.5. (Wechsler, 1991, pp. 170–172) present the various scores obtained by the samples used to investigate the stability of the WISC–III. The tables present the means and standard deviations for the subtest, IQ and Index scores for the two testings. The tables also present the uncorrected and corrected correlation coefficients for the two test administrations; the retest coefficients were corrected for the variability on the first testing in order to obtain accurate estimates of score consistency in the standardization population.

Corrected test-retest correlations for the Verbal, Performance and Full Scale IQs for the 6–7-year-olds are .90, .86, and .92, respectively. For the 10–11-year-old subjects, the corrected test-retest correlations for the Verbal,

Performance and Full Scale IQs are .94, .88, and .95, respectively. And for the 14–15-year-old subjects, the corrected test-retest correlations for the Verbal, Performance and Full Scale IQs are .94, .87, and .94, respectively. Corrected test-retest correlations for the four Index scores for the three age groups are all .80 or above except for the Freedom from Distractibility Index for the 6–7 year age group, which is .74. These correlations indicate that the WISC–III provides adequate stability in measurement of examinee's performance over a relatively short time interval.

WISC–III SCORE STABILITY AND PRACTICE EFFECTS

Sattler (1992) analyzed the data provided by Wechsler (1991) further by examining changes in examinee performance from the first to the second testing. He determined that in the 6–7 year age group, Verbal IQ increased by 1.7 points, Performance IQ increased by 11.5 points, and Full Scale IQ increased by 7.0 points. In the 10–11 year age group, Verbal, Performance and Full Scale IQs increased by 1.9, 13.0, and 7.7, respectively. In the 14–15 year age group, Verbal, Performance, and Full Scale IQs increased by 3.3, 12.5, and 8.4 points, respectively. All of these increases were significant at least beyond the .01 level of significance.

Sattler (1992) suggests that the large gains on the WISC–III Performance Scale when readministered after a short interval reflect practice effects due to the examinees' recall of the types of items they were given and the strategies they used to solve the items on the first test administration. The findings reported in the WISC–III manual (Wechsler, 1991) and discussed by Sattler (1992) of course indicate that examinees are likely to do much better on a second administration of the WISC–III when it is given soon after the first testing. Furthermore, examinees are likely to do much better on the Performance than the Verbal Scale.

The WISC–III manual ideally should have reported results with the test when the interval between first and second administrations was perhaps six months or a year rather than 60 days. Relevant to this issue, using the WISC–R, Haynes and Howard (1986) and Naglieri and Pfeiffer (1983) reported highly stable test performance with Verbal, Performance and Full Scale IQ test changes less than three points over a two-year period.

Also using the WISC–R, Bauman (1991) investigated the stability of subtest scores over an approximate two-year period among 130 learning disabled elementary school-children ranging in age from 6-1 to 11-10. He found that the stability coefficients of the subtests ranged from .61 to .76 for the total sample. Although the scatter of correlations within the subgroups was noteworthy, none of the subtests reached Sattler's (1990) criterion of .80 or higher for reliability coefficients except for the subtests of Information and Block Design for the above-8 age group. Hence, it will be necessary to obtain further research data on the WISC–III over longer periods of test-retest intervals for normal and various learning disabled groups to determine the stability of scores in these instances.

As far as the clinical use of the WISC–III, a vital issue not addressed by Wechsler (1991) or Sattler (1992) is the frequency with which an examiner tests a child who has taken the WISC–III very recently. It would only be in this circumstance, perhaps when a child has recently moved into a new community or changed schools, that the examiner might administer the WISC–III to an examinee who has just had the test.

If the examiner knows an examinee has been tested recently with the WISC–III, she or he should certainly be aware of the above-noted practice effects when interpreting test results. If the examiner does not know the examinee has been previously tested with the WISC–III, the examinee will sometimes spontaneously mention, "Oh, I did this at school," or "I did this last week," in which case the examiner will know that he or she must consider the effect of recent practice on the examinee's performance. Alternatively, at the conclusion of testing, the examiner may routinely ask the examinee if he or she has ever taken this test or one like it. This would make the examiner aware of those few examinees who might be familiar with the test but not spontaneously inform the examiner of this fact.

Perhaps more relevant to the issue of practice effects would be Sattler's (1992) analysis of the specific subtest changes observed for examinees of different ages. Sattler (1992) reports that the largest gains were for the Picture Arrangement subtest, with increases of 2.7 to 3.3 scaled score points and the smallest increases were for Vocabulary with increases of 0 to .2 scaled score points and Comprehension with increases of from 0 to .5 scaled score points.

There does not appear to be a subtest by age interaction such that individuals of any of the three age groups display a more significant effect of practice on particular subtests than do individuals of other age groups. Since "practice effects" involve some degree of incidental or even focused learning by the examinee, the findings presented in Tables 5.3., 5.4., and 5.5. in Wechsler (1991) may be viewed as normative for these processes.

If the examiner encounters an examinee who has had the test recently, the examiner may analyze the test results and determine if the examinee displays a relatively normative pattern of practice effects or some unusual pattern of practice effects. This information might be helpful in generating recommendations for instruction for the child who has been evaluated since the results would provide information about the child's ability to learn and/or retain information which he or she had not specifically attempted to learn.

VALIDITY OF THE WISC-III

According to the standards for educational and psychological testing (American Educational Research Association, American Psychological Association & National Council on Measurement in Education, 1985), evidence regarding the validity of a test is the result of numerous investigations which explore the multiple kinds of validity which may characterize a test. Thus the establishment of a test's validity requires many studies which, over time, provide accumulated evidence that the test measures those constructs intended by its developers and that performance on the test is related to performance on instruments that measure similar or related constructs while being uncorrelated with performance on tasks that assess unrelated constructs.

Wechsler (1991) notes that because of the similarities between the WISC-III and its predecessor, the WISC-R, the accumulated research evidence for the validity of the WISC-R should be considered in determining the validity of the WISC-III.

Studies of the WISC-R

Wechsler (1991) points out that the WISC-R is one of the most extensively researched and cited tests in the professional literature (Kaufman, 1979a; Kaufman et al., 1990). Numerous studies of the test have appeared since its publication in 1974 and many of these contribute to the establishment of the test as a valid instrument for measuring intelligence and various aspects of this construct.

In view of the substantial correlations between the WISC-R and the WISC-III and because of the significant item overlap from the WISC-R to the WISC-III (aside from the Symbol Search subtest, approximately 80% of the items on the WISC-III were taken from the WISC-R), evidence regarding the validity of the WISC-R is felt to support the validity of the WISC-III.

Construct-Related Evidence Regarding the WISC-R

Both the WISC-R and the WISC-III are tests which have been designed to measure the variety of cognitive abilities which reflect and underlie what Wechsler described as an individual's "aggregate or global capacity" to act purposefully, think rationally, and to deal effectively with his or her environment (Wechsler, 1958). Evidence from many years of research has demonstrated the existence of a broad or "global" construct described as *g* or general intelligence which has been seen as related to such criteria as individuals' educational attainment, academic performance and occupation (e.g., Brody, 1985; Crano, Denny & Campbell, 1972).

Utilizing factor analysis as an investigative tool, various authors (e.g. Vance & Wallbrown, 1977) have analyzed examinees' performances on the WISC–R and identified the presence of a general factor in this test. Kaufman (1975) analyzed the scores of each of the age groups in the WISC–R standardization sample and interpreted the first factor that emerged in the analysis of each age group as a general intelligence, or g factor.

Five WISC–R subtests (Information, Similarities, Block Design, Vocabulary and Comprehension) had loadings on this general factor of above .70. The best measure of g on the WISC–R is felt to be the Full Scale IQ score, which is based on the scores of 10 subtests, nine of which are on Kaufman's (1975) list of subtests which he considered to be acceptable measures of g.

Jensen (1987) reported the average percentage of variance accounted for by the g factor across 20 data sets which involved more than 70 ability tests and which included the Wechsler scales was 42.7%.

Sattler (1990) has reported that the WISC–R Full Scale IQ correlates with a variety of other measures of global intellectual ability at from .61 (with the Slosson Intelligence Test) to .82 (with the Stanford-Binet: Form L–M); with measures of academic achievement at from .52 (with the Wide Range Achievement Test Arithmetic subtest) to .71 (with the Peabody Individual Achievement Test); and .39 with school grades. Hence there is significant evidence in the literature to conclude that there is a global or g factor which underlies performance on many tests of cognitive function and that the WISC–R assesses this construct.

Numerous investigations have also demonstrated the existence of two primary factors underlying performance on the WISC–R. These factors are the Verbal or Verbal Comprehension factor and the Performance or Perceptual Organization factor. These factors emerged in Kaufman's (1975) analysis of the WISC–R standardization data as evident in each of the 11 age groups and as aligned with the Verbal and Performance Scales. A number of subsequent investigations with various populations have obtained factor structures of the WISC–R that parallel the Verbal-Performance organization of the test (e.g., Carlson, Reynolds & Gutkin, 1983; Dean, 1980; Groff & Hubble, 1982; Kaufman et al., 1990).

Kaufman (1975) introduced evidence for a third factor, which he called Freedom from Distractibility, and which he felt was relevant to interpreting the WISC–R. He based his conclusions on a series of exploratory analyses of the WISC–R standardization data. Further research on this third factor, which was composed of the Arithmetic and Digit Span Subtests and with Coding having a smaller factor loading, has been somewhat inconsistent.

However, investigations of a variety of groups of children have identified the third factor (Kaufman et al., 1990). For example, studies of learning disabled children have often identified the third factor (e.g., Juliano, Haddad,

& Carroll, 1988). Van Hagen and Kaufman (1975) and Groff and Hubble (1982) identified the third factor in their investigations of mentally retarded children. And studies of children of different ethnic backgrounds, such as Hispanic-American children (Boodoo, Barona, & Ochoa, 1988), African-American children (Juliano et al., 1988), and Hong Kong Cantonese children (Chan, 1984), have also found evidence of the third factor.

Possible aspects of the Freedom from Distractibility factor have included emphasis on its attentional qualities (Kaufman, 1975), the fact that third factor subtests all involve sequential processing (Bannatyne, 1974), and the fact that the subtests on this factor are all sensitive to test anxiety (Lutey, 1977). Others (e.g., Osborne & Lindsey, 1967) have stressed the numerical- and quantitative-ability aspect of the factor while Wielkiewicz (1990) has described the role of executive processes as underlying performance on the third factor subtests.

Certainly, the meaning and interpretation of the third factor have continued to be topics of debate since Kaufman (1975) discussed the factor. Gutkin (1978) has noted that the WISC–R's third factor does not meet the .90 reliability standard to justify its use in making decisions regarding individual children, and Hale (1991) points out that even when the factor is found in some analyses, the reliability of the factor is not high enough to make it useful for practitioners.

Criterion-Related Evidence Regarding the WISC-R

Wechsler (1991) reviews a number of studies (e.g., Sandoval, Sassenrath, & Penaloza, 1988) in which the WISC–R has been compared to a variety of other intelligence tests and the correlations between the WISC–R IQs and the IQs on the other test have been reported. These investigations deal with a variety of normal and special education samples and cover a variety of age groups. Correlations of these various other intelligence tests with the WISC–R Full Scale IQ range from .65 to .96 with a median correlation of .83. Correlations for Verbal IQs with other tests range from .75 to .96 with a median correlation of .80, while correlations with Performance IQs range from .55 to .82 with a median correlation of .77. Thus, the findings reviewed by Wechsler (1991) indicate that there is a reasonable degree of concurrent validity for the WISC–R.

EVIDENCE REGARDING THE VALIDITY OF THE WISC-III

WISC-III Measurement of General Intelligence

Sattler (1992) notes that examination of the loadings on a first unrotated factor in either a principal components or maximum-likelihood factor analysis of the WISC–III permits the determination of the degree to which the test as a whole and the individual subtests measure general intelligence, or *g*. He states that overall, the WISC–III is a fair measure of general intelligence in that 43% of the variance on the test is attributable to *g*.

Sattler (1992) states that the WISC–III subtests form three clusters in terms of their reflection of *g*: Vocabulary, Information, Similarities, Block Design, Arithmetic, and Comprehension are good measures of *g*, with from 50% to 62% of the variance on these subtests being attributable to *g*; Object Assembly, Picture Completion, Symbol Search, Picture Arrangement, and Digit Span are fair measures of *g*, with from 26% to 44% of the variance on these subtests being attributable to *g*; and Coding and Mazes are poor measures of *g*, with 13% and 20% of the variance on these subtests attributable to *g*.

The verbal subtests typically have higher loadings on *g* than do the performance subtests, with verbal subtests averaging 52% of their variance attributable to *g* while performance subtests average 36% of their variance attributable to *g*. The best measures of *g* on the verbal scale include Vocabulary, Information and Similarities, while on the performance scale only Block Design appears to be a good measure of *g*.

Roid et al. (1993) report that their results verify the presence of a *g* factor on the WISC–III with their findings parallelling Sattler's (1992) observations. Although the actual percentages they report are slightly lower than those reported by Sattler (1992), in their investigation Vocabulary, Information, Similarities, Comprehension, Arithmetic, and Block Design have the highest loadings on *g*, while Coding and Mazes have the lowest. These findings suggest that there is general consensus that the test provides a reasonable measure of children and adolescent's general intelligence.

Internal Validity

As one approach to exploring the internal validity of the WISC–III, the relationships among various subtests and scales were examined by the test developers. Tables C.1.–C.12. (Wechsler, 1991, pp. 270–281) present the resulting intercorrelation matrices of subtest scaled scores and sums of scaled scores for Verbal, Performance and Full Scale IQs and for the four

Index scores for each of the 11 age groups. Table C.12. (Wechsler, 1991, p. 281) presents the average intercorrelations across all of the 11 age groups combined.

Examination of these intercorrelations indicates that there are higher within-scale correlations than across-scale correlations: verbal subtests typically correlate more highly with each other than they do with performance subtests, and performance subtests typically correlate more highly with each other than they do with verbal subtests. This pattern of higher correlations within each scale is an indication of the convergent validity of the WISC–III subtests while the lower correlations between the verbal and performance scales is an indication of the discriminant validity of the WISC–III subtests (Campbell & Fiske, 1959).

Examination of the average intercorrelations for the entire standardization sample (see Table C.12., Wechsler, 1991, p. 281) indicates that for the total group, intercorrelations range from .14 for Mazes with Digit Span to .70 for Vocabulary with Information. The Vocabulary subtest has the highest correlation with the Verbal scale (.78) while the Block Design subtest has the highest correlation with the Performance Scale (.65).

Factor-Analytic Approaches to WISC–III Validity

A second approach to exploring the internal validity of the WISC–III was the use of factor analysis. A number of different factor-analytic methods, including both exploratory and confirmatory analyses, were performed on the WISC–III standardization data and the results of these analyses were compared and contrasted with one another. Each of these analyses and methods were applied to the total sample of 2200 subjects and to four age-group subsamples: Ages 6–7 (n = 400), Ages 8–10 (n = 600), Ages 11–13 (n = 600), and Ages 14–16 (n = 600) (see Wechsler, 1991, pp. 187–196, for a detailed description of the factor analyses).

Wechsler (1991) approached the interpretation of the results of their factor analyses in terms of a criterion of "psychological meaningfulness" which was based on research with the WISC–R as well as the model of global intelligence propounded by Wechsler (1974).

Factor models which ranged from one to five factors were examined and compared in terms of goodness of fit, and Wechsler states that the results of their analyses "converge to strongly suggest a four-factor solution for the WISC–III" (Wechsler, 1991, p. 187); these four factors included two major factors and two smaller supplementary factors.

The first two factors, those of Verbal Comprehension and Perceptual Organization, are the same as have been obtained in factor analyses of the

WISC–R (Kaufman, 1975, 1979a; Kaufman et al., 1990). The Verbal Comprehension factor is comprised of four subtests: Information, Similarities, Vocabulary and Comprehension. The Perceptual Organization factor is also comprised of four subtests: Picture Completion, Picture Arrangement, Block Design and Object Assembly.

The third factor obtained in the analyses of the WISC–III differs slightly from that obtained with the WISC–R. On the WISC–R the third factor consisted of the Arithmetic, Digit Span and Coding subtests. But on the WISC–III the third factor consists of only the Arithmetic and Digit Span subtests, although this factor continues to be labelled Freedom from Distractibility just as it was on the WISC–R. On the WISC–III, the Coding subtest now loads on a fourth factor, along with the newly devised Symbol Search subtest, and this factor is labelled the Processing Speed factor.

Wechsler (1991) also examined the factor structure of the WISC–III for groups other than the standardization sample in order to determine whether the four-factor solution was generalizable to other populations. Clinical, high-ability and low-ability groups were chosen for investigation.

For the study of the clinical group, Wechsler (1991) used data which had been obtained on one of the special groups studied to examine the validity of the WISC–III. The clinical group sample consisted of 167 subjects including children with learning disabilities, reading disorders or attention-deficit disorders. These children were 82% males and ranged in age from 6 to 16 (median = 10 years). The results indicated that the four-factor model fit the data best, with the only exception to this being that the Picture Arrangement subtest had split loadings on three of the four factors, a result that had also occurred for the 6–7 year Age group in the standardization sample.

The high-ability group was formed by combining the gifted students who were studied to examine WISC–III validity with all those children in the standardization sample who had Full Scale IQs of 125 or greater. This resulted in a sample of 157 children aged 6–16 (median = 10 years). Confirmatory factor analyses again indicated that the four-factor model fit the data best of the five factor models considered. The fifth factor that emerged in this analysis appeared to be composed primarily of the Picture Arrangement subtest.

In the final study examining the consistency of the four-factor structure of the WISC–III across groups, a sample of children with low ability were studied. This group was comprised of 32 children with mental retardation who were part of the WISC–III validity studies and 109 children from the standardization sample who had Full Scale IQs of 75 or less, with the resulting sample in this group consisting of children aged 6–16 (median = 11). The best fit to the data was once again the four-factor model with an insignificant improvement in fit when the five-factor model was evaluated.

In contrast to Wechsler's (1991) results, Sattler (1992) reports his own maximum-likelihood factor analysis of the standardization sample for each age group and for the total sample. His results differed from those reported in the Wechsler (1991) manual and suggested that a three-factor model fit the WISC–III data best. However, he notes that this model is somewhat weak at ages 6 and 15 where only two factors emerged clearly. Sattler (1992) labels the three factors obtained in his analysis: Verbal Comprehension, which accounts for 25% of the test variance; Perceptual Organization, which accounts for 16% of the test variance; and Processing Speed, which accounts for 10% of the test variance.

Sattler (1992) also notes that although his third factor, Processing Speed, is typically represented by Coding and Symbol Search, this is not true for all ages. Thus, Arithmetic and Digit Span largely represent the third factor at age 11, but Symbol Search, Arithmetic, Picture Arrangement and Coding primarily represent the third factor at age seven. For the entire sample, however, Sattler notes that Coding and Symbol Search do have substantial loadings on the Processing Speed factor.

In justifying his position, Sattler (1992) notes that he conducted a four-factor analysis for each of the 11 separate age groups in the standardization sample, which Wechsler (1991) did not. At each age group and for the total sample, the eigenvalues (a mathematical value pertaining to the proportion of variance that a given factor accounts for) fell below a commonly used criterial eigenvalue of 1 for the Freedom from Distractibility factor. Additionally, the Freedom from Distractibility factor did not emerge in the 6, 8, 10 and 16 year age groups. Sattler's (1992) conclusion is thus that the Freedom from Distractibility factor on the WISC–III should be disregarded until there is further evidence to support its use. Thorndike (1992) also concluded that although there was evidence to support the Processing Speed factor, there was little evidence to support the Freedom from Distractibility factor.

Roid et al. (1993) note that Sattler's (1992) and Thorndike's (1992) conclusions are contradicted by certain technical considerations of factor-analytic methodology which were incorporated in Wechsler's (1991) approach. Roid et al. (1993) offer a statistical basis to justify the existence of the Freedom from Distractibility factor on the WISC–III, noting that such a factor was evident in Cohen's (1959) original investigation of the factorial structure of the WISC and which Cohen (1959) also labelled Freedom from Distractibility.

Roid et al. (1993) note that the WISC–III, although closely related to the WISC–R, differs from its predecessor in several ways: approximately 30% of the items are new, more stringent scoring rules are used in the WISC–III, and the test includes the new Symbol Search subtest. Hence one cannot assume that the WISC–R factor structure will automatically apply to the WISC–III.

Partly in response to questions raised by Sattler (1992) and Thorndike (1992) about the factor structure of the WISC–III, Roid et al. (1993) report a study of the WISC–III factor structure with an independent sample. One year after the standardization of the WISC–III, as part of the standardization of the Wechsler Individual Achievement Test (WIAT; The Psychological Corporation, 1992a), 1118 children were tested with both the WISC–III and the WIAT. This sample included approximately one hundred children at each full year of age (6–16) who had been selected based on a stratified random sampling plan using the variables of ethnicity/race, parent educational level, geographic region, and gender.

A number of exploratory and confirmatory factor-analytic methods were applied to the data from this newly obtained WISC–III sample. Although noting that they explored up to a five-factor solution, Roid et al. (1993) felt that a four-factor model yielded the most psychologically meaningful solution for the data.

In the four-factor solution, the Verbal Comprehension factor accounted for almost 44% of the variance, the Perceptual Organization factor for over nine percent, the Freedom from Distractibility factor six percent and the Processing Speed factor eight percent of the variance. Hence the authors conclude that their results are highly similar to those presented in the WISC–III manual (Wechsler, 1991) and contribute to the justification of using a four-factor approach to interpreting the WISC–III.

Kamphaus, Benson, Hutchinson, and Platt (1994) note that after decades of factor-analytic research, the latent traits assessed by the Wechsler scales continue to be a topic of debate. Criticizing the authors of the WISC–III manual for making the presumably contradictory conclusion that Wechsler's (1991) factor analyses support *both* the Verbal-Performance scale dichotomy *and* the four-factor solution, Kamphaus et al. (1994) report their own examination of the fit of two-, three-, and four-factor models to the WISC–III standardization data.

The sample used by Kamphaus et al. (1994) consisted of the standardization group described in the WISC–III manual (Wechsler, 1991). The sample was the 2200 subjects from the WISC–III standardization, divided into 11 age groups from ages 6 to 16 in one-year intervals, with 200 children at each age level.

The analyses carried out were based on three confirmatory factor models. The first was a two-factor model based on Wechsler's original verbal-performance dichotomy (Wechsler, 1958, 1974) and used all the WISC–III subtests except Symbol Search. The second model was a three-factor model based on Kaufman's (1979a) division of the Wechsler subtests into a verbal, a performance, and a freedom from distractibility factor, and divided the WISC–III subtests except Symbol Search into three groups. The third model was a four-factor model, based on Wechsler's (1991) division of the WISC–III subtests into four groups: verbal comprehension, perceptual organization, freedom from distractibility, and processing speed.

Kamphaus et al. (1994) use a number of statistical procedures to evaluate the fit of each of the factor models to the data, and note that there is very little difference between the three- and four-factor models for ages 6 and 9, while for all of the other age groups none of the models fit very well. Kamphaus et al. report examination of the standardized factor loadings for each model tested for each age group. For all three models, the standardized factor loadings are significant although there is some variation in the size of the loadings for different subtests.

Kamphaus et al. (1994), however, conclude that their findings do not support routine application of the four Index scores in clinical practice, as the statistical fit of the four-factor model is lacking for most age groups. They note that, at the same time, some of the statistics used to evaluate the data favor the four-factor model over the two-, and three-factor models. Apparently, the Mazes, Digit Span, and Coding subtests weaken the various factors in all three models. Finally, Kamphaus et al. close their article by noting the need for further research on the latent variables underlying the WISC–III and saying, "the four-factor model advocated by Wechsler (1991) is somewhat supported by the current analyses, but the theoretical or clinical importance of the additional factors and the Index is unclear" (p. 185).

As suggested by the foregoing material, the present author assumes that there will be continuing debate regarding whether a three- or four-factor model is the most appropriate solution to the WISC–III. This phenomenon occurred with respect to the existence of a third factor on the WISC–R (e.g., Kaufman et al., 1990), although, over the life of the WISC–R, the existence of the third factor became well established with a wide variety of populations (e.g., Cadwell & English, 1983; Chan, 1984; Groff & Hubble, 1982).

The essential conclusion that is possible based on these investigations is that as with the controversy which surrounded the existence or nonexistence of the WISC–R third factor, there is likely to be a continuing debate regarding whether or not the four-factor model is appropriate for the interpretation of the intellectual performance of a wide variety of subject populations evaluated with the WISC–III. The question of which model is more appropriate to explain the WISC–III will be addressed by a variety of research investigations in the coming years.

The present author will assume that a four-factor solution is appropriate for the interpretation of the WISC–III, although the controversy about whether three or four factors best explain WISC–III results should stand as a reminder to the clinician that her or his own beliefs will determine the strategy selected for interpreting any kind of data and that a cautious, thoughtful and conservative approach to utilizing any test is the most reasonable strategy for the clinician to use.

STUDIES OF THE WISC-III: COMPARISON STUDIES

The following section discusses the relationship between the WISC–III and other intelligence scales on the one hand, and between the WISC–III and various measures of academic achievement on the other, in order to provide evidence of two kinds of validity: convergent validity is demonstrated by high correlations between measures purported to assess the same construct (e.g., the VIQ on the WISC–R and the VIQ on the WISC–III); discriminant validity is demonstrated by low correlations between measures purported to assess different constructs (e.g., the lower correlations between WISC–III verbal subtests and PIQ, and between the performance subtests and VIQ).

Correlation with the WISC-R

Wechsler (1991) reports two studies examining the correlation between the WISC–III and WISC–R. In one study, the WISC–III and the WISC–R were administered in counterbalanced order to a sample of 206 children between 6 and 16 years of age, with a median age of 11. The intertest interval ranged from 12 to 70 days (median = 21 days). The sample consisted of 55% female and 45% male subjects with 70% Whites, 19% Blacks, 8% Hispanics, and 3% children of other racial/ethnic origin.

The correlations between the two tests, corrected for the variability of the WISC–III scores, were .90 for the Verbal IQ, .81 for the Performance IQ, and .89 for the Full Scale IQ. Over the two administrations, the average Full Scale IQ on the WISC–III was 5.3 points lower than the average Full Scale IQ on the WISC–R (WISC–III FSIQ = 102.9, SD = 14.7; WISC–R FSIQ = 108.2, SD = 15.1). The average WISC–III Verbal IQ was 2.4 points lower than the average WISC–R Verbal IQ (WISC–III VIQ = 101.5, SD = 14.5; WISC–R VIQ = 103.9, SD = 14.7) and the average WISC–III Performance IQ was 7.4 points lower than the average WISC–R Performance IQ (WISC–III PIQ = 104.2, SD = 15.1; WISC–R PIQ = 111.6, SD = 15.4). These findings are consistent with the observation by Flynn (1987) that ordinarily individuals obtain lower IQ scores on newly developed tests.

In comparing the 12 subtests that the WISC–III and WISC–R both include, the lowest correlation was between the Picture Arrangement subtest scores on the WISC–III and the WISC–R with a correlation of .42; the highest subtest correlation was for the Information subtest, with a correlation of .80 between the Information subtest scores on the WISC–III and the Information subtest scores the WISC–R. The verbal subtests tended to correlate more highly between the two tests than did the performance subtests.

In the second study, WISC–III and WISC–R scores of a clinical sample were compared. This sample involved 104 children, with 57% of the children having various learning or reading disabilities, 35% having attention-deficit hyperactivity disorder, and 8% having depression or an anxiety disorder. The children were from 7 to 14 years of age with a median age of 10. The sample consisted of 81% male and 89% White children, with 5% Blacks, 4% Hispanics, and 2% children of other racial/ethnic background.

Although Wechsler (1991) does not provide complete information on this study, for this sample, the corrected correlations between the WISC–III and WISC–R were .86 for the Full Scale IQ, .86 for the Verbal IQ and .73 for the Performance IQ. In this sample, the WISC–III Full Scale IQ was 5.9 points less than the WISC–R Full Scale IQ; the WISC–III Verbal IQ was 5.4 points less than the WISC–R Verbal IQ; and the WISC–III Performance IQ was 5.1 points lower than the WISC–R Performance IQ. Hence the overall correlations, the IQ scores and differences between the sets of scores are of similar size and in the same direction as the results obtained for the non-clinical sample.

Correlation with the WAIS–R

Wechsler (1991) reports one study in which the WISC–III and the WAIS–R were administered in counterbalanced order to a sample of 189 16-year-old children. Intertest intervals between occasions of testing ranged from 12 to 70 days (median = 21 days). The sample consisted of 55% females and 45% males with 71% of the sample Whites, 10% Blacks, 16% Hispanics, and 3% children of other racial/ethnic origin.

The correlations between the WISC–III scores and the WAIS–R scores, corrected for the variability of the WISC–III scores, were .86 between the Full Scale IQs on the two tests; .90 between the Verbal IQs on the two tests; and .80 between the Performance IQs on the two tests. These results suggest that the two tests measure a similar underlying construct.

Across the counterbalanced administrations, the average Full Scale IQ on the WISC–III was 3.9 points lower than the WAIS–R Full Scale IQ (WISC–III FSIQ = 101.4, SD = 15.0; WAIS–R FSIQ = 105.3, SD = 14.9). The WISC–III Verbal IQ was 1.5 points lower than the WAIS–R Verbal IQ (WISC–III VIQ = 101.0, SD = 14.7; WAIS–R VIQ = 102.5, SD = 13.3).

And the WISC–III Performance IQ was 5.9 points lower than the WAIS–R Performance IQ (WISC–III PIQ = 101.8, SD = 15.9; WAIS–R PIQ = 107.7, SD = 14.3).

For the 11 subtests which the WISC–III and the WAIS–R have in common, the lowest correlation was .35 for the Picture Arrangement subtest while the highest correlation was .85 for the Vocabulary subtest.

Correlation with the WPPSI-R

Wechsler (1991) reports one study in which the WISC–III and WPPSI–R were administered in counterbalanced order to a sample of 188 6-year-old children. The intertest interval ranged from 12 to 62 days (median = 21 days), and the sample consisted of 53% female and 47% male children with 67% Whites, 12% Blacks, 14% Hispanics, and 7% children of other racial/ethnic origin.

The correlations between the two scales, corrected for the variability of the WISC–III scores, were .85 for the Full Scale IQ, .85 for the Verbal IQ, and .73 for the Performance IQ. Across the counterbalanced administrations, the average WISC–III Full Scale IQ was 106.5 (SD = 12.5) as compared to the WPPSI–R Full Scale IQ of 102.5 (SD = 12.5) with the WISC–III being 4.0 points higher than the WPPSI–R. The WISC–III Verbal IQ was 1.9 points higher than the WPPSI–R Verbal IQ (WISC–III VIQ = 104.2, SD = 13.2; WPPSI–R VIQ = 102.3, SD = 14.4) while the WISC–III Performance IQ was 5.9 points higher than the WPPSI–R Performance IQ (WISC–III PIQ = 108.2, SD = 12.8; WPPSI–R PIQ = 102.3, SD = 11.4).

Although the correlation of .73 between the PIQs on the WISC–III and WPPSI–R for these 6-year-old children is lower than would be desirable, Wechsler (1991) concludes that the magnitude of the correlation between the FSIQs on the two tests suggests that, overall, the WISC–III and the WPPSI–R measure similar constructs.

Correlations Between the WISC-III and Other Tests

Wechsler (1991) reports the correlations between the WISC–III and a number of other tests of intellectual or academic performance (Tables 6.14. & 6.15.; Wechsler, 1991, pp. 204–205; see Wechsler, 1991, pp. 203–209 for the full discussion of these correlations).

Examination of Tables 6.14. and 6.15. in Wechsler (1991, pp. 204–205) indicates that the WISC–III correlates quite highly with some other measures of individuals' intellectual or academic performance. For example, the WISC–III and the *Otis-Lennon School Ability Test Sixth Edition, Form I* (OLSAT; Otis & Lennon, 1989) were both administered to 65 children aged 6–16 (median = 9 years). The correlation between the WISC–III Full Scale IQ and the Otis-Lennon Total School Ability Index was .73. The correlation between the WISC–III VIQ and the OLSAT Verbal School Ability Index was .69, and the correlation between the WISC–III PIQ and the OLSAT Nonverbal School Ability Index was .59.

Wechsler (1991) reports that standard scores on the *Differential Ability Scales* (DAS; Elliott, 1990) were obtained for 27 children aged 7–14 (median = 9 years) who were also administered the WISC–III. The WISC–III FSIQ correlated .92 with the DAS General Conceptual Ability score, while the WISC–III VIQ score correlated .87 with the DAS Verbal Ability score. The WISC–III PIQ correlated .78 with the DAS Nonverbal Reasoning score and .82 with the DAS Spatial Ability score. Furthermore, the DAS Speed of Information Processing score correlated .67 with the WISC–III Processing Speed Index score.

Table 6.15. in Wechsler (1991, p. 205) also presents the correlations of the WISC–III IQ and Index scores with the DAS achievement test scores. These correlations vary from .26 (for the WISC–III POI and the DAS Basic Number Skills score) to .61 (for the WISC–III FDI and the DAS Word Reading score).

Correlations between the WISC–III IQ scores and the Wide Range Achievement Test-Revised scores range from .11 (between the WISC–III PIQ and the WRAT–R Spelling subtest) to .62 (between the WISC–III VIQ and the WRAT–R Reading subtest). However, the WISC–III factor scores correlate at a higher level with WRAT–R subtests, for example, with the WISC–III PSI correlating .73 with the Arithmetic subtest of the WRAT–R. Correlations between WISC–III IQs and the newest version of the WRAT, the WRAT3 (Wilkinson, 1993), range from .51 (between the WISC–III PIQ and the WRAT3 Arithmetic Combined score) to .70 (between the WISC–III VIQ and the WRAT3 Reading Combined score).

Wechsler (1991) reports an investigation of 358 children aged 6 to 16 (median = 11 years) who were administered both the WISC–III and one of a number of different group achievement tests. Wechsler (1991) reports the average correlations, across the five achievement tests used, of the WISC–III IQ and Index scores with Total Achievement, Reading, Mathematics, and Written Language Normal Curve Equivalent scores on the achievement tests. A correlation of .74 was obtained between the WISC–III FSIQ and Total Achievement, and with the WISC–III VIQ and Total Achievement. The WISC–III FSIQ correlated .68 with the Mathematics Achievement score.

Finally, correlations between the WISC–III Verbal, Performance and Full Scale IQs and Index scores correlate from .28 to .48 with school grades.

Hishinuma and Yamakawa (1993) investigated the construct and criterion-related validity of the WISC–III with a sample of 78 students attending a private school for gifted and/or learning disabled students. These authors utilized the WISC–III as well as a number of other standardized tests such as the Peabody Picture Vocabulary Test, Revised (PPVT–R; Dunn & Dunn, 1981); the Detroit Tests of Learning Aptitude, 3rd ed. (DTLA-3; Hammill, 1991); Woodcock Reading Mastery Tests Revised (WRMT–R; Woodcock, 1987); the Wide Range Achievement Test-Revised (WRAT–R; Jastak & Wilkinson, 1984); and the KeyMath, Revised (Connolly, 1988), among others.

Of the 78 students who participated in the study, 15 (19%) were identified previously as high potential (gifted); 9 (12%) were high potential/remedial (gifted/learning disabled); 31 (40%) were remedial (learning disabled); and the remaining 23 (30%) were classified as other, since they did not fall into any of the previous three categories. Fifty-five (70.5%) of the students were male and 23 (29.5%) were females. One percent of the students were African-American, 28% were Asian-American/Pacific Islander, 55% were Anglo, and the remaining 16% were of mixed origin.

To determine whether the WISC–III differentiated among groups, means and standard deviations were calculated for the IQs, Index scores, and subtest scaled scores for the entire sample and for each of the four groups.

The order of the four groups Full Scale IQs was as follows: high potential = 118.7; high potential/remedial = 112.0; other = 100.2; and remedial = 98.9, which the authors conclude supports the construct validity of the WISC–III. In examining the intercorrelation patterns among the subtests, the authors note that since correlations were higher for verbal subtests with the Verbal IQ and for performance subtests with the Performance IQ, their findings support the convergent validity of the test. Hishinuma and Yamakawa (1993) note that the discriminant validity of the test also was supported since lower correlations were obtained when verbal subtests were correlated with the Performance IQ and when performance subtests were correlated with the Verbal IQ.

Hishinuma and Yamakawa (1993) note that intercorrelations between the WISC–III and other measures of cognitive functioning generally support the construct validity of the WISC–III. Thus there was a correlation of .70 between the WISC–III Full Scale IQ and the DTLA-3 General Mental Ability score. A correlation of .66 was obtained between the WISC–III Verbal IQ and the DTLA-3 Verbal composite, and a correlation of .54 between the WISC–III Performance IQ and the DTLA-3 Nonverbal quotient was obtained. Correlations between the WISC–III Full Scale IQ correlated at from .51 to .76 with the WRAT–R subtests, but correlations between the WISC–III Verbal IQ and the WRAT–R subtests were generally higher (.65 with the Reading subtest; .63 with the Spelling subtest; and .76 with the Arithmetic subtest).

Hishinuma and Yamakawa (1993) also carried out unrotated and rotated factor analyses of the major scores of the various tests they had administered. Although their results did support Wechsler's (1991) four-factor model for interpreting the WISC–III, they did find that the Perceptual Organization factor did not include the Picture Arrangement subtest, which instead loaded on the Processing Speed factor.

Teeter and Smith (1993) investigated the predictive and discriminant validity of the WISC–III and the Woodcock-Johnson Psychoeducational Battery-Revised (Woodcock & Johnson, 1977) with a group of 60 adolescents, 30 with severe emotional disturbance, and a control group of 30 adolescents without academic or emotional problems. These authors administered the WISC–III, two subtests of the WJ–R Cognitive Battery designed to measure fluid reasoning, and nine subtests of the WJ–R Achievement Battery to their subjects.

Teeter and Smith (1993) found that the emotionally disturbed students scored below average and below the control students' IQs on the WISC–III Verbal, Performance and Full Scale IQ scores. Their data also provided support for the predictive validity of the WISC–III in regard to the broad achievement scores of their sample on the WJ–R factors that were studied. A discriminant function analysis permitted the WISC–III factor scores and the WJ–R reasoning score to correctly classify emotionally disturbed students with 100% accuracy and control students with 86.7% accuracy.

Wechsler (1991) reports that correlations between the WISC–III and non-academic tasks, such as components of the Halstead-Reitan Neuropsychological Test Battery or the Revised Benton Visual Retention Test range from −.64 (TPT Total Time with WISC–III PIQ) to .45 (TPT Memory with WISC–III PIQ).

The above-noted studies provide evidence of the concurrent, construct, predictive, and discriminant validity for the WISC–III. Nonetheless, the sizes of some of the correlations obtained in the above-noted investigations indicate that predictions of an individual examinee's ability to succeed in a given academic program should be made with considerable thoughtfulness and with due caution since many factors other than intellectual ability as measured by the WISC–III may enter into the individual's functioning in a real-world situation.

Chapter Seven

OTHER PSYCHOMETRIC FEATURES
OF THE WISC-III

DIFFERENCES BETWEEN IQ AND INDEX SCORES
ON THE WISC-III

Since the initial development of the Wechsler Scales, interpretation of an individual's performance on the test has involved consideration of differences between various parts of the scale (Wechsler, 1955). In discussing this issue regarding the WISC–III, Wechsler (1991) notes that in the interpretation of differences between IQ scores or between factor-based Index scores, two issues must be considered: the statistical significance of a difference between scores, and the base rate, or frequency with which a given difference occurs in the total population.

The statistical significance of a difference between two scores, say the Verbal and Performance IQs, pertains to the probability that this difference might have occurred because of chance or error variation in the scores. In this framework, low probability levels (e.g., $p < .05$ or $p < .01$) indicate that the obtained difference is highly unlikely to occur if the actual difference between the two scores is zero.

On the other hand, the base rate of the difference between two scores refers to the frequency with which a given difference between two scores is found to occur in the total population. In this framework, it is often the case that while the difference between an examinee's Verbal and Performance IQs may be statistically significant, it is not a rare occurrence among examinees in general. These two frameworks—the statistical significance of a difference and the frequency of occurrence of given differences—are not the same and both need to be considered independently when interpreting an individual's test performance.

Table B.1. (Wechsler, 1991, p. 261) presents the smallest difference between an examinee's Verbal and Performance IQs, or between any pair of Index scores, which is necessary to conclude that the obtained difference is statistically significant at either the .15 or .05 level of confidence. Wechsler's Table B.1. provides the data for each age group in the standardization sample on the differences required for statistical significance between two IQ or index scores. Table 14 in the present volume, "Differences Between WISC–III IQ and Index Scores Required for Significance by Age," adapted from Naglieri (1993), provides such data when corrections have been made in the experimenterwise error rate as discussed by Naglieri (1993), and the examiner who wishes to use a more conservative standard for evaluating VIQ–PIQ or Index Score differences can utilize this table instead of Wechsler's (1991).

Table B.2. (Wechsler, 1991, p. 262), on the other hand, indicates the frequency of VIQ–PIQ differences of various sizes which occurred in the entire WISC–III standardization sample. Analyses of variance found no significant differences in the average discrepancy between VIQs and PIQs, or between various Index scores across age groups or ability levels. Hence Table B.2. summarizes the findings for the entire standardization sample. The VIQ–PIQ column, for example, shows the percentage of subjects whose VIQs and PIQs differed by at least the given amount, regardless of which IQ score was higher.

In using these tables, for example, if one had tested a 10-year-old child and she or he obtained a VIQ of 95 and a PIQ of 107, referring to Table B.1. (Wechsler, 1991, p. 261) one could determine that the 12-point difference between these IQ scores is statistically significant; that is, there is less than five chances in 100 that the true difference between them is actually zero. This examinee thus displays a real difference between his or her abilities for handling verbal as opposed to nonverbal tasks.

On the other hand, inspection of Table B.2. (Wechsler, 1991, p. 262) indicates that almost 36% of examinees in the standardization sample obtained VIQ and PIQ scores that differed by 12 or more points; hence the finding on this 10-year-old is statistically significant but not uncommon and this should be considered by the examiner in determining what he or she might say in a psychological report describing the examinee's intellectual functioning.

DIFFERENCES BETWEEN A SINGLE SUBTEST SCALED SCORE AND AN AVERAGE OF SUBTEST SCORES ON THE WISC-III

Ordinarily, an examinee's subtest scaled scores on the WISC–III will be characterized by some degree of variability. Just as with the interpretation of differences between IQ or Index scores, the interpretation of differences between one subtest score and the average of some subset of subtest scores should be carried out with an appreciation of the statistical characteristics of observed differences and estimates of population base rates.

Kaufman (1979a, 1990) has proposed and popularized a method called "profile analysis" for the interpretation of the variability in an examinee's Wechsler performance. In this approach, the meaningfulness of a specific subtest scaled score is interpreted by comparing it to the examinee's average score on all subtests (or on a particular subset of scores that includes the subtest in question).

From within this interpretive framework, an examinee's score on, for example, the Block Design subtest could be compared with the examinee's average score on any of the various subsets which contain this subtest (e.g., the five performance subtests included in the PIQ calculation; the six performance subtests excluding Mazes; all seven performance subtests; the 10 subtests included in the calculation of the examinee's IQ scores; 12 subtests excluding Mazes; all 13 subtests of the WISC–III; or the four subtests included in the Perceptual Organization factor).

This strategy, which views an examinee's score on any subtest in relation to her or his other subtest scores, is considered an *ipsative* approach; it characterizes the examinee's strengths or weaknesses with respect to his or her *own* profile of abilities. Hence the performance of an examinee whose overall intellectual functioning may be average, above average or below average with respect to the standardization sample may be evaluated this way to determine the examinee's *own* relative strengths or weaknesses in cognitive ability.

Although there has been disagreement with the concept of this interpretive approach (McDermott, Fantazzo, & Glutting, 1990; McDermott, Fantuzzo, Glutting, Watkins & Baggaley, 1992; Naglieri, 1993), Table B.3. (Wechsler, 1991, pp. 263–264) provides information regarding the differences needed for statistical significance at the .15 and .05 levels and the cumulative percents in the normative population of differences of various sizes for comparing individual subtest scores with the average of various other subtest scores of the examinee.

Table B.3. (Wechsler, 1991, pp. 263–264) did not include the .01 level of significance because it was felt that when examining subtest and composite score differences, one is in a hypothesis-generating mode and a type II error would be as problematic as a type I error. Hence it was felt that the .05 and .15 levels were a reasonable range for the clinician to use when balancing type I and type II errors (A. Prifitera, personal communication, July 12, 1993).

In the same way as in the case of differences between composite scores such as Verbal and Performance IQs, a difference between a single subtest score and the average of a group of subtest scores may be statistically significant but occur frequently or infrequently among the standardization population. Hence Table B.3. (Wechsler, 1991, pp. 263–264) provides data on how frequently the various tabled differences occur in the entire standardization sample. Although the manual does not state it explicitly, one would assume that the cumulative percentages for the entire sample are relevant to the performance of an examinee of any particular age.

The examiner can use Table B.3. by noting that, for example, 25% of the standardization population obtained a difference of 2.00 or more points between their score on the Information subtest and the average of their scores on the five verbal subtests. On the other hand, only one percent of the standardization population obtained a difference of 4.80 or more points between their score on the Information subtest and the average of their scores on the five verbal tests.

DIFFERENCES BETWEEN INDIVIDUAL SUBTEST SCORES ON THE WISC-III

In some instances when interpreting the WISC–III the examiner may also be interested in the difference between two specific subtest scaled scores on an examinee's test profile. For example, an examinee may have obtained a Comprehension subtest score of 8 and a Picture Arrangement subtest score of 12 and the examiner would like to comment on this difference in the psychological report. Before doing so, the examiner should determine whether or not this difference is significant since the difference could have occurred purely by chance.

For every possible pair of WISC–III subtests, the size of intersubtest score difference which is required for statistical significance appears in Table B.4. (Wechsler, 1991, p. 265). The differences required between subtest scores for significance at the .15 level appear above the diagonal of the table while the differences required for significance at the .05 level appear below the diagonal. Examination of the table indicates that a difference of 2.98 points between the Comprehension and Picture Arrangement subtests is significant at the .15 level; however, a difference of 4.06 points would be needed between these two subtests for significance at the .05 level.

Intersubtest scatter refers to the degree of variability of scaled scores within an individual's test profile (Kaufman, 1976a). While the degree of such variability is often used in interpretation of the examinee's test performance, before drawing conclusions about this aspect of the examinee's functioning, it is important to know how frequently any given degree of scatter occurs.

Wechsler (1991) uses as the index of scatter the difference between an examinee's highest and lowest subtest scaled scores. Table B.5. (Wechsler, 1991, p. 266) indicates the cumulative percentages within the standardization sample of intersubtest scatter for various groups of subtests (e.g., 5 or 6 verbal subtests). Wechsler (1991) reports that analyses of variance were conducted to determine whether intersubtest scatter varied as a function of age or ability level. There were no significant differences in average scatter across age groups and although significant differences among ability levels were obtained, these were small and hence a single set of scatter frequences for examinees of all age and ability levels is presented in Table B.5.

If an examinee has obtained a difference of six points between the examinee's highest and lowest verbal subtest scaled scores, the examiner can refer to Table B.5. and note that approximately thirty percent of the standardization sample had differences between their highest and lowest verbal subtest scores of at least six points. This indicates that a six-point variation among an examinee's verbal subtests is quite common and of limited interpretive significance.

The WISC–III Digit Span score is based on the combined raw scores of digits forward and backwards. It has been suggested, however, that the cognitive processes involved in these two tasks may differ and that performance on the tasks may differ according to the presence or kind of information processing deficit the individual may have (Rudel & Denkla, 1974).

To facilitate the interpretation of the examinee's performance on the Digit Span subtest (which is one of the subtests in the Freedom from Distractibility factor), Wechsler (1991) provides Table B.6. (p. 267), which indicates cumulative percentages of examinees' longest digit spans forward and longest digit spans backwards for each of the 11 age groups in the standardization sample and for all ages combined. Additionally, Wechsler (1991) provides Table B.7. (p. 268) which indicates cumulative percentages of the differences between examinees' longest digit spans forward and their longest digit spans backwards for each of the 11 age groups and for all ages combined. In those instances where the examiner wishes, she or he may provide a more specific analysis of an examinee's performance on the Digit Span subtest and describe the examinee's abilities for basic attention (Digits Forward) and more complex internal mental processing (Digits Backward).

WISC–III SUBTEST SPECIFICITY

The idea of interpreting individual subtests on the Wechsler was discussed by Wechsler himself (Wechsler, 1955), and in the manual of the Wechsler Intelligence Scale for Children-Revised (1974), he notes the relevance of individual subtest scores in differential diagnosis. Sattler (1974) and Kaufman (1979a) have given further impetus to this approach to test interpretation by providing summaries of the unique and shared abilities assessed by the Wechsler scales.

On the other hand, McDermott et al. (1990) note that Wechsler (Wechsler, 1958) advanced the contradictory ideas that, on the one hand, the subtests had no special meaning other than to contribute to the composite of global intelligence while, on the other hand, he proposed that the subtests had particular significance. McDermott et al. (1990) thus criticize the use of subtest analysis on a number of methodological grounds and point out that the consideration of Wechsler profiles adds nothing to that achieved by simply examining global IQ measures.

Bracken et al. (1993) note that despite these counterarguments, the WISC–III manual includes extensive information to enable the examiner to determine the significance of differences between various WISC–III subtest scores, which supports and facilitates the use of profile analysis. Assuming that this clinical practice will continue, Bracken et al. (1993) provide information on subtest specificities.

Examinees' subtest scores on the WISC–III include three components: common variance (shared with other subtests), specific variance (unique to a particular subtest), and error variance (reflecting measurement error). In statistical terms, the specificity of a subtest refers to the proportion of a subtest's variance that is reliable (not due to measurement error) and unique to that particular subtest (Sattler, 1992).

The determination of subtest specificity is based on a rule of thumb proposed by Kaufman (1975). This rule is that subtests display "ample" specificity when the subtest's specific variance equals 25% or more of the subtest's total variance and exceeds the subtest's error variance. Subtests display "adequate" specificity when their specific variance is between 15% and 24% of the subtest's total variance and exceeds the subtest's error variance. And subtests display "inadequate" specificity when they have specific variance that is either less than 15% of the subtest's total variance or is equal to or less than the subtest's error variance.

Kaufman (1975) states that it is reasonable to interpret subtests with "ample" specificity as measures of unique constructs. Although one may interpret subtests with "adequate" specificity as reflecting unique constructs, Kaufman (1975) suggests a more cautious approach in this case. Lastly, he believes that those subtests with "inadequate" specificity should not be interpreted as measuring unique constructs although they may be interpreted as measuring general intelligence or as part of one of the broad factors (e.g., perceptual organization) that comprise the test.

Table 16, "WISC–III Subtest Specificities," adapted from Bracken et al. (1993), is reprinted in the present volume for the reader's information and use.

Examination of Table 16 indicates that Digit Span, Coding, Picture Arrangement and Block Design have ample specificity over the entire age range of the WISC–III. Mazes has ample specificity at 10 of the 11 age levels, and Picture Completion has ample specificity at nine of the 11 age levels. Each of the remaining subtests has its own unique pattern of specificity in terms of those age levels where the subtest has ample, adequate or inadequate specificity.

Comparison of the data of Bracken et al. (1993) with that of Sattler (1992, p. 1049) indicate some disagreement in the categorization of the specificity of the various subtests. For example, Sattler (1992) notes that Coding has ample specificity at 10 of 11 ages while it has inadequate specificity at age eight.

In using this information, before making the interpretation that an examinee's performance on a particular subtest reflects the examinee's strength or weakness on the presumed underlying ability, the examiner must consider whether the subtest in question demonstrates ample, adequate or inadequate specificity. Object Assembly is the one subtest that across almost the entire age range of the WISC–III lacks sufficient specificity to justify interpreting it as unique.

Bracken et al. (1993) note that the interpretation of performance on a single subtest should be done with caution. Interpretation of normative or ipsative strengths or weaknesses should rely on more global estimates of functioning, such as clusters or factor scores, which will permit interpretations to rest on more reliable and accurate estimates of an examinee's abilities.

SUBTEST COMPOSITE RELIABILITIES

One issue regarding the interpretation of the Wechsler Intelligence Scale for Children-Revised was whether the various subtest composites (e.g., Information and Vocabulary taken together as a measure of the construct of Fund of Information) identified by such authors as Sattler (1974) and Kaufman (1979a) were sufficiently reliable to permit meaningful interpretation. Piotrowski and Siegel (1984) calculated the subtest composite reliabilities for 46 such WISC–R composites that had been identified by Sattler (1974) and Kaufman (1979a).

Piotrowski and Siegel (1984) found that WISC–R subtest composites ranged from a reliability of .76 for Paper and Pencil Skill (comprised of the Coding and Mazes subtests) to a reliability of .94 for Cognition (comprised of the Similarities, Arithmetic, Vocabulary, Picture Completion, Block Design, Object Assembly and Mazes subtests).

All of the WISC–R subtest composites except three met the .80 minimum criterion proposed by Salvia and Ysseldyke (1988) for screening purposes, and 18 of 46 composites met the more stringent criterion of .90 felt necessary for making important educational decisions regarding students.

Bracken et al. (1993) note that in using the WISC–III, many clinicians will continue the practice of subtest composite interpretation and hence it is important that the reliabilities of these composites be known. Although the WISC–III includes 12 of the subtests that were on the WISC–R, the new version of the Wechsler also includes an additional subtest, the Symbol Search subtest. The inclusion of this subtest has altered the factor structure of the WISC–III by resulting in a fourth factor, Processing Speed, and in the shift of the Coding subtest to load on this Processing Speed factor instead of the WISC–R third factor of Freedom from Distractibility.

In addition, since the Symbol Search subtest does share underlying characteristics with some of the former WISC–R subtest composites (e.g., Paper and Pencil Skill), its inclusion in these composites must also be considered. Thus, subtest composite reliabilities for the WISC–III must be re-established to reflect all 13 subtests and the impact of the Symbol Search subtest on some of the WISC–R composites.

Bracken et al. (1993) report the subtest composite reliabilities for the WISC–III standardization sample for three age levels: the two extreme age levels (i.e., 6 and 16) and the middle-most age level in the standardization sample (i.e., age 11). Furthermore, Bracken et al. (1993) averaged and then rank ordered the composite reliabilities by magnitude across the three age levels.

Bracken et al. (1993) calculated the reliabilities for each of the 46 subtest composites which had been identified by Piotrowski and Siegel (1984) but modified the composites to reflect the contributions of the Symbol Search subtest; they also added one additional composite, that of Processing Speed, resulting in a total of 47 WISC–III subtest composites. Finally, since the WISC–III factor analyses indicate that Mazes does not load significantly on the Perceptual Organization factor as it did on the WISC–R, the subtests on this composite on the WISC–III were changed from those which were included on the composite for the WISC–R.

In contrast to the procedure used by Piotrowski and Siegel (1984) who simply averaged the reliability coefficients across the three age levels, Bracken et al. (1993) converted all reliabilities to Fisher's Zs before averaging, then reconverted each averaged Z to a resulting reliability coefficient, which is a more sensitive statistical technique than had been used by Piotrowski and Siegel (1984).

Bracken et al. (1993) found the ranges of composite reliabilities for the WISC–R and WISC–III to be quite similar (.80 to .94 for the WISC–III and .79 to .94 for the WISC–R). However, they observed a trend for the WISC–III to reveal higher composite reliabilities than the WISC–R, suggesting that the clinician who does interpret subtest composites can do so with confidence in the internal consistency of those composites on the WISC–III. Despite these findings, Bracken et al. (1993) note that there are several arguments for not interpreting subtest composites as meaningful psycho-educational constructs.

A major issue in this regard is that when individual subtests or small clusters of subtests are interpreted as measuring a unique ability, the clinician is ignoring the largest portion of the subtest's reliable variance, which is that variance it shares with the remainder of the test. Further, Bracken and Fagen (1988) have noted that there is often little consensus among researchers as to which psychoeducational abilities underlie specific subtests, or presumably groups of subtests. The less precise the construct (e.g., holistic processing), the less agreement there is in terms of the meaning of the construct.

Thus, although the interpretation of subtest composites may make report writing more interesting and exciting for the clinician, the process must be approached from a thoughtful, cautious and conservative perspective. In view of these concerns regarding the interpretation of subtest composites, the present author has not included the tables from Bracken et al. (1993) which deal with subtest composites. The author recommends that any reader who does include such composites in her or his reports consult Bracken et al. before doing so.

Part II of the present volume, "Development and Nature of the WISC–III," has thus described the background, development, and various aspects of the psychometric characteristics of the WISC–III. This material provides a vital context for the clinical use of the test since the interpretation of the WISC–III relies on the test's statistical and psychometric features. Although there may be some concern about such characteristics as the reliabilities of individual subtests (Kaufman, 1994), in general, the basic reliability and validity of the WISC–III appear to justify its use for the assessment of children and adolescent's intellectual abilities.

Part III
FOUNDATIONS OF TESTING
WITH THE WISC-III

Chapter Eight

ISSUES IN THE CLINICAL USE OF THE WISC-III

One of the major activities of clinical and school psychologists during the past 50 years has been the psychological evaluation of individuals and groups. At the present time, psychological assessment comprises a wide variety of approaches applied to an equally wide variety of clients for a number of different purposes (Anastasi, 1988; Goldstein & Hersen, 1990).

While the examiner may focus on the use of psychological tests in order to evaluate a given individual, it is important to realize that testing and the outcome of testing fits within and may also serve a variety of political and social imperatives (Hale, 1991), and that testing of any child or adolescent must be understood in terms of the cultural context within which the child has developed and lives (Miller-Jones, 1989).

In any instance where an individual child or adolescent is to be evaluated, one can assume that such an evaluation is one step in a series of events that began prior to the evaluation proper. The process that eventuates in an individual being formally evaluated thus involves a number of sequentially organized steps or stages, with each step involving a decision-making process and a selection among alternative paths. Although the clinician actually testing a child may become involved in this sequence of events at any of several points, it is relevant for the psychologist to be aware of the total sequence of events so that he or she can address the issues among the spectrum of individuals for whom the testing may have meaning.

Viewed from the perspective of a set of sequentially organized events that may culminate in, or include, the psychological testing of a child or adolescent, the specific steps in such a process include the following:

1) Identification of the individual as possibly being in need of some specific evaluation. For a child, this would ordinarily involve some adult in the child's world indicating concern about the child's status on one or more dimensions as compared to the child's reference group;

2) Referral of the child to some more specifically trained or qualified person(nel) whose task is to gather initial data regarding the referral question and to determine whether or what strategy is indicated: no action; defer and review the child's status at some future date; or to

proceed with some specific current evaluation (whether medical, social, psychological and/or educational);

3) Proceed to obtain that further evaluation or multiple evaluation data; interpret the data gathered and generate a verbal or written report of findings, conclusions and recommendations;

4) Review the evaluative information that has been obtained and, based on that information, formulate a plan of action (intervention);

5) Share the evaluation results, conclusions and recommended plan with the relevant individuals (e.g., child, parent, teacher, pediatrician, therapist) and determine a future review point;

6) Implement the plan, i.e., provide some specific intervention for the child who has been evaluated;

7) At the predetermined review point, re-evaluate the individual; review the outcome of the plan that has been implemented and determine whether the original evaluation and plan were sufficient to address the concerns raised, whether the plan should be continued, or whether new data and a different plan are indicated.

The above-noted sequence refers to a cycle that is relevant for essentially any instance in which a child or adolescent is considered for possible assessment. It is based on the assumption that ordinarily, one intervenes in those situations where a child's functioning is discrepant from an expected pathway, whether the individual's functioning is below expectation (e.g., a child failing in school) or above (e.g., a child who is succeeding well beyond grade-level placement). The author is aware of the value of preventive approaches in mental health (Forgays, 1991). However, the current volume is organized to view assessment of a child as occurring in the context of the child's questioned variance from, or similarity to, a referent population.

Regardless of the particular setting in which the clinician is functioning, whether in a school, hospital, community clinic or private office, the above sequence of events is likely to occur. The clinician who is responsible for administering the WISC–III will enter the above-noted sequence of events at some point in the sequence, depending on the specific setting in which she or he is functioning.

According to the sequence described above, the first issue that arises is the identification of an individual as possibly or definitively in need of psychological, or more specifically intellectual, assessment. Fundamentally, the child or adolescent, in his or her functioning, would have displayed behaviors which raise a question regarding the nature of the individual's adaptation, possibly including her or his intellectual functioning.

Information leading to the conclusion that psychological assessment, and particularly intellectual assessment, is indicated would come from the various systems within which the individual functions (Fine, 1992) and the adequacy with which he or she deals with the demands of the major spheres of living for the child: self, family, community and school.

Aside from information the child her- or himself might provide, information regarding the individual's functioning within the family system would typically be provided by the child's parenting figures based on their observations of their son's or daughter's ability to deal with the ordinary tasks of development.

In the school realm, a second system within which the child functions, the usual source of information would be a teacher's observations of a student's ability to perform adequately on either a particular learning task or on a variety of academically related tasks.

Regarding the child's behavior in the community, it is rare to obtain information directly from a person in the community who is familiar with the child or adolescent's behavior; instead, information about a child's functioning in the community is likely to come from either a parent or school-related figure.

Based on the above kinds or sources of information, and conceptualized within the above sequential framework of clinical process, the clinician must decide whether the utilization of an intelligence test, and particularly the WISC–III, is appropriate and justified for the particular child and at the specific point in time being considered. Although the present author strongly believes in the value of intellectual assessment if one is testing a child or adolescent, it is nonetheless vital to see the decision to test as one that must be thought about carefully and decided based on whether, and in what way, assessment will serve the best interests of the specific child being considered.

In order for the clinician to attempt to make a decision which places the child's welfare as the foremost issue, the clinician should consider each of the following questions before deciding whether testing of the child at all or specifically with the WISC–III is indicated.

1) What is (are) the *specific* purpose(s) or objective(s) for testing this child with the WISC–III?
2) In what way will the data derived from the WISC–III be used to benefit this child?
3) What would be the best possible outcome of the testing for this child?
4) What would be the worst possible outcome of the testing for this child?
5) What specific benefits, risks or impact can the clinician identify for the child (or the child's family) depending on either the best or worst test outcomes for this child?

6) Who else in any of the above-noted systems has something to gain by the testing of the child other than the child?

7) What specific action or decisions will be based on the results of assessment with the WISC–III?

8) What does the clinician providing the testing have to gain by doing the testing?

9) How will the results of testing be shared with this child and with this child's family?

10) What will be a meaningful framework to make the test understandable for the child who is to be tested?

11) How will the clinician deal with any adverse consequences he or she anticipates may result from the testing?

12) Can the examiner identify any ethical violations involved in the planned assessment of this child?

It is only by attempting to address the above-noted questions regarding each child that the clinician is approaching the assessment task in a professional manner that maintains primary respect and concern for the child who is the focus of the assessment.

WHEN AND WHY TO TEST INTELLIGENCE

If one asks the specific reasons for testing intelligence, there are several possible answers. Perlman and Kaufman (1990), for example, note that reasons for the administration of intelligence tests include identification of such things as mental retardation or learning disabilities; placement of a child into gifted or other specialized programs; or as an adjunct to a clinical evaluation.

In their answer to the question of when to test intelligence, Reynolds and Kaufman (1985) note that from the ages of approximately 5 to 18, children typically attend school, with the focus of this experience being to permit the individual to become an independent, contributing member of the society. Implying that intelligence is a facet of the child that is crucial to understanding the individual and her or his interaction with school and the surrounding culture, Reynolds and Kaufman (1985) state that their response to the question of when to assess intelligence in the context of a psychological evaluation is "virtually always."

Hale (1991) notes that if psychologists in public schools are asked why they give intelligence tests to children, they frequently answer that it is to measure the child's intelligence, which means they are using a test to measure a theoretical construct. Although this would imply that the psychologist should be able to define the construct of intelligence and relate it to the test's measurement function, Hale (1991) indicates this is often not the case.

Wechsler (1991) notes that as a measure of general intellectual ability, the WISC–III is useful and appropriate for several purposes. These include "psychoeducational assessment as part of educational planning and placement, diagnosis of exceptionality among school-aged children, clinical and neuropsychological assessment, and research" (p. 7).

In terms of why a child's intelligence should be tested, there is considerable evidence to indicate that measures of intelligence have median correlations with measures of academic achievement at from the .50s to the low .70s (Sattler, 1990). Correlations between WISC–III IQ scores and academic achievement (Wechsler, 1991) indicate that WISC–III VIQ correlates .70 with Reading Achievement scores, .63 with Mathematics Achievement scores, and .56 with Written Language Achievement scores. WISC–III PIQ correlates .43 with Reading Achievement scores, .58 with Mathematics Achievement scores, and .46 with Written Language Achievement scores. WISC–III FSIQ correlates .66 with Reading Achievement scores, .68 with Mathematics Achievement scores, and .57 with Written Language Achievement scores. Correlations between WISC–III factor scores and scores in Reading, Mathematics, and Written Language Achievement range from .37 to .70.

Correlations of WISC–III IQ scores with school grades are somewhat lower than with other measures of achievement, with WISC–III VIQ correlating .42 with GPA (estimated as the average of grades in Mathematics and English); WISC–III PIQ correlates .39 with GPA; and WISC–III FSIQ correlates .47 with GPA (Wechsler, 1991). Hence, although the WISC–III would not provide one with anywhere near perfect ability to predict a child or adolescent's academic performance, measuring a child's intellectual functioning can provide an estimate of his or her ability to demonstrate the kind of learning that is expected in an ordinary classroom situation.

There are thus a variety of ways to consider the question of when and why one should assess a child or adolescent's intelligence. The different viewpoints noted above all rest on a set of interrelated assumptions: that intelligence is itself a valid construct; that it is a primary characteristic of individuals; that it can be measured in a reliable and unbiased fashion; that the construct as measured can be demonstrated to have a meaningful relationship to other variables, both concurrently and predictively; and that measurement of this quality of individuals provides information that is useful for the individual, or for those systems that interact with the individual.

SPECIFIC REFERRAL QUESTIONS

As indicated above, there are several kinds of referral problems where the child or adolescent's intellectual functioning may be of concern, whether in a very specific way or only as related to other aspects of the individual's overall adaptation. The next sections will focus on ways in which specific referral questions relate to the use of the WISC–III in the evaluation of the individual.

The Question of Level of Intellectual Functioning

One of the fundamental questions that may be addressed through an intellectual assessment is evaluation of a child's general level of intellectual functioning. Referrals with this as the major question to be addressed ordinarily arise in young children, when the individual encounters the academic demands of beginning school.

Before and often during the first grade, parents and/or teachers may be unsure as to whether a given child is performing inadequately because of generalized immaturity, some attentional deficit, or any of a variety of emotional problems. Hence, the question of a child's basic intellectual competence may not be raised until she or he is partway through the first grade, particularly if the child's functioning is somewhat uneven, or if the child's level of functioning is not very obviously below average. However, one relatively straightforward referral question where intellectual assessment would be indicated is that of the presence and/or degree of intellectual or cognitive deficit in the child.

The *Diagnostic and Statistical Manual of Mental Disorders, Fourth Edition* (DSM–IV; American Psychiatric Association, 1994) notes that the essential feature of mental retardation is significantly subaverage general intellectual functioning which is accompanied by significant limitations in adaptive functioning in at least two of several skill areas: communication, self-care, home living, social/interpersonal skills, use of community resources, self-direction, functional academic skills, work, leisure, health and safety, and the onset of the condition must be before age 18. Mental retardation has a number of different etiologies but "may be seen as a final common pathway of various pathological processes that affect the functioning of the central nervous system" (DSM–IV, p. 39).

The American Association on Mental Deficiency (Grossman, 1983) referred to mental retardation as involving significantly below average general intellectual functioning resulting in or associated with simultaneous impairments in adaptive behavior, which is manifested during the developmental period in the child's life.

More recently, the American Association on Mental Retardation (1992) has put forth a more elaborated definition which forms the basis of the DSM–IV (American Psychiatric Association, 1994) criteria. This new definition notes that mental retardation refers to substantial limitations in the individual's current functioning; the condition is evident before the individual reaches the age of 18; and the condition is characterized by "significantly subaverage intellectual functioning" (American Association on Mental Retardation, 1992, p. 5) which exists along with limitations in two or more of the following adaptive abilities: self-care, communication, home living, social skills, community use, self-direction, health and safety, functional academics, leisure, and work.

In explaining their definition, the American Association on Mental Retardation (1992) notes that mental retardation involves a fundamental difficulty in learning and performing particular skills of daily living. By significantly subaverage intellectual functioning is meant an IQ score of approximately 70 to 75 or below, with this IQ score being based on one or more individually administered tests of the kind which have been developed to assess intellectual functioning.

The person's intellectual limitations occur simultaneously with limitations in adaptive skills which are more closely related to intellectual deficiencies than to other circumstances, and evidence of adaptive skill restrictions is needed because intellectual functioning alone is insufficient for a diagnosis of mental retardation. Further, the impact of these limitations on the individual must be broad enough to encompass at least two major areas of life functioning, such as communication, social skills and the like. And mental retardation appears before age 18, the approximate point in American society where individuals usually assume adult roles.

The authors also note and explain four assumptions which are essential to the application of the definition of mental retardation (American Association on Mental Retardation, 1992). The first is that valid assessment of the individual must take into consideration cultural and linguistic diversity as well as differences in communication and behavior. This means that failure to consider these factors may result in an invalid assessment of the individual's functioning. The second assumption is that limitations of adaptive skills occur within the context of community environments typical for people the individual's age, and that analysis of the person's limitations also includes determination of needed supports that may facilitate the individual's adaptation.

The third assumption is that particular adaptive limitations of the person often coexist with other strengths or adaptive capacities of the individual and that assessment of the person should include evaluation of both the individual's deficits and his or her competencies. The fourth assumption is that with suitable supports over extended periods, the life functioning of the individual with mental retardation will generally be enhanced. This refers to the fact that with an array of services provided according to the individual's needs, which may vary over time, the quality of the individual's life experience can be improved.

Both the DSM–IV and the AAMR approaches to defining mental retardation indicate that more than simply level of intelligence is a requisite for the diagnosis of the condition. While the individual's intellectual functioning is a critical element in defining and diagnosing mental retardation, there must also be consideration and delineation of the individual's adaptive strengths and limitations, as well as determination of the individual's needs for supports that will enhance his or her life functioning.

Sattler (1990), discussing the WISC–R, notes that the WISC–R is a reliable and valid test for assessing mild levels of mental retardation in children. Factor-analytic studies (e.g., Cummins & Das, 1980; Van Hagen & Kaufman, 1975) indicate that the factor structure of the WISC–R is basically similar for mentally retarded and normal children, although the Freedom from Distractibility factor appears less stable for mentally retarded than for normal IQ children.

In terms of the WISC–III, according to Wechsler (1991), individuals with IQs of 69 and below comprise 2.2% of the theoretical normal curve and 1.9% of the actual WISC–III standardization sample. Individuals with IQs falling in this portion of the distribution are classified as "Intellectually Deficient."

As reported in the WISC–III manual (Wechsler, 1991), the WISC–III was administered to 43 children aged 6–16 years (median 11 years) who had been diagnosed as mildly mentally retarded based on their performances on the WISC–R and separate measures of adaptive functioning.

The mean VIQ of this group of children was 59.2; the mean PIQ of the group was 59.2; and the mean FSIQ was 55.8. The standard deviation of IQ scores within this group was approximately 8–9 points, which is much less than the 15-point standard deviation found in the general population.

The children with mental retardation obtained the following average scores on the four factor-based indices: VCI, 61.3; POI, 59.4; FDI, 62.5; PSI, 70.2. For the 28 children in the sample who had previously been tested with the WISC–R, with an average intertest interval of 2 years and 2 months, the mean WISC–III VIQ, PIQ and FSIQ scores are 8.9, 6.8, and 8.9 points lower respectively than the WISC–R scores obtained by these children. The usual WISC–R–WISC–III difference is approximately 5 points, suggesting that for children with less ability, this difference may be more pronounced (see Post & Mitchell, 1993, in "Test Reviews" section).

Hence the WISC–III would be an important instrument for use in assessing a child with suspected intellectual deficiency. However, the examiner would also need to include one or more additional measures of the child's adaptive behavior in terms of self-care, communication, and the child's functioning at home and in the community, information which would ordinarily be obtained by interviewing the child's parent with a survey schedule dealing with the child's adaptive behavior. In addition, as Shaw, Swerdlik, and Laurent (1993) have noted, one limitation of the WISC–III for assessing the cognitive functioning of intellectually deficient individuals is the high floor of the test, in that a child cannot obtain an articulated IQ score below 46. Hence the WISC–III would not be usable to evaluate the cognitive performance of a child with severe intellectual deficiency.

The Question of Learning Disability

There are many ways to approach and define the concept of learning disability. The original definition formulated by the National Advisory Committee on Handicapped Children stated that learning disabilities include "disorders of listening, thinking, talking, reading, writing, spelling, and arithmetic" (U.S. Office of Education, 1968, p. 34). The definition provided in U.S. Public Law 94-142 (1977) indicates that learning disabilities are reflected in problems in oral expression, listening comprehension, written expression, basic reading skill, reading comprehension, mathematics calculation, and mathematics reasoning (p. 65083).

According to a position paper by the National Joint Committee on Learning Disabilities (1983), this group states that learning disability is a generic term referring to "a heterogeneous group of disorders manifested by significant difficulties in the acquisition and use of listening, speaking, reading, writing, reasoning, or mathematical abilities" (p. 336). The definition proposed by the National Joint Committee on Learning Disabilities also makes clear that these disorders are intrinsic to the individual, presumably reflecting central nervous system dysfunction, and that, although other handicapping conditions may also be present in the individual, the learning disability is not a direct result of those other conditions.

These various definitions of learning disability define such a disability as a deficit in academic achievement when the individual is of at least average intelligence, has been exposed to adequate instruction, and is not suffering from any obvious physical/neurological disorder or from some primary emotional disorder that might prevent the child from utilizing her or his adequate intellectual potential for actual learning.

Such definitions implicitly, or explicitly, state that a "learning disability" thus reflects some impairment in the child's cerebral function. This means that the child who displays a learning disability actually suffers from some subtle impairment in neurological integrity, which might involve physical, structural or chemical deficits in those aspects of the central nervous system that underlie competent learning performance.

Taylor (1989) notes that the definitions currently in use to conceptualize learning disabilities are not completely satisfactory since they do not acknowledge either the individual variation within groups of disabled learners or the importance of psychosocial, motivational, and environmental influences on learning problems (Keogh, 1982; Smith, 1985). In addition, most definitions of learning disabilities currently in use exclude children who do not meet certain IQ requirements.

Taylor (1989) points out that psychometric intelligence is itself a function of learning history (Taylor, 1988). The same skill deficits that underlie a given learning problem may also contribute to poor performance on an IQ test. Hence Taylor (1989) notes that using IQ test results to distinguish children with learning disabilities from other non-retarded low achievers seems inappropriate since many children with IQs in the 70s or 80s have learning problems similar to children with higher IQs. Additionally, there is no empirical basis for the belief that children with IQs in the low average or borderline range are less able to profit from remedial assistance than are children with higher IQs.

Taylor (1989) suggests a broader view of learning disabilities, one that proposes that learning problems occur when children fail to meet expectations for academic achievement and productivity. These problems likely reflect the impact of a number of variables, including the child's actual school-related skills, cognitive and behavioral characteristics, as well as environmental and biological factors.

Kavale and Forness (1994), however, point out the complex relationship between intelligence and learning disability and note that if one allows the concept of learning disability to be applied to individuals with IQs in the 70–85 range, who usually display low levels of academic achievement, the result will be a greater confounding between the concepts of mental retardation on the one hand and learning disability on the other.

Perhaps more pertinent to the present volume, Kavale and Forness (1984, 1994) have also discussed efforts of various investigators (e.g., Dudley-Marling, Kaufman, & Tarver, 1981; Kaufman, 1979c; Rugel, 1974) to find diagnostic indicators of learning disability on WISC profiles. Kavale and Forness (1984, 1994), after reviewing many such investigations of WISC and WISC–R studies seeking particular WISC learning disability profiles, conclude that no such distinctive profiles exist and that one cannot use the Wechsler scales for accurate identification and diagnosis of individuals with learning disabilities.

There is also controversy in terms of whether it is more appropriate to use simple discrepancy scores between a measure of a child's intelligence and his or her academic achievement or to use a method based on concepts of statistical regression in order to identify learning disabled children (Braden & Weiss, 1988; Wilson & Cone, 1984). Braden and Weiss (1988) point out that the size of simple difference discrepancies between IQ and achievement varies with IQ level, while regression discrepancies do not vary as a function of IQ level. Hence Braden and Weiss (1988) contend that regression methods are more appropriate than simple difference methods for determining learning disability eligibility, although they would not use either method as the sole criterion for learning disability placement.

Learning Disability and the WISC-III

Based on the publications of Kavale and Forness (1984, 1994), which review a large number of studies dealing with the issue, the present author's basic conclusion is that the WISC-III cannot be used as an instrument by itself for the diagnosis of learning disability in a child. To diagnose a learning disability in an individual, the examiner would have to utilize *both* a measure of the child or adolescent's general intellectual ability *and* some measure of the child or adolescent's academic achievement. It is fundamentally in the discrepancy between an examinee's presumed general intellectual ability and her or his actual academic achievement that a reasonable concept of learning disability may be found.

It is also important to realize that if one uses a simple intelligence-achievement discrepancy on the one hand, or a statistical regression concept on the other, the result will be differential identification of children as learning disabled or not. Similarly, if one assumes an intelligence-achievement discrepancy regardless of the general level of intelligence the individual displays, this also will complicate the definition of who is learning disabled and who displays some intellectual deficit which results in low academic achievement.

In terms of the WISC-III, this test was administered to 65 children aged 6–14 years (median 10 years) who were considered to have learning disabilities (Wechsler, 1991). The sample included children with a variety of learning disabilities and was comprised of both females and males and included Whites, Blacks, Hispanics and Asians.

This group of children with defined learning disabilities obtained an average WISC-III VIQ of 92.1, a PIQ of 97.2, and a FSIQ of 93.8, with a lower VIQ than PIQ, which is not unexpected (Sattler, 1990). Their average scores on the factor-based indices were as follows: VCI, 93.8, POI, 100.5, FDI, 87.1, and PSI, 89.1, which indicates an even more pronounced VCI–POI than VIQ–PIQ difference, and with depressed scores on the FD and PS scales. Although these subjects did have FDI and PSI scores that fell in the low average range, it is interesting to note, as Kavale and Forness (1984, 1994) describe, that, as a group, the learning disabled children obtained Verbal, Performance, and Full Scale IQs which are all in the normal range.

No matter what theoretical or conceptual position regarding learning disabilities and their definition one adopts, whenever a question is raised in the mind of a referral source, the referred individual, or the clinician about the presence of a learning disability within a child, it is necessary to obtain a measure of the child's general cognitive abilities. And for this purpose, the WISC–III is highly appropriate. Findings on the WISC–III can certainly provide cues or indications that a child has difficulties with certain kinds of information processing or has deficits in certain cognitive skills. However, reviews of research which has attempted to identify learning disabled individuals by their Wechsler profiles alone indicate that the diagnosis of a learning disability with a Wechsler Intelligence Scale by itself is virtually impossible (e.g., Kavale, & Forness, 1984, 1994) and therefore should not be attempted.

The Question of Neuropsychological Impairment

Questions of whether or to what degree a child suffers from neuropsychological impairment can arise at any point during infancy or childhood, whether the question is related to atypicalities of child development, neurological disorders, possible learning problems, or as a result of exposure to traumatic injuries (Boll & Barth, 1981).

Telzrow (1989) notes that there are two major orientations which may be considered in regard to the neuropsychological assessment of children. One variant of the first of these is exemplified by the Halstead-Reitan Neuropsychological Test Battery (Goldstein, 1990; Reitan, 1979; Reitan & Davison, 1974; Rourke, 1981; Rourke, Bakker, Fisk, & Strang, 1983). A second variant of this approach is in the Luria-Nebraska Neuropsychological Battery (Golden, 1981a, 1981b; Goldstein, 1990) based on the writings of the Russian neuropsychologist A.R. Luria (1966, 1973). The Reitan (1979) and Golden (1981b) approaches both utilize a standardized battery of tasks designed to identify brain impairment. This standard-battery approach typically involves the administration of an invariant set of identical tasks to each examinee, regardless of his or her presenting problems or specific history.

The second approach to neuropsychological assessment of children involves the use of a flexible or varied combination of traditional psychological, educational and neuropsychological tests, with the elements of the battery being dependent upon such child variables as age, history, functioning level, and presenting problem of the child (Telzrow, 1989).

The test batteries which Reitan has developed, modified, and researched extensively (Reitan & Wolfson, 1992, 1993, 1994) based on the original work of Halstead (1947) have typically included administration of the age-appropriate Wechsler Intelligence Scale, whether for adults (e.g., the WAIS–R), children (e.g., the WISC–R), or young children (e.g., the WPPSI–R), and interpretation of these intelligence tests is included with the interpretation of the neuropsychological tests. The test batteries devised by Golden (1981a, 1981b) include an Intellectual Processes scale as part of the test battery itself.

Telzrow (1989) notes WISC–R test results which demonstrate various deficits in particular populations of children with neuropsychological impairments such as learning disabilities (e.g., V < P or V > P, depending on subtype; Rourke, 1983). However, Shaw, Swerdlik, and Laurent (1993) point out that although intelligence tests are considered an important part of neuropsychological test batteries, this is based more on clinical tradition than empirical evidence. They note there is no consistent body of literature that supports the use of the WISC–R Full Scale score, factor scores, or profile analysis for making differential diagnoses between brain-damaged and non-brain-damaged children (Goldstein & Levin, 1984).

Shaw, Swerdlik, and Laurent (1993) note that although children with brain damage do have lower Full Scale IQs than non-brain-damaged children, most children with low Full Scale IQs have no demonstrable neuropsychological impairment (Chadwick, Rutter, Thompson, & Shaffer, 1981). Their essential conclusion is that it is not appropriate to consider the WISC–III as suitable for the measurement of neuropsychological impairment.

The present author would concur with this view if Shaw, Swerdlik and Laurent (1993) refer to an attempt to utilize the WISC–III by itself for the *diagnosis* of neuropsychological impairment without data from other neuropsychological instruments. However, the present author believes that whether one utilizes the Reitan (1979) or Golden (1981a, 1981b) standard-battery approach or a flexible-battery approach (Fennell & Bauer, 1989; Telzrow, 1989) in the assessment of possible neuropsychological impairment in a child, the WISC–III should be included as one of the tests administered.

The data obtained from the WISC–III can provide additional information on the nature of the child's intellectual status, cognitive strengths and weaknesses, and can be utilized as part of a systematic strategy of hypothesis formation, inferential reasoning and clinical experimentation (Fennell & Bauer, 1989) to delineate a child's cognitive abilities and to determine whether or not the child displays convincing evidence of neuropsychological impairment.

The Question of Giftedness

A critical issue in thinking about giftedness is the definition of this term that one utilizes. Sattler (1990) points out the distinction made by Gagne (1985) between the concepts of *giftedness* and *talent*. Giftedness refers to significantly and perhaps uniquely above-average competence in intellectual, creative or sensorimotor performance. In contrast to giftedness, talent refers to uniquely above-average competence in one or more fields of human endeavor, such as in the fine or performing arts.

The use of intelligence scores as the only criterion for determining giftedness among children has certainly been questioned (Kaufman, 1990; Sternberg, 1986; Treffinger & Renzulli, 1986). However, if one considers giftedness as involving only individuals with extremely high IQs (over 130), according to Wechsler (1991), this would involve the IQ classification labelled "Very Superior" and would include 2.2% of the theoretical normal curve and 2.1% of the actual WISC–III standardization sample. Sattler (1990) notes that approximately 2 in 100 children have IQs over 130 while only about 3 in 100,000 children have IQs of 160 or higher.

Those who argue in favor of using intelligence tests in the selection of gifted individuals (e.g., Kaufman & Harrison, 1986) do not recommend using *only* intelligence tests for the identification of giftedness, but believe that intelligence tests provide the most objective assessment of gifted ability and that such tests have the most adequate psychometric properties of instruments used to assess gifted individuals. Intelligence tests also are the best predictors of academic achievement, and they provide several scores for a more differentiated interpretation of an individual's profile of cognitive abilities.

Factor analyses of the WISC–R with gifted students have ordinarily found at least a two-factor solution (Kames & Brown, 1980). However, Brown, Hwang, Baron, and Yakimowski (1991) suggest that a three-factor model may be a better model for interpreting the scores of gifted students than a two-factor model, while Brown and Yakimowski (1987) have reported a four-factor model which accounted for 65% of the total variance among their sample; these four factors are: Verbal Comprehension, Perceptual Organization, Acquisition of Knowledge, and Spatial Memory. On the other hand, McMann, Plasket, Barnett, and Siler (1991) examined the factor structure of the WISC–R for a sample of children with IQs over 120 and concluded that the most parsimonious interpretation of their data favored a one-factor solution, which appeared to reflect verbal rather than general ability.

In terms of the WISC–III, this test was administered to 38 children aged 7–14 (median = 10) who had been identified as gifted by independent evaluations (Wechsler, 1991). On the WISC–III, this group of children obtained an average VIQ of 128.0, a PIQ of 124.6, and a FSIQ of 128.7. The group obtained the following scores on the four factor-based indices: VCI, 126.9, POI, 125.8, FDI, 123.0, and PSI, 110.2. The sample obtained its lowest score and displayed more variability on the Processing Speed scale, although Wechsler (1991) does not offer any explanation of this finding except to note that scores on the Freedom from Distractibility and Processing Speed scales vary independently of FSIQ.

In terms of approaching the identification of gifted individuals, Kaufman and Harrison (1986) suggest guidelines for using intelligence tests in the assessment of individuals who may be gifted. They suggest that intelligence scores should never be used as the only basis for determining gifted abilities, and particular criterion scores should not be utilized to exclude individuals from programs for the gifted since this may exclude individuals who actually have specialized talent or a handicap which impedes their performance on an intelligence test. These authors also note, first, that confidence intervals around an obtained score should be considered when determining an individual's gifted status rather than using only the scores the child achieved on the test administered; and second, that test scores can be used for selection *and* for educational or program planning. Lastly, Kaufman and Harrison (1986) emphasize that intelligence test scores should not be used to make decisions about people. People make such decisions, with the aid of test scores.

As the foregoing discussion indicates, there are a number of issues to consider in thinking about giftedness or talent, and additional issues to consider in regard to use of an intelligence test as part of any systematic strategy to assess and select gifted individuals for special programs. While one may need a flexible approach to dealing with this selection process, there is little question in the author's mind that while it should not be the only instrument utilized, the WISC–III can make an enormous contribution to the evaluation and selection of children being considered for accelerated or specialized academic programs.

The Question of Career Counseling

In terms of the ability of intelligence to predict subsequent outcome, whether in academic achievement, level of education achieved, adult occupational accomplishment, or job performance, there is extensive data (Kaufman, 1990; Matarazzo, 1972) to support the conclusion that, whether causally related or not, intellectual status is a powerful predictor of future performance in a variety of aspects of life adaptation and functioning.

In discussing the WAIS–R, Kaufman (1990) notes the increasing levels of average IQ as one proceeds through a range of occupational groups from unskilled workers to professional and technical workers. Although Kaufman (1990) points out that the variations in IQ scores *within* any occupational group may be quite significant, the overall findings are consistent with the conclusion that higher levels of intelligence are ordinarily associated with higher levels of socioeconomic accomplishment.

There are thus situations when a clinician may be dealing with a middle adolescent who is attempting to determine a potential future career path. To the extent that admission to particular academic programs and particular professions are associated with basic intellectual requirements, the inclusion of an intellectual assessment in the evaluation of such an individual would be highly appropriate.

Such an evaluation would permit the clinician to evaluate the adolescent's general intellectual level of functioning with respect to others his or her age; determine the relative verbal and nonverbal reasoning skills the individual displays; and observe the personal characteristics of motivation, problem-solving strategy and reaction to success and failure that may be relevant to the young person's selection of a particular academic and/or career pathway.

While the clinician might not provide definitive conclusions or recommendations based on the intellectual evaluation, the assessment of the adolescent's intellectual abilities (either with the WISC–III or the WAIS–R) would be an important component of any career-counseling assessment of an adolescent that the clinician might provide.

Questions Regarding the Adequacy of the Child or Adolescent's Personal or Social Adjustment

The foregoing questions have focused on issues pertaining to the child or adolescent's intellectual or cognitive abilities, cerebral integrity, or learning potential. Wechsler (1958), in discussing the WAIS, described a variety of WAIS subtest patterns presumably characteristic of each of a variety of psychological disorders, and it is clinically appealing to think that the Wechsler scales for children can provide discriminative information about a child's emotional condition.

Relevant to this issue, Hodges and Plow (1990) report an investigation of psychiatrically hospitalized children who received diagnoses of conduct, oppositional, anxiety, and affective disorders on the basis of structured interviews. These authors found IQ to vary as a function of diagnosis, with conduct-disordered children displaying a relative deficit in verbal abilities, anxiety-disordered children displaying lower global intelligence, and oppositional-disordered children displaying no cognitive deficit. The authors also considered the presence or absence of an anxiety disorder diagnosis on Bannatyne's (1974) sequential category and the ACID profile (Prifitera & Dersh, 1993). Significant differences were obtained between anxiety-disordered and non-anxiety-disordered children on these subtest groups, leading the authors to conclude that anxiety-disordered children scored below non-anxiety-disordered children on groups of subtests which have typically been associated with learning disability or attentional problems.

In contrast to the findings of Hodges and Plow (1990), Zimet, Zimet, Farley and Adler (1994) examined 178 children with a variety of psychiatric disorders and found no significant differences among the disorder groups for any of the IQ test scores they examined.

Plante, Goldfarb, and Wadley (1993) studied the records of 100 children ranging in age from 6 to 16 who had been referred for multidisciplinary diagnostic testing during 1989–1990. Data from the WISC–R (Wechsler, 1974) and the Woodcock-Johnson Test-Revised (Woodcock & Johnson, 1977) were examined from the patient's clinical records. These authors found that stress in the lives of the children—particularly physical and/or sexual abuse as well as parental separation and divorce—was associated with lowered aptitude (and achievement) test performance among the children in this investigation.

Thus there are mixed findings reported on whether or not children's cognitive functioning varies according to their psychological condition. The present author would conclude that even if children's intellectual performance does vary depending on psychiatric diagnosis, there are no distinctive Wechsler patterns that would permit an examiner to draw reliable conclusions about an examinee's psychopathology based only on the child's WISC–III protocol. Nonetheless, intelligence is fundamental to a child or adolescent's adaptation in essentially every aspect of her or his life. In view of this fact, and because the WISC–III samples such a wide range of specific content areas as well as a number of different problem-solving capacities on the part of the child, it is the author's view that the WISC–III should be included in any child or adolescent assessment, even if the individual has been referred for evaluation because of concerns that are seemingly unrelated to intellectual functioning per se.

In view of the increasing restrictions on mental health utilization brought about by managed care, it seems probable that evaluation of individuals will have to be made more economical, and hence briefer and including fewer tests. The examiner will need to determine which test or investigative procedure will be most valuable and provide the most meaningful clinical information to address the widest number of variables in the examinee's life.

Under these circumstances, the author believes that the assessment of a child's intellectual functioning will be among the most important aspects of the child or adolescent to assess. Information derived from an intellectual assessment can supply the examiner with material that would be useful in dealing with the child's school and parents and also provide information to assist in deciding on the kind of therapy which may be pursued with the child, i.e., one that relies to a greater or lesser extent on verbal mediation.

The WISC-III Versus the WPPSI-R and the WAIS-R

Insofar as the WISC-III was developed for use with examinees between the ages of 6 years, 0 months and 16 years, 11 months, the WISC-III overlaps with the WPPSI-R (Wechsler, 1989) and the WAIS-R (Wechsler, 1981) for examinees who are at the extremes of the age distribution for which the WISC-III was designed. The WISC-III overlaps with the WPPSI-R for ages 6-0 to 7-3-15, and with the WAIS-R for ages 16-0-0 to 16-11-30.

Wechsler (1991) reports a study which involved the administration of the WISC-III and WPPSI-R in counterbalanced order to a sample of 188 6-year-old children with the intervals between the two testings ranging from 12 to 62 days (median = 21 days). The correlations between the WISC-III and WPPSI-R Verbal, Performance, and Full Scale IQs were .85, .73, and .85, respectively.

In terms of IQ scores, the WISC-III Verbal, Performance, and Full Scale IQs were 104.2, 108.2, and 106.5 respectively, while for the WPPSI-R, the Verbal, Performance, and Full Scale IQs were 102.3, 102.3, and 102.5 respectively. This means that the WISC-III Verbal IQ was 1.9 points higher than the WPPSI-R, the WISC-III Performance IQ was 5.9 points higher than the WPPSI-R Performance IQ, and the WISC-III Full Scale IQ was 4.0 points higher than the WPPSI-R Full Scale IQ.

In terms of ranges of expected WISC-III IQ scores for various WPPSI-R IQ scores, Wechsler (1991) notes that the ranges of WISC-III IQ scores for particular WPPSI-R IQ scores are narrower near the average range and wider at both the upper and lower extremes. This finding suggests that the equivalence of the WISC-III and the WPPSI-R varies as a function of where on the normal IQ distribution the examinee is located. This would also have implications for testing an examinee with the WISC-III who has been tested with the WPPSI-R in the past, as one might expect greater change in scores for an examinee near the upper or lower extreme of the IQ distribution. In addition, the differences between WISC-III and WPPSI-R PIQs are larger than the differences between the VIQs of these two tests.

Sattler and Atkinson (1993) report an investigation of item equivalence for the WPPSI-R and WISC-III. Although they did find age discrepancies between individual items on the two scales, they found an overall correlation of .88 between the test-age equivalents based on the 23 items that appeared (similar in wording, concept or pictorial content) on both scales. These authors concluded that their investigation demonstrated the parallelism of the WISC–III and the WPPSI–R beyond the level of subtests and IQs, but reaching even to the level of specific item selection, which also indicates the interchangeability of these two tests for the age range where they overlap.

In terms of recommendations for using the WISC–III or the WPPSI–R for a particular examinee, Wechsler (1991) suggests that in general, for a six-year-old child whose intellectual performance is anticipated to be below average, the WPPSI–R would provide the more adequate and accurate assessment. For examinees of above age six who appear to be of at least average ability, the WISC–III would be appropriate.

Sattler (1992), based on personal communication with Atkinson (January, 1992; cited in Sattler, 1992), notes a somewhat different recommendation for deciding on use of the WISC–III versus the WPPSI–R. Sattler (1992) states that the WPPSI–R is a better choice for examinees with [presumed] below-average ability, while the WISC–III is a better choice for examinees with [presumed] above-average ability, and either test would be adequate for children with [presumed] average ability.

Sattler (1992) notes that for ages 7-0 to 7-3, the WISC–III has superior subtest reliabilities, higher subtest ceilings, and better item gradients, and hence the WISC–III is a better choice for all children between the ages of 7-0 and 7-3.

In terms of choosing between the WISC–III and the WAIS–R, Wechsler (1991) reports a study which involved the administration of the WISC–III and the WAIS–R in counterbalanced order to a sample of 189 16-year-olds. The intervals between testing ranged from 12 to 70 days (median = 21 days).

The correlations between the WISC–III and the WAIS–R Verbal, Performance, and Full Scale IQs were .90, .80, and .86 respectively. In terms of IQ scores, the WISC–III Verbal, Performance, and Full Scale IQs were 101.0, 101.8, and 101.4 respectively, while for the WAIS–R, the Verbal, Performance, and Full Scale IQs were 102.5, 107.7, and 105.3 respectively. This means that the WAIS–R Verbal IQ was 1.5 point higher than the WISC–III Verbal IQ, the WAIS–R Performance IQ was 5.9 points higher than the WISC–III Performance IQ, and the WAIS–R Full Scale IQ was 3.9 points higher than the WISC–III Full Scale IQ.

In terms of ranges of expected WISC–III IQ scores for various WAIS–R IQ scores, Wechsler (1991) notes that the ranges of WAIS–R IQ scores associated with particular WISC–III scores are relatively narrow near the average range, but wider at the upper and lower IQ score levels. Thus while the average difference between the WISC–III and the WAIS–R FSIQ is approximately four points, the WAIS–R FSIQ may be as much as 8 points greater than the WISC–III FSIQ at the upper or lower extremes of the IQ distribution. Additionally, the WISC–III and WAIS–R PIQ scores will differ more than do the VIQ scores.

In terms of the WISC–III versus the WAIS–R, Kaufman (1990), in discussing the WAIS–R versus the WISC–R, notes that whenever one is evaluating an individual of known or suspected low IQ, the WISC–R would be recommended. However, Kaufman (1990) goes on to note that in view of the questionable WAIS–R norms for ages 16–19, and the low WAIS–R subtest reliabilities for ages 16–17, it is probably wiser to use the WISC–R to test any 16-year-old of any ability level.

In view of the general concept that it is usually best to use the test with the most recent norms, and in view of the very careful test construction of the WISC–III (Kaufman, 1993), Kaufman's (1990) recommendation regarding the WAIS–R versus the WISC–R would suggest that one should use the WISC–III rather than the WAIS–R for any examinee under 16-11-30 who is being tested. Use of the WISC–III under these circumstances would provide the more accurate measurement of the examinee's intellectual functioning and would also permit the individual's reassessment at some future date with the WAIS–R (or the WAIS–R's replacement, assuming the WAIS–R will be revised in the not-too-distant future).

Sattler (1992) notes that his recommendations regarding the WISC–III versus the WPPSI–R and the WAIS–R are based on internal psychometric data regarding the tests involved. But he notes that in the final analysis, the choice between two tests that deal with the same age should depend on the validity of the inferences the examiner can make from the scores on one or the other test.

The present author assumes that Sattler (1992) is referring to the establishment of statistical validity regarding either of the tests in question. The present author believes that when examiners use a particular test frequently, they develop "intuitive norms" regarding that test. These intuitive norms involve the body of clinical experience that a particular clinician gathers in using a certain test with a wide range of examinees, and this information is extremely valuable for the examiner in knowing when to question a response, how to accurately score the response, and how to interpret the examinee's performance on the test.

Thus, the present author would recommend that the examiner attempt to decide on use of one scale or the other based on: (1) choosing the most recently published scale if possible; (2) choosing the test with which the examiner is most familiar and comfortable. The reason for this is that the examiner is much more likely to provide an accurate, reliable, and valid administration and interpretation of a test he or she uses routinely than a test which must be reviewed and administered only once in a great while.

Chapter Nine

MODELS IN PSYCHOLOGY

The present author believes that there are several fundamental conceptual models which are relevant to clinical practice and which are therefore relevant to a discussion of the clinical use of the WISC–III. These models include a gradient and non-gradient, a hierarchy and a systems perspective.

Gradients and Non-Gradients

The first model to be discussed is that of a gradient (see Figure 1). This concept has a long history in psychology (Dollard & Miller, 1950; Miller, 1948) and refers to the fact that an individual's behavior can be observed to vary in a systematic fashion according to a number of dimensions: for example, the state of the organism (Gjesme, 1974; Losco & Epstein, 1977); the spatial relationship between an individual and a goal (Udin, Olswanger & Vogler, 1974); the temporal relationship between an individual and an event (Gjesme, 1975); and the increasing or decreasing goal-relevance of information or stimuli presented to the individual (Epstein & Fenz, 1962).

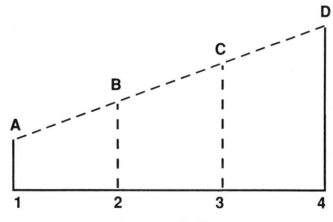

Figure 1. A Gradient.

While much of what has been written about gradients relates to approach-avoidance conflict (e.g., Losco & Epstein, 1974; Epstein, 1978), it is possible to simply focus on the underlying and essential concept of a gradient as representing the gradual change of a given variable from one extreme to the other along a particular dimension (see Figure 1). One can observe the presence of such a gradient concept in personality theory (Farley, 1990) as well as in the clinical procedures involved in interviewing (Shea, 1990); systematic desensitization (Wolpe, 1985); shaping (Ross, 1981); exposure treatment (Barlow, 1988); and parent guidance (Powell, 1987).

On Figure 1, the points labelled 1, 2, 3 and 4 represent different points along any dimension or continuum (e.g., space, time, structure, goal-relevance), with point 1 representing one extreme on the dimension and with point 4 representing the other extreme on that dimension. The points labelled A, B, C and D represent levels of increasing arousal, anxiety or affect as one moves from one extreme of the dimension (point 1) to the other extreme of that dimension (point 4).

The gradient or continuum depicted may be used to conceptualize changes in the individual's state of arousal or adequacy of performance as a function of changes in any of a number of variables, for example, the approach of an event in time (as an aversive event approaches temporally, the individual's anxiety increases); locus of control (as the individual has more control of the situation, he or she feels less anxious; as the individual has less control of the situation, she or he feels more anxious); or task difficulty (as test items become more difficult, the child being tested feels increased anxiety or anger). Figure 1 indicates the more or less *gradual* changes which occur in the individual as a function of changes in his or her movement along the particular dimension being considered.

In contrast to the gradient concept, one must also consider the non-gradient concept (see Figure 2). While the gradient model reflects a *gradual* change in an individual's state of arousal, the non-gradient illustrates a *rapid* change in activation on the part of the individual from relative calm or non-arousal (point A on Figure 2) to a state of extreme arousal or activation (point D on Figure 2). This rapid change in state of arousal may be observed in individuals whose systems of self-regulation are deficient and whose states of activation thus change precipitously (e.g., conduct-disordered children). The models of the gradient and non-gradient will be relevant to a number of aspects of WISC–III test administration and interpretation.

Hierarchies

A third model which is relevant to psychological practice and which is thus relevant to the clinical use of the WISC–III is that of a hierarchy (see

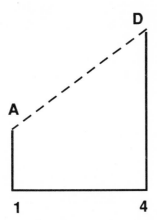

Figure 2. A Non-Gradient Response. (See text for explanation.)

Figure 3). This concept has been adapted from Gagne (1970) who proposed that there are eight basic kinds of learning. These different forms of learning can be conceptualized as existing in a hierarchical fashion with very simple stimulus-response learning at the base and with complex learning involving the abstraction of principles and problem solving at the apex.

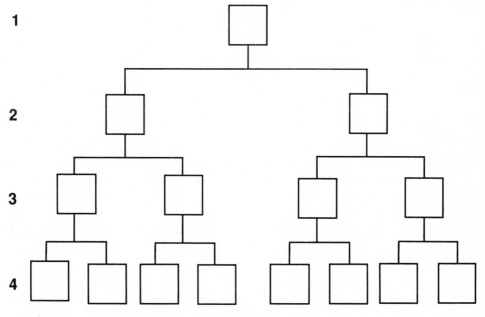

Figure 3. A Hierarchy. (See text for explanation.)

According to Gagne (1970), one can analyze any instructional task in terms of this hierarchical model and determine the specific kinds of learning that are involved. The apex of the hierarchy represents the highest form of learning required by a specific task (e.g., ordering numbers). In order to determine the instructional requirements of teaching the highest level task, one analyzes the task downward to determine the component skills (e.g., forming sets of numbers) which the learner must master before he or she can accomplish the highest level task.

Although the task-analytic approach proposed by Gagne (1970) may be applied to the interpretation of specific aspects of the WISC–III (e.g., in considering what component skills a child may need or lack in her or his handling of a particular subtest), the present author will view the hierarchy primarily as a conceptual structure for organizing the examiner's analysis of the overall test as well as for understanding the role of the psychologist who uses the WISC–III.

A Systems Perspective

The fourth model which is relevant to psychological practice and to the use of the WISC–III is that of a systems perspective (see Figure 4). Until the last half of the twentieth century, strategies of scientific thought have reflected methods now often referred to as *Newtonian, classical or mechanistic* (Plas, 1992). These approaches assumed that the world in which we live functions in much the same way as does a machine. From within this conceptual framework, the solution to problems was seen as involving a linear process in which there is a systematic search for the part or parts in an organism that are damaged, impaired or missing, and hence responsible for inefficiency in the transfer of energy from one part of the organism to another.

More recently, however, von Bertalanffy (1968) has proposed a *general systems theory,* which focuses on the nature of organization itself, since he believed that the principles that govern organization are similar across all aspects of existence. Von Bertalanffy's (1968) *general systems theory* thus attempts to formulate conceptual principles that are valid for systems in general regardless of the specific elements or kinds of energy or information that they may involve.

Ideas which shift the frame of focus in psychological disorders have also occurred since the 1950s. For example, Bateson and his colleagues (Bateson, 1972; Bateson, Jackson, Haley & Weakland, 1956) developed an approach to psychotherapy which focused on the family as the unit of intervention rather than on the identified patient, thus addressing the way in which a total system functions rather than focusing only on an individual component within that system.

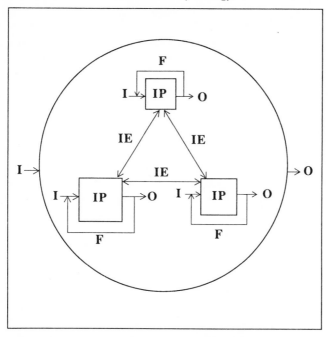

Figure 4. A Systems Perspective. (See text for explanation.) Ledgend. I = Input; IP = Information Processing; O = Output; F = Feedback Loop; IE = Information Exchange

Fine and Carlson (1992) present a number of viewpoints which relate systems concepts to the school setting in an approach labelled a "systems-ecological" perspective (Fine, 1992). From within this view, individuals are understood within the context of their relationships and interactions with others rather than primarily on the basis of their individual psychological characteristics. This means that any individual can be best understood when he or she is viewed in terms of the various systems within which she or he functions.

Fundamentally, a system may be defined as "a set of components interacting with each other and a boundary which possesses the property of filtering both the kind and rate of flow of inputs and outputs to and from the system" (Berrien, 1968, pp. 14–15). Open systems take in information or energy from their environments, process it and then put forth the transformed energy or information in some modified form.

Boulding (1968) points out that one can conceptualize systems themselves as hierarchically organized from frameworks at the lowest level to ultimate concepts of systems at the highest level. This view allows us to conceive of the universe as comprised of systems nested hierarchically within systems. It is also a perspective that permits us to view the use of the WISC–III as existing within multiple systems, those that involve the child or adolescent who is tested, the examiner who does the testing, and the environment within which the testing occurs. From this perspective, it is necessary to understand the multiple forces that operate, and systems which are involved, when a psychologist tests a particular child or adolescent with the WISC–III.

Adopting such a systems perspective on the use of the WISC–III views the assessment as an element within a total process, as a dynamic phenomenon embedded in a wider set of meanings and implications for the child tested, his or her teachers and her or his parents and siblings. Similarly, the testing, both the actual event of interacting with a child to obtain the raw data and the writing of a report, may have numerous meanings for the psychologist, who must maintain an awareness of the multiple factors and perspectives involved when he or she evaluates a child or adolescent with the WISC–III.

The various models discussed above—the gradient, nonilized in discussing various aspects of the clinical use of the WISC–III.

Chapter Ten

MODELS IN PSYCHOLOGICAL ASSESSMENT

The present author believes that whether one is providing a psychological assessment or engaging in any other activity as a psychologist, having a conceptual model for one's behavior is helpful if not essential (Miller, Galanter, and Pribram, 1960). In the case of an assessment, the purpose of such a framework is to provide the clinician with a set of principles or strategies to organize and guide his or her own thinking and behavior in approaching the task and to make the assessment meaningful to both the examiner and the person being evaluated. The following discussion will present both a general and a more specific model for assessment as well as an application of the model for testing children and adolescents with the WISC–III.

A GENERAL MODEL FOR ASSESSMENT

Sloves, Docherty, and Schneider (1979) present a general model of psychological assessment which is congruent with the present author's own view of this process and which will be presented here in slightly modified form. Sloves et al. (1979) base their model on the concept of the "scientific problem-solving model" developed by Comtois and Clark (1976; cited in Sloves et al., 1979).

Sloves et al. (1979) contend that much of the confusion and misconception regarding psychological assessment which existed at the time they published reflected the failure to differentiate between two conceptually distinct aspects of psychodiagnosis: psychological assessment and psychological testing, a distinction that has also been discussed by Matarrazzo (1990).

According to this viewpoint, psychological assessment involves a broad, complex and comprehensive process which includes problem solving, decision making, evaluation procedures, and the integration of multiple sources of data. The goal of psychological assessment is to yield information that is relevant to intervention in the broadest sense and to generate decisions which will be helpful to clients. Psychological testing, on the other hand, may be defined as a set of specific skills which represent only one of the potential strategies which may be used by the psychologist in the process of an assessment.

Psychological assessment is oriented towards multiple systems and is problem oriented, dynamic, and conceptual, while psychological testing is oriented towards measurement, description, and the application of specific test instruments. Psychological assessment is thus the broader concept, subsuming psychological testing as the narrower and more specific function. In terms of the hierarchical model the author has presented earlier, psychological assessment would be the apex of a hierarchy (Level 1). Level (2) of this hierarchy might involve assessment of the client him- or herself directly versus obtaining information from other observers about the person. Level (3) of the hierarchy would include psychological testing of the individual as one possible strategy, along with, for example, interviewing of the individual, observation of him or her in real-life situations or in interactional testing with one or more significant others (e.g., parents or a partner). Level (4) would involve the specific tests or sample situations utilized in the testing of the client.

SLOVES ET AL.'S SCIENTIFIC PROBLEM-SOLVING MODEL

According to Sloves et al. (1979), the scientific problem-solving model is meant to describe what practitioners do when they are practicing most effectively. These authors note the model they describe is called "scientific" because it is based on a scientific method and reflects the application of scientific thinking to clinical practice. It is considered a "problem-solving" model because problem solving is viewed as the core feature of any clinical endeavor, whether one is engaged in individual therapy or program consultation. The model consists of three interrelated parts: the problem-solving process, levels of organizational action (which the present author will label levels of organizational structure), and specific methods, with the various components interacting in a continuing, dynamic and non-linear fashion.

The Problem-Solving Process

The problem-solving process consists of six sequentially organized steps that the psychologist can utilize in an assessment: clarifying the problem, planning the assessment, locating resources, implementing the evaluation, determining the outcome, and disseminating the findings (Solves et al., 1979).

The problem clarification step involves the determination of the specific purpose or objective of an assessment; this involves the thoughtful analysis by the psychologist of a variety of factors which provide the context for any evaluation. In this step, the psychologist must consider such things as the referral process within the social system of which it is a part; the referral agent and precipitant for the referral; what constraints may be operating against various resolutions of the problem; the availability of resources needed for assessment and resolution of the problem; and the social, organizational, and structural context within which the problem is embedded.

The second step in the problem-solving process involves planning. This entails the enumeration or development of hypotheses which may explain the referral problem. Once the psychologist has generated his or her hypotheses regarding the referral issues, assessment goals may then be specified that will address and evaluate these hypotheses.

The third step in the problem-solving process involves developing strategies and refers to the gathering of resources necessary to examine the hypotheses which have been generated. This may involve the design of observational approaches, the selection of specific tests, or the reviewing of the methods for administration of the particular tests one will utilize.

The fourth step is implementation, which involves actually carrying out the assessment with the person being evaluated. This step includes preparation of individuals and/or settings for an assessment, informing people of their rights in the assessment process, and maintaining standard testing procedures when formal tests are actually administered.

The fifth step involves outcome determination, which entails the analysis and interpretation of the assessment data which has been obtained, including determination of whether appropriate information was gathered and whether or not one's hypotheses were adequately evaluated.

The sixth and final step of the problem-solving process involves dissemination of the information obtained in the assessment. At this point, the examiner must decide what is useful or pertinent information to communicate, to what audience, and what is the most relevant and effective method for dissemination of this information (e.g., a written report, an individual consultation, or a case conference).

Although Sloves et al.'s (1979) model is applicable to the broader issue of assessment, it is relatively straightforward to perceive the application of their six-step model specifically to intelligence testing of a child or adolescent.

Levels of Organizational Structure

Levels of organizational structure refers to the second component of the scientific problem-solving model. Levels of organization in systems range from the lowest level of a hierarchy of organizations, the individual level, through increasingly comprehensive systems which encompass an ever larger number of individuals (e.g., an individual child, a classroom group, or family, a special service department in a school, a school district, a state or federal agency, or another suprasystemic organization).

In dealing with this aspect of the problem-solving process, the examiner should ask in what way a given organizational level facilitates or hinders the solution of the problem the psychologist is seeking to solve and in what way the findings of the assessment relate to or have implications for the various levels of organizational structure within which the psychologist and the examinee are operating.

Methods

The third component of the model is that of the particular methods used to obtain information relevant to the objectives of the assessment, which in turn are intended to address the hypotheses which one has generated. These methods consist of an array of specific skills, tactics, and strategies from which the examiner may choose those which promise to provide information regarding her or his hypotheses about the problem to be solved. In the area of assessment, methods include (although they need not be limited to) the set of test instruments that are used in psychological testing of the individual.

The "scientific problem-solving model" thus provides a general framework for thinking about assessment in its broadest terms, and this model is clearly applicable when one is considering the assessment of a child or adolescent. The following discussion will involve additional views of the assessment process, specifically regarding the use of the WISC–III in the evaluation of a child or adolescent client.

A SPECIFIC MODEL FOR PSYCHOLOGICAL ASSESSMENT

Within the context of a broad problem-solving view of clinical activities such as that proposed by Sloves et al. (1979), whether one is performing only an intellectual assessment or a broader and more thorough evaluation of the person's overall adaptation, it is vital for the clinician to have a conceptual framework that guides the examiner's approach to the assessment situation.

The present author believes the most reasonable model for conceptualizing an assessment situation is that of psychotherapy, and the model utilized must therefore consider similarities and differences between psychological assessment and psychotherapy. An additional variable which must be considered with respect to the use of the WISC–III is that whenever this instrument is used, the assessment situation involves an adult and a child as opposed to two adults.

While it would be possible to conceive of psychological assessment in relation to many forms of psychotherapy, Clair and Prendergast (1994) discuss the parallel between psychological assessment and brief individual psychotherapy, essentially focusing on three aspects of brief psychotherapy which they feel are applicable to psychological assessment: entering a relationship with the client, establishing a focus, and providing feedback.

Clair and Prendergast (1994) note that in recent years a variety of factors have resulted in the development and articulation of many forms of brief individual psychotherapy which reflect numerous theoretical and technical viewpoints (e.g., Beck, Rush, Shaw, & Emery, 1979; Davanloo, 1978; Klerman, Weissman, & Rounsaville, & Chevron, 1984).

Based on the fundamental assumption that psychological treatment can be conducted within a limited time frame, brief psychotherapies place great emphasis on the ability of the therapist and client to enter into a relationship with one another that is understood to be short-term and collaborative. Utilizing the concept of respect for the individual as articulated in client-centered therapy (Rogers, 1961), these brief therapies stress the validation of the client's perspective, the therapist's willingness to actively engage the client, and the therapist's capacity to respond to the client openly, honestly and directly as components of the development of a constructive therapist-client relationship.

Paralleling the therapist's willingness to relate directly to the client in brief therapy, Clair and Prendergast (1994) note that in their assessment procedure, they invite the client to discuss his or her understanding of why a referral for psychological testing was made and what the client hopes to derive from the testing. They feel that, in this way, they are emphasizing the collaborative nature of psychological assessment and are inviting the person to actively participate in the process.

Consistent with the first interview in brief therapy, the purpose of this strategy is to obtain the client's view of his or her problem, how it may relate to events in the client's life, and how psychological assessment may help address these concerns. If the person has no idea regarding how psychological assessment may be helpful, these authors suggest that the purpose of testing should be explored before beginning the assessment.

Clair and Prendergast (1994) note that in addition to entering into a relationship with the client, the therapist engaging in brief therapy also attempts to integrate historical, developmental and interpersonal data into a focal theme or conflict which will provide an organizing focus for the treatment (Budman & Gurman, 1988).

The specific manner of developing such a focus depends on the theoretical orientation of the therapist, and this may differ across therapists and orientations (e.g., Mann, 1973; Sifneos, 1987; Strupp & Binder, 1984). However, regardless of her or his particular therapeutic orientation, each therapist using a brief therapy model communicates his or her formulation of the client's central issue to the client, obtains feedback from the client, and seeks to develop a mutually agreed upon focus for the therapeutic treatment.

Clair and Prendergast (1994) feel that such an approach is also useful in psychological assessment, since it assists the clinician to organize the data into a clinical formulation, and integrates the client's perception with historical, interview and test data. They note that the search for a focus in the context of an assessment involves review and integration of the client's history, the examiner-examinee relationship, and the test data itself.

The development of a focus in psychological assessment can provide an integrated formulation of the client's difficulties and current condition, which is useful for communication to the referral source. This focus, however, is also relevant as a vehicle for conveying the client's central concerns back to the client her- or himself in the interpretive or feedback component of the testing process.

The third and final aspect of Clair and Prendergast's (1994) discussion deals with interpretation and feedback to the client. They note that in brief psychotherapy, feedback to clients is offered in the form of trial interpretations. These interpretations may be seen as a method of assessing the client's ability to engage in a process of self-exploration, but also the client's response may modify, and render more accurate, the therapist's own formulation. This feedback component thus recognizes the client's capacity to tolerate feedback, to utilize it, and to respond in a way that may clarify the thinking of the therapist.

Clair and Prendergast (1994) note that the provision of feedback during and at the conclusion of testing represents a continuation of the collaborative examiner-examinee relationship which has been present throughout the evaluation process. They point out that the psychologist should not assume someone else will provide adequate and meaningful communication to the examinee about the findings of the psychological assessment.

Instead, consistent with the structure of brief therapy, the examiner should view feedback as an integral component of the assessment process. And continuous with the direct, active and respectful relationship that has been established during the evaluation, the psychologist him- or herself should provide feedback to the client on the assessment findings as a way to make the findings meaningful to the examinee and to provide the examinee with an opportunity to express her or his feelings regarding the assessment experience and findings.

APPLICATION OF THE MODEL TO THE INTELLECTUAL ASSESSMENT OF CHILDREN AND ADOLESCENTS

As noted above, the present author believes it is most reasonable to conceptualize psychological assessment as analogous to psychotherapy. The author concurs with Clair and Prendergast (1994) in their noting of similarities between psychological assessment and brief psychotherapy in terms of the importance of establishing a relationship with the examinee, developing a focus for the assessment, and providing feedback to the examinee regarding test findings. However, the author would note other issues which should also be considered in conceptualizing assessment in general and in applying this view to the testing of children and adolescents with the WISC–III in particular.

First of all, the above model focuses on the similarity or analogy between psychotherapy and psychological assessment. But the differences should also be noted. One significant difference is in the control of the situation. In psychotherapy, the client is ordinarily able to exercise significant control regarding which topics he or she wishes to focus on and to what extent she or he wishes to reveal information. In testing in general, but particularly in intellectual assessment, the examiner (and the test itself) controls what topics or tasks will be dealt with and thus determines the client's revelation of areas of strength or weakness.

Second, Clair and Prendergast (1994) discuss the psychological assessment of adults while the present volume pertains to children and adolescents, and the experience of adults dealing with psychological assessment differs from that of children and adolescents dealing with this experience. For example, it must be kept in mind that adults are usually more willing participants in psychological assessment or treatment than are children or adolescents. Referral of children and adolescents ordinarily begins with someone other than the child or adolescent, and hence their approach to a testing situation may be different from that of an adult.

Third, as discussed elsewhere (see section on "Ethics and the WISC–III"), adults have certain rights in psychotherapy or assessment that they may choose to exercise. Children's rights before the law and in terms of their ability to refuse to participate in testing may be less clear, and most children may not know of or feel able to exercise their rights not to be tested or to not answer questions posed by an adult authority.

Fourth, in contrast to the model described by Clair and Prendergast (1994), since the present volume focuses on the WISC–III and not an entire test battery, the development of a focus of testing during the course of an assessment may be less applicable to the current presentation than to a comprehensive psychological assessment of either a child or an adult.

However, in considering those aspects of Clair and Prendergast's (1994) approach which apply to the testing of children and adolescents, one can delineate four issues: (1) the short-term or brief nature of the examiner's contact with the child or adolescent; (2) the articulation of the purpose for the assessment, which is basically to contribute to the betterment of the child's life circumstance by providing knowledge about and understanding of his or her intellectual functioning; (3) the potential provision of feedback to the child or adolescent about her or his test performance; and (4) possible use of the test results by the examiner and child in collaboration to identify one or more steps the examinee may take to change his or her functioning based on the knowledge gained from the testing.

Implementing such an approach to the testing of children means adopting a model in which the examiner conveys a basic respect for the child or adolescent, clearly indicating that the contact between the two will be relatively brief; discussing the purpose (instead of Clair and Prendergast's focus) of testing with the child; and being prepared to give the child some degree of constructive and supportive feedback about his or her perform-ance should the child desire that information.

The rationale for using such a procedure with children and adolescents is that it is the child whose behavior or classroom performance resulted in a referral for testing, it is the child who is being evaluated, and it is the child or adolescent whose future may be significantly influenced by the outcome of the assessment. Further, it is the examiner who has the best knowledge of the WISC–III and of the child's performance on the test. It is thus the examiner who is in the best position at the completion of testing to communi-cate at least some feedback to the child about his or her performance and the implications of that performance for the child or adolescent's future. Finally, such an approach is consistent with the *Ethical Principles of Psychologists and Code of Conduct,* which states that "psychologists ensure that an explanation of the results [of an assessment] is provided using language that is rea-sonably understandable to the person assessed or to another legally author-ized person on behalf of the client" (American Psychological Association, 1992, p. 1604).

From within this perspective, the present author would note seven basic aspects of the engagement and testing process: (1) informing the child of the brief nature of the examiner-examinee relationship; (2) obtaining at least basic identifying information about the child and his or her living circum-stances; (3) establishing rapport and appropriate task set in the child, by asking and/or discussing with the child her or his understanding of who the examiner is, and why the child is being evaluated—i.e., the *purpose* of testing (as opposed to Clair and Prendergast's *focus* for testing) and possi-bly providing a motivating instructional set; (4) utilizing a set of test-administration strategies; (5) offering and/or providing feedback to the child about his or her performance once testing has been completed; (6) explaining to the child what will happen to the test information and its meaning for the child's own future, and possibly determining specific ways the child may change his or her behavior based on the results of testing; and (7) within the limits of test security, attempting to answer any questions the child or adolescent may have regarding the testing or testing process.

In terms of these seven aspects of testing, the first issue to consider is the short-term or brief nature of the contact with the child. A complete psychological evaluation of a child or adolescent may involve between three and four or more hours. The WISC–III manual (Wechsler, 1991) suggests that the standard battery takes, on the average, 50 to 70 minutes to administer, with an additional 10 to 15 minutes if the supplementary tests are also given. However, Edwards and Edwards (1993) note that in their experience, average testing time has been 80 to 90 minutes for the standard battery.

One can assume that assessment of a child or adolescent with the WISC--III if one adds any other tests (e.g., Figure Drawings, Bender-Gestalt, WRAT-3) or some brief interviewing will require at least two to two-and-a-half hours or more. Because of the significance of the decisions that may depend on the child's WISC–III performance, the examiner must decide on a general strategy for engaging, or attempting to engage, the child in the testing as Clair and Prendergast (1994) discuss with respect to adults.

If one assumes that the testing represents any degree of threat or anxiety arousal for the child, one may conceive of the beginning of testing as involving an effort to reduce the child's anxiety. In this regard, the literature on health psychology indicates that with respect to any medical procedure, the most fundamental intervention entails preparation of the child for the experience he or she will undergo (Dolgin & Jay, 1989; Melamed & Seigel, 1975), which involves discussing what will be happening, and dealing with any of the child's fears.

In applying this concept to psychological testing of children, the *first* aspect of the engagement involves the concept of honesty and directness with the child. This entails informing the child that one's relationship with him or her will be brief. For example, in a school setting, the examiner might say, "You and I will be getting together for about two hours or so this morning. I might see you around school after this, but I think this is the only time we will be getting together." If the child is young and/or might have difficulty with time concepts, the examiner may say, for example, that the child will return to her or his room before lunch.

The purpose of this introduction is to provide temporal structure for the child and to remind the child that he or she will be returning to familiar surroundings shortly. In addition, this introduction also indicates the fact that the examiner and child may only meet on this one occasion.

The *second* component of testing should include at least a minimum number of questions (see "Pre- and Post-WISC–III Questions"). The purpose of these questions is to provide the examiner with a basic knowledge of the examinee's living circumstances and to give the examiner and child a shared referent; that is, the child can know that the examiner has a basic knowledge of the examinee's life which has just been provided by the child her- or himself.

Beyond this, however, the examiner can consider a strategy intended to involve the examinee more fully and actively in the assessment and decide, based on the child's initial reaction and level of anxiety, to what extent to implement the strategy. This *third* component of the testing process involves asking the child for his or her understanding of the reason for the testing. This issue can be broached by asking the examinee an appropriate variant of the question, "Do you know how come we're getting together today?" Using the gradient model discussed earlier and varying the strategy depending on the examinee's age, the examiner may need to focus this question more clearly, for example, if the child replies "To talk" or "To be tested." Related to asking the child the reason why she or he is being seen, or tested, the examiner may also ask if the examinee has any idea how the testing can be of help to the child.

The child is asked for her or his understanding of why she or he is being seen and how testing may help in order to provide the child with a cognitive framework for the *purpose* for the testing experience. The examiner may at some point in this discussion need to explain his or her own understanding of the assessment in terms appropriate to the child's age. For example, with a younger child the examiner might say, "Well, your teacher seemed to feel it was kind of hard for you to do some of your schoolwork. We felt that some of the things I will ask you to do will help us figure out why things seem hard and what we can do to make school better."

The examiner must be able to express the idea of testing at a level which is understandable for a child the age of the examinee, or which makes some sense to the resistant middle adolescent who feels that testing is for the school rather than for him or her. Once having provided an explanation, the examiner may again ask the child to explain to the examiner the child's understanding of the purpose of the testing.

Assuming that the examiner and child are able to agree on a reasonably clear statement regarding the purpose of the testing and how it may be helpful to the child, this provides a framework within which the testing can proceed, moves in the direction of Clair and Prendergast's (1994) involvement of the client in testing, and also provides a structure for the examiner to use in giving feedback to the child or adolescent at the conclusion of testing.

Additionally, as part of this third component of the assessment process, the examiner may deal with what the Wechsler (1991) manual refers to as "Establishing and Maintaining Rapport" (pp. 36–37). Assuming the instructions in the manual provide guidelines for the examiner, the gradient model is relevant for the examiner to use in determining a specific set of instructions for the examinee. One may thus conceptualize a continuum of test instructions that vary from minimal through maximal structure and from those that do not emphasize optimal performance to those that do.

This means the examiner can focus simply on the fact of testing (i.e., "I'm going to ask you some different questions, and to figure out different kinds of problems, things like that."), or the examiner can use instructions which will attempt to motivate the child to approach the tasks in a particular way (i.e., "I am going to be asking you some different questions and to solve different kinds of problems. *I'd like you to really try hard to do the best you can.*").

The examiner can go still further in the demand nature of her or his instructions (i.e., "I'm going to be asking you some different questions, and to solve some different problems, with puzzles and pictures. Some of the things will be easy for you and some will probably be hard, so I don't expect you to get everything right. *But I do expect you to try your best on everything.*").

In determining at what level of the gradient to provide instructions, the examiner should realize that the more extreme instructions may have a positive *or* negative impact on the examinee's functioning. The child might work much harder than he or she might ordinarily, resulting in an estimate of the child's capability when very highly motivated. On the other hand, these more extreme instructions may also stimulate the examinee's achievement anxiety or negativism, resulting in the child performing less well than he or she might ordinarily.

Hence the examiner must decide whether she or he should attempt to shape the examinee's test-taking attitude, or simply provide minimal direction and motivation with pre-test statements, and observe the way in which the child or adolescent spontaneously approaches the assessment tasks. This decision will depend on whether the examiner's orientation is to obtain a sample of the child's *typical* functioning or presumed *optimal* functioning.

Whether the examiner is seeking a sample of the examinee's typical or optimal test performance may influence the examiner's introductory statements as well as the examiner's behavior during testing. The present author assumes that factors which may adversely affect the child's test performance include: anxiety, motivation, attentional problems, verbal style, and aspects of the child's self-perception, such as diffidence or low self-esteem. Table 6,

"Examiner Behaviors Used to Elicit Typical or Optimal Child Test Performance," indicates ways in which the examiner can approach these aspects of the child's test performance depending on whether the examiner is seeking a sample of the child's typical or optimal functioning.

The *fourth* component of the testing process involves obtaining an "adequate" sample of the examinee's performance during the administration of the subtests themselves. This will involve competent administration of the tasks, observation of the child's behavior, and an ability to respond appropriately to reactions the child may have to particular aspects of the testing experience. Again, the examiner's behavior during this phase of the test administration will depend to some extent on whether the examiner is seeking a typical or an optimal sample of the examinee's functioning.

The *fifth* component of testing involves offering feedback to the child immediately after testing on how he or she performed on the WISC–III. In order to carry out this fifth component, the examiner should have a basic familiarity with children's performance on the WISC–III so that he or she can have a reasonable "feel" for how well a child has done. To prepare for actually providing feedback to the examinee, however, the examiner must take certain steps before and during the test administration.

First of all, in order to be able to provide feedback to the child immediately after testing, the examiner must choose a sample of subtests and score these during or immediately after testing is completed. To prepare for this phase of the testing, before the actual testing, the examiner can mark points on several of the subtests on the WISC–III test booklet as to what a target raw score might be on those subtests for the child who is to be tested.

Sattler (1992) describes short forms of the WISC–III, noting also that because of several statistical phenomena, it is virtually certain that short-form IQs and Full Scale IQs will very often lead to different classifications of the individual's intelligence. Although the present author does not recommend the use of short forms of the WISC–III, for the purpose of immediate feedback to the examinee, these can be used.

To prepare for this feedback, the examiner must first select a group of subtests to comprise a short form of the WISC–III. Sattler (1992) provides a table (Table L-11, p. 1170) which indicates reliability and validity coefficients for WISC–III dyads, triads, tetrads, and pentads. Although the examiner could use a two- or three-subtest short form for this purpose, the present author recommends use of a four-subtest, or tetrad, short form. The present author recommends the use of the four subtests of Information, Similarities, Picture Completion, and Block Design (although an examiner could select a different set of subtests). Calculated according to the formulas presented in Sattler (1992), which are based on the classic paper by Tellegen and Briggs (1967), this tetrad has a reliability coefficient of .929 and a validity coefficient of .881. The author would suggest use of these four subtests for feedback purposes as they involve 40% of the subtests used to calculate the examinee's IQ scores; include both verbal and performance tasks; include only one of the "ACID" subtests (Information; see section on "ACID" subtests); include one of the easiest WISC–III subtests (Picture Completion; Kavale & Forness, 1994; Kaufman et al., 1990); and, except for the Similarities subtest, they require relatively little judgment during scoring.

For many children, the examiner can roughly score the individual's Similarities subtest during administration of the subtest; scoring can be rechecked, for example, while the child is working on the Symbol Search subtest. Scoring of the Information and/or the Picture Completion subtests may be done while the examinee is working on the Coding subtest, and scoring of the Block Design subtest can be done as one proceeds through the subtest.

In order to determine the child's scaled scores (or estimated IQ), the examiner can proceed in one of two ways. In the first method, prior to the actual testing, the examiner can locate the appropriate raw score in Wechsler (1992, Table A.1., pp. 217–249) that would yield a particular scaled score (or IQ) for the child being tested. Depending on the focus of the examiner's concern, the scaled-score target could be set at 7, 8, 9, or higher.

For example, if one were testing a child of 10 years, 2 months of age, one would use Table A.1. on page 229. The examiner would locate the raw scores for the short-form subtests which would be necessary for the child to obtain scaled scores of 7 on each subtest (since an average score of 7 on five verbal subtests would yield a Verbal IQ of 83, and an average score of 7 on five performance subtests would yield a Performance IQ of 81, which would result in a Full Scale IQ of 81). The necessary raw scores for each of the subtests of Information, Similarities, Picture Completion, and Block Design would be copied from Table A.1., and written on the WISC–III test form.

As the examiner proceeds through the WISC–III or immediately after, he or she can calculate the examinee's raw score for each of these subtests. If the child's raw score on each subtest is at least the target value, the examiner can conclude that the child will have an estimated IQ which can be considered in at least the low average range (or above). If the examiner requires a few minutes to check the subtest scores or to calculate the estimate of the child's IQ scores after testing, the examinee can be asked to do something for a moment while the examiner completes this task.

The second method involves the examiner simply scoring these four subtests during or immediately after the WISC–III has been administered and then checking the child's raw scores in the appropriate section of Table A.1. in Wechsler (1991, pp. 217–249) to determine the examinee's scaled scores on these subtests. This approach would take longer than the first method but would permit the examiner to obtain the exact scaled score for each raw score.

Once the examiner has prepared in this way to discuss the examinee's test performance, the child can be asked if he or she would like to talk about how she or he did on the various tasks. If the examinee wishes to, the examiner can first ask how well the child thinks he or she did compared to other children of the same age—worse, the same, or better. The examinee may also be asked if there were any tasks which he or she thought were difficult or easy or on which she or he did very well or very poorly.

Using the child's response as a guide, the examiner can provide some direct and immediate feedback to the examinee regarding his or her test performance. Depending on what the examiner and child had originally agreed was the purpose of the testing, the examiner can at this point relate the examinee's test performance to the original purpose for the current evaluation.

Three additional points may be noted here. First, if the examinee's performance falls in or below the borderline range, the examiner may wish to have the test results shared with the examinee's parent(s) before these results are shared with the child in any fashion. However, since the examiner does not provide a label for the child's performance, the strategy noted below can still be used in a discussion with the examinee. Second, if the examiner includes discussion of the test results with the child, he or she should inform the child that the scores must be rechecked and could be somewhat different when all the scores are calculated. Third, if the examiner scores these subtests at the time of the testing, they should be rescored carefully when the entire test is scored and the results written up.

In providing feedback to the examinee, the examiner can begin by stating that the test involves tasks where the child answers questions in words and tasks where the child does things with his or her hands and eyes, and that usually children do better on some parts of the test than others. The examiner can say that he or she checked *some* parts of the test, and that on those parts, the examinee (either) performed as well as (or better than) most children his or her age, or seemed to find some of the tasks harder than many children her or his age.

If the results on the verbal and performance subtests are very obviously different, and if the examiner feels that this is true of the examinee's handling of the other subtests, the examiner might point out that the child seems to do better when using words, or when working on things with his or her hands and eyes. The examiner at this point can also provide feedback regarding the behavioral observations of the examinee during testing, for example, by nothing that the examinee seemed to give up on some of the tasks, and that if he or she had been able to stick at them, she or he might have been able to do even better, or that the child's nervousness seemed to make things harder for the examinee.

Whether or not the examiner chooses to offer the examinee an opportunity to discuss his or her test performance, the examiner proceeds to the *sixth* component of the testing, which involves explaining to the child what will happen with the results of the testing. This refers to informing the examinee of the chain of events that link the present testing to other aspects of the child's world, or other systems within which the child or adolescent lives: school and home.

The examiner can explain that the test results will be discussed with other professionals (e.g., the child's teacher) and with her or his parent(s) (with or without the child present). Based on the child's performance, recommendations may be made for ways to assist him or her with those difficulties that had resulted in the child being tested. If the examiner and examinee have discussed the child's test performance, the two may collaboratively discuss how the findings of the testing can be transferred from the testing situation into the child's academic world to facilitate his or her improved functioning. This step thus entails involving the examinee in determining what changes may be required in order to make her or his functioning more adequate. Hence this last step introduces the child or adolescent's own responsibility for participating in making changes in his or her own life and behavior based on the outcome of the testing.

The *seventh* and final component of the testing process calculated to make the evaluation meaningful to the examinee involves asking if the child or adolescent has any questions she or he would like to ask the examiner about the testing which has just been completed. Within the limits of test security, the examiner can attempt to answer the examinee's questions openly and honestly although with a recognition of the need to be psychologically sensitive and supportive to the individual.

The major concern with implementing the above framework for involving a child or adolescent client in intellectual assessment is the fact that this procedure adds time to the clinical process. There is little doubt that approaching the examinee as suggested may add as much as half an hour to the testing time. If the examiner is pressured with a heavy workload, she or he may feel that such an approach is not worth the additional time.

On the other hand, if one considers that the intelligence testing of a child or adolescent is an important part of the child's life, with significant consequences for that individual, then the additional time becomes more worthwhile as a demonstration of concern and respect for the examinee. Furthermore, such an approach to testing promises to provide a model for the individual child as to how she or he can and should approach future assessments: expecting that a psychological assessment will be a collaborative venture between the examinee and a concerned adult; that the child can decide how he or she will be involved in the assessment; that the purpose of the evaluation is to be helpful to the child; and that the examinee may choose whether or not to obtain immediate feedback on her or his performance.

Finally, such an approach as this one has the potential to shift the testing encounter from one in which the examiner only "finds out" about the examinee into a situation where the testing can conclude with the examiner and child collaborating to discuss what has been found, and how the examiner and child can jointly determine how to use this information for the improvement of the child's academic or other life experience. Thus this approach makes the psychological testing more like a psychotherapeutic intervention in which the examiner obtains information about the child which is then used with the child to facilitate her or his future adaptation. The approach also provides the examiner with a much more fulfilling role in regard to the individual being evaluated. The examiner is not merely being a psychometrician gathering a set of scores during testing, but is actively engaged in noting the examinee's intellectual and behavioral functioning for use in a meaningful and constructive post-test dialogue with the child.

Part IV
ADMINISTRATION, ANALYSIS, AND INTERPRETATION OF THE WISC–III

Chapter Eleven

GENERAL ISSUES IN TEST ADMINISTRATION

Assessment in clinical psychology involves the use of a range of techniques and strategies to obtain particular information about an individual or unit of two or more individuals (Goldstein & Hersen, 1990). Insofar as the present volume deals with the administration of the WISC–III, assessment may be understood as involving an interpersonal situation that includes two individuals, one an adult, the other an individual from early childhood through middle adolescence. The situation has been set up so that one of the participants, the examiner, can obtain a variety of kinds of information about the other, the child or adolescent being evaluated.

From within this perspective, a number of variables may be considered that have a bearing on the functioning of these two individuals within the test situation and on the ultimate test protocol that results from their interaction:

(a) Characteristics of the examiner and her or his role;
(b) Characteristics of the child and his or her role;
(c) Aspects of the test situation;
(d) Test administration and scoring.

CHARACTERISTICS OF THE EXAMINER AND HER OR HIS ROLE

One characteristic of the examiner that may have an effect on the testing situation and its outcome includes the professional role and status of the examiner, which in turn reflects the place of psychology within the mental health field. Historically, in clinical settings, the psychologist had been relegated to the role of providing assessment of patients, who were then turned over to a psychiatrist for actual treatment. In recent years, as psychology has developed its own independent status as a health profession, there has been a movement away from the psychologist only as examiner; many psychologists feel that such a role is demeaning or at least less important or satisfying to them than other aspects of their professional roles and functions.

However, the perception that the examiner has of him- or herself professionally will enter into the way the examiner perceives testing, and this in turn will have an impact on the way the examiner functions when administering a given psychological test.

An issue related to the concept of the examiner's professional identity is the training that psychologists receive regarding testing. Slate and Hunnicut (1988) discuss this as one of the sources of examiner errors on the Wechsler scales. These authors note that the primary skill deficit found in clinical psychology graduate students has been the lack of assessment skills (Garfield & Kurz, 1973), and surveys of internship directors (e.g., Sturgis, Verstegen, Randolph, & Garvin, 1980) have noted assessment and diagnostic skills as among new interns' most prominent skill deficits. Drabman (1985) has noted that interns often arrive at their internship sites "not knowing how to administer, score, and interpret the standardized tests used for educational evaluation" (p. 624). Hence the background, training, and attitude towards assessment of the examiner (Garfield & Kurz, 1973) will affect his or her approach to the assessment of any particular individual.

A third aspect of the psychologist's role that may affect the administration of a test is the psychologist's perception of the meaning of the results of testing and within what context the test data will have significance. This issue refers to the way in which psychological test data is to be used and the extent to which it may be depended on for making specific decisions regarding the child who has been evaluated.

With the advent of legislation such as P.L. 94-142 (U.S. Public Law 94-142, 1977) that provides guidelines for the evaluation of handicapped children, the school psychologist and psychological test data have come to carry considerable weight in decisions made in regard to children. Arasim and Frankenberger (1989) surveyed a sample of school psychologists and found that school psychologists played a primary role in MDT assessment processes, as they received referrals, appointed MDT members, and did the majority of the assessments. Frankenberger and Harper (1988) analyzed rating scales obtained from 235 MDT participants after parent conferences and found that professionals most often participating on the teams (e.g., school psychologists) were also those rated most important to the teams' decisions.

In interdisciplinary settings, the politics of the system as well as the particular interpersonal organization of the specific decision-making group may make psychological test data of major importance or of relatively little significance in the decision made about any particular child. However, the psychologist's perception of where psychological test data fits into the overall process of clinical decision making will also influence the way the psychologist approaches a particular test administration.

A fourth factor that may affect the psychologist's approach to test administration lies in the psychologist's own personal identity, particularly those factors that led the person to become a psychologist in the first place. One would assume that the individual who has become a psychologist has some desire to be of help to others, to enable them to achieve their potential, and to assist others to adapt more successfully. The intellectual desire to know about and understand people and their motivations, to have a vocation involving mental rather than physical exertion, and to work with interesting and stimulating colleagues would also be operating in the individual who becomes a psychologist.

On the other hand, less socially desirable motives may also operate in the psychologist's personality. These motives may include, for example, a desire to have control over others, to deal with people who are weak and hence less threatening, or to have the opportunity to see into others' minds, or their private and personal feelings may also be involved in the psychologist's personal identity. Hence, many aspects of the psychologist's own sense of self and internal conflicts may emerge in the way he or she approaches and administers a given test or test battery.

Another examiner variable to be considered in terms of the administration of a psychological test is the sex of the examiner (Black & Dana, 1977; Bradbury, Wright, Walker, & Ross, 1975; Quereshi, 1968). Sattler (1990) notes that in some studies, children performed better for female than male examiners, but no systematic trends are evident. However, the present author feels that it is important to consider the nature of examiner-child interaction as a function of the various combinations of age and sex of the child, and sex of examiner, particularly in view of more recent knowledge of the prevalence of sexual abuse histories in children (e.g., National Center on Child Abuse and Neglect, 1988), and in view of the realization that psychologists are not immune from boundary violations in regard to their patients (Pope, Tabachnick, & Keith-Spiegel, 1987). This means at the very least that the examiner's sex may have an effect on the testing situation and may affect the outcome of testing.

Another examiner variable that may affect testing is that of the examiner's test administration style. For example, Saigh (1981) investigated the effects of positive examiner verbal comments on children's WISC–R performance. Children in the experimental group were verbally praised after their responses while children in the control group received only non-evaluative procedural comments. Full Scale IQs were found to average 10 points higher under the verbal praise condition than under the control procedure, indicating that the examiner's use of verbal praise may affect the test outcome.

Related to the use of verbal praise during testing, Buckhalt (1990) examined comments made by experienced and novice examiners during intelligence testing. Considering attributional comments (regarding task difficulty, effort, ability or knowledge, practice or experience, and fatigue of the examinee), and encouraging comments (statements that praised or supported the examinee), it was found that the pattern of comments for both experienced and beginning examiners related to the structural aspects of the test (e.g., the apparent task difficulty evident on particular subtests). It was also found that experienced examiners made many more attributional comments and encouraging comments than did novice examiners. Buckhalt (1990) notes that with greater experience, examiners may learn that both attributional and encouraging comments are instrumental in maintaining the examinee's interest and motivation throughout the testing session.

On the other hand, in terms of reinforcement as a variable in testing, Fish (1988), in his meta-analysis of the effects of reinforcement during intelligence testing, concluded that although reinforcers do enhance the performance of some examinees, one cannot draw the general conclusion that systematic reinforcement will always increase the performance of all examinees under all conditions. Buckhalt (1990) notes that the testing situation is comprised of a number of different kinds of tasks, and the effects of incentives may vary as a function of the interaction of child, examiner, and task demand variables. Hence it may not be possible to make general conclusions about the effects of reinforcers on test performance. However, from the perspective of reinforcement as a variable in testing, the examiner might attempt to observe what reinforcers do operate in the examinee's on-task behavior: those which appear internal to the examinee, such as satisfaction when he or she succeeds on an item or subtest; or those which appear examiner-controlled, such as praise or verbal comments.

Related to the examiner's test administration style is the issue of whether the examiner attempts to obtain the typical performance or the optimal performance of the child being evaluated. This relates to whether the examiner attempts to have the child demonstrate his or her optimal test performance, in which case the examiner may be more active, ask more questions, and encourage the child to persist when she or he is inclined to give up; or whether the examiner allows the child to approach the test in his or her own natural fashion, whether or not this involves significant or minimal effort, easy distractibility, or lack of elaborated verbal responding (see Table 6).

Still another variable that may affect test administration is the examiner's impression of the child being evaluated. This factor involves the "halo" effect, the tendency for the examiner to establish a global perception of the child, either positive or negative, and then for this global perception to influence a variety of aspects of test administration or scoring.

Sattler, Hillix, and Neher (1970) conducted two experiments to explore the halo effect. By having graduate students score ambiguous Comprehension and Vocabulary subtest responses on identical WISC protocols but by leading the students to believe the examinees were bright, dull, or of

Table 6
EXAMINER BEHAVIORS USED TO ELICIT
TYPICAL OR OPTIMAL CHILD TEST PERFORMANCE

Examiner Behavior to Elicit:	Typical Performance	Optimal Performance
Area of Child Experience:		
Anxiety	Use little pre-test conversation, explanation, do not explore any child anxieties regarding testing	Use significant pre-test conversation, explore any examinee anxieties regarding testing
	During testing, use minimum comments recognizing or reducing examinee's anxiety	During testing, use comments to empathize with or reduce child's anxiety
Motivation	Display friendly neutrality, little conversation during testing	Display engagement, spontaneity during test administration
	Provide minimal motivation in pre-test instructions	Provide maximal motivating pre-test instructions
	During testing, do not provide supportive comments during subtests	During testing, provide supportive comments, encouragement during subtests
Attention	Make no specific attempts to have child focus on test or subtests	Use focusing instructions at various points during testing
Verbal Style	Do not ask additional clarifying questions on verbal subtests	Ask additional clarifying questions on verbal subtests readily
Self-Perception	Make no comments regarding examinee's ability to do his or her best, or ability to succeed or to keep trying on subtests; let child give up when she or he wants to	Use comments regarding examinee's ability to do her or his best, or ability to keep on trying on difficult items; encourage child to continue when he or she wants to give up

unknown ability, Sattler et al. (1970) found that the mean scores of the "bright" examinees were 3.8 points higher than those of the "dull" examinees on the Vocabulary subtest. Hence the examiner's overall perception of the examinee may provide a source of variation in test administration or scoring.

Another aspect of the effect of the examiner's impression of the examinee on the outcome of testing was explored by Wheeler, Adams, and Nielsen (1987), although their investigation used undergraduates rather than actual psychologists as subjects. In their study, Wheeler et al. (1987) trained 42 male and 42 female undergraduates in the scoring of WISC–R verbal subtests and then had them score a protocol which was accompanied by a photo of an attractive or unattractive child who had presumably taken the test. The attractiveness or unattractiveness of the subject did not result in differential scoring, but the subjects in the study did differentially attribute positive characteristics to attractive versus unattractive children.

One final variable regarding the examiner and her or his role involves the race of the examiner. Sattler (1990) notes that with ethnic minority children, the examiner's race plays a negligible role, and Sattler and Gwynne (1982) state that the hypothesis that the race of the examiner yields different IQ scores for blacks and for whites is a myth. However, Jenkins and Ramsey (1991) point out that it may be premature to conclude that the race of the examiner effect is a myth, noting that Graziano, Varca, and Levy (1982) argue that the reasons for differences observed in African-American and white intelligence test scores is a complex issue and that much research remains to be done on this matter. Hence, the race of the examiner is a variable that should also be considered as potentially affecting test administration and test outcome.

Overall, then, there are a number of variables that involve the examiner and his or her role that may impact on the testing situation and may thus have an effect on the course of the assessment and its outcome. The examiner should realize the potential effect of these variables on his or her functioning during testing. By being aware of the potential effects of these variables, the examiner may attempt to minimize the effect they actually do have, or realize that any one or more of these variables may have had an effect on the testing of a particular child, or on the examiner's testing more generally.

CHARACTERISTICS OF THE EXAMINEE
AND HIS OR HER ROLE

There are a number of characteristics of the examinee apart from his or her intellectual ability that may also have an impact on the test situation, and consequently on the outcome of the testing. The first of these is the meaning to the child or adolescent of being a client or patient. The very idea of being tested indicates to the child or adolescent that he or she is somehow different from others in her or his referent group. By definition, testing means that the child has been selected for some reason to undergo an experience that not all of his or her peers will undergo, and this may stimulate behaviors in the child that might not otherwise be present.

The examiner must be aware of the fact that the child being tested may enjoy being singled out and appreciate the special attention, but also that the experience of being tested may arouse different kinds and degrees of anxiety among different children, and that these tensions may contribute to the examiner-child interaction and the ultimate test protocol that results from the interaction.

Relevant to this issue, Wigfield and Eccles (1989) reviewed the literature on the development of test anxiety in elementary and secondary school children. They viewed anxiety as a multidimensional construct having its roots in how parents react to children's early achievement strivings. The development of anxiety was seen as related to children's developing ability to interpret their school performance relative to their previous performance; their view of the performance of other children; and the increasingly strict evaluative experiences they encounter as they progress through school. Hence the child who is to be tested may experience heightened anxiety about the prospect of testing, and this may affect his or her approach to the entire testing situation.

A second aspect of the child's behavior that should be considered is the issue of power during the testing interaction. For virtually all children, of course, the issue of powerlessness is a relatively central one. Hence for any child or adolescent, the dynamics of having to expose him- or herself and to display her or his inadequacies, or to attempt to avoid such exposure, would be expected to emerge in the child's test functioning and behavior.

One way in which the issue of power may appear in testing would be in control of the test situation. In this regard, some children accept the position of powerlessness and vulnerability and readily expose their abilities or disabilities without using many self-protective strategies. On the other hand, some children attempt by any of a variety of behaviors to conceal their own weaknesses from themselves or from the examiner, and this may involve their efforts to shift the control of the situation from the examiner to themselves. Alternatively, Wapner and Connor (1986) have suggested that impulsive boys in whom defensiveness and impulsivity are correlated may present a facade of unconcern to mask their underlying anxiety; their impulsive response may occur in part because they are defensive about appearing incompetent, equate rapidity of response with competence, and hence respond quickly in order to appear competent.

A third potential issue regarding the examinee is that of the child's developmental status, since her or his stage of development may interact with, or highlight, particular aspects of the child's functioning. Thus the referred child of early school age may display difficulties in the area of self-regulation and of acceptance of both familial and extra-familial authority. The child of this age may also have various concerns regarding dependency or separation that appear in his or her test functioning.

The slightly older child, of age eight to ten, may have been referred because of school learning, behavior, or attentional problems. Ordinarily, children of this age are able to distinguish among various adults in their lives; they may thus appreciate the special attention involved in testing and the opportunity to miss school, and may cooperate eagerly with the assessment. On the other hand, if such children are acutely aware of having been referred because of academic difficulties, they may display significant anxiety during the assessment since the WISC–III includes many school-related tasks.

The individual who is in pre- or middle adolescence, from age eleven to thirteen or fourteen, may have been referred for behavioral, academic, or even antisocial behavior, and may also be experiencing a recent reaction to the onset of puberty or the movement into adolescence with an already problematic life history. The youth at this stage may view the evaluation as a necessary step towards obtaining some help and therefore may participate appropriately. On the other hand, the individual at this stage may not differentiate among adults, may perceive the examiner as just one more adult enemy and as someone to be resisted or thwarted, and hence the individual may approach the testing in a highly uncooperative fashion.

Finally, the middle adolescent, from age fifteen to essentially age seventeen, may approach the testing situation in many ways as an adult might. The youth may be as physically large and developed as the examiner, and the implied power in the situation may be brought to a heightened level of awareness in both the adolescent and the examiner if the adolescent displays anger, overt resistance, or refusal to cooperate with the assessment. In addition, the interactional effects of the sex of the examiner and the sex and developmental stage of the individual being tested must also be considered (Hetherington, 1972).

Another variable that may affect the child in the testing situation is that of the child's race. As noted above, Sattler (1990) has stated that research indicates race of examiner does not have a significant effect on the measurement of minority children's IQ, and Reynolds and Kaiser (1990), Hale (1991), and Reynolds and Kaufman (1985) have reviewed a number of studies indicating that the Wechsler scales are not significantly biased in the assessment of minority group members' intellectual functioning (see section on "Bias and the Wechsler Scales"). Nonetheless, the present author believes that the child's racial background may have both direct and indirect influences on the testing situation and the outcome of testing.

The first issue involved if the examinee is a member of a minority group and the examiner is not is the child's perception of a non-minority examiner, and the feelings or anxieties this experience may stimulate in the child which may interfere with the examinee's performance. The second issue involves the difference in cultural background between the non-minority examiner and the minority child, in terms of acculturation, language and values. These factors may all affect the nature of examiner-child communication and understanding during testing, particularly if the examinee is bilingual, and may render the testing situation more complex and vulnerable to greater error in measurement than in the case of a non-minority child.

Hence there are a number of aspects of the examinee's role, including the fact of being tested, the reason the examinee perceives for the testing, the examinee's developmental stage, and the examinee's race, that may enter into his or her behavior and functioning during the assessment and that the examiner should be aware of during any evaluation.

ASPECTS OF THE TEST SITUATION

The first issue that should be considered in regard to the characteristics of the test situation is that of the physical surroundings in which testing is to occur. The optimal situation is one in which testing takes place in a comfortably appointed, quiet and well-lighted office, whether this office is located in a school, clinic, or hospital. If possible, the examiner should consider the route to the office, since the trip there from the classroom or waiting room may provide additional unnecessary sources of anxiety for the examinee.

The examiner's office should be reasonably neat with a minimum of distractions that might interfere with an examinee's ability to focus on test tasks, even if the examinee does not have particular difficulty with paying attention. Thus, if the examiner has a number of toys present in her or his office, these probably should be reduced in number or removed if the examinee is a young child.

There are of course times when testing must take place under less than optimal circumstances. For example, an examinee may need to be tested in a hospital, in the examinee's own home, or in an available room in a school building. In each of these circumstances, the examiner should attempt to reduce sources of stimulation that might interfere with the test procedure. For example, if the examinee is tested at home, parents might be asked not to interrupt the testing procedure. Similarly, if the examinee is tested in a hospital, nursing staff might be asked for their cooperation in not entering the testing room during testing, to the extent that this can be arranged.

Wechsler (1991) notes that as a rule, only the examinee and the examiner should be in the room during testing. The author would note that with the young or any highly anxious examinee, such as a child who refuses to attend school, the examiner can utilize the gradient model (see section on "Models in Psychology"). Thus, the examiner may attempt to have the parent wait in the waiting room (or another room in the examinee's home) and inform the child that he or she can see the parent: (1) after testing; (2) after a while, or periodically during testing. If these positions are met with the examinee's resistance, the examiner should allow the parent to be present when assessment begins since this will reduce the examinee's anxiety and permit testing to proceed. Under this circumstance, periodically during testing, the examinee may be asked if his or her parent can leave the situation.

In terms of specific physical arrangements of the testing situation, ordinarily testing will be carried out at a desk or table, most of which are rectangular in shape. Wechsler (1991) suggests that the examinee be seated directly across from the examiner. The present author believes that in standardizing the WISC–III, a variety of different seating arrangements should have been employed since there is actually great variability in the testing situations where psychologists use the WISC–III.

Although the present author could find no recent studies in the literature dealing with spatial relationships between examiners and children, he believes that interpersonal distance is a critical factor in the anxiety a child experiences during testing. Steyaert and Snyder (1985) report an investigation of the effects of seating arrangement and sex of the subject on performance on the Digit Span and Digit Symbol subtests of the WAIS–R. These authors found that seating arrangement (whether the subject sat across a desk from the experimenter, or with the corner of a desk between the subject and experimenter) had no significant effect on WAIS–R subtest scores.

Related to this issue, Hetherington (1972) reported an investigation of the effects of father absence on personality development in adolescent females and found that when adolescent females chose seats with a male interviewer, daughters of divorcees tended to choose the seat closest to the interviewer, females from intact families chose the seat directly across the table from the interviewer, and daughters of widows chose the seat most distant from the male interviewer. Other aspects of the female adolescents' behavior also varied as a function of family status.

Hetherington's (1972) research was carried out before there was much awareness of the prevalence of sexual abuse in children, and the present author would suggest that such histories exist unknown in many examinees. Hence the physical dimension of the testing situation is certainly important. The present author recommends that the examinee sit at one of the short sides of the table or desk while the examiner sits at the long side of the desk or table. For the right-handed examiner, the examinee sits to the examiner's left, while for the left-handed examiner, the examinee sits to the examiner's right.

This arrangement allows the examiner to keep the WISC–III kit a maximal distance from the examinee, so that the examinee is unable to see the test materials if the kit is open. Additionally, this arrangement allows the examiner to write notes without the examinee being able to read them very readily.

With the seating arrangement the author recommends, the examiner can sit further from the examinee if the examinee's history or behavior suggest that physical proximity is anxiety producing; the participants do not have to adopt a posture that involves a frontal orientation, and this seating reduces the likelihood of the feet or knees of the examiner and examinee touching. It might also be possible for the examiner to have chairs in both the position recommended by Wechsler (1991) and at the short side of the table, and allow the examinee to select her or his seat according to preference.

Another important aspect of the testing situation is that sufficient time should be allowed to complete the testing in one session, without having to rush the examinee and without preventing him or her from working on items up to (and in some cases beyond) the time limit allowed on the test. Wechsler (1991) notes that the administration of the regular battery of 10 subtests requires approximately 50–70 minutes, although Edwards and Edwards (1993) report administration times of 80–90 minutes for the standard battery. Testing would be expected to take longer if one is testing a young but quite intelligent examinee, or an older but unevenly functioning examinee, or if one utilizes the model for testing described in this volume.

While the author believes it is usually best to complete the entire WISC–III administration in one session, there is obviously no absolute rule on this matter. Under a variety of circumstances, for example, illness in the examinee, weakness in a medically ill child, or intense resistance to testing, testing may need to be interrupted and resumed on another occasion.

A final aspect of the discussion of the test situation involves the application of the gradient model to conceptualizing the WISC–III and its clinical use. From within this perspective, one can consider several basic dimensions as pertinent to the WISC–III: structure, control, item difficulty, and response latitude.

First of all, if one conceives of tests (or samples of examinee functioning) as distributed along a continuum from those that are highly structured at one pole to those which are highly unstructured at the other, one would place the WISC–III at the highly structured pole of such a continuum, and one can consider structure to be a primary characteristic of the test. If one is using the WISC–III as part of a battery of tests or procedures, it will clearly be one of the more structured tasks to be utilized (and thus might be deliberately administered in a certain sequence within the examination procedures). By structure is meant that the tasks are organized, focused, with specific instructions to guide the examinee's behavior, and that there are ordinarily specific criteria which are utilized to evaluate the examinee's responses.

Thus in considering the examinee's handling of the WISC–III, the examiner should be cognizant of the fact that this test represents a sample of the child or adolescent's responding under highly structured task conditions.

A second feature of the WISC–III from within the gradient perspective is on the dimension of control. If one presumes that one pole of a gradient (or continuum) involves control by the examiner and the other pole represents control by the examinee, the WISC–III is a task that entails control primarily by the examiner. The rate of item presentation, the changing from one task to another, and the timing of the examinee's responses are all aspects of the examiner's control of the test situation. Viewed from this perspective, the examiner may remember that the interpersonal aspects of the test situation represent the examinee's efforts to deal with interpersonal control. Some children comply with this essential feature of testing, while other children may display a variety of behaviors calculated to avoid or transform this aspect of the situation, for example, by trying to take the examiner's watch, turning the pages on the Picture Completion or Block Design subtests, or in other ways seeking to alter the examiner's control of the testing.

A third way in which the gradient model may be applied to conceptualizing the WISC–III is in terms of item difficulty. Each of the subtests may be conceived of as a continuum of items distributed along a dimension of (presumably gradually) increasing difficulty. Considered this way, the examiner has the opportunity to observe the way in which the examinee deals with increasing challenge or stress. As noted earlier in the discussion of the gradient and non-gradient responses (see section on "Models in Psychology"), the child or adolescent may respond to the increasing item difficulty with an equally graduated response, or with an undercontrolled, non-gradual and even explosive reaction to the task situation. During test administration, the examiner can keep in mind that he or she is witnessing the child's handling of gradually increasing stress on his or her problem-solving and adaptive abilities.

A final way in which the gradient model may be applied to the WISC–III is in terms of response latitude. Thus one may consider examinee behaviors or responses during an assessment as varying along a continuum of latitude or breadth. In some aspects of an assessment (e.g., Rorschach, Thematic Apperception Test, interviewing), the examiner may desire the child to have access to a wider range of thoughts, cognitions, or affects. However, the WISC–III involves a relatively narrow range of acceptable response alternatives for the child or adolescent. Viewed from within a Structure of Intellect perspective (Guilford, 1967), this means that the WISC–III involves primarily convergent rather than divergent cognitive processes. In administering the WISC–III, the examiner can keep in mind the fact that the test tasks assess the degree to which the examinee is able to organize her or his abilities to produce these convergent rather than divergent problem-solving skills.

TEST ADMINISTRATION AND SCORING

In terms of actually administering the WISC–III, the author recommends that the examiner memorize the various administration procedures for the entire test and all of the subtests. It is assumed that the examiner who has only recently begun using the WISC–III will need to use the manual initially. However, it is felt that the examiner should set as a personal goal the ability to administer the test without needing to use the manual, since being able to administer the test this way will permit the examiner to focus her or his attention on establishing and maintaining rapport with the examinee, recording verbatim what the examinee says, and recording important observations about the examinee's test behavior.

Once the examiner reaches the point where she or he can administer the WISC–III without reference to the manual, he or she should still periodically consult the manual, at times during test administration and certainly when scoring the test. The reason for this is that over time, the examiner may inadvertently alter the standard administration procedures, and re-checking the manual at least periodically will allow the examiner to correct her or his test administration and scoring procedures.

In terms of the test materials themselves, the author recommends keeping the WISC–III test kit on one or the other side of the desk or table away from the examinee or on another chair next to the examiner. The author does not use the crackback manual standing on the examination table, as this may provide an obstacle to seeing or relating to the examinee. The author also does not use the inside of the front page for recording information about the child since the examiner's observations occur during the testing, and it would be inconvenient to return to this location to record information. Instead, the author uses a regular pad (in conjunction with the "Child Test Behavior Observation Form"; Table 8) on which test observations are recorded during testing.

Standard Procedures: Wechsler (1991) notes that the purpose of the WISC–III is to assess a child's performance under a fixed set of conditions, and changes in the presentation of test items, or other deviations from standard subtest directions, could reduce the validity of test results. The purpose of such standard administration procedures is to reduce the error of measurement that could arise from differences between examiners, and to reduce such error variance should the examinee be tested on more than one occasion.

The concept of standardized test administration is certainly relevant from a psychometric viewpoint. However, research results (e.g., Slate & Hunnicutt, 1988) suggest that errors in Wechsler test administration and scoring are extremely common, and Hanna, Bradley, and Holen (1981) estimated that the actual WISC–R Full Scale IQ standard error of measurement is +/− 6.6 points, which is double the figure reported in the WISC–R manual. While the examiner should certainly strive for standard test administration, it is important to realize that in a clinical situation, the examiner must be somewhat flexible and consider the WISC–III as a tool to be utilized in assessing an examinee's intellectual and/or overall adaptive ability.

From within this framework, the examiner may be seeking a variety of kinds of information about the child or adolescent being evaluated, and the gathering of this information might be obscured by a too rigid administration of the test. Thus standard test administration must be viewed as necessary when the goals of evaluation are focused, and pertain specifically to an assessment of the examinee's intellectual performance under quite specific and easily repeatable conditions. When the examinee is a member of a nontypical population—for example, a nonverbal delinquent; an extremely anxious or phobic child; or an examinee who has experienced a serious head trauma—the examiner may need to recognize that establishment and maintenance of rapport, and the optimal test administration, may not be identical for each examinee and hence may not be completely standardized.

Behavioral Observations of the Examinee: In terms of the gradient model which is utilized throughout this volume, the author will provide three strategies for describing examinee behavior during testing with the underlying dimension being that of examiner latitude in describing the child's functioning.

The first strategy involves an open description of the child, based on the examiner's usual manner of organizing his or her observations of a child during testing. If the examiner chooses this approach, Table 7, "Aspects of the Child and Child Behavior to be Observed During Testing," provides a number of aspects of the child and her or his behavior that the examiner may consider in describing the examiner-child interaction during testing.

A second level of approach to describing the examinee's behavior during testing is the "Child Test Behavior Observation Form" (see Table 8), which provides a more structured format for the organization of the examiner's observations of child behavior during testing. This form offers a set of characteristics of the child that can be noted during the administration of each subtest and also provides space for the examiner to record other observations which may be made of the examinee during testing. The examiner may use this form instead of, or in conjunction with, a regular pad during test administration.

The form is designed according to the gradient model and in consideration of the way in which the examiner is likely to process and thus notice or not notice examinee behavior. Thus, the items are arranged sequentially from attention, the first behavior of the examinee likely to be noticed by the examiner, through effort and cooperation, qualities of child likely to be noted by the examiner as the child moves to more challenging subtest items on a particular subtest.

The seven behavioral categories with definitions are as follows: *Attention,* reflecting the examinee's focusing on subtest instructions and the task itself, and may also include concentration; *Reflective,* pertaining to the examinee's thoughtful and reflective or impulsive response style and tempo; *Effort,* which refers to the energy the examinee invests in the task, for example, in persistence despite frustration; *Flexibility,* reflecting the child's ability to change set or to attempt different solution strategies to the various subtest items; *Systematic,* which refers to the degree of organization of the examinee's efforts in approaching a given subtest, whether logical or haphazard; *Information Processing,* which refers to any aspects of the child's processing of the information on the subtest, for example, visual or auditory perception, or motor coordination; and *Cooperative,* referring to whether the examinee displays basic cooperation or negativism in regard to the examiner and the particular subtest.

The coding system that can be used with this form involves essentially four scores: the item is left blank if the examiner does not notice any behavior of the child in a particular category (e.g., if the examiner does not notice that the child displays flexibility); the examiner records a "−" if the child displays noticeably negative or inadequate functioning on a given dimension on a particular subtest (e.g., if the examinee is very inattentive on the Arithmetic subtest); the examiner would record a "+" if the child

Table 7
ASPECTS OF THE CHILD AND CHILD BEHAVIOR
TO BE OBSERVED DURING TESTING

1. Separation and Engagement. This would include the child's separation from the situation he or she is in prior to testing, whether this is with a parent in the waiting room, or other children in a classroom, and how the child initially approaches the examiner in the testing situation, and whether the child expresses the desire to interrupt testing and leave prematurely.

2. Physical Characteristics. This would include a physical description of the child, including age, sex, stature, racial/ethnic characteristics (the child may be asked what label he or she uses for this characteristic), developmental status, whether the child uses any prostheses, such as glasses, hearing aids or other such devices. Also included here would be the child's posture, gait and gross and fine motor coordination, and whether or not the child displays any tremor or tic behavior. Also included may be observations regarding the child's physical attractiveness or unattractiveness, cleanliness, and any distinctive features the child may have, such as misaligned teeth or scars. Also included would be the child's handedness and manner of holding a pencil.

3. Speech and Language Performance. This would include the child's speech, articulation, syntax, language usage, whether the child's native language is English, and whether the child is bilingual or not.

4. Nonverbal Communication. This would include observation of whether or not and to what degree the child utilizes nonverbal communicative strategies, for example, indicating not knowing an answer by shrugging, or using facial expression rather than words to communicate with the examiner.

5. Engagement with the Examiner. This includes the nature of the child's relationship to the examiner, ranging on a gradient from cooperative, trusting and responsive through neutral or indifferent, to negative, resistant or oppositional and defiant. Included here would be the nature of the child's connectedness with the examiner, as expressed, for example, in eye contact with the examiner. This would also include observation of the child's need for limits, having to be brought back to the task, or needing encouragement and praise, and whether the child allows the examiner to control the situation or whether the child seeks control of the test situation.

6. Engagement with Tasks. This involves the child's approach to the test tasks themselves, whether the child is focused and motivated, retreats and gives up easily or refuses one or more tasks. Also included would be the child's treatment of test materials, whether respectfully or aggressively, for example, in dropping or flipping test materials.

7. Activity Level. This would include the child's physical activity level including large and small motor movements, moving his or her chair, getting up frequently and moving around the room, and looking at the examiner and test materials or elsewhere.

8. Attention, Concentration and Persistence. This would include the child's ability to focus her or his attention on the task at hand and to persist. The child's attention and concentration would be evident on such subtests as Arithmetic, and Digit Span, but would also be involved on Picture Completion and Picture Arrangement. Concentration would be evident on Coding and Symbol Search as well, and persistence or impersistence would be evident in the child's approach to most Performance subtests. The child's frustration tolerance, or ability to persist despite lack of success, could also be noted here.

9. Problem-Solving Style. This would include the child's approach to the test items, whether impulsive or reflective, and whether flexible or rigid. Also included would be whether the child approaches tasks in a systematic and efficient way, seeking or using a strategy, or in a haphazard, trial-and-error and planless fashion.

10. Reaction to Success and Failure. This would include the child's reaction to success, whether without much response or by becoming insecure or over-confident; and the child's reaction to failure, by persisting or giving up, or by becoming discouraged, or angry at the tasks, the examiner, or the child him- or herself. The child's frustration tolerance could also be noted here.

11. Self-Awareness and Attitudes Toward Self. This would include the child's ability to regulate her or his own behavior and approach, whether the child makes any self-guiding, self-reinforcing or self-deprecatory comments, and whether the child seeks feedback on his or her performance from the examiner. This aspect of the child's behavior may be further evaluated by asking the child after testing how the child thought she or he did compared to others her or his age.

12. Reaction to discussion of test results. If the examiner offers to discuss the results of testing with the child, the child's reaction would be noted here and would include whether the child was interested, asked any questions, how the child reacted to any feedback, and whether the child appeared to understand the meaning of the testing for her- or himself.

13. Ending the Testing Session. This includes how the child ends the contact with the examiner, whether the child is eager to leave, says good-bye to the examiner, or appears to feel better, worse or the same as at the beginning of the testing session.

displays noticeably positive behavior on a given dimension (e.g., if the child demonstrates effort or flexibility on the Object Assembly subtest); and the examiner would record a "/" if the child displays noticeably variable behavior on a particular subtest.

Using this format would also permit the examiner to review the various categories after testing to determine whether the examinee tended to display any consistent pattern in her or his test behavior (i.e., usually being attentive, or persistent). Since the examiner is likely to analyze the child's functioning according to verbal and performance scales of the WISC–III, the form is designed to group the subtests by scale.

Table 8

CHILD TEST BEHAVIOR OBSERVATION FORM

Name _____ DOE _____

At = Attention; Refl = Reflective; Ef = Effort; Flx = Flexibility; Sys = Systematic; IP = Information Processing; Coop = Cooperative. [− = Negative; = Neutral; + = Positive; / = Variable]

PC At___ Refl___ Ef ___ Flx___ Sys___ IP ___ Coop___   IN At___ Refl___ Ef ___ Flx___ Sys___ IP ___ Coop___

CD At___ Refl___ Ef ___ Flx___ Sys___ IP ___ Coop___   SM At___ Refl___ Ef ___ Flx___ Sys___ IP ___ Coop___

PA At___ Refl___ Ef ___ Flx___ Sys___ IP ___ Coop___   AR At___ Refl___ Ef ___ Flx___ Sys___ IP ___ Coop___

BD At___ Refl___ Ef ___ Flx___ Sys___ IP ___ Coop___   VO At___ Refl___ Ef ___ Flx___ Sys___ IP ___ Coop___

OA At___ Refl___ Ef ___ Flx___ Sys___ IP ___ Coop___   CO At___ Refl___ Ef ___ Flx___ Sys___ IP ___ Coop___

SS At___ Refl___ Ef ___ Flx___ Sys___ IP ___ Coop___   DS At___ Refl___ Ef ___ Flx___ Sys___ IP ___ Coop___

MZ At___ Refl___ Ef ___ Flx___ Sys___ IP ___ Coop___

A third, and most highly structured, level of observation of the child's test behavior involves use of the *Guide to the Assessment of Test Session Behavior for the WISC-III and the WIAT* (GATSB; Glutting & Oakland, 1993). The GATSB is a 29-item behavior rating instrument which allows the examiner to evaluate the examinee's behavior during the administration of either the WISC–III (Wechsler, 1991) or the WIAT (The Psychological Corporation, 1992).

The GATSB was designed for use with children between 6 years, 0 months and 16 years, 11 months, and is statistically linked with the WISC–III and the WIAT, to allow the examiner to determine whether a child's behavior during the administration of either of these tests differs substantially from the test session behavior of other children of the same age. Depending on the child's score (or scores) on the GATSB, the examiner can determine whether the test which has been administered, the WISC–III in this case, does or does not provide a reliable estimate of the child's functioning.

The GATSB includes three scales: Avoidance, Inattentiveness, and Uncooperative Mood. Glutting and Oakland (1993) state that these dimensions are theoretically congruent, fit with past findings regarding children's test behavior, and are similar to established dimensions used to evaluate children's adjustment and well-being. The GATSB provides empirically derived standard scores for each of the three scales and for a Total Score, which is a combination of the scores on the three scales.

Glutting and Oakland (1993) note several salient reasons for routinely using the GATSB in the evaluation of children: the GATSB permits the examiner to focus on and evaluate important test behaviors that may affect a child's scores on the WISC–III; the GATSB is brief and can be completed after the test so it does not interfere with testing; the GATSB scores have high reliability, thus minimizing examiner bias; the GATSB scales and Total Score were derived empirically according to the results of factor-analytic procedures; and the GATSB provides norms that are a requirement for any instrument designed to be used for interindividual comparisons or decision making.

The GATSB involves the examiner rating a child's test session behavior on each of 29 items on a three-point scale: Usually applies, Sometimes applies, or Doesn't apply, with the GATSB being completed immediately after the WISC–III has been administered. Raw scores are translated into T-score units with M = 50 and SD = 10 for three age groups: Age Group 1 (6–0 to 8–11); Age Group 2 (9–0 to 12–11); and Age Group 3 (13–0 to 16–11).

Glutting and Oakland (1993) provide an extensive discussion of the background, development and statistical treatment of the normative data regarding the GATSB. The authors note that the norms they present were derived from a standardization sample of 640 children representative of the United States population of children. The variables they describe include:

age, gender, race/ethnicity, parent education level, and child ability level. However, they do not mention geographic region, which was a variable utilized in developing the WISC–III (Wechsler, 1991) standardization sample.

Glutting and Oakland (1993) note that the GATSB scores were designed to be interpreted in a general-to-specific direction, so that the examiner first considers the Total Score T value, since this is the most reliable of the scores obtained. A highly elevated GATSB Total Score T value (i.e., =/> 70) can be interpreted as reflecting the presence of unusual test session behaviors since only 5.3% of the children in the GATSB standardization sample had Total Score T values of this size.

If the child has a Total T Score value of =/> 70, the authors recommend obtaining information about the child's functioning in situations other than the test session itself. The information obtained from parents or teachers can either be consistent or inconsistent with the child's test session behavior—i.e., the child may display test-situation specific behavior (Glutting, Oakland, & McDermott, 1989) or what the authors describe as transituationally general behavior.

If the child's test session behavior does not occur in other settings, the examiner may interpret the test findings conservatively, or even consider retesting the child, although the present author believes this is an unlikely strategy. If the child's test session behaviors are also reported by parents or teachers, the examiner can be more confident that the behaviors observed during testing are enduring qualities of the child. In this case, the way the results are interpreted will depend on whether the examiner believes test performance should reflect *typical* or *optimal* performance.

The examiner who believes that testing should reflect the way a child *typically* functions will accept the WISC–III test results as valid since they view the child's inappropriate behaviors as having a negative impact on both the child's test behavior and his or her academic functioning within the classroom. On the other hand, examiners who believe that testing should represent the child's *optimal* performance will question the test results when the child's test session behaviors are significantly inappropriate even if the child's behavior in most settings reflects this same inappropriateness.

Perhaps the area where this issue may be most relevant would be if the results of testing are questioned by parents or legal agencies. The GATSB provides the examiner with a norm-referenced instrument that allows him or her to state that the child's test session behavior was or was not similar to that of other children taking the test.

Discontinuation Criteria: When to begin and when to discontinue each of the WISC–III subtests is discussed in the WISC–III manual, and discontinuation criteria are printed on the WISC–III form at the beginning of each subtest where this is appropriate. Although the color coding of the

WISC–III test form may make it attractive, it is not always functional. The specific discontinue criterion at the top of each subtest (e.g., 4 or 5 failures) should be color-coded, since the examiner is likely to want to simply glance up during test administration to check on this vital bit of information. The examiner might underline this piece of information on certain subtests or until it is memorized. Also, the present author folds the WISC–III test form back so that only one side is showing during test administration. The Vocabulary and Comprehension subtests each span two pages, but in each case, the discontinue criterion is not printed on the second page. The examiner may simply write the criterion in on these subtests as a prompt each time he or she uses the test.

On several subtests, especially Vocabulary, Similarities, Information, and Comprehension, scoring has been reported as problematic (Slate & Hunnicutt, 1988). When administering these subtests, the examiner may be uncertain of the correctness of an examinee's response while the test is being administered. The author suggests that the examiner continue testing unless she or he is certain that a given subtest should be discontinued. Although this approach may lengthen the testing somewhat, it is preferable to sample a few extra items rather than too few on these subtests.

Repetition and/or Explanation of Test Items: With the exception of the Digit Span subtest items, all of the verbal test items may be repeated if the examinee requests this. It is probably a good idea to make note of such repetitions when they occur, since they may reflect the examinee's anxiety, attentional deficits, or delaying tactics, and this observation may be relevant when writing up the test findings.

On the performance items, since each item is continuously in front of the examinee, the concept of item repetition is not relevant. If on a performance item (e.g., a Picture Arrangement item), the examinee asks to redo the item after the examiner has recorded the examinee's response, the examiner should permit this and score both responses since this also provides information about the examinee's style of intellectual functioning. In terms of explaining items, for example, when a young child reaches the higher level Information or Comprehension items, the author does not recommend explanation of what a particular word or object means.

Inquiry Regarding the Examinee's Responses: It is the author's view that the examiner should attempt to have a reasonable idea of how each response is to be scored without checking in the manual. Although the design of the WISC–III includes the responses with the items in the test manual, it is difficult for the examiner to scan the responses in the manual while administering the test. If the examiner has an idea of the correct response, and if the examinee offers a vague, unscorable or questionable response, the examiner can inquire further to clarify what the examinee meant. However, the author feels that inquiry of the examinee should be used minimally. For example, if the examiner feels that constant questioning of the shy or nonverbal examinee will only increase the examinee's anxiety and result in further withdrawal from the test, the examiner may be better off maintaining an overall rapport and sacrificing a marginal increase in information on a few items.

Recording the Examinee's Responses: The author recommends that all of the examinee's responses be recorded in as verbatim a fashion as possible, for several reasons. First of all, once the examinee has said or done something, if it is not recorded, it is gone forever. Hence, if the examiner wishes to check his or her own scoring later, this becomes impossible. Also important is that the interpretation of the examinee's protocol depends to some extent on what the examinee did during the testing, what he or she said, how she or he went about responding, and how the examinee dealt with success or failure. Only if these aspects of the test situation have been recorded will they be of use when the results are being developed into a report.

In addition, if the examiner only checks off the examinee's correct responses but writes down his or her incorrect ones, the examiner is introducing a feedback system whereby the examinee may be informed unwittingly of the correctness of her or his responses.

Reinforcement Variables in Test Administration: A number of investigations over the years have focused on the impact of a variety of reinforcement variables on children's Wechsler test performances (e.g., Fabes, McCullers, & Hom, 1986; Galbraith, Ott, & Johnson, 1986; Sweet & Ringness, 1971; Terrel, Taylor, & Terrel, 1978; Witmer, Bornstein, & Dunham, 1971). These investigations have included focusing on the influence of verbal (e.g., Witmer, Bornstein, & Dunham, 1971; Terrel, Taylor, & Terrel, 1978; Saigh & Payne, 1976) and tangible (e.g., Fabes, McCullers, & Hom, 1986; Keiffer & Goh, 1981; Sweet & Ringness, 1971) rewards on the test performances of children.

The findings of these investigations appear somewhat inconsistent. Although it seems that in general, reinforcement variables can operate to enhance children's test functioning, the effects may vary in complex ways depending on the socioeconomic status or the general intellectual level of the children studied, the nature of the reinforcements used, whether verbal, nonverbal, or tangible, and as a function of which specific subtests, either verbal or performance, are being considered. Fish (1988) noted that while reinforcers do enhance the performance of some examinees, one cannot draw the general conclusion that systematic reinforcement always increases the test performance of all examinees under all conditions.

The most reasonable conclusion for the user of the WISC–III to make is that rewards can ordinarily have a positive effect on children's Wechsler performances. However, since these reward factors may interact (at times in unknown ways) with other child, examiner, or test variables, it is probably wisest to keep the use of specific reinforcers to a minimum under ordinary test administration conditions. Only where the examiner a priori knows that he or she will be testing a very atypical examinee—for example, a hyper-resistant child, or one who has been untestable in the past—might the planned utilization of a specific reward strategy seem worthwhile.

Possible Introductions to the WISC–III: Several studies with the WISC (e.g., Bridgeman, Strang, and Buttram, 1974; Strang, Bridgeman, and Carrico, 1974) have described investigations of the impact on children's test perform-ance of telling them that they were going to be taking several tests versus telling them that they were going to be playing several games. The findings of these investigations vary, with outcomes depending on the grade level of the children and on whether the subtests administered involved verbal or performance tasks.

Unless the examiner is going to utilize the model discussed in the present volume, perhaps the most neutral introduction involves informing the examinee that he or she and the examiner will be doing some things together which will involve the examinee answering some questions and putting things like puzzles together.

Pre- and Post-WISC–III Questions: If the examiner uses the model described in this book (see section on "Models in Psychological Assessment"), the introduction to the WISC–III and post-WISC–III discussion will be included in that model. The following questions are recommended whether the examiner uses the more elaborate model or chooses a less extensive approach to assessment. It should also be noted that many psychologists include the WISC–III as a component of a more extended assessment that includes interviewing, and these questions play a role in the entire evaluation. However, they are no less important if one is only evaluating an examinee's intellectual or cognitive performance since they set the testing session by providing the examiner and examinee with a shared knowledge base.

The following is a list of the questions which may be asked of the examinee prior to beginning the WISC–III itself. The questions may be phrased at a higher vocabulary level if the examinee is an older child or adolescent.

1. How old are you?
2. When is your birthday? The examiner should also ask the examinee the year of her or his birth if the child does not give the year spontaneously.
3. What is your address, where you live?
4. What town/city is that in?
5. What is your phone number? What is your phone number backwards?

6. What school do you go to?
7. What grade are you in?
8. Are you in regular or special class?
9. Have you ever repeated a grade or stayed back? If the examinee says she or he has, the examiner should ask which grade(s) was (were) repeated and the reason.
10. Who lives at home with you? The examiner should also ask the ages of the examinee's siblings.
11. Do you speak English at home, or do you speak some other language?
12. How tall are you?
13. How much do you weigh?
14. Are you right-handed or left-handed?
15. Do you have any really bad (serious) sickness (illness)?
16. Do you take any medicine or pills everyday? If the examinee says that he or she does, the examiner should ask what medication, what it is for, and when it was last taken.
17. Do you have anything like a headache or stomachache today?
18. Do you think of yourself as a black person, or an Hispanic, or a Latino, or Asian, or white, or Native American, or in some other group of people?
19. Do you know how come we're getting together today?

If the examiner is utilizing the model presented in this book, once the WISC–III has been completed, the examiner would proceed as suggested by the model. If the examiner is not proceeding according to the model, the examiner may ask the examinee if she or he has any questions to ask about the test or what will happen with the results of testing, and attempt to provide appropriate answers to the examinee's questions.

Scoring: A number of investigations over many years have examined the accuracy of scoring and other clerical tasks with the Wechsler scales. Many studies (e.g., Bradley, Hanna, & Lucas, 1980; Brannigan, 1975; Conner & Woodall, 1983; Franklin, Stillman, Burpeau, & Sabers, 1982; Miller & Chansky, 1972; Miller, Chansky, & Gredler, 1970; Slate & Chick, 1989; Slate & Jones, 1990; Slate, Jones, & Covert, 1992; Warren & Brown, 1972) have shown that there are very frequent scoring, administrative, and clerical errors in psychology graduate students' and professional psychologists' WISC, WISC–R, WAIS, and WAIS–R protocols.

Slate and Hunnicutt (1988) examined a number of potential hypotheses that might explain the reasons why examiners make errors on Wechsler intelligence test protocols. These included: (a) lack of proper training and instructional preparation; (b) lack of appropriate testing supervision; (c) ambiguity, lack of clarity, and lack of sufficient scoring examples in test manuals; (d) carelessness on the part of the examiner that results in clerical and mathematical errors; (e) examiner-examinee relationship issues that result in unintentional feedback during testing or influence test scoring; and (f) job stress, fatigue, and boredom with testing that results in job dissatisfaction on the part of the examiner and influences test administration and scoring.

In later studies, Slate, Jones, and Murray (1991) and Slate, Jones, Coulter and Covert (1992) pointed out several additional specific errors made in test administration and scoring, such as failure to record examinee's responses, assigning too many or too few points to answers, inappropriate questioning, and they also noted that when examiners practiced administering these tests, instead of becoming more proficient in test administration, they tended to practice their errors.

Although scoring errors tend to occur more on verbal than performance subtests, and occur primarily on the Vocabulary, Similarities, and Comprehension subtests, errors also frequently occur on other subtests, such as Information, Picture Completion, and Coding. Slate et al. (1992) point out that errors are extensive enough that when they are corrected, the resulting changes in Full Scale IQ have the potential to influence labelling and placement decisions.

Kaufman (1990) has reviewed the findings of investigations of administration and scoring performance with respect to the WAIS–R, and notes that scoring errors are just as common for this test as they have been for other Wechsler scales. Kaufman (1990) notes that subjects made errors on almost half of the ambiguous responses they had to score; more errors were made on Vocabulary than on Comprehension or Similarities; errors tended to be biased toward leniency in scoring; neither specific cautions about care in scoring nor the examiner's experience was related to scoring accuracy; and that an examiner's personality appears related to his or her scoring accuracy.

Hence there is extensive evidence to indicate that administrative, scoring, and clerical errors abound with respect to all of the Wechsler scales that have been developed and utilized since the inception of these test batteries, and that the variety of errors that are made have a significant effect on overall IQ scores, and consequently on the decisions made based on those scores.

Slate and Jones (1989), in an effort to explore methods for improving Wechsler test administration and scoring, used a quasi-experimental design to investigate their hypotheses. The experimental treatment involved providing the experimental group with detailed information about frequent errors made by the control group, and giving the experimental group explicit rules for avoiding these commonly made errors. The experimental group made fewer errors and assigned more accurate IQ scores than did the control group.

McQueen, Meschino, Pike, and Poelstra (1994) explored the impact of improved lecture and laboratory strategies on the test administration performance and the grades of clinical psychology graduate student subjects. These authors found that such interventions as weekly quizzes, alerting the students to the most commonly made errors in testing, having students use a ruler to read tables in the manual, and having students use a WISC–R scoring criteria supplement improved the test administration and academic performance of their subjects.

The foregoing discussion of studies dealing with the WISC, WAIS, WISC–R, and WAIS–R indicate that there is ordinarily some degree of disagreement or variability among scorers and hence among scores given to individual responses, subtests, and IQ scores on the Wechsler scales. Although scoring errors are most frequent on the subtests involving more extended verbal responses (e.g., Vocabulary), errors actually occur in all aspects of the test.

It is thus important for the examiner to be aware of various potential sources of error that may enter into her or his administration and scoring of an examinee's WISC–III and to keep in mind several strategies to improve the level of accuracy in overall test administration.

First, as noted earlier, while memorization of the test instructions is important, the examiner should realize that it is quite easy to incorrectly memorize the instructions, particularly if one uses a variety of tests, or even several different Wechsler scales. Hence, it is worthwhile to periodically review the manual to see if the examiner is correctly administering the test.

Second, although many psychologists are able to memorize the test instructions and hence to administer the test largely without reference to the manual, few if any psychologists can remember all of the various scoring criteria for each item. Hence, the safest rule for the psychologist to use in guiding his or her test administration behavior is that on verbal subtests, such as Vocabulary, Similarities, Comprehension, and even Information, it is better to obtain more information rather than less on any given item. This will usually, although not always, permit the easiest and most accurate scoring of a particular response.

The fundamental strategy of seeking more information per item must be weighed against the realization that a resistant examinee may become even more angry, negativistic or uncommunicative with repeated questioning. Rather than running the risk of completely alienating an already defensive examinee, the sensitive examiner may forego clarifying questions on many items in order to allow the examinee to at least respond to more items on a given subtest.

A third consideration, based on the findings dealing with the effect of reinforcement variables on test performance, is that examiner behavior can certainly have some degree of impact on the examinee's performance. It is probable that as the examiner moves along a gradient from minimal to maximal use of reinforcement (e.g., increased use of praise), the variability attributable to examiner behavior or examiner by child interaction will be increased. Hence, feedback, such as praise, comments about how well the examinee is doing, or indications that particular responses are correct or incorrect, should be carefully considered by the examiner before utilizing such an approach.

In terms of scoring items themselves, it is always wise to consult the manual, even though the examiner may believe he or she is certain how a given response is to be scored. If it still does not seem possible to determine into which category a given response falls, several strategies may be considered. If there is one or very few such ambiguous responses on a protocol, the examiner might simply flip a coin to determine whether a response should be place in the higher or lower of two categories (i.e., two points versus one, or zero versus one point).

A second approach to determining whether to give an examinee's response more or less points might consider the examinee's performance on items beyond the one being scored. Thus, if the examinee is able to earn credits on items above the one which the examiner cannot score, it seems reasonable to infer that the examinee's performance on the difficult-to-score item was better rather than worse, and hence the examinee should receive the higher credit for the item. If the examinee cannot correctly answer items more difficult than the one being scored, it is reasonable to conclude that the examinee did worse rather than better on the item that was difficult to score. If there are several such difficult-to-score items on a given protocol, the examiner may use the above strategies, but might also attempt to balance the scoring, by giving one unclear response the higher score and the next unclear response the lower score.

A final possibility in terms of handling one or several particular responses that cannot be scored readily would involve double scoring of any of the responses being considered. Utilizing this approach, the examiner would assign the score that seems most appropriate or most conservative to a given response, and next to that, in parentheses, the higher level score would be recorded. The examiner would then calculate the subtest score, the Verbal IQ score, the Performance IQ score, and the Full Scale IQ score twice, once using the conservative scoring of the unclear items and a second time using the liberal scoring of the unclear items. In writing the psychological report, the examiner can then at least consider the two sets of scores as indicative of the range of functioning the examinee is able to display.

If an examinee's protocol is characterized by many difficult-to-score or ambiguous responses, whatever strategy the examiner uses to score the protocol, the nature of the examinee's test functioning should be emphasized in the psychological test report, since this quality of the examinee's behavior is likely to be quite typical of his or her overall adaptation and would thus have implications for anyone dealing with the individual.

Lastly, in terms of seeking an accurate test administration, it is important for the examiner to recheck the various clerical tasks involved in scoring. Thus the examiner should routinely recheck her or his calculation of the examinee's age (the Pre-WISC–III question of the child's age helps with this), the sum for one or several subtests, and the various sums of scaled scores.

The clerical tasks have increased on the WISC–III over the WISC–R because of the potential to calculate the four factor scores, and the tables in the WISC–III manual, particularly the supplementary tables, are not well designed to reduce errors on the part of the examiner. Hence, there are more opportunities for clerical errors on the WISC–III than on the WISC–R. This means that the examiner should be more contemplative or cautious than impulsive in the scoring and clerical tasks on the test, and maintain a thoughtful realization that in determining an examinee's IQ, or in calculating various statistical qualities of the examinee's test performance, it is quite possible to be in error.

Chapter Twelve

THE INDIVIDUAL SUBTESTS

The WISC–III is comprised of a total of 13 individual subtests, 10 regular and three supplementary subtests. The WISC and WISC–R have been thoroughly researched in the past forty years (e.g., Kaufman, 1979a; Sattler, 1990), and the WISC–III is at the beginning of its own cycle of research (Bracken, 1993). And although there has been a long tradition of interpreting the clinical significance and meaning of Wechsler subtest patterns and individual subtest scores (e.g., Holt, 1968), there has been relatively little research reported on the specific subtests themselves for use in clinical interpretation.

The following sections are intended to provide the examiner with a variety of perspectives on the meaning and significance of each subtest on the WISC–III. This material is intended to furnish the examiner with a number of ways to think about each subtest as it is administered; and to offer ideas about potential interpretive hypotheses regarding the child or adolescent's performance on any given subtest, whether the examinee's performance is viewed: (1) in relation to the average performance of the normative sample (i.e., in relation to a scaled score of 10); (2) in relation to the examinee's own average performance (i.e., Kaufman's [1979a, 1990] profile analytic approach); or (3) in terms of potential provision of clinical information about the examinee.

The material contained in this chapter is drawn from Wechsler (1958, 1991), Kaufman (1979a, 1990), Matarrazzo (1972), Sattler (1990, 1992), Horn (1985), Bannatyne (1968, 1971, 1974), Glasser and Zimmerman (1967), and the author's own clinical experience and perspectives, as well as other research relevant to the various Wechsler subtests (dealing with the WISC, WISC–R, and occasionally the WAIS or WAIS–R).

PICTURE COMPLETION

What the Picture Completion Subtest Measures

Wechsler (1958) notes that the Picture Completion subtest of the Wechsler-Bellevue and the Wechsler Adult Intelligence Scale "merely require the subject to discover and name the missing part of an incompletely drawn picture" (p. 77). Wechsler (1958) notes that "[O]stensibly, it [the subtest] measures the individual's basic perceptual and conceptual abilities insofar as these are involved in the visual recognition and identification of familiar objects and forms. . . . In a broad sense the test measures the ability of the individual to differentiate essential from non-essential details" (p. 78).

According to Wechsler (1991), the Picture Completion subtest is a component of the Perceptual Organization factor (with Picture Arrangement, Block Design and Object Assembly).

Sattler (1992) states that the Picture Completion subtest requires the child to identify the one most important detail missing in each of 30 drawings of common objects, animals, or people. Sattler (1992) also states that the child must recognize the object that is depicted, appreciate its incompleteness, and determine the part that is missing, and he points out that the task requires concentration, reasoning, visual organization and long-term visual memory. According to Sattler (1992), the Picture Completion task may also measure perceptual and conceptual abilities, while perception, judgment and delay of impulses may also influence the individual's subtest performance.

Kaufman (1979a, 1990) notes that the Picture Completion subtest reflects the individual's holistic or right-brain processing, ability to distinguish essential from non-essential details, and the individual's visual perception and processing of meaningful stimuli. The subtest's unique ability involves measurement of the individual's visual alertness and her or his abilities for visual recognition and identification, which involve long-term visual memory.

Kaufman (1979a, 1990) notes that factors which influence performance on the subtest include: the individual's ability to respond when uncertain; her or his alertness to the environment; whether the person has a field dependent or independent cognitive style; and the individual's ability to concentrate and work under time pressure.

According to the Fluid-Crystallized model of intelligence (Horn, 1985; Kaufman, 1990), the Picture Completion subtest is one of the subtests that reflects Fluid Intelligence (with Picture Arrangement, Block Design, Object Assembly, Similarities, and Digit Span).

According to Bannatyne's (1974) categorization, the Picture Completion subtest is included in the Spatial Ability Category (with Block Design and Object Assembly).

Glasser and Zimmerman (1967), in discussing the WISC, state that the Picture Completion subtest calls for visual identification of familiar objects, forms, and living things and the further capacity to identify and separate essential from nonessential characteristics. Additionally, they note that attention and concentration play an important role in performance on this subtest.

The present author views the Picture Completion subtest as assessing several aspects of the examinee's functioning. The first is that of visual attention and/or concentration on ordinarily familiar materials when the child's attention is specifically focused on a single stimulus (as opposed to, for example, the Picture Arrangement subtest, where the examinee must deal with several pictorial stimuli).

Additionally, the Picture Completion subtest also measures long-term visual memory for static information; that is, this subtest in some sense is a visual version of the Information subtest (the average intersubtest correlation for the Picture Completion subtest and the Information subtest for the WISC–III sample is .47, which is the third highest correlation between the Picture Completion subtest and any other subtest, and it is the second highest correlation between the Information subtest and any performance subtest).

Hence, the Picture Completion subtest may be conceptualized as a task that involves the following sequence of events: a visual stimulus is presented to the examinee, who must then recall from memory the image of that object she or he has stored in long-term memory; the examinee must then match or compare the test stimulus with the visual memory image, find the missing part in the test stimulus, and respond. Thus, the subtest may be viewed as assessing the following:

1) the examinee's visual search and/or scanning strategies and thus her or his ability to visually attend;
2) the adequacy of the child's visual memory images, i.e., his or her store of visually coded static knowledge;
3) to some extent, the examinee's ability to recall verbal labels for objects or parts of objects and hence her or his ability to link visual and verbal information;
4) moreover, the subtest measures the child or adolescent's ability for such processing of familiar visual information as opposed to processing of the kind of abstract information involved in the Block Design subtest.

Insofar as the subtest is influenced by the examinee's alertness, the subtest can also provide some estimate of the degree to which the examinee has a hyperalert or overly vigilant attitude toward her or his surroundings and feels impelled to carefully examine, notice and retain the details of his or her visual environment.

Another kind of information about the examinee that can be provided by the Picture Completion subtest is the examinee's ability to name objects. Essentially, on this subtest, the child is asked to indicate the part missing from each picture. While some examinees may point to the part missing, most attempt to name the part, and in so doing, the individual reveals the adequacy of her or his ability to provide verbal labels for his or her visual perceptions.

One other consideration in terms of what the Picture Completion subtest measures is that of the degree of organization evident in the examinee's visual processing as well as the child's behavioral tempo, whether reflective or impulsive. Thus, the examiner may note the nature of the examinee's visual scanning or visual search of the subtest stimuli to see whether the examinee appears haphazard or more systematic in his or her scrutiny of each picture.

Additionally, the examiner should note the time the child spends in inspecting each picture, since one would expect that if the examinee is impulsive or described as having a short attention span, then the Picture Completion subtest is one place where the examinee might display such behavioral characteristics.

In terms of what the Picture Completion subtest measures, during the subtest administration, the examiner may periodically remember that he or she is observing a sample of the examinee's Performance IQ, perceptual organization (Wechsler, 1991), fluid intelligence (Horn, 1985; Kaufman, 1990), or spatial ability (Bannatyne, 1974).

Research Pertaining to the Picture Completion Subtest

A number of research investigations using the WISC–R with various learning disabled (e.g., Anderson, Kaufman, & Kaufman, 1976; Mishra, 1984; Schiff, Kaufman, & Kaufman, 1981), emotionally or behaviorally disturbed (e.g., Hale & Landino, 1981; Ollendick, 1979), and mentally retarded (e.g., Clarizio & Bernard, 1981; Kaufman & Van Hagen, 1977) children have reported that the Picture Completion subtest is the easiest or among the easiest for these populations.

In their consensus rankings of subtest means for the 10 regular WISC–R subtests across a number of studies, Kaufman et al. (1990) report that the Picture Completion subtest ranks second for learning-disabled and emotionally disturbed children and ranks first for mentally retarded children.

Paralleling these findings was an investigation by Share, Silva and Adler (1987), who studied 925 children from ages 3 to 11. Of those children in this sample who displayed both reading and spelling retardation, the children revealed poor verbal subtest performance relative to non-retarded learners, but they displayed superior performance on the Picture Completion and Object Assembly subtests of the WISC–R.

In contrast to these findings, Whipple, Parker, and Noble (1988) reported a study of 15 sons (mean age 10.1 years) of alcoholic fathers who had at least one first- or second-degree alcoholic relative and compared these children to 15 sons of non-alcoholic fathers who had at least one first- or second-degree alcoholic relative. The first group, considered high risk, displayed an atypical neurocognitive profile in terms of their event-related potentials during a complex visual discrimination task and in their reduced visuo-perceptual performance as reflected in significantly lowered scores on the WISC–R Object Assembly, Block Design, and Picture Completion subtests.

In general, however, research findings suggest that Picture Completion is among the easiest subtests on the WISC–R for a variety of populations of children.

Information Processing Aspects of the Picture Completion Subtest

For the Picture Completion subtest, input to the examinee is in the form of pictorial information accompanied by verbal instructions to locate the part missing from each of a series of pictures. Cognitive operations involved on this subtest include visual scanning and visual search of the pictorial stimuli; search and recall of items in visual memory; comparison of the visual stimulus and visually recalled image; and determination of the part missing from each picture. Output involves verbal labelling or pointing to indicate the part missing from each picture.

Observation of the examinee during this subtest entails noting the nature of the examinee's visual search/scanning strategies, his or her reflective or impulsive response tempo, and the adequacy of the examinee's ability to provide verbal labels for pictorial materials.

Examination of the Picture Completion items indicate that the items require three kinds of responses on the part of the examinee: analysis of the configuration or outside of the object to notice the part missing; analysis of the internal details of the object to determine the part missing; or reasoning about the pictured object to determine what part is missing. Observation of the items on which the examinee offers incorrect responses may indicate which kind of information processing the examinee has difficulty with. Items 1, 3 and 5 involve an analysis of the item configuration. Items 2, 4, and items 6 through 30 involve primarily an analysis of internal details of the item, while items 13, 16 through 21, 23, 24, 28, and 29 also involve reasoning about the item.

Information processing deficits that might be reflected on the Picture Completion subtest would include difficulties in visual perception, visual search or scanning, visual memory, and a language deficit evident in the examinee's difficulty with naming the parts missing from the stimulus items. Hence the examiner should be alert to the examinee who points to a part missing from each of the pictures or else refers to them with a generic label rather than a specific name.

Statistical Characteristics of the Picture Completion Subtest

The Picture Completion subtest has an average split-half reliability coefficient across all ages of the WISC–III of .77 with reliability coefficients that range from .72 to .84 across the 11 age groups. The Picture Completion subtest has an average test-retest stability coefficient for all ages of .81.

According to Sattler's (1992) categorization, which groups subtests into good, fair, and poor measures of *g,* the Picture Completion subtest is a fair measure of *g.* In the original WISC–III sample, the Picture Completion subtest ranks eighth among all WISC–III subtests in its *g* loading while in the Roid et al. (1993) replication study, the Picture Completion subtest ranks seventh among all WISC–III subtests in its *g* loading.

Kamphaus and Platt (1992) report subtest specificities for the WISC–III and indicate that the Picture Completion subtest has adequate specificity for the combined age groups on the WISC–III. Bracken et al. (1993; see Table 16 in the present volume) and Sattler (1992) indicate that the Picture Completion subtest has inadequate specificity for age 12. For the remaining ages, the subtest has ample specificity.

Relationships Between the Picture Completion Subtest and Other Aspects of the WISC–III

The Picture Completion subtest correlates .58 with the WISC–III Full Scale IQ, .52 with the Verbal IQ and .54 with the Performance IQ.

The Picture Completion subtest displays a range of correlations with the other WISC–III subtests. It correlates best with Information (.47) on the Verbal Scale and with Block Design (.52) on the Performance Scale. The Picture Completion subtest correlates least well with the Coding (A & B) subtest (.18).

The relatively high correlation between the Picture Completion and Information subtests may reflect the fact that both of these subtests do reflect the individual's coding and retention of information, one in a verbal format, the other in a visual format. The correlation between the Picture Completion and Block Design subtests may reflect the fact that both of these subtests deal with visual analytic and perceptual processing skills, which supports the grouping of these subtests in the Perceptual Organization factor.

From a clinical standpoint, the Picture Completion subtest may be seen as involving static visual information and, in this sense, may be considered in relation to the individual's static verbal knowledge or information. Such a comparison can indicate the relative amount of verbal and visual stored information the examinee has regarding her or his environment.

The Picture Completion subtest may also be viewed as a measure of focused or static visual attention in comparison to the examinee's Picture Arrangement subtest performance. The latter utilizes visual details in order to facilitate the examinee's grasping the logical sequence of social events. In this sense, comparing the examinee's Picture Completion and Picture Arrangement subtest scores can indicate the degree to which the individual does better when his or her visual attention is focused, as in the Picture Completion subtest, or when the examinee is given the support of multiple images and may use this context in order to facilitate problem-solving performance. In this regard, one may consider the Picture Completion subtest as involving a single stop-action photo, whereas the Picture Arrangement subtest presents the individual with a series of frames from a continuous action which must be organized logically.

Insofar as Picture Completion and Block Design both involve visual analytical skills, one with recognizable stimuli and the other with abstract stimuli, the examinee's scores on these two subtests may be compared in order to determine whether the examinee performs more adequately where she or he is called upon to visually analyze novel stimuli in the present (Block Design) or familiar stimuli which also call upon the examinee's long-term visual memory (Picture Completion).

Interpretation of the Handling of the Picture Completion Subtest by the Examinee

Utilizing the gradient model discussed above, one can view the Picture Completion subtest as involving a series of increasingly difficult items which will range from within the examinee's capacity to at or beyond it. The initial items should be relatively obvious and easily dealt with, while the later items are more subtle, may require more careful visual examination, and may even involve reasoning rather than simply recalling the visual image of an object.

Viewing the child's responses from within this framework allows the examiner to observe the way in which the examinee reacts to gradually increasing cognitive demands in the domain of visually stored information.

There are two basic aspects of the examinee's handling of the Picture Completion subtest that may be noted by the examiner. The first involves the way in which the examinee deals with the subtest itself, and the second involves the pattern of the examinee's successes and failures on the subtest and how the examinee deals with this pattern. In regard to the first issue, one important consideration is that the subtest stimuli are contained in a spiralbound booklet.

The examiner should note whether the examinee allows the examiner to turn the pages in the booklet, or whether the examinee attempts to turn the pages him- or herself. This latter behavior on the part of the examinee may reflect either impulsivity or an attempt on the examinee's part to shift control of the testing situation from the examiner to the examinee.

A second aspect of the examinee's handling of the subtest itself deals with the impulsivity or reflectivity displayed by the child in examining each stimulus before offering a response. Assessment by the examiner of this aspect of the examinee's functioning may be facilitated by the examiner's timing of how long it takes for the examinee to generate a response to each Picture Completion item.

Another aspect of the examinee's handling of the Picture Completion subtest per se involves the nature of what the examinee says is missing from a particular item. The examiner should observe the examinee's response to each item, but perhaps particularly to items 4, 6, 7, 12 and 27, which have human content and which thus indicate the examinee's ability or inability to notice visual cues regarding people. Also of importance are the examinee's responses to items 4, 6, 7, 8, 11, 12, 18, 20, 22, and 28 since these items may stimulate the examinee's associations to, and anxiety regarding, aggression, punishment or past abuse experiences.

A second general aspect of the child's handling of the Picture Completion subtest involves the way in which the examinee deals with failure on any of the items, whether by simply saying she or he does not know what is missing in a given item; by saying nothing is missing; or by giving an erroneous response without any awareness that the response is incorrect. Observation of the child's individual item responses can provide information regarding the child's strategies for coping with increasing stress and/or failure experiences.

The examiner should also note the pattern of the child's successes and failures on the subtest, whether the examinee displays a generally consistent or highly erratic sequence of correct and incorrect responses, as this pattern provides some indication of the efficiency or inefficiency of the examinee's functioning when dealing with the kind of information contained on the Picture Completion subtest. The examiner may also note the cumulative effect on the child of several failures in a row, whether the examinee continues to exert effort on the task, or retreats readily after encountering one or two failures.

INFORMATION

What the Information Subtest Measures

Wechsler (1958) notes that "[T]he fact is, all objections considered, the range of a man's knowledge is generally a very good indication of his [sic] intellectual capacity" (1958, p. 65). Wechsler (1958) also states that items on an information subtest should call for the kind of knowledge that an average individual with average opportunity might be able to acquire for him- or herself.

According to Wechsler (1991), the Information subtest is a component of the Verbal Comprehension factor (with Similarities, Vocabulary and Comprehension).

Sattler (1992) states that the amount of information a child has may depend on the individual's natural endowment as well as the extent of education and the cultural opportunities to which the child has been exposed. He notes that the subtest samples knowledge that the average child with average opportunities should be able to acquire.

Kaufman (1979a, 1990) notes that the Information subtest reflects the individual's fund of information and long-term memory. The subtest's unique ability involves measurement of the individual's range of general factual knowledge.

Kaufman (1979a, 1990) notes that factors which influence performance on the subtest include: the individual's alertness to the environment and her or his cultural opportunities; whether or not the individual has a foreign language background; the individual's intellectual curiosity, striving or interest patterns; whether the individual suffers from any learning disability; the degree to which he or she does outside reading; the richness of the individual's environment; and the extent of academic learning by the individual.

According to the Fluid-Crystallized model of intelligence (Horn, 1985; Kaufman, 1990), the Information subtest is one of the subtests that reflects Crystallized Intelligence (with Vocabulary, Comprehension and Similarities) and is also one of the subtests which reflects Retrieval (with Arithmetic and Digit Span).

According to Bannatyne's (1974) categorization, the Information subtest is included in the Acquired Knowledge Category (with Arithmetic and Vocabulary).

Glasser and Zimmerman (1967), in their discussion of the WISC, note that the Information subtest is oriented to determining how much general information the child has abstracted from his or her surrounding environment.

The individual is not asked to find relationships between facts but rather the task assesses whether or not the child has obtained and stored facts as general knowledge. Thus, according to Glasser and Zimmerman (1967), the subtest reflects the child or adolescent's capacities for remote memory, ability to comprehend and to think associatively, as well as the interests and reading background of the child.

The present author would note that an individual's general information and knowledge are often viewed as central features of his or her intelligence (Wechsler, 1958). Intelligent individuals are able to gain a large store of verbally coded knowledge about the world which they can retrieve either spontaneously or on specific demand. Hence, performance on this subtest assesses the degree to which an individual has in the past or is currently exploring the environment, coding knowledge in verbal form, retaining the information in long-term memory and is able to retrieve the information volitionally.

Performance on this subtest may thus reflect genetically determined facility or a more deliberate and effortful pattern on the part of the child for encoding verbal knowledge. It may also reflect the breadth and richness of the individual's social and intellectual background and the exposure to models who provide the child or adolescent with specific verbal encoding of information and possibly with reinforcement to the child for acquiring such knowledge.

The material on the Information subtest is coded or codable in verbal form, and thus the means by which the individual gains the knowledge assessed by this subtest is often by direct experience or by listening to sources of verbal information in her or his surroundings. In the past, this would have included parents, siblings or other individuals including teachers. More recently, this would include radio, television and computers as major sources of auditory-verbal information.

Additionally, if a child is able to demonstrate knowledge of higher level subtest items, the author would infer that the individual has well-developed reading skills since the knowledge assessed at the upper level of the subtest is unlikely to be gathered by the child through direct experience or only by listening to auditory sources of information.

Examination of the items on the subtest indicates that the initial items, from 1 to 3, likely involve the child's direct experience. Items 4 through 15 or 16 involve information transmitted to the child from parents or other adults in school or by reading. Items from 17 to 30 are likely to involve the child obtaining the knowledge through reading or in a school context.

In terms of what the Information subtest measures, during the subtest administration, the examiner may periodically remember that this subtest is providing a sample of the examinee's Verbal IQ, verbal comprehension

(Wechsler, 1991), crystallized intelligence and retrieval ability (Horn, 1985; Kaufman, 1990), verbal conceptualization ability and acquired knowledge (Bannatyne, 1974), and that the subtest is one component of the ACID profile (Ackerman, Dykman, & Peters, 1976, 1977).

Research Pertaining to the Information Subtest

A number of research investigations using the WISC–R with learning disabled (e.g., Henry & Wittman, 1981; Smith, Coleman, Dokecki, & Davis, 1977a; Zingale & Smith, 1978), emotionally or behaviorally disturbed (e.g., Dean, 1977; Hale & Landino, 1981; Ollendick, 1979), and mentally retarded (e.g., Clarizio & Bernard, 1981; Henry & Wittman, 1981; Kaufman & Van Hagen, 1977) children have reported that the Information subtest is the most difficult or among the most difficult for these populations.

In their consensus rankings of subtest means for the 10 regular WISC–R subtests across a number of studies, Kaufman et al. (1990) report that the Information subtest ranks tenth for learning disabled and emotionally disturbed children and ranks ninth for mentally retarded children.

In terms of the Information subtest as one of the subtests in the ACID pattern, some studies (e.g., Ackerman et al., 1977; Joschko & Rourke, 1985) have found this pattern of low performance on the subtests of Arithmetic, Coding, Information, Digit Span, among learning-disabled children, as well as in samples of children with attention-deficit hyperactivity disorder (e.g., Dykman, Ackerman, & Oglesby, 1980), although Kavale and Forness (1984), in their meta-analysis of the validity of Wechsler profiles, conclude that no Wechsler profile is distinctive enough to permit the differential diagnosis of a learning disability.

Kaplan, Beardslee, and Keller (1987) report an investigation utilizing the WISC–R (and the WAIS) of the intellectual competence of 41 children one or both of whose parents were depressed. As one aspect of their study, they examined a diagnostic sign which had been proposed by Saccuzzo and Lewandowski (1976), of low Information and high Similarities. According to this view, a Wechsler score pattern indicative of emotional disturbance involves the Information subtest being the lowest or second lowest on the group of scores constituting the verbal scales, and Similarities being the highest or second highest score of the scores on the verbal scale.

Kaplan et al. (1987), using strict criteria, compared their sample to a normative sample and found that both the high Information and the low Similarities subtest pattern occurred significantly more frequently in the at-risk children than in normal controls. This pattern was not more common in children with two depressed parents than in children with one depressed parent, and neither this nor other features of the children's profiles varied depending on the children's own psychiatric diagnosis. Hence, although this finding may be of interest, it would not imply that the WISC–R (or WISC–III) subtest patterns are specifically diagnostic for examinees' psychological status.

In general, a number of research studies have indicated that the Information subtest is one of the most difficult on the Wechsler children's scales. This subtest has also been noted as one of the ACID group of subtests on which learning disabled children frequently perform more poorly than they do on the remaining Wechsler subtests.

Information Processing Aspects of the Information Subtest

For the Information subtest, input to the examinee is in the form of a series of verbally presented questions. The internal cognitive operations of the examinee involve analysis of the auditory input/questions, search of long-term memory, and formulation of an appropriate verbal response. Output is in the form of a verbal statement of a relatively specific bit of verbally coded information.

Observation of the examinee during this subtest entails noting the adequacy of the examinee's hearing, the competency and nature of the examinee's expressive English language performance, whether the examinee displays any speech impediment such as stuttering, stammering or blocking, and whether the examinee displays any word-finding difficulty.

Information processing deficits that might be reflected on the Information subtest would include difficulties in auditory reception, verbal encoding of material, visual-verbal associative learning, verbal memory, and verbal or linguistic expression.

Statistical Characteristics of the Information Subtest

The Information subtest has an average split-half reliability coefficient across all ages of the WISC–III of .84 with reliability coefficients that range from .73 to .88 across the 11 age groups. The Information subtest has an average test-retest stability coefficient for all ages of .85.

According to Sattler's (1992) categorization, which groups subtests into good, fair, and poor measures of g, the Information subtest is a good measure of g. In both the original WISC–III sample and in the Roid et al. (1993) replication study, the Information subtest ranks first among all WISC–III subtests in its g loading.

Kamphaus and Platt (1992) report subtest specificities for the WISC–III and indicate that the Information subtest has adequate specificity for the combined age groups on the WISC–III. Bracken et al. (1993; see Table 16 in the present volume), and Sattler (1992), indicate that the Information subtest has inadequate specificity for ages 6–7. For the remaining ages, the subtest has at least adequate specificity.

Relationships Between the Information Subtest and Other Aspects of the WISC–III

The Information subtest correlates .72 with the WISC–III Full Scale IQ, .75 with the Verbal IQ and .55 with the Performance IQ.

The Information subtest displays a range of correlations with the other WISC–III subtests. It correlates best with Vocabulary (.70) and Similarities (.66) on the Verbal Scale and with Block Design (.48) on the Performance Scale. The Information subtest correlates least well with the Mazes subtest (.18).

The relatively high correlations between Information with Vocabulary and Similarities support the grouping of these three subtests in the Verbal Comprehension factor, and suggest that these subtests all assess a similar underlying construct of verbal ability.

There are several ways to consider the Information subtest clinically. If one assumes that the Information subtest assesses static verbal information (knowledge that is specific and coded in verbal form), then the Information subtest may be viewed in relation to the Picture Completion subtest, which may be seen as assessing static visual information, or knowledge about the world coded in visual form. In this regard, the examiner may compare the examinee's knowledge of specific verbal facts with her or his knowledge of specific visual facts by comparing the examinee's performance on these two subtests.

On the other hand, Information viewed as a measure of the examinee's static verbal knowledge may also be compared to the examinee's performance on the Comprehension subtest, viewing the latter as a measure of the examinee's knowledge of the dynamic flux of social events around him- or herself. Hence, by comparing an examinee's Information and Comprehension subtest scores, it may be possible to compare the examinee's static verbal knowledge with his or her capacity to reason about events that are socially, dynamically or temporally organized.

Interpretation of the Handling of the
Information Subtest by the Examinee

Utilizing the gradient model discussed above, one can view the Information subtest as involving the examinee progressing along a gradient marked by increasing difficulty of the items, with the initial items presumably representing little challenge to the examinee's abilities and with subsequent items representing increasing and ultimately maximal challenge to her or his capacities. Viewing the examinee's responses from within this framework allows the examiner to observe the way in which the examinee responds to gradually increasing cognitive demands in the domain of verbal knowledge.

To the extent that the examiner assumes the examinee's performance on this subtest reflects the way in which the child typically handles information, the pattern of failures and successes on the subtest can suggest how efficiently or inefficiently the child deals with this aspect of intellectual performance. The examinee who answers several questions correctly, then fails five items in a row may be an individual who is able to utilize his or her abilities adequately, demonstrate her or his knowledge, and then discontinue effort.

The examinee who displays an erratic series of successes and failures may be an inefficiently functioning individual who may have difficulties with maintaining attention; this may have characterized the examinee's initial learning of factual information or the child's performance in the testing situation itself.

It is important for the examiner to observe carefully the examinee's reaction to success *and* failure since these observations may provide information to use in making recommendations to the child's teachers about whether or how to relate to the child and how effective social reinforcement may be. The examiner should note the examinee's verbal style, qualities of his or her enunciation, and whether or not the examinee makes eye contact and the degree of confidence or diffidence the child displays in responding to subtest items. It is also important for the examiner to make note of the child's or adolescent's nonverbal reactions, since these may also provide a relevant source of data about the examinee's functioning.

With respect to items to which the examinee does not know the answer, the child may simply acknowledge this; say he or she has not been taught the material; unknowingly give an incorrect answer; or indicate that he or she will guess. Perhaps the major framework the examiner may use to evaluate the child's response strategy is the degree to which the examinee's response reflects a more or less adequate handling of the issue of knowing what he or she knows, and the issue of taking personal responsibility for what she or he knows, and possibly feeling secure enough to risk guessing.

In terms of the issue of the child taking responsibility for his or her own knowledge, in these days of greater awareness of the abuse of children (Newberger, 1991), whenever the clinician observes an avoidant strategy in an examinee, the clinician should at least raise the hypothesis of the examinee having developed such a strategy because in the examinee's past, acknowledging ignorance may have been associated with parental anger, or else that the examinee's rapid retreat away from a challenge may reflect some specific aspect of the child's interpersonal learning history.

The examiner should also note the examinee's seeming awareness of the subtest organization. Thus some children will make the observation that the questions are becoming more difficult. The subtest's content seems readily relatable to school learning, and hence this subtest may easily stimulate feelings in the examinee that he or she may have for an academic situation.

In this regard, the examiner should attempt to note the examinee's response to failure of one, two or several items in a row. The examiner should note whether the child appears to shake off the failure and attempt to invest in the next item, or whether failures seem to have a cumulative effect, resulting in the examinee's increasing discouragement, faster retreat on subsequent items, comments regarding his or her being dumb, or the child expressing the wish to give up entirely and leave the situation altogether.

In addition, depending upon the pattern of response successes and failures the individual displays, the examiner may infer that anxiety might be disrupting the examinee's recall process or that anxiety or inattention interfered with the child's original learning of the material involved in particular items.

The indication that presently experienced anxiety was causing the examinee to miss items might be reflected in rapid giving up on a particular item, suggesting that the individual had not attempted to retrieve the information from memory, or with the individual giving a markedly inappropriate content response.

A pattern suggestive of long-standing deficits in the assimilation of information would be where successes and failures are distributed across the entire range of the child's responses, since this would suggest that the individual has been attentive to input of environmental stimulation on a variable basis and has thus learned some things while failing to learn others.

Since one aspect of the testing should be to attempt to determine if the examinee is a victim of past or ongoing trauma, the examiner should be alert to the examinee's handling of items which deal with aspects of the self (e.g., Item 1 or 2); or which deal with situations where abuse could be involved (e.g., Item 5) since the child's responses to these items may provide some indication of the examinee's anxiety regarding these issues.

Finally, the examiner should note the examinee's reaction to success and whether this stimulates feelings of confidence in the examinee, with the individual behaving as though he or she expected to be successful, whether the child instead interprets success as due to luck, or whether she or he becomes unrealistically overconfident and finds it difficult to focus on the next subtest.

CODING

What the Coding Subtest Measures

Wechsler (1958) states that the Digit Symbol subtest, the adult version of the Coding subtest, is one of the oldest and best established of all psychological tests, and he notes, "[T]he subject is required to associate certain symbols with certain other symbols, and the speed and accuracy with which he does it serve as a measure of his intellectual ability" (p. 81).

Wechsler had taken the Digit Symbol subtest from the Army Beta Examination, noting its advantages in that it involved a sample demonstration which allows the examiner to be certain that the examinee understands the task. A second advantage is that the subject is required to reproduce the unfamiliar symbols rather than the associated numbers, which lessens the advantage individuals having facility with numbers would enjoy. Although these observations were made regarding the adult version of this subtest, they also apply to the Coding subtest of the WISC–III.

According to Wechsler (1991), the Coding subtest is a component of the Processing Speed factor (with Symbol Search).

Sattler (1992) states that the Coding subtest requires the child to copy symbols paired with other symbols. The subtest has two separate parts, A and B, and each part uses a sample. Sattler (1992) states that the subtest assesses the child's ability to learn an unfamiliar task. It reflects the speed and accuracy of the child's visual-motor coordination, attentional skills, visual scanning and tracking (involving shifts from the code to the answer spaces), short-term memory or new paired associate learning of an unfamiliar code, cognitive flexibility, handwriting speed and possibly motivation.

According to Sattler (1992), the subtest also involves speed of mental operations and, to some degree, the child's visual acuity. Success on the subtest reflects not only understanding of the task but also on skillful use of pencil and paper, and the subtest is also sensitive to visuoperceptual problems.

Sattler (1992) also points out that Coding B may additionally involve a verbal encoding process if the child attaches verbal descriptions to the symbols, and hence Coding B may also be described as measuring the ability to learn combinations of symbols and shapes and to make such associations quickly and accurately. Hence, to at least some extent, Coding

A and B may involve separate information processing modes. The speed and accuracy with which the child performs the task provides a measure of the examinee's intellectual ability.

Kaufman (1979a, 1990) notes that the Coding (or Digit Symbol) subtest reflects the individual's encoding of information for further processing, facility with numbers, learning ability, the ability to reproduce models, the individual's sequential or left-brain processing, visual perception of abstract stimuli and visual sequencing ability. The subtest's uniqueness involves measurement of the individual's ability to follow directions, her or his clerical speed, accuracy and pencil and paper skill as well as the individual's psychomotor speed and visual short-term memory.

Kaufman (1979a, 1990) notes that factors which influence performance on the subtest include: the individual's anxiety, concern for accuracy and detail, distractibility, the individual's capacity to work under time pressure and to persist, and whether the individual has a learning disability.

According to the Fluid-Crystallized model of intelligence (Horn, 1985; Kaufman, 1990), the Coding (or Digit Symbol) subtest is the only member of the Speed category, although the present author would also include Symbol Search in this category).

According to Bannatyne's (1974) categorization, the Coding subtest is included in the Sequential Ability Category (with Digit Span and Arithmetic).

Glasser and Zimmerman (1967), in discussing the WISC, state that the Coding subtest appears to measure visual motor dexterity, particularly pencil manipulation, more than anything else. They also believe the task involves the individual's ability to absorb new material in an associative context while speed and accuracy in making associations will also determine an individual's success on the subtest.

The present author feels that both Coding A and Coding B reflect the examinee's ability to associate various pairs of symbols (a symbol with a geometric shape on Coding A and a symbol with a number on Coding B). In addition, both tasks involve sequential shifting, scanning, and focusing; coordination and very distinct integration of visual fine motor performance; and the possibility of a varying degree of paired-associate learning (i.e., learning which symbol is associated with a given geometric shape or with a particular number).

Both tasks also involve the examinee's ability to focus his or her attention on sets of external stimuli (as opposed to the Digit Span or Arithmetic Subtests, for example). Both Coding A and Coding B reflect the speed with which the examinee's information processing apparatus can deal with the flow of the task itself. The present author believes that the examinee's approach to the task reflects her or his efficiency or ability to formulate a best strategy for dealing with the subtest.

The task permits ongoing learning by the individual, i.e., he or she can learn the paired associates while moving through the task itself. However, if the examinee attempts to look at each item in the task, then check his or her memory to determine if the correct association has been learned and if not to then check the key, the examinee's performance will be erratic or slowed. Hence, the most efficient subtest-taking strategy is one in which the examinee does not deliberately attempt to learn the paired associations but simply identifies the shape or number in the item, searches the key (or looks back to the last identical pair dealt with) for the correct symbol and correctly marks the item.

Both Coding A and B thus reflect the efficiency of the child or adolescent's approach to a redundant task; they also reflect the degree of energy that the examinee can focus and sustain for at least a relatively extended period of time (of all the timed items on the WISC–III, only four Object Assembly items have longer time limits; all other timed items have time limits equal to or less than the time allowed on Coding A or B).

There are several differences between Coding A and B that should be noted. Coding A uses geometric shapes rather than numbers as the stimuli printed on the form. Processing of these geometric shapes by the child would seem to differ from Coding B, where the examinee perceives the form of the numbers, reads each as a number, then searches for its associated symbol and records it. With Coding A, the examinee sees the form, may label the figure verbally (e.g., square, cross), searches for that figure in the key, locates the proper symbol, and records it within the geometric shape. In addition, Coding A has only five figure-symbol combinations rather than the nine for Coding B, so the search through the key is less time consuming and less demanding for the individual working on Coding A.

Overall, then, Coding A and B are similar because both require visual sequential processing of primarily visual as opposed to verbal stimuli; visual and motor-coordinated performance; possible paired-associate learning; and the development by the examinee of a problem-solving strategy that may aid or hinder task performance. The two tasks differ in that Coding A uses five different items that involve symbol-shape pairs, while Coding B uses nine different symbol-number pairs. Both tasks are sensitive to the amount of focused energy the examinee can invest in a sequential and redundant task in which the examinee regulates the pace at which he or she will work, independent of specific feedback or cues provided by the examiner.

In terms of what the Coding subtest measures, during the subtest administration, the examiner may periodically remember that this subtest is providing a sample of the examinee's Performance IQ, processing speed (Wechsler, 1991), sequential ability (Bannatyne, 1974), speed of processing (Horn, 1985;

Kaufman, 1990), and that the subtest is one component of the ACID profile (Ackerman et al., 1976, 1977).

Research Pertaining to the Coding Subtest

Research investigations using the WISC–R with learning-disabled (e.g., Clarizio & Bernard, 1981; Mishra, 1984; Schiff et al., 1981) and emotionally or behaviorally disturbed (e.g., Fischer et al., 1985; Henry & Wittman, 1981) have found the Coding subtest to be among the more difficult for these populations. Investigations of mentally retarded children with the WISC–R (e.g., Clarizio & Bernard, 1981; Reilly, Wheeler & Etlinger, 1985) have found the Coding subtest to vary in its degree of difficulty for this population.

In their consensus rankings of the subtest means for the 10 regular WISC–R subtests across a number of studies, Kaufman et al. (1990) report that the Coding subtest ranks eighth for learning-disabled samples and ninth for emotionally or behaviorally disturbed samples. These authors report that the Coding subtest ranks fourth among samples of mentally retarded individuals, suggesting that it is less difficult for mentally retarded individuals than for either learning disabled or emotionally or behaviorally disturbed children.

The Coding subtest is one of the four subtests in the ACID pattern, and hence has often been identified as among the most difficult for learning disabled children (Ackerman et al., 1977; Reynolds & Kaufman, 1985; see section on the ACID pattern in "Frameworks for the Interpretation of the WISC–III").

Differential performance on the WISC–R Coding subtest has been reported by Kaufman (1979a), Phelps and Ensor (1987), and Vance (1978) for males and females. Kaufman (1979a) reported that females outperformed males on the Coding subtest.

O'Donnell, Granier, and Dersh (1991) reported research investigating whether handedness or gender of the examinee affected performance on the WISC–III Coding subtest. These authors found that handedness did not affect performance on the Coding subtest, but they did find that there was a gender difference in Coding subtest performance, with females outperforming males.

A study by Gatewood (1987) assessed the effects of using a lead pencil or a felt-tip pen on the WISC–R Coding subtest performance of 40 10–12-year-old children and found that the type of writing implement did not affect writing speed.

Massman, Nussbaum, and Bigler (1988) explored the relationship between hyperactivity and performance on several psychological tests. These authors found that for children between 6 and 8, there was no significant relation-ship between hyperactivity/attentional problems as measured by the Child Behavior Checklist (Achenbach, 1991a, 1991b) Hyperactivity scale and per-formance on the WISC–R Freedom from Distractibility subtests (Coding, Arithmetic, and Digit Span). However, for a sample of children between 9 and 12, there was a significant and large negative correlation between CBC hyperactivity scores and Coding subtest performance, which the authors interpreted to mean that hyperactivity/inattention has a deleterious effect on test performance (relative to peers) as age increases.

Williams et al. (1993) investigated the use of frequently administered nonverbal tasks to predict performance on the Writing Fluency subtest of the Woodcock-Johnson Tests of Achievement for 146 subjects aged 6–16 years. These authors found that for the Coding subtest, a scaled score $= / < 7$ would be highly predictive of writing dysfluency, especially for boys, and such a finding should be pursued by further evaluation and/or modifica-tions in classroom instructional procedures for the child.

Overall, then, the Coding subtest appears to vary in terms of difficulty for different populations, being among the more difficult subtests for learning disabled and emotionally disturbed children, and being somewhat less difficult for mentally retarded children and adolescents. The subtest is one of the ACID group of subtests on which learning disabled individuals often perform more poorly than they do on the remaining Wechsler subtests.

Information Processing Aspects of the Coding Subtest

For the Coding subtest, input to the examinee is in the form of printed numerical or geometric information plus verbal and modeled instructions for the examinee to substitute symbols for numbers or for geometric forms. Cognitive operations on the part of the examinee include visual scanning and shifting of visual focus combined with fine motor coordination, rapid associative processing, or associative learning. Output on the subtest involves production of a string of written symbol-for-number or symbol-for-geometric-form substitutions.

Observation of the child or adolescent during this subtest entails noting the nature of the examinee's organization in space in relation to the task, the smoothness of the child's visual focus shifts, the nature and accuracy of the examinee's motor control and coordination, the child's persistence or distractibility, and whether or not the examinee develops and utilizes a learning strategy or a copying strategy. Additionally, the examiner should note the examinee's pencil grip and whether he or she holds the paper down as indices of the child's ability to adapt to a school-related task.

Information processing deficits that might be reflected in performance on the Coding subtest would include difficulties in visual perception, visual search or scanning, difficulties with new learning or developing a learning strategy, and difficulties with attention, concentration or fine motor coordination. The examinee's handedness and the nature of his or her pencil grip can provide information regarding the development of lateral preference and possible central nervous system dysfunction (Kinsbourne, 1989).

Statistical Characteristics of the Coding Subtest

The Coding subtest has an average split-half reliability coefficient across all ages of the WISC–III of .79 with reliability coefficients that range from .70 to .90 across all ages of the scale; however, there are no reliability coefficients reported in the WISC–III manual for five age groups (8, 9, 12, 13 and 16) because no children were retested at these ages. The Coding subtest has an average test-retest stability coefficient of .70 for Coding A and an average test-retest stability coefficient of .77 for Coding B.

According to Sattler's (1992) categorization, which groups subtests into good, fair, and poor measures of *g*, the Coding subtest is a poor measure of *g*. In the original WISC–III sample, and in the Roid et al. (1993) replication study, the Coding subtest ranks twelfth among all WISC–III subtests in its *g* loading.

Kamphaus and Platt (1992) report subtest specificities for the WISC–III and indicate that the Coding subtest has adequate specificity for the combined age groups on the WISC–III. Bracken et al. (1993; see Table 16 in the present volume) also indicate that the Coding subtest has ample specificity for all ages of the WISC–III. Sattler (1992) indicates that the Coding subtest has inadequate specificity for age 8; for the other 10 age groups, the subtest has ample specificity.

Relationships Between the Coding Subtest and Other Aspects of the WISC–III

The Coding subtest correlates .33 with the WISC–III Full Scale IQ, .29 with the Verbal IQ and .32 with the Performance IQ.

The Coding subtest correlates best with the Vocabulary subtest on the Verbal Scale (.26) and with the Symbol Search subtest (.53) on the Performance Scale. The Coding subtest correlates least well with the Mazes subtest (.15).

The relatively high correlation between the Coding and Symbol Search subtests may reflect the fact that both of these subtests deal with a similar kind of mental processing of visual information and supports the grouping of these two subtests in the Processing Speed factor.

Comparison of these two tasks indicates that the Coding subtest is more redundant in its demand characteristics, and the examinee can even learn the associations between particular symbols and their numerical or geometric counterparts. The Symbol Search subtest requires that the child alter his or her specific processing on each item. In addition, the pencil manipulation task required of the examinee differs on these two subtests so that they share some perceptual processing requirements, yet also require somewhat differing performance of the child or adolescent.

In terms of the fact that the Coding and Symbol Search subtests are both included in the Processing Speed factor, it is important to realize that these two subtests can and should be interpreted as reflecting a unitary factor only if they are not significantly different from one another. If they do differ significantly, they should be interpreted separately although they may be viewed in relation to one another.

To determine whether these two subtests are significantly different from one another, Table B.4. (Wechsler, 1991, p. 265) indicates that a difference between them of 4.02 is significant at the .05 level. Hence if the Coding and Symbol Search subtest scaled scores differ by 4.02 units (4 or more to be realistic), the examiner can conclude that they do not reflect a unitary factor and the two subtests should be interpreted separately.

If one considers the gradient model discussed earlier and conceives of these two tasks as distributed on a gradient of passive versus active demand of the examinee, one can think of the Symbol Search task as requiring predominantly visual processing by the child while the Coding subtest requires visual processing plus a specific motor output component as well as possible associative learning and memory components. By comparing the examinee's performance on these two subtests, one may observe how the child handles these related but differing task demands.

Interpretation of the Handling of the Coding Subtest by the Examinee

The first issue to consider in terms of the handling of this subtest by the examinee is whether the child or adolescent is right- or left-handed. Although the subtest form is designed so that the task is easier for a left-handed child to accomplish than with the WISC–R (Wechsler, 1974), it may be noted that non-righthandedness is more common among the mentally retarded, autistic, and language and learning delayed, but even within these populations, the non-right-handed subgroups are often more severely affected by the deficit in question (Kinsbourne, 1989).

Kinsbourne (1989) notes that non-right-handedness occurs relatively frequently in stuttering, language delay and dyslexia. Several different explanations have been proposed for this finding. These include an absence of central lateralization; a consequence of early left hemisphere pathology (Satz, Orsini, Saslow, & Henry, 1985); or some influence in early development which adversely affects language lateralization and also diminishes the functions of the language hemisphere (Geschwind & Behan, 1982). Hence if the examinee is left-handed, this should alert the examiner to the possibility of the examinee having some significant information processing deficit.

Beyond the examinee's handedness, the examiner should note whether and how well the examinee uses his or her other hand to hold the page down. The behavior of holding the page down while writing on it is an adaptive response that should be learned by most children soon after they enter school, when they realize that if they do not hold the page down as they write on it, the page will move. The child who fails to hold the page down is one who either suffers from lapses in adaptive thinking or is relatively inefficient in awareness of fundamental properties of the world in which she or he lives.

With respect to the task performance itself, there are several basic strategies that may be observed. The examiner should note whether the examinee focuses visually on the item or whether he or she uses the non-writing hand to point to each item. In the latter case, one may infer that the child is anxious and unconfident or else the examinee is aware of difficulties in attentional tasks, and has developed a compensatory strategy to allow better visual focusing and tracking.

A second strategy that may be noted at times is the use by the examinee of verbal encoding of the task, such as saying aloud the names of the shapes in Coding A or using verbal labels for some of the symbols in Coding B. This approach suggests that the individual needs to rely on more than the visual system for processing visual information and may spontaneously utilize a vocal, and perhaps a kinesthetic, system to assist in visual processing.

The next issue to consider is the examinee's performance while actually working on the Coding task. Three possibilities may be noted. The first is when the examinee stops the task at the end of the first row. This is an indication of the child's possible failure to have attended to, or retained, the original instructions.

A second kind of behavior seen occasionally is that of a child who begins to complete the task by doing all of the same kind of item (for example, all of the star or circle items on Coding A, or all of the #1 or #3 items on Coding B). This behavior suggests that the examinee has not listened to the instructions carefully, or else ignored them in favor of a strategy which occurred to the examinee during the task and which appears quite efficient.

Observing this behavior in an examinee suggests, first, that in approaching problems, this examinee is capable of generating innovative strategies; but second, the child may have difficulty in placing constraints on her or his problem-solving approaches by virtue of limits or instructions provided in a given situation. Stated otherwise, such an examinee might feel that the end justifies the means, and he or she might display such an approach in other than the testing situation as well.

Still another aspect of the examinee's performance which should be noted is the degree of pencil pressure the child uses; the examinee may make her or his pencil marks too light or too dark, reflecting the examinee's anger, anxiety or efforts at self-control. Also to be noted by the examiner is whether the examinee stays within the limits of the task: within the geometric designs for Coding A or within each box on Coding B, as this will indicate the accuracy of the child's fine motor control.

A final consideration is that of the examinee who erases one or more symbols during the task. This implies several things: first, that the examinee (either in general or when attempting to work quickly) makes mistakes, which in turn suggests that the examinee may be impulsive or careless. However, since the examinee erases something, it means he or she is alert to her or his performance, notices errors that have been made, and attempts to undo or correct them, which also suggests that the examinee has some standards and self-monitoring capacity which the examinee applies to his or her performance.

In observing the examinee working on the task, the examiner may also note the examinee's eye movements and may be able to determine if the child is utilizing a strategy involving direct copying from the key or from items already completed, or, finally, if the examinee seems to be trying to memorize the symbols. Finally, if the examiner wishes, it is possible to record how many items the examinee completes during various portions of the task (Kaplan et al., 1991), and to compare the examinee's performance on these different chunks, or to examine the child's incidental learning of the number- or form-symbol associations once the task has been completed.

SIMILARITIES

What the Similarities Subtest Measures

Wechsler (1958), in describing the Similarities subtest of the WAIS, notes that "while a certain degree of verbal comprehension is necessary for even minimal performance, sheer word knowledge need only be a minor factor. More important is the individual's ability to perceive the common elements of the terms he is asked to compare and, at higher levels, his ability to bring them under a single concept" (p. 73).

Wechsler (1958) notes the several advantages of the Similarities subtest: that it is easy to give, appears to be interesting to the average adult; that it is a good reflection of *g,* or general intelligence; and that the subtest provides information about the logical character of the subject's thinking processes.

According to Wechsler (1991), the Similarities subtest is a component of the Verbal Comprehension factor (with Information, Vocabulary and Comprehension).

Sattler (1992) states that the Similarities subtest requires the child to answer questions about how concepts or objects are alike. He notes that in addition to perceiving the common elements of paired items, the child must bring these elements together in a single concept. Hence the subtest may measure verbal concept formation, defined as the ability to place objects or events together in a meaningful group. In order to do this, the child may need to organize, abstract and discover relationships that are not initially apparent.

Sattler (1992) notes that while concept formation can be a voluntary and effortful process, it can also reflect merely well-automated verbal conventions. Thus performance on this task may be related to cultural opportunities, interest patterns and memory.

Kaufman (1979a, 1990) notes that the Similarities subtest reflects the individual's ability to handle abstract verbal concepts, the ability to distinguish essential from nonessential details, verbal reasoning and verbal expression. The subtest's unique ability involves measurement of the individual's logical abstractive or categorical thinking.

Kaufman (1979a, 1990) notes that factors which influence performance on the subtest include: the individual's flexibility, interests, negativistic style, overly concrete thinking and outside reading experiences.

According to the Fluid-Crystallized categorization of intellectual tasks (Horn, 1985; Kaufman, 1990), the Similarities subtest reflects both Crystallized Intelligence (with Information, Vocabulary and Comprehension) and Fluid Intelligence (with Picture Completion, Picture Arrangement, Block Design, Object Assembly and Digit Span).

According to Bannatyne's (1974) categorization, the Similarities subtest is included in the Verbal Conceptualization or Conceptual Category (with Vocabulary and Comprehension).

Glasser and Zimmerman (1967), in discussing the WISC, note that this subtest is constructed to measure the qualitative aspects of relationships that the child has abstracted from his or her environment. The subtest involves remote memory, the ability to comprehend, the capacity for associative thinking, interests and reading patterns of the subject, and the ability to select and verbalize appropriate relationships between two ostensibly dissimilar objects or concepts. In addition, Glasser and Zimmerman (1967) note that the subtest measures the individual's ability to hierarchize abstract and essential as opposed to concrete and nonessential features of objects or events as a basis on which to categorize them.

The present author views the Similarities subtest as measuring the ability of the examinee to form verbal concepts or to perceive relationships between apparently diverse aspects of her or his experience or environment. The Similarities subtest is felt to be a good measure of g; it is viewed as reflecting more of the examinee's innate or natural capacity for intelligent reasoning than school-dependent subtests, such as Information or Vocabulary. Thus, as a measure of abstract verbal reasoning, one can view the Similarities subtest as reflective of the examinee's capacity for intelligent and logical thinking as distinct from school subject learning; that is, whether or not the examinee has been exposed to a particular learning experience, or has performed well in school, this subtest indicates the child's potential to independently perceive and articulate relationships among manifestly different aspects of the world.

An additional way of viewing the Similarities subtest is that it may provide an indication of the examinee's potential for the kind of insightful thinking found in dynamic forms of psychotherapy. That is, if one reasons that insight requires the child be able to see relationships between manifestly different situations or events (for example, that one's father and one's school principal are both authority figures), then the child who performs well on the Similarities subtest at least has one ability needed for insightful understanding of his or her life experience. However, adequate performance on this subtest is not a guarantee that the child will be able to apply insightful thinking to all aspects of her or his life or behavior.

Information about the strategies of cognition the examinee utilizes can also be revealed in the subtest responses, with the individual's replies suggesting whether he or she has adopted a verbal or visual orientation to the items to be categorized. The examiner may thus infer from the child's responses whether she or he has pictured the items visually or placed them in a verbal categorical scheme.

This may allow inferences regarding the examinee's conceptual style—concrete and visual or characterized by a linguistic code for thinking about the world. Many if not most of the subtest items permit a strategy in which the child can visualize the components in the item, and the examinee can then articulate a concrete or abstract linguistic concept to group the elements. Items 10, 15, 16, and 18 do not have concrete visual referents as the other items do.

In terms of what the Similarities subtest measures, during the administration of this subtest, the examiner may periodically remember that the subtest is providing a sample of the examinee's Verbal IQ, verbal comprehension (Wechsler, 1991), both crystallized and fluid intelligence (Horn, 1985; Kaufman, 1990), and verbal conceptualization ability (Bannatyne, 1974).

Research Pertaining to the Similarities Subtest

Research investigations using the WISC–R with learning disabled (e.g., Fischer et al., 1985; Kaufman & McLean, 1986), emotionally or behaviorally disturbed (e.g., Clarizio & Bernard, 1981; Reilly et al., 1985), and mentally retarded (e.g., Henry & Wittman, 1981; Kaufman & Von Hagen, 1977) children have reported that the Similarities subtest is of intermediate difficulty for these populations.

In their consensus rankings of subtest means for the 10 regular WISC–R subtests across a number of studies, Kaufman et al. (1990) report that the Similarities subtest ranks sixth for learning disabled, emotionally or behaviorally disturbed, and mentally retarded children.

A number of research investigations (e.g., Slate & Chick, 1989; Slate & Jones, 1990) have indicated that scoring errors occur frequently on the Similarities subtest, suggesting that it is important for examiners to use extra caution when scoring this subtest.

Kaplan et al. (1987) report an investigation using the WISC–R (and the WAIS) of the intellectual competence of children, one or both of whose parents were depressed. As one aspect of their investigation, they examined a diagnostic sign which had been proposed by Saccuzzo and Lewandowski (1976), of low Information and high Similarities. According to this view, a Wechsler score pattern indicative of emotional disturbance involves the Information subtest being the lowest or second lowest on the group of scores constituting the verbal scale, and Similarities being the highest or second highest score on the scores of the verbal scale.

Kaplan et al. (1987) compared their sample to a normative sample and found that both the high Information and the low Similarities subtest pattern occurred significantly more frequently in the at-risk children than in normal controls. Although this finding may be of interest, it would not imply that the WISC–R (or WISC–III) subtest patterns are specifically diagnostic for examinees' psychological status.

Thus overall, the Similarities subtest has been found to be of intermediate difficulty for learning disabled, emotionally or behaviorally disturbed and mentally retarded. This subtest is also one that is one of the more difficult to score reliably.

Information Processing Aspects of the Similarities Subtest

For the Similarities subtest, input to the examinee is in the form of auditory verbal word pairs. Internal cognitive operations on this subtest include auditory analysis, comparison, abstraction and logical thinking. Output on the subtest is in the form of a categorization by the child or adolescent of the two elements presented, with the examinee's response varying in degree of concreteness-abstractness.

Observation of the examinee during this subtest involves noting the nature of her or his attentiveness, evident hearing or auditory perceptual processing difficulties (e.g., if the child mishears any of the stimulus words), and the examinee's reflectivity or impulsivity in responding to each item.

Examination of the Similarities subtest items indicates that items 10, 15, 16 and possibly 18 may impel the examinee to respond with an abstract concept; the other subtest items all have features which may permit the child to respond with a concrete or perceptually based categorization.

Information processing deficits that might be reflected in performance on the Similarities subtest would include specific auditory or language problems.

Statistical Characteristics of the Similarities Subtest

The Similarities subtest has an average split-half reliability coefficient across all ages of the WISC–III of .81 with reliability coefficients that range from .74 to .84 across the 11 age groups. The Similarities subtest has an average test-retest stability coefficient for all ages of .81.

According to Sattler's (1992) categorization, which groups subtests into good, fair, and poor measures of *g*, the Similarities subtest is a good measure of *g*. In both the original WISC–III sample and in the Roid et al. (1993) replication study, the Similarities subtest ranks third among all WISC–III subtests in its *g* loading.

Kamphaus and Platt (1992) report subtest specificities for the WISC–III and indicate that the Similarities subtest has inadequate specificity for the combined age groups on the WISC–III. Bracken et al. (1993; see Table 16 in the present volume) and Sattler (1992) indicate that the Similarities subtest has inadequate specificity for ages 7–10 and age 13. For the remaining ages, the subtest has at least adequate specificity.

Relationships Between the Similarities Subtest and Other Aspects of the WISC-III

The Similarities subtest correlates .72 with the WISC–III Full Scale IQ, .75 with the Verbal IQ and .55 with the Performance IQ.

The Similarities subtest correlates best with Vocabulary (.69) on the Verbal Scale and with Block Design (.49) on the Performance Scale. The Similarities subtest correlates least well with the Mazes subtest (.18).

The relatively high correlation between the Similarities and Vocabulary subtests may reflect the fact that both of these subtests involve the child's use of verbal language, both are good measures of *g* and indicate the examinee's ability to express him- or herself verbally, and thus support the inclusion of both subtests in the Verbal Comprehension factor. The correlation between the Similarities and Block Design subtests may reflect the fact that both of these tasks are good measures of *g;* hence both involve the examinee's ability to think abstractly and logically, one with verbal symbols, the other with visuospatial information.

Interpretation of the Handling of the Similarities Subtest by the Examinee

From within the gradient model discussed above, one can view the Similarities subtest as involving a series of item pairs that progress from those that are relatively more concrete and immediate in terms of the child's experience to those which are more abstract and remote; hence the examinee is called upon to perceive and articulate increasingly more abstract and less obvious principles that unite the item pairs.

One of the first issues for the examiner to note on this subtest is the speed with which the examinee replies to the subtest items. Some examinees respond quickly and effortlessly to the items, suggesting a kind of free and flexible thinking capacity or, alternatively, an impulsive behavioral style. Other examinees may respond to the items slowly, which may suggest their more reflective cognitive style, or else indicating the effort they are willing to invest in what for them may be a challenging task.

As the subtest progresses, the examiner may note a shift in response time by the examinee, from shorter to longer reaction times, suggesting that the specific items presented have reached or surpassed the conceptual capacity of the examinee.

The examiner should note whether the child or adolescent generates one response or several to an item, since this again indicates the examinee's approach to such a reasoning task. The individual may approach the task as a divergent one, where he or she associates to the stimuli and produces several possible ideas, or go beyond this divergent strategy to a convergent one and select from among her or his thoughts the one that best fits the subtest requirements.

If the examinee does develop more than one response, the sequence of responses (whether toward increasing abstractness or toward increasing concreteness) should be noted. These observations can indicate whether the child seems to typically respond adequately and then undo his or her performance, or whether the examinee begins poorly but on further reflection is able to think more clearly or at a higher level. Beyond this, if the examinee produces several responses and is asked to choose one, the examiner can observe whether the child chooses the more or less adequate response.

Observation of these response behaviors on the part of the child can indicate whether the examinee does her or his thinking and response selection covertly, or verbalizes the process; and whether or how the individual selects among alternative responses. This information can then become part of the examiner's recommendations for working with the examinee in school or therapy.

In terms of the examinee's handling of this subtest it is important to note the child's responses to the early subtest items when he or she is being exposed to the *set* of the subtest. For children who have some difficulty in catching on to the idea of the task, it is important to note whether they are able to benefit from examiner questioning or explanation and then to demonstrate higher level abstract thinking during the subsequent items of the subtest to which they are exposed. Such an observation of a child's handling of this subtest (as well as in her or his handling of other subtests) may indicate that the examinee is a person who may not move into new tasks very readily, but with support, guidance or modeling, the individual may recognize what is expected and then proceed more adequately.

Another consideration in terms of the examinee's handling of this subtest is in the scoring of the items. Thus the examinee who obtains some or many 2's displays greater capacity for abstract thinking than the examinee who obtains primarily 1's. Similarly, the examinee who displays more unevenness in the pattern of his or her scores (for example, 2, 1, 0, 2, 2, 0, 1, 2) would be expected to function erratically when faced with tasks requiring abstract or logical reasoning while the examinee whose pattern is 2, 2, 1, 2, 2 would be expected to demonstrate more even, consistent and efficient capacity for thinking logically.

Since this subtest provides a sample of the examinee's verbal communication, it is also important to observe the clarity of the child's expression; this can be assessed by noting how easily the examiner can assign a score to the child's responses. Some examinees' responses to the subtest are readily scored as 0, 1 or 2. Other examinees may respond to a number of items in ways that challenge the examiner to assign scores to the items, and this quality of the child's communication and thinking should be noted by the examiner since it is an important feature of the individual's intellectual functioning.

PICTURE ARRANGEMENT

What the Picture Arrangement Subtest Measures

Wechsler (1958) notes that "[T]he Picture Arrangement Subtest consists of a series of pictures which, when placed in the right sequence, tell a little story" (p. 74), and that the subtest "effectively measures a subject's ability to comprehend and size up a total situation. The subject must understand the whole, must get the idea of the story, before he [sic] is able to set himself effectively to the task.... Secondly, the subject matter of the test nearly always involves some human or practical situation. The understanding of these situations more nearly corresponds to what other writers have referred to as 'social intelligence' " (p. 75).

According to Wechsler (1991), the Picture Arrangement subtest is a component of the Perceptual Organization factor (with Picture Completion, Block Design and Object Assembly).

Sattler (1992) states that the Picture Arrangement subtest requires the child to place a series of pictures into a logical order, and hence the subtest measures the child's ability to comprehend and evaluate a total situation. In order to accomplish the task, the examinee must grasp the general idea of a story and although the child may sometimes use trial-and-error, she or he usually needs to appraise the total situation depicted in order to succeed.

Sattler (1992) also notes that the subtest may be seen as a measure of nonverbal reasoning that involves planning ability, anticipation, visual organization, and temporal sequencing. Additionally, the subtest measures the ability to anticipate the consequences of initial acts or situations, as well as the ability to interpret social situations. Since some children may generate covert verbal descriptions of alternate story sequences, the subtest may also measure verbal sequencing processes in the child as well.

Kaufman (1979a, 1990) notes that the Picture Arrangement subtest reflects the individual's ability to demonstrate common sense by understanding cause-effect relationships, the ability to distinguish essential from nonessential details, nonverbal reasoning, sythesis, visual perception/processing of meaningful stimuli (people and things) and visual sequencing. The subtest's unique ability involves measurement of the anticipation of consequences, planning ability (comprehending and sizing up a total situation) and temporal sequencing and time concepts.

Kaufman (1979a, 1990) notes that factors which influence performance on the subtest include: creativity, cultural opportunities, exposure to comic strips and working under time pressure.

According to the Fluid-Crystallized categorization of intellectual tasks (Horn, 1985; Kaufman, 1990), the Picture Arrangement subtest reflects Fluid Intelligence (with Picture Completion, Block Design, Object Assembly, Similarities and Digit Span).

According to Bannatyne's (1974) categorization, the Picture Arrangement subtest, which had been included in the Sequential Category (Bannatyne, 1968), is not included in any of the four groups of Wechsler subtest scores.

Glasser and Zimmerman (1967), in discussing the WISC, note that such factors as perception, visual comprehension, planning (which involves understanding sequential and causal events), and synthesis into intelligible wholes are involved on this subtest. Glasser and Zimmerman (1967) also note that performance on the Picture Arrangement subtest may indicate social alertness and common sense or intelligence applied to social or interpersonal situations.

The present author views the Picture Arrangement subtest as reflecting the capacity of the individual to logically and sequentially organize visual or pictorial information that is socially or interpersonally meaningful. From this perspective, the Picture Arrangement subtest requires that the examinee have some stored knowledge or repertoire of typical or ordinary sequences of social behavior. Hence the subtest reflects to some extent the examinee's social awareness or sensitivity. The task requires the examinee to examine an array of related but separate and nonsequentially organized images and determine a hypothesis as to what the total sequence or story involves.

Probably two solution strategies on the part of the child are possible: in one the examinee abstracts from the array of pictures a theme he or she believes accurate and then the examinee puts the separate cards into a sequence consistent with that overall theme; in the second, the examinee picks up partial information from one or two of the cards and gradually attempts to build up the correct sequence by using a more focused rather than a holistic strategy. In either of these approaches, the individual is involved in a process of hypothesis testing, in which she or he puts the cards in a particular sequence, obtains feedback and decides that the arrangement is or is not an adequate one.

The subtest also reflects to a significant degree the child's ability to reason logically about pictorial or nonverbal social information. The child needs to have some understanding of the concept of implication, insofar as one action or behavior depicted implies a next action or behavior; the examinee must also be able to draw inferences from separate images as to how different features of a continuous flow of events may be logically related to one another.

The capacity to handle the task thus involves the examinee's ability to take in visual, interpersonally relevant information and to determine the sequence in which the separate items might be organized in a logical progression. This may involve aspects of the ability to use foresight or to plan ahead and to understand social behavior within a temporal context. This also involves the child's ability to notice visual details within a broad framework and hence to shift from a broad perceptual focus to a narrow focus.

Related to this is the examinee's capacity to delay responding on the task itself until he or she has sufficient information to generate an adequate hypothesis regarding the overall idea of the item. One would assume that children differ in regard to how much information they take in before taking action. In this situation, children differ in the length of time they examine the array of pictures before they begin to rearrange them into a particular sequence. Thus the subtest can provide information regarding the examinee's impulsivity or reflectivity in dealing with social information.

In terms of what the Picture Arrangement subtest measures, during the administration of the subtest, the examiner may periodically recall that the subtest is providing a sample of the examinee's Performance IQ, perceptual organization, and fluid intelligence (Horn, 1985; Kaufman, 1990).

Research Pertaining to the Picture Arrangement Subtest

A number of research investigations using the WISC–R with learning disabled (e.g., Fischer et al., 1985; Henry & Wittman, 1981; Smith et al., 1977a), and emotionally or behaviorally disturbed (e.g., Hale & Landino, 1981; Reilly et al., 1985) children have reported that the Picture Arrangement subtest is one of the easier subtests on the WISC–R for these populations. Various studies with mentally retarded children using the WISC–R (e.g., Clarizio & Bernard, 1981; Kaufman & Van Hagen, 1977) have reported the Picture Arrangement subtest to be of varied difficulty for this population.

In their consensus rankings of subtest means for the 10 regular WISC–R subtests across a number of studies, Kaufman et al. (1990) report that the Picture Arrangement subtest ranks third for learning disabled and emotionally or behaviorally disturbed children, while the subtest ranks fifth for mentally retarded children.

There have been numerous research investigations of the validity of the Picture Arrangement subtest, with the WISC (e.g., Krippner, 1964; Lipsitz, Dworkin, & Erlenmeyer-Kimling, 1993), the WAIS–R (e.g., Nobo & Evans, 1986; Ramos & Die, 1986; Reiff & Gerber, 1990; Segal, Westen, Lohr, & Silk, 1993; Sipps, Berry, & Lynch, 1987) and the WISC–R (e.g., Browning & Quinlan, 1985).

These investigations have focused on the view that the Picture Arrangement subtest (often with the Comprehension subtest) reflects the individual's capacity for social reasoning or sensitivity. The results of these studies are somewhat mixed with some investigations obtaining positive results in terms of relationships between Wechsler measures of "social intelligence" and external criteria (e.g., Reiff & Gerber, 1990; Sipps et al., 1987).

For example, Reiff and Gerber (1990) investigated possible explanations for social skill deficits in students with learning disabilities. They administered the Comprehension, Picture Arrangement and Digit Span subtests of the WISC–R and the Profile of Nonverbal Sensitivity, a test which measures the ability to understand or decode nonverbal information (e.g., facial expression), to 32 elementary school-age students.

Using a multiple regression analysis, these authors found that Picture Arrangement was the most important variable in predicting the students' performances on the test of nonverbal sensitivity, and they concluded that these students' difficulties in making central inferences and noticing social cues were reflected in both their social difficulties and in their performance on the WISC–R Picture Arrangement subtest.

However, other investigations have found that there is little justification for utilizing the Picture Arrangement subtest as an index of an individual's social competence (e.g., Lipsitz et al., 1993; Nobo & Evans, 1986) and suggest that the subtest should not be used to draw personality inferences about the examinee until appropriate validity data has been obtained to justify such inferences.

Thus, overall, the Picture Arrangement subtest has been found to be one of the easier subtests for learning disabled and emotionally or behaviorally disturbed children, while it is of varying difficulty for populations of mentally retarded children. Although the subtest has long been viewed as reflective of an individual's social sensitivity or social intelligence, research results on this question have been mixed, and the consensus is that drawing conclusions about an examinee's social competence from this subtest is unwarranted.

Information Processing Aspects of the Picture Arrangement Subtest

For the Picture Arrangement subtest, input to the examinee is in the form of pictorial information with verbal and modeling instructions to sequentially organize a number of discrete pictures into a logical story. Internal cognitive operations include visual scanning and visual search of the pictorial stimuli; logical thinking regarding the integration of the stimuli into a coherent and meaningful sequence; processing of general visual themes as well as visual details; and motor organization and coordination. Output involves the production of a logical sequential organization of pictorial information.

Observation of the child during this subtest entails noting the examinee's visual search/scanning strategies, the individual's reflective or impulsive response tempo, and the nature of the examinee's fine motor coordinated behavior. For example, the examiner should note whether the child picks up the cards or slides them on the work surface (the latter strategy is faster and hence more efficient). The examiner should also note the dexterity the child displays in handling the cards, and whether the examinee uses only one hand or both, which may indicate the child or adolescent's flexibility in dealing with visual motor tasks.

Information processing deficits that might be reflected on the Picture Arrangement subtest would include difficulties in visual acuity or perception, problems in visual search or scanning, difficulties in sequential or spatial organization, or difficulties with impulsivity and self-regulation.

Statistical Characteristics of the Picture Arrangement Subtest

The Picture Arrangement subtest has an average split-half reliability coefficient across all ages of the WISC–III of .76 with reliability coefficients that range from .70 to .84 across the 11 age groups. The Picture Arrangement subtest has an average test-retest stability coefficient for all ages of .64.

According to Sattler's (1992) categorization, which groups subtests into good, fair, and poor measures of *g,* the Picture Arrangement subtest is a fair measure of *g.* In the original WISC–III sample, the Picture Arrangement subtest ranks tenth among all WISC–III subtests in its *g* loading, while in the Roid et al. (1993) replication study, the Picture Arrangement subtest ranks ninth among all WISC–III subtests in its *g* loading.

Kamphaus and Platt (1992) report subtest specificities for the WISC–III and indicate that the Picture Arrangement subtest has ample specificity for the combined age groups on the WISC–III. Bracken et al. (1993; see Table 16 in the present volume) and Sattler (1992) indicate that the Picture Arrangement subtest has ample specificity for all ages of the WISC–III.

Relationships Between the Picture Arrangement Subtest and Other Aspects of the WISC–III

The Picture Arrangement subtest correlates .52 with the WISC–III Full Scale IQ, .45 with the Verbal IQ and .49 with the Performance IQ.

The Picture Arrangement subtest displays a range of relatively low correlations with the other WISC–III subtests. It correlates best with Information

(.40) and Vocabulary (.40) on the Verbal Scale and with Block Design (.41) on the Performance Scale. The Picture Arrangement subtest correlates least well with the Digit Span Subtest (.20).

The correlations between the Picture Arrangement subtest with the Information and Vocabulary subtests may reflect the degree to which these three subtests all reflect general intelligence, while the correlation between the Picture Arrangement and Block Design subtests may reflect the visual, visual-organizational and general intellectual factors these latter subtests share. Although Picture Arrangement and Block Design are both included in Wechsler's (1991) Perceptual Organization factor, Sattler (1992) does not include Picture Arrangement in his Perceptual Organization factor because of the high loading of Picture Arrangement on the Verbal Comprehension factor.

The Picture Arrangement and Picture Completion subtests may be viewed in relation to one another as a motion picture and a still photograph. The Picture Arrangement subtest calls upon the child to understand visual information as dynamic and temporally organized. The examinee's task is thus to relate visual details to a larger thematic context similar to grasping the flux of events depicted in a motion picture.

As with the Picture Arrangement subtest, the Picture Completion subtest also requires processing of visual information, but, in contrast to the Picture Arrangement subtest, the examinee's attention is focused on a particular item or event; the examinee need not relate the information in a particular picture to any thematic structure beyond the single picture. By the same token, the examinee cannot use context to assist in solving the task. In addition, the Picture Completion subtest involves substantial visual memory, while the Picture Arrangement subtest relies more on the examinee's current problem-solving strategies.

Thus by comparing the examinee's performance on these two subtests, the examiner may see how well the examinee observes visual details when he or she has only one object with which to deal (Picture Completion) or when she or he must notice visual details embedded in a social context (Picture Arrangement).

The Picture Arrangement subtest may also be viewed in relation to the Comprehension subtest. The Comprehension subtest may be seen as assessing the examinee's ability to understand and to verbally explain social behavior and the rationale of conventional social action. The Picture Arrangement and Comprehension subtests may be compared to provide an indication of the examinee's abilities to verbally state the rules or basis of social behavior on the one hand and to demonstrate knowledge of the sequential organization of social events presented visually on the other.

Interpretation of the Handling of the Picture Arrangement Subtest by the Examinee

The first issue for the examiner to note in terms of the child's handling of the Picture Arrangement subtest is whether the examinee appears to grasp the idea of the subtest from the sample item or whether the examinee continues to have difficulty through the first two or three items to which he or she is exposed.

The child who does have difficulty in understanding the basic idea of the subtest from the sample may be one who is intellectually limited or who may suffer from some deficit in visual processing or in visual sequential ability.

A second aspect of the examinee's handling of the subtest involves which hand the examinee uses in manipulating the Picture Arrangement cards. For the individual who has both hands with neither one being physically impaired, the child may use his or her right or left hand preferentially, may vary on different items, or may use both hands for each item.

If the subtest is viewed as an opportunity for the individual to display adaptive motor behavior (i.e., using her or his eyes and hands in order to solve a given problem), then the examiner may note the degree to which the examinee's strategy is adaptive or not. The most adaptive strategy is likely the one in which the child uses both hands to move the subtest cards. If the examinee's handedness is strongly lateralized, he or she may consistently use his or her preferred hand, which is still an adaptive response. The least adaptive behavior would be where the child varies, sometimes using one hand or the other, or both.

Another issue to be observed is the speed of processing by the child or adolescent, whether the examinee's approach appears reflective or impulsive. This may be assessed in a more accurate way by simply noting the length of time it takes before the child moves the first card out of its initial sequence. It can be assumed that this period of time—anywhere from one second up—reflects the time the child is using to examine the array of cards before acting. Assessment of this may be facilitated by dividing the Completion Time box for each item in half. The examiner can focus on the stopwatch and note, out of the corner of his or her eye, when the child moves the first card out of its original placement. This reflects the examinee's initial processing time. One would assume that more impulsive children will act more quickly while more contemplative children will study the array for a longer period before responding.

Still another aspect of the examinee's handling of the subtest that may be noted is the utilization by the examinee of verbalization or vocalization while attempting to deal with the task. Thus some individuals will spontaneously verbalize the story they believe goes along with, or essentially provides organization for, the sequence of cards they are constructing.

Such behavior suggests that the examinee may not have a well-developed internal language; instead, when dealing with situations requiring motor problem solving, the examinee may be inclined to actually verbalize what she or he is doing in order to guide his or her problem-solving behavior. Such an observation may be valuable to the examiner who may inform the examinee's teachers that the child appears able to utilize verbalization to assist in solving problems that many children might approach silently or by using internal language.

Another aspect of the child's handling of this subtest involves the examinee who, if not interrupted, would continue working on the item beyond the acceptable time limit. In those instances where the examiner feels that he or she can permit the individual to continue working on the item, valuable information may be obtained in terms of whether or not the examinee is able to solve the problem or would ultimately give up. If the child is able to solve the problem by working overtime, this may also be important information to share with school personnel, namely, that the child is able to persist and, if given sufficient time, may be able to perform at a higher level than if he or she must work quickly.

A final aspect of the examinee's handling of the subtest that may be noted is his or her reaction to failure. Partly because of the nature of this subtest, where the examinee may organize the pictures and not be certain whether his or her solution is correct, a child may ask if the response she or he offered was the correct one. This in itself indicates concern on the part of the examinee with obtaining feedback regarding her or his performance, and this in turn suggests concern on the examinee's part with his or her adequacy. However, as noted earlier (see discussion on gradient and non-gradient responses), on those items where the child gives up, or the examiner stops the examinee, the child's reaction—whether frustration, discouragement, or an abrupt display of anger—should be noted.

ARITHMETIC

What the Arithmetic Subtest Measures

Wechsler (1958) notes that "[T]he ability to solve arithmetical problems has long been recognized as a sign of mental alertness... arithmetical reasoning tests correlate highly with global measures of intelligence" (p. 69). Although Wechsler (1958) states that an individual's performance on an arithmetic reasoning task reflects the individual's education and occupational pursuit, this is not relevant in the case of children. He also states that individual test scores may be affected by transient changes in attention or emotional reactions of the subject. And lastly, Wechsler (1958) also mentions that it appears that children who do poorly in arithmetic reasoning also have difficulty with other academic subjects.

According to Wechsler (1991), the Arithmetic subtest is a component of the Freedom from Distractibility factor (with Digit Span).

Sattler (1992) states that the Arithmetic subtest requires the child to answer problems dealing with arithmetical concepts and numerical reasoning that vary in complexity. He notes the subtest taps various skills in that the problems require the child to follow verbal directions, concentrate on particular parts of questions and utilize numerical operations. Hence the child must have knowledge of the basic arithmetical operations, although the emphasis is more on mental computation and concentration than on mathematical knowledge per se.

According to Sattler (1992) the Arithmetic subtest measures numerical reasoning but requires the use of such noncognitive functions as attention and concentration in combination with the cognitive functions of numerical operations. Success on the subtest is influenced by the child's education, interests, shifts in attention and momentary affective reactions. The subtest taps memory and prior learning but also requires the active application of particular skills to new or unique situations.

Sattler (1992) also notes the subtest may involve information processing strategies as well as mathematical skills; these may include rehearsal to retain the information in an item and recognition of an appropriate response. Mathematical skills include comprehension and integration of verbal information presented in a mathematical context, in combination with numerical ability.

Kaufman (1979a, 1990) notes that the Arithmetic subtest reflects the individual's ability for auditory sequencing, the ability to encode information for further cognitive processing, facility with numbers, mental alertness, sequential, linear or left-brain processing, long-term memory and numerical reasoning ability. The subtest's unique ability involves measurement of computational skill.

Kaufman (1979a, 1990) notes that factors which influence performance on the subtest include: attention span, anxiety, concentration, distractibility, the presence of a learning disability (the ACID profile), school learning and working under time pressure.

According to the Fluid-Crystallized categorization of intellectual tasks (Horn, 1985; Kaufman, 1990), the Arithmetic subtest reflects Retrieval (with Information and Digit Span).

According to Bannatyne's (1974) categorization, the Arithmetic subtest is included in the Sequential Ability Category (with Digit Span and Coding).

Glasser and Zimmerman (1967), in discussing the WISC, note that the Arithmetic subtest requires meaningful manipulation of complex thought patterns, and reflects the child's ability to translate verbal into mathematical problems and to utilize abstract concepts of number and numerical operations. These processes reflect the child's cognitive development, but since the subtest also involves attention and concentration which are essentially noncognitive functions while numerical operations are cognitive, the subtest provides an indication of how the child relates cognitive and noncognitive factors in thinking and performance.

The present author views the Arithmetic subtest as measuring a number of different functions at different points in the subtest. The first five items utilize concrete visual stimuli to assess the child's basic ability to count and subtract objects. Thus, at this initial level, the task appears to assess some fundamental physical and sensory integrities on the part of the examinee in terms of his or her ability to coordinate pointing and counting. The early items also provide an indication of the examinee's basic grasp of numbers as associated with objects.

At item 6, the items shift from using concrete props and require the examinee to display internal and increasingly complex cognitive processing. First, the child is required to attend to a sequential auditory presentation, to hold the information in short-term memory, and then to abstract the essential mathematical problem from the verbal statement. The examinee must then recall from her or his own long-term memory the appropriate arithmetic operations, and once retrieved from long-term memory, the examinee must apply those operations or rules to the data held in consciousness.

At item 19, the examinee is required to read a series of items aloud, which may reduce the load on auditory short-term memory, but if the child or adolescent has any difficulty with reading, this part of the subtest may involve increased anxiety for the individual which may then interfere with his or her handling of the essential mathematical task.

Thus, depending on the examinee's age, the ability to perform adequately on the Arithmetic subtest requires the child to be able to focus on and then process the visual and/or auditory information presented, to determine the arithmetic problem involved, to select the indicated operation from long-term memory and apply it correctly, and thus to be resistant to either internal or external sources of distraction during a chain of interconnected cognitive activities.

In terms of what the Arithmetic subtest measures, during the subtest administration, the examiner may periodically recall that this subtest is providing a sample of the examinee's Verbal IQ, freedom from distractibility

(Wechsler, 1991), sequential ability and acquired knowledge (Bannatyne, 1974), retrieval ability (Horn, 1985; Kaufman, 1990), and that the subtest is one component of the ACID profile (Ackerman et al., 1976, 1977).

Research Pertaining to the Arithmetic Subtest

A number of research studies using the WISC–R with learning disabled (e.g., Clarizio & Bernard, 1981; Fischer et al., 1985; Henry & Wittman, 1981), emotionally or behaviorally disturbed (e.g., Hale & Landino, 1981; Reilly et al., 1985), and mentally retarded (e.g., Henry & Wittman, 1981; Kaufman & Van Hagen, 1977) children have reported the Arithmetic subtest to be one of the most difficult for these populations.

In their consensus rankings of subtest means for the 10 regular WISC–R subtests across a number of investigations, Kaufman et al. (1990) report that the Arithmetic subtest ranks ninth among samples of learning disabled children and eighth for emotionally or behaviorally disturbed and for mentally retarded children.

The Arithmetic subtest is one of the three subtests in the WISC–R Freedom from Distractibility factor (with Digit Span and Coding). There has been extensive research over the years exploring this factor and the role of the three subtests within it (Kaufman et al., 1990). Woodcock (1990) presented an explanation of the abilities assessed by the Freedom from Distractibility factor and, using a multiple-instrument factor analysis, concluded that Arithmetic was a measure of quantitative abilities.

Kaufman et al. (1990) review a number of studies investigating the Freedom from Distractibility factor and report that in analyses of the WISC–R standardization data, a distractibility factor was obtained for each age group in the sample (Kaufman, 1975). Arithmetic loaded on this factor at all ages in the sample. However, Kaufman et al. (1990) note that in [only] 21 of the 31 studies they review, meaningful distractibility factors emerge, and in most of the studies, the distractibility factor consisted primarily of two or all three of the subtests of Arithmetic, Digit Span, and Coding.

Since the Arithmetic subtest is one of the four subtests on the ACID profile, the Arithmetic subtest has also been investigated in studies of the ACID profile (e.g., Ackerman, Dykman & Peters, 1971; Sandoval, Sassenrath & Penaloza, 1988). These investigations have typically found that Arithmetic emerges consistently as part of a distractibility factor, and in the WISC–III, Wechsler (1991) reports loadings of Arithmetic on a Freedom from Distractibility factor (involving only the Arithmetic and Digit Span subtests) across the four age groupings that were factor analyzed. However, Sattler (1992), in his factor analysis of the WISC–III standardization data, did not find a

Freedom from Distractibility factor, and instead found Arithmetic to load on the Verbal Comprehension factor.

Overall, research regarding the Arithmetic subtest has noted that it is among the most difficult on the Wechsler scales for learning disabled, emotionally disturbed, and mentally retarded children. Much research has suggested that the subtest is a component of a Freedom from Distractibility factor, and it has also frequently been found as part of a group of subtests, the ACID subtests, on which learning disabled individuals often perform more poorly than they do on the remaining Wechsler subtests.

Information Processing Aspects of the Arithmetic Subtest

For the Arithmetic subtest, input to the child is an auditory verbal question in which is embedded an arithmetic or numerical problem. For the first five items, the examinee also has concrete visual information presented. For each of the last six items, the child or adolescent is required to read the problem aloud. Internal cognitive operations involve short-term recall, analysis of visual, auditory linguistic or printed information into verbal and mathematical components, selection and retrieval from long-term memory of an appropriate mathematical cognitive operation, and application of this operation or rule to the visual data or the data held in consciousness. Output on the subtest is in the form of a combined verbal numerical and motor response, or a verbal numerical response.

Observation of the examinee during the first four items of this subtest entails noting the individual's visual focusing and the accuracy of coordination of the examinee's verbal and motor behavior. Observation of the child during items from 6 to 18 involves noting the adequacy or inadequacy of the examinee's focused attention and the degree to which the individual appears distracted by internal or other external stimuli, as well as the nature of the examinee's linguistic processing of the items presented. On items 19 and beyond, observation should include the adequacy of the examinee's reading ability and the degree to which inefficiency in reading interferes with the child's ability to process the arithmetic problems presented.

Information processing deficits that might be reflected in performance on the Arithmetic subtest would include difficulties in visual processing and visual motor functioning as well as numerical reasoning on the first five items; difficulties with attention, concentration, and receptive or expressive linguistic performance on items 6 to 18; and difficulties with reading competence on items 19 to 24.

Statistical Characteristics of the Arithmetic Subtest

The Arithmetic subtest has an average split-half reliability coefficient across all ages of the WISC–III of .78 with reliability coefficients that range from .71 to .82 across the 11 age groups. The Arithmetic subtest has an average test-retest stability coefficient for all ages of .74.

According to Sattler's (1992) categorization, which groups subtests into good, fair, and poor measures of *g,* the Arithmetic subtest is a good measure of *g.* In the original WISC–III sample, the Arithmetic subtest ranks fifth among all WISC–III subtests in its *g* loading, while in the Roid et al. (1993) replication study, the Arithmetic subtest ties with the Block Design subtest for the fourth rank among all WISC–III subtests in loading on *g.*

Kamphaus and Platt (1992) report subtest specificities for the WISC–III and indicate that the Arithmetic subtest has adequate specificity for the combined age groups on the WISC–III. Bracken et al. (1993; see Table 16 in the present volume) and Sattler (1992) indicate that the Arithmetic subtest has ample specificity for ages 6–7, 10, 13, and 15; adequate specificity for age 16; and inadequate specificity for ages 8–9, 11–12, and 14.

Relationships Between the Arithmetic Subtest and Other Aspects of the WISC-III

The Arithmetic subtest correlates .65 with the WISC–III Full Scale IQ, .62 with the Verbal IQ and .54 with the Performance IQ.

The Arithmetic subtest correlates best with Information (.57) on the Verbal Scale and with Block Design (.52) on the Performance Scale. The Arithmetic subtest correlates .43 with the Digit Span subtest with these two subtests comprising the Freedom from Distractibility factor. The Arithmetic subtest correlates least well with the Mazes subtest (.22).

The correlation between the Arithmetic and Information subtests may reflect the fact that these subtests are both good measures of *g,* both involve auditory verbal processing, and both reflect the examinee's motivation to acquire knowledge in school. The correlation between Arithmetic and Block Design may reflect the spatial and visual spatial aspects involved in both of these tasks.

From a clinical standpoint, the Arithmetic Subtest may be seen in relation to the Digit Span subtest. Because of the seeming sensitivity of the Arithmetic subtest to distraction or to the inability to concentrate on material that may be readily lost from consciousness, the Arithmetic subtest is typically seen in relation to the Digit Span subtest. These two subtests both may be considered as reflecting the child's ability to focus her or his attention on sequentially organized verbal numerical information; stated otherwise, both subtests require that the examinee be free from internal or external distractions.

From the perspective that both subtests reflect the examinee's ability to attend, or to be free of the interfering effects of distraction, Wechsler (1991) has categorized these two subtests on the Freedom from Distractibility factor. However, in order to interpret the two subtests as reflecting a unitary factor, they must not be significantly different from one another. If they are, they should not be viewed as reflecting a unitary factor but should be viewed separately, although they can be interpreted in relation to one another.

To determine whether these two subtests are significantly different from one another, Table B.4. Wechsler (1991, p. 265) indicates that a difference of 3.59 is significant at the .05 level. Hence if the Arithmetic and Digit Span scaled scores differ by as much as 4 units (3 or more if the examiner wishes to use a conservative criterion), the examiner would conclude that they do not reflect a unitary factor and the two subtests should be interpreted separately.

When viewed separately, however, the Arithmetic and Digit Span subtests may be seen as existing on a gradient of passive-active attention and concentration. Interpreted from this perspective, the Arithmetic subtest requires a more active mode of information processing; the examinee must not only attend to and temporarily store but also actively operate on the information held in consciousness, while the Digit Span subtest, particularly Digits Forward, requires only that the examinee passively receive and then repeat the information presented.

From this viewpoint, a high Arithmetic and low Digit Span score suggests that the child has difficulty with relaxed attention, but when he or she is more actively concentrating, the examinee can perform at a higher level. If the examinee displays a higher Digit Span and lower Arithmetic subtest score, this suggests that the individual is able to respond to a simple task, where only passive attention and repetition is required, but when required to actively concentrate and carry out more complex cognitive processing, the examinee performs less adequately.

Interpretation of the Handling of the Arithmetic Subtest by the Examinee

The first issue to note in terms of the examinee's handling of the Arithmetic subtest depends on the child's age. For the examinee who begins with item 1, the examiner should note which hand the child uses and the adequacy of the examinee's motor coordination in pointing at the stimuli to be counted.

For all children and all items, the next issue to be noted is the length of time it takes for the individual to generate a response to each item. This can be facilitated by dividing the Completion Time column on the test form in half. The examiner can record how long it takes for the examinee to start responding to the left of the dividing line, and the child or adolescent's final response to the right of the line. Timing the examinee's response in this way provides the examiner with information regarding how long it took the child to generate a response or, stated otherwise, whether the examinee responded impulsively or reflectively to the Arithmetic subtest items.

Second, the examiner should note and record when the child or adolescent asks to have an item repeated. The examinee's asking to have an item repeated indicates that he or she did not hear the item, was uncertain of the item content, or is requesting that the item be repeated to allow more time for approaching a solution to the problem. Apart from the child's specific score on the Arithmetic subtest, the individual's need to have one or several items of the subtest repeated is an indication of his or her varying attention or concentration during the task, as well as the fact that the examinee is sufficiently capable of self-assertion to request that the item be repeated.

A next issue for the examiner to consider in the child's handling of the Arithmetic subtest involves the strategies the examinee uses to carry out the arithmetic calculations themselves. Ordinarily, calculation on the Arithmetic subtest beyond the first five items is done internally. However, at least some children may count items on their fingers, count out loud, or try to write numerical symbols on the examiner's desk. Any of these strategies suggest that the examinee needs an externalized or concrete referent and that the child does not have a well-internalized or automatized symbol system to use in dealing with simple arithmetic tasks.

In considering the examinee's handling of the Arithmetic subtest, the subtest may be conceived of as involving a set of hierarchically organized skills (see discussion on "Models in Psychology"). If it is assumed that the apex of the hierarchy represents successful performance by the child on a given item, then failure on that item may be due to any of several possible errors in the levels of the examinee's functioning below the apex (e.g., lack of attention or concentration, or lack of mathematical knowledge).

In order to determine at what level of such a hierarchy the child has difficulty, the examiner may proceed down the hierarchy by having the examinee repeat an item to determine if the child is able to recall the problem, or by presenting the mathematical task (e.g., division) not embedded in a linguistic problem to determine if the examinee can carry out the relevant arithmetic operation when he or she does not have to abstract the arithmetic problem from a linguistic statement.

BLOCK DESIGN

What the Block Design Subtest Measures

Wechsler (1958) notes that the Block Design subtest was originated by Kohs, who viewed it as a comprehensive measure of nonverbal intelligence. Wechsler (1958) notes "[T]he Block Design is not only an excellent test of general intelligence, but one that lends itself admirably to qualitative analysis. One can learn much about the subject by watching 'how' he takes to the task set him" (p. 79).

Wechsler (1958) notes that important information may be obtained by observing whether the examinee follows the design pattern as a whole or breaks it up into its component parts. Similarly, one may also note differences in attitude and emotional reaction on the part of the individual, and it is possible to distinguish the impulsive person from the deliberate and careful type, or the subject who gives up easily from the one who persists and keeps on working even after the time is up.

According to Wechsler (1991), the Block Design subtest is a component of the Perceptual Organization factor (with Picture Completion, Picture Arrangement and Object Assembly).

Sattler (1992) states that the Block Design subtest requires the child to perceive and analyze forms by breaking down a whole design into its component parts and then assembling the components into an image identical to the original design, a process referred to as analysis and synthesis. In order to succeed at the task, the child must utilize visual organization and visual-motor coordination as well as logic and reasoning applied to problems involving spatial relationships. Hence, Block Design may be considered to be a nonverbal concept formation task requiring perceptual organization, spatial visualization and abstract conceptualization. It can also be viewed as a constructional task involving spatial relations and the separation of figure and ground.

Kaufman (1979a, 1990) notes that the Block Design subtest reflects the individual's ability to reproduce models, his or her simultaneous, holistic or right-brain processing, the individual's ability for synthesis, trial-and-error learning and visual perception/processing of abstract stimuli. The subtest's unique ability involves measurement of the analysis of a whole into component parts, nonverbal concept formation, and spatial visualization.

Kaufman (1979a, 1990) notes that factors which influence performance on the subtest include: cognitive style (field independence versus field dependence), visual-perceptual problems, and the ability to work under time pressure.

According to the Fluid-Crystallized categorization of intellectual tasks (Horn, 1985; Kaufman, 1990), the Block Design subtest reflects Fluid Intelligence (with Picture Completion, Picture Arrangement, Object Assembly, Similarities and Digit Span).

According to Bannatyne's (1974) categorization, the Block Design subtest is included in the Spatial Ability Category (with Picture Completion and Object Assembly).

Glasser and Zimmerman (1967), in discussing the WISC, note that the Block Design subtest involves visual perception, analysis, synthesis, and reproduction of abstract designs. Additionally, the subtest requires that the individual apply logic and reasoning to spatial relationships. Further, non-verbal concept formation involving implicit verbal manipulation as well as visual-motor coordination are also measured by the subtest.

The present author views the Block Design subtest as involving a variety of aspects depending on the age of the child. For the young examinee, the subtest includes aspects of visual observation and matching to the model demonstrated by the examiner; manipulation of tangible three-dimensional objects; and the integration of various visual processes with the construction of structures that have form (two by two or three by three block configurations) and design (the designs to be reproduced) characteristics.

The Block Design task thus involves various kinds of finger dexterity or fine motor coordination as well as the examinee's ability to reproduce what she or he observes in an external visual model (either the examiner's actual block model on designs #1 to 3 or the picture design shown to the examinee on designs #4 to 12) by manipulating tangible materials in the process.

Hence the Block Design subtest measures both visual receptive as well as motor constructive abilities on the part of the examinee. Since the content of the subtest involves abstract materials, the task is not likely to stimulate personal associations that might interfere with the examinee's functioning.

Insofar as the task involves certain principles that can be recognized or learned on the initial designs and then applied on the later ones (e.g., the idea that the half-red and the half-white side can be used to create angles and may be used to create a line), the entire subtest can be viewed as a kind of learning experiment, to see the degree to which the child can abstract principles from his or her own activity and then apply these principles to a range of increasingly complex problem situations.

While there are many abilities involved in this task, the present author feels that critical ones involve the child's ability to visually analyze and synthesize or re-integrate the stimulus material. This means that the stimulus presented (to the examinee over age eight) is a pictorial one that is integrated into a total pattern. For the younger examinee and for designs #3, 4, and 5, a variety of prompts or cues are presented in the examiner's demonstration or in the additional block lines on the item. The examinee's task is thus one in which she or he must visually examine the stimulus presented and analyze or fragment the total pattern into its parts, determine the correct components and each component's correct spatial orientation, then integrate or synthesize the several individual blocks, correctly oriented, to reproduce the pictured design.

Although the present author believes that this task is fundamentally a visual analytic one, mediated predominantly by the right cerebral hemisphere with a left cerebral hemispheric contribution, there do appear to be two basic approaches to the subtest. One of these appears to be a holistic, Gestalt-oriented approach in which the examinee appears to move rapidly and without much reflection towards the solution, as though from a grasp of the overall pattern in which the parts fit readily, and the solution is accomplished quickly and efficiently.

The other approach is one in which the child appears to more carefully examine the parts of the design, seemingly visually segmenting the overall pattern into its components, and checking each block as to its correct orientation, then placing it in the block construction being made with this latter approach seemingly utilizing a part-focused and analytic strategy.

The subtest may thus be viewed as assessing the examinee's natural cognitive style, whether the individual is inclined to view an entire problem and readily see the way components fit within the whole; or whether the child tends to focus on parts of a problem and gradually integrate these to yield an overall solution. The subtest can also offer information regarding the examinee's ability to make the shift from one strategy to the other as required by the task being dealt with.

In terms of what the Block Design subtest measures, during the administration of this subtest, the examiner may periodically recall that this subtest provides a sample of the examinee's Performance IQ, perceptual organization (Wechsler, 1991), spatial ability (Bannatyne, 1974), and fluid intelligence (Horn, 1985; Kaufman, 1990).

Research Pertaining to the Block Design Subtest

A number of research studies using the WISC–R with learning disabled (e.g., Anderson et al., 1976; Fischer et al., 1985; Vance, Blaha, Wallbrown & Engin, 1975), emotionally or behaviorally disturbed (e.g., Henry & Wittman, 1981; Vance & Fuller, 1983), and mentally retarded (e.g., Clarizio & Bernard, 1981; Henry & Wittman, 1981) children have reported the Block Design subtest to be of variable difficulty for these samples, but typically to fall in the moderately difficult range for these populations.

In their consensus rankings of subtest means for the 10 regular WISC–R subtests across a number of studies, Kaufman et al. (1990) report that the Block Design subtest ranks fifth for learning disabled and mentally retarded children and ranks fourth for emotionally or behaviorally disturbed children.

Grote and Salmon (1986), using the Block Design subtest of the WAIS–R with 69 right-handed adults, noted the amount of time each subject's hand was in contact with the blocks during each reproduction attempt. It was observed that subjects used their right hands with greater frequency only on tasks of low and moderate spatial complexity. The authors suggest that the degree of usage of the hand varies as a function of the spatial complexity of the task.

Spelberg (1987) reports an investigation of whether the choice of an analytic or a synthetic strategy for solving Block Design items depends on chronological age, intelligence or Block Design total score. Using an experimental version of the Block Design subtest in the Netherlands, Spelberg (1987) found that all subjects tended to use the analytic strategy, which suggested that the choice of problem-solving approach may depend on stimulus characteristics rather than on individual processing preference.

Whipple et al. (1988) reported the finding that among sons of men who were alcoholic and had at least one first- or second-degree relative who was alcoholic, the sons displayed an atypical neurocognitive profile consisting of amplitude reduction on an event-related potential during a complex visual discrimination task, and significantly lower scores on the Object Assembly, Block Design and Picture Completion subtests of the WISC–R.

Although not involving a research investigation, Killian, Campbell, and Diston (1986) note that a game called Trac 4 is quite similar to the Block Design subtest, and exposure to this game could conceivably artificially inflate an examinee's performance on the Block Design subtest. Hence, significant elevations on this subtest might suggest the need for inquiry into the examinee's past experience with certain kinds of toys.

Overall, research involving the Block Design subtest suggests that it is of variable difficulty for learning disabled, emotionally or behaviorally disturbed, and mentally retarded children. There is some suggestion that the subtest reflects right-hemisphere functioning and that problem-solving approaches to the task may reflect the nature of the task itself rather than characteristics of the examinee.

Information Processing Aspects of the Block Design Subtest

For the Block Design subtest, input to the examinee is in the form of three-dimensional multicolored blocks, three-dimensional models or pictured designs, and verbal instructions and modeling demonstrations to indicate that the child's task is to reproduce modeled or pictured block designs. Cognitive operations for the examinee involve visual analytic and synthetic processing, and logical reasoning applied to tangible materials combined with visual-motor integration and coordination. Output is in the form of block constructions reproducing modeled or pictured designs.

Observation of the child or adolescent during this subtest involves noting the examinee's visual inspection strategies, the examinee's reflective or impulsive response tempo, the nature of the child's logical operations in dealing with the task (e.g., whether the individual uses a systematic or random trial-and-error approach) and the nature of the examinee's fine motor coordinated behavior (e.g., whether he or she displays any fine motor incoordination, clumsiness or tremor). The examiner should note the dexterity the examinee displays in handling the blocks, whether the child picks the blocks up or slides them, and whether the examinee uses his or her dominant hand, non-dominant hand, uses both hands or shifts from item to item.

The examiner should also note indications of possible visual perceptual or visual organizational problems in the examinee. Commonly observed indications of such difficulties include rotation of individual blocks within an overall design, rotation of an entire design 45, 90 or even 180 degrees from the direction in which the design is presented to the examinee, or various kinds of fragmentation of the design such that the examinee loses the concept of figure and ground in her or his reproduction of the design.

Information processing deficits that might be reflected in performance on the Block Design subtest would include difficulties in visual acuity or perception, visual analysis, difficulties in spatial orientation, or difficulties in visual motor integration and coordination.

Statistical Characteristics of the Block Design Subtest

The Block Design subtest has an average split-half reliability coefficient across all ages of the WISC–III of .87 with reliability coefficients that range from .77 to .92 across the 11 age groups. The Block Design subtest has an average test-retest stability coefficient for all ages of .77.

According to Sattler's (1992) categorization, which groups subtests into good, fair, and poor measures of *g*, the Block Design subtest is a good measure of *g*. In the original WISC–III sample, the Block Design subtest ranks fourth among all WISC–III subtests in its *g* loading, while in the Roid et al. (1993) replication study, the Block Design subtest is tied with the Arithmetic subtest for fourth among all WISC–III subtests in its *g* loading.

Kamphaus and Platt (1992) report subtest specificities for the WISC–III and indicate that the Block Design subtest has ample specificity for the combined age groups on the WISC–III. Bracken et al. (1993; see Table 16 in the present volume) and Sattler (1992) indicate that the Block Design subtest has ample specificity for all ages of the WISC–III.

Relationships Between the Block Design Subtest and Other Aspects of the WISC–III

The Block Design subtest correlates .66 with the WISC–III Full Scale IQ, .57 with the Verbal IQ and .65 with the Performance IQ.

The Block Design subtest correlates best with Arithmetic (.52) on the Verbal Scale and with Object Assembly (.61) and Picture Completion (.52) on the Performance Scale. The Block Design subtest correlates least well with the Coding subtest (.27).

The correlation between the Block Design and Arithmetic subtests may reflect the degree to which both of these subtests reflect general intelligence or involve some spatial reasoning abilities. The correlation between the Block Design and Object Assembly subtests may reflect the visual, spatial and visual analytic and synthetic factors both of these subtests share as well as confirming the inclusion of both subtests on the Perceptual Organization factor.

From a clinical standpoint, the Block Design subtest may be viewed in relation to the Similarities subtest and to the Object Assembly subtest. If the Block Design subtest is viewed in relation to the Similarities subtest, the examinee's performance on the Block Design subtest may be seen as a measure of his or her capacity for abstract, logical reasoning when she or he is dealing with tangible materials. On the other hand, his or her performance on the Similarities subtest may be viewed as indicative of the child's ability for abstract or categorical reasoning and logic when the child is dealing with verbal or linguistic stimuli.

In addition, the Block Design subtest, as a measure of primarily visual analytic abilities, may be seen in relation to the Object Assembly subtest, which may be viewed as primarily a measure of visual synthetic or integrative abilities. Examination of the individual's performance on these two subtests can indicate whether the examinee is more capable of visual analytic processes (Block Design) or visual synthetic processes (Object Assembly).

Similarly, the Block Design subtest involves processing without much reliance on memory abilities, while the Object Assembly subtest may require more visual memory ability on the part of the child, and hence the examinee's performances on these two subtests can be viewed from the perspective of their relative reliance on, or utilization of, visual memory.

Interpretation of the Handling of the Block Design Subtest by the Examinee

One of the major aspects of this subtest as compared to other subtests is that the Block Design task requires the manipulation of objects; the objects are abstract or unfamiliar rather than recognizable; the items are all similar except that the difficulty of the items generally increases sequentially; and the number of elements with which the examinee must deal, or the overall dimensions of the task, increases at item #10.

If the examinee is under age eight, the examiner can observe the way in which the child deals with the models demonstrated by the examiner. Some children will wait and watch carefully while the example is constructed by the examiner; other examinees will rush ahead as though they are eager to perform the task themselves. Observation of the child or adolescent's behavior in this situation may provide clues for the examiner as to whether the examinee has the necessary capacity to delay responding and to thus learn from a model or whether the child is too impulsive to benefit from such an intervention strategy.

Consistent with the gradient model discussed earlier, the Block Design task, with the same materials but with increasingly complicated items, permits the examiner to observe the child's reaction to increased pressure (particularly at design #10 when the number of blocks increases from four to nine).

When item #10 is reached, some examinees will exclaim that they cannot do the item as soon as the item is exposed, but then proceed to try, with this pattern suggesting a child who may be uncertain about his or her own adequacy or sense of competence.

Another possible pattern involves the examinee beginning a particular item, then giving up or shaking her or his head to indicate that he or she cannot succeed. This approach also provides information about the child's tendency to become overwhelmed by problem situations or instead to apply her or his effort when faced by a challenging task.

The particular methods of object manipulation the examinee uses should also be noted. These include whether the child consistently uses his or her preferred hand, shifts from using one hand to the other, or tends to use both hands simultaneously. The nature of the examinee's grip of the blocks, whether smoothly coordinated or awkward, provides some indication of the examinee's fine motor control and/or neurological maturity. Additionally, because the Block Design task involves the placement of light plastic blocks in close juxtaposition to one another, tremors of the examinee's fingers, mild incoordination and the carelessness or precision of the child's placement of blocks may also be noted.

Important information can also be obtained regarding the child's tolerance for frustration, or precisely how long the individual will work at a problem she or he seems unable to solve. Aside from the length of time the child is willing to work on an item, changes in the examinee's strategy may be noted. For example, a child may deal with the early subtest designs with an overall or Gestalt approach, and when the examinee encounters the more difficult items, he or she may shift to a more focused analytical strategy. The examiner can observe whether or at what point this shift occurs and how the child reacts to the increased stress this represents.

One approach that is often observed is when a child or adolescent concludes that one block face is unsatisfactory, puts that block down and picks up another block, or identifies a block in the wrong spatial rotation and continues to rotate the block but continually misses the correct rotation. These responses suggest that under stress conditions, such an examinee cannot make the most logical or adaptive response and instead reveals an inefficiency in his or her problem-solving efforts.

As on other subtests, it is important to note the sequence of the child's successes and failures on this subtest. An uneven pattern of success and failure may reflect anxiety, impulsivity or carelessness, which may cause the examinee to make simple errors, such as one block incorrectly placed that the examinee does not notice.

Alternatively, the child may have such difficulty with the kind of reasoning required by this task that he or she can only succeed at several of the designs by working at them for longer than the time limit. However, this performance provides information regarding the examinee's ability to persist, and, given this kind of approach, the examiner might recommend that in school this child be given support and more time than usual to complete assigned tasks.

Another possible interpretation of an uneven pattern of success and failure on the subtest would be that the child has difficulty in abstracting principles from experience and then using them consistently to deal with similar but not identical problem situations. Hence, although an examinee may correctly solve some of the earlier subtest items, he or she may in fact be using a trial-and-error approach while failing to grasp the principles involved in working with the blocks, and, thus on later designs, she or he may be unable to succeed.

The examinee's reaction to his or her own performance should of course also be noted. Some children or adolescents will work for the entire time limit in a disorganized fashion without ever seeming to develop a strategy for processing the task, while other examinees will more systematically attempt to deal with even designs they may fail. Finally, some individuals will display a moderate reaction to failure, while others may respond with an undercontrolled, non-gradient expression of frustration and anger.

VOCABULARY

What the Vocabulary Subtest Measures

Wechsler (1958) notes that "[T]he size of a man's vocabulary is not only an index of his schooling, but also an excellent measure of his general intelligence. Its excellence as a test of intelligence may stem from the fact that the number of words a man knows is at once a measure of his learning ability, his fund of verbal information and of the general range of his ideas" (p. 84).

Wechsler (1958) also notes that a test calling for the definition of words is often of value because of its qualitative aspects. Thus the specific way in which an individual defines a word provides some understanding of the person's cultural background. Further, the semantic character of the word definition offered by an individual may provide some insight into that person's thought processes.

According to Wechsler (1991), the Vocabulary subtest is a component of the Verbal Comprehension factor (with Information, Similarities and Comprehension).

Sattler (1992) states that the Vocabulary subtest requires the child to listen as the examiner reads words aloud to her or him and then to define the words. The subtest is a test of word knowledge, and it may tap cognition-related factors, including the child's learning ability, fund of information, richness of ideas, memory, concept formation, and language development; these factors may be related to his or her experience and educational environment.

Sattler (1992) further notes that since the number of words known by a child correlates with her or his ability to learn and accumulate information, the subtest provides an excellent estimate of the child's intellectual ability.

Kaufman (1979a, 1990) notes that the Vocabulary subtest reflects the individual's fund of information, her or his ability to handle abstract verbal concepts, the individual's long-term memory and his or her learning ability. The subtest's unique ability involves measurement of the individual's language development and her or his word knowledge.

Kaufman (1979a, 1990) notes that factors which influence performance on the subtest include: cultural opportunities, a foreign language background in the individual, the individual's intellectual curiosity and striving, his or her interests, outside reading and reading ability, richness of the individual's early environment, and her or his school learning.

According to the Fluid-Crystallized categorization of intellectual tasks (Horn, 1985; Kaufman, 1990), the Vocabulary subtest reflects Crystallized Intelligence (with Information, Comprehension and Similarities).

According to Bannatyne's (1974) categorization, the Vocabulary subtest is included in the Verbal Conceptualization Category (with Comprehension and Similarities) and in the Acquired Knowledge Category (with Information and Arithmetic).

Glasser and Zimmerman (1967), in discussing the WISC, note that the Vocabulary subtest is probably the best single measure of general intellectual level and that it provides an indication of the examinee's learning ability, fund of information, richness of ideas, kind and quality of language, degree of abstract thinking, and character of thought processes.

According to Glasser and Zimmerman (1967), the Vocabulary subtest also reflects an examinee's level of education and his or her environmental background. The subtest is of particular value because of the qualitative aspects that may be observed in different examinee's unique definitions of the same item, which may vary in abstractness, detail or degree of sophistication.

Glasser and Zimmerman (1967) note that, from a clinical point of view, the most important feature of verbal definitions is the insight they can provide into the nature of the child's thought processes, particularly among those children who display impaired reality testing.

The present author feels that the Vocabulary subtest is one of the most purely verbal of all the subtests on the WISC–III, and since language is one of the most fundamental characteristics of human beings, this subtest reflects that most uniquely human ability of individuals to understand and to express themselves in words. Hence, the subtest provides a broad measuring system for assessing the competency the examinee displays in using language in his or her adaptation.

The Vocabulary subtest provides information regarding the degree to which the child has utilized her or his auditory apparatus to receive linguistic information; the extent to which the examinee has retained that information in meaningful form; and the degree to which the individual is able and/or willing to provide adequate and accurate alternative meanings for the words on the subtest. Hence the subtest provides an indication of the degree to which the examinee is able and willing to participate in an interpersonal community insofar as such participation will involve use of a verbal or linguistic code for communication.

The Vocabulary subtest may also be seen as an index of the number of verbalizable concepts the examinee has available. Assuming that at least some forms of psychotherapy involve either the child's development of self-instructions, relabelling of experience, or attaching verbal labels to particular experience, the Vocabulary subtest can provide an indication of the pool of accurate, consensually valid verbal labels the examinee has available to utilize in this task. Hence, the Vocabulary subtest can provide some indication of the feasibility of a more verbally oriented psychological treatment approach for the child being evaluated.

Research Pertaining to the Vocabulary Subtest

A number of research investigations using the WISC–R with various learning disabled (e.g., Anderson et al., 1976; Fischer et al., 1985; Mishra, 1984) and emotionally or behaviorally disturbed (e.g., Hale & Landino, 1981; Henry & Wittman, 1981; Vance & Fuller, 1983) children have found the Vocabulary subtest to be of moderate difficulty for these populations. Studies of mentally retarded children with the WISC–R (e.g., Clarizio & Bernard, 1981; Kaufman & Van Hagen, 1977) have found the Vocabulary subtest to be among the most difficult for this population.

In their consensus rankings of subtest means for the 10 regular WISC–R subtests across a number of investigations, Kaufman et al. (1990) report that the Vocabulary subtest ranks seventh for learning disabled and emotionally or behaviorally disturbed children, while the subtest ranks tenth for mentally retarded children.

A number of research studies on the administration and scoring of the Wechsler scales (e.g., Slate & Chick, 1989; Slate & Jones, 1990) have reported that scoring errors occur quite frequently on the Vocabulary subtest, suggesting that examiners should use extra caution when scoring this subtest.

A study by Sandler, Watson, and Levine (1992) investigated the characteristics of 37 females attending clinics for routine health care. These authors found three groups among their sample: those who were sexually active and used contraception reliably; those who were sexually active but did not use contraception reliably; and those who were not sexually active. Those who were sexually active and using contraception reliably had higher WISC–R Vocabulary scores than those females who were sexually active but not using contraception reliably.

Rescorla, Parker, and Stolley (1991) compared 83 homeless children (aged 6–12 years) with 45 inner-city domiciled children (aged 6–12 years) on measures of intellectual ability, academic achievement, and emotional/ behavioral adjustment. These authors found that homeless 6–12-year-olds scored significantly lower on the WISC–R Vocabulary subtest than did the comparison group.

Thus, research investigations have demonstrated that the Vocabulary subtest is of moderate difficulty for learning disabled and emotionally disturbed individuals, while it is among the most difficult for mentally retarded children. In addition, the Vocabulary subtest appears to be among the Wechsler subtests which are more difficult to score reliably.

Information Processing Aspects of the Vocabulary Subtest

Input on the Vocabulary subtest involves auditory input of the subtest items as they are stated by the examiner. In terms of the instructions themselves, with the WISC–R it was not infrequent that, when asked to tell what each word meant, the child would respond by stating what the word made the examinee think of. The Vocabulary words on the WISC–III are presented in a way that makes the task of defining the stimulus words more readily understandable to the examinee. Internal cognitive operations for the child involve analysis of the auditory input, search of the examinee's memory store to identify the spoken word, and then formulation of an appropriate explanation or definition of the target word that has been presented. Output on the subtest is in the form of a verbal response which provides an explanation or definition of the original stimulus word.

Observation of the child or adolescent during this subtest involves noting the examinee's auditory and visual orientation, the length of time the child takes to formulate a response and the linguistic structure of the examinee's response as well as the adequacy of the individual's pronunciation.

Information processing deficits that may be reflected in performance on the Vocabulary subtest would be in various aspects of language performance, either in auditory receptive or perceptive functions as well as in verbal expressive functions.

Statistical Characteristics of the Vocabulary Subtest

The Vocabulary subtest has an average split-half reliability coefficient across all ages of the WISC–III of .87 with reliability coefficients that range from .79 to .91 across the 11 age groups. The Vocabulary subtest has an average test-retest stability coefficient for all ages of .89.

According to Sattler's (1992) categorization, which groups subtests into good, fair, and poor measures of *g*, the Vocabulary subtest is a good measure of *g*. In the original WISC–III sample as well as in the Roid et al. (1993) replication study, the Vocabulary subtest ranks first in its *g* loading.

Kamphaus and Platt (1992) report subtest specificities for the WISC-III and indicate the Vocabulary subtest has inadequate specificity for the combined age groups on the WISC-III. Bracken et al. (1993; see Table 16 in the present volume) and Sattler (1992) indicate that the Vocabulary subtest has ample specificity for ages 6 and 11, adequate specificity for ages 7–8 and 12–16, and inadequate specificity for ages 9–10.

Relationships Between the Vocabulary Subtest and Other Aspects of the WISC-III

The Vocabulary subtest correlates .74 with the WISC-III Full Scale IQ, .78 with the Verbal IQ and .56 with the Performance IQ.

The Vocabulary subtest correlates best with Information (.70) on the Verbal Scale and with Block Design (.46) on the Performance Scale. The Vocabulary subtest correlates least well with the Mazes subtest (.17).

The correlation between the Vocabulary and Information subtests may reflect the high loading on *g* shared by both of these subtests, and their correlation may also reflect their loading on the Verbal Comprehension factor of which both are components.

From a clinical standpoint, the Vocabulary subtest may be considered with the Information subtest, as both involve the examinee's long-term retention of verbally coded material; both seem to be affected by the richness of the child's early environment, by the examinee's reading activities, and by his or her schooling. Hence it is assumed that an examinee should have equal or nearly equal scale scores on the Vocabulary and Information subtests. However, one may view the Information subtest as reflecting the child's assimilated knowledge, while the Vocabulary subtest reflects the examinee's ability to use language for the purpose of communicating with other people.

Thus the examinee whose Information score is higher than his or her Vocabulary score is one who may know more than she or he shares effectively with others, while the individual with a higher Vocabulary than Information subtest score is one who may impress others verbally despite her or his actual lack of knowledge.

Interpretation of the Handling of the Vocabulary Subtest by the Examinee

The first aspect to observe in terms of the child's handling of the Vocabulary subtest is the length and linguistic quality of his or her responses. Thus the examinee's actual score on this subtest may not indicate much about the qualitative aspects of the definitions the individual offers, or on the general stylistic features of her or his expressive language.

As with other subtests, the gradient model discussed earlier is relevant in terms of observing the examinee's reaction to a series of increasingly difficult and challenging words to define.

The gradient model, however, may also be thought of as illustrating a continuum, with elements varying from one extreme to the other, and this way of conceptualizing the child's responses may also be helpful to the examiner. Thus, for example, the examiner can conceive of the examinee's verbal facility as existing on a continuum from vague at one pole to precise at the other, wordy at one pole to concise at the other, and concrete at one pole to abstract at the other.

Viewed from within this framework, the examiner should note whether the child's definitions are clear or diffuse, concrete or abstract and wordy or brief. To the extent that the examinee's responses are short but abstract, they suggest that the individual has a clear understanding and knowledge of verbal communication; the child who defines words this way would be expected to be capable of clear verbal communication when he or she chooses. On the other hand, the examinee whose definitions are lengthy but vague would be expected to have much greater difficulty with clear and accurate interpersonal communication.

A second aspect of the child's handling of the Vocabulary subtest that should be noted is the nature of the examinee's syntax and the organization of his or her verbal expression. In this regard, some children or adolescents display quite adequately formulated explanations or definitions of the words on the subtest. These individuals express themselves in complete, clear and grammatically correct sentences, reflecting careful and well-thought-out responses to the items presented.

On the other hand, some examinees' responses reflect inadequate linguistic performance, and these individuals may express themselves in incomplete or poorly organized sentences. These features of verbal expression also provide the examiner with information regarding not only the examinee's vocabulary but about her or his general ability for verbal interpersonal communication as well.

An important issue to consider is the child or adolescent who gives unclear or too brief responses leading the examiner to want to inquire further. While it is ordinarily better to ask questions to clarify whether the examinee does or does not know a given word, the examiner must weigh whether asking clarifying questions might increase the child's defensiveness to such an extent as to jeopardize the remainder of the subtest or the remainder of the entire WISC–III.

Examinees who respond in a laconic or seemingly withholding manner may in fact be displaying during the subtest itself the difficulty they have with verbal interpersonal communication in general. The examiner may infer from such behavior that these are children for whom verbal communication is fraught with a variety of affects, including anxiety, fear or anger. Other aspects of the child's behavior may involve the examinee who mishears a particular word or words, which may reflect an auditory perceptual problem or, more rarely, an anxiety-based defensive operation that prevents the individual from accurately hearing certain words.

Finally, the examinee's pattern of success and failure, and the child's reaction to failure on the subtest, should be noted. These features of the examinee's functioning provide some indication of how consistently the child is able to perform in the realm of verbal interpersonal communication, and whether he or she reacts to failure with increased motivation, or else with increased frustration, anger or withdrawal, and these observations may be useful in making recommendations for approaching the child in the school setting or in a therapeutic intervention.

OBJECT ASSEMBLY

What the Object Assembly Subtest Measures

Wechsler (1958) notes that the Object Assembly subtest was included in his test battery after much hesitation; he felt that whatever value object assembly tests might have for testing children, such tests were often ill-adapted for testing adults. Wechsler (1958) felt most standardized form-boards were too easy for the average adult, at high levels had little discriminative value, have large scatter, and taken singly, most have low reliability.

Despite these reservations, because of the subtest's merits, it was kept in the WAIS. Wechsler (1958) notes the best features of the Object Assembly subtest are its qualitative ones, as examiners had praised the subtest because it provided information regarding the subject's thinking and working habits.

Of importance from this vantage point was the subject's approach to the task, which might be one of several kinds. "The first is an immediate perception of the whole, accompanied by a critical understanding of the relation of the individual parts.... A second type of response is that of rapid recognition of the whole but with imperfect understanding of the relations between the parts.... Still a third type of response is one which may begin with complete failure to take in the total situation, but which after a certain amount of trial and error manifestation leads to a sudden though often belated appreciation of the figure" (Wechsler, 1958, p. 83).

Wechsler (1958) states that the subtest has particular clinical value because it often reveals the individual's mode of perception, the degree to which he or she relies on trial-and-error methods of problem solving, and the individual's manner of reacting to her or his mistakes. The subtest may also reflect the individual's ability to deal with part-whole relationships, the ability to work for an unknown goal, and the individual's capacity to persist at a task.

According to Wechsler (1991), the Object Assembly subtest is a component of the Perceptual Organization factor (with Picture Completion, Picture Arrangement and Block Design).

Sattler (1992) states that the Object Assembly subtest requires the child to put together jigsaw pieces to form common objects, and he views the subtest as primarily a test of the skill at synthesis—putting things together to form familiar objects. Sattler (1992) notes the subtest requires visual-motor coordination, with motor activity guided by visual perception and sensori-motor feedback.

According to Sattler (1992), the subtest is also a test of visual organizational ability since the child must produce an object that may not be immediately recognizable from the separate parts, and the child must be able to grasp the entire pattern by anticipating the relationship among the parts. The task also requires some constructive ability and perceptual skill. Additionally, the subtest relates to the rate and precision of the child's motor activity, the child's persistence and his or her long-term memory of the objects to be constructed.

Kaufman (1979a, 1990) notes that the Object Assembly subtest reflects synthesis, simultaneous (holistic or right-brain) processing, trial-and-error learning, and visual closure. The subtest's unique ability involves measurement of the ability to benefit from sensory-motor feedback and the anticipation of relationships among parts.

Kaufman (1979a, 1990) notes that factors which influence performance on the subtest include: the ability to respond when uncertain, cognitive style (field dependence/field independence), experience with puzzles, flexibility, persistence, and the ability to work under time pressure.

According to the Fluid-Crystallized categorization of intellectual tasks (Horn, 1985; Kaufman, 1990), the Object Assembly subtest reflects Fluid Intelligence (with Picture Completion, Picture Arrangement, Block Design, Similarities and Digit Span).

According to Bannatyne's (1974) categorization, the Object Assembly subtest is included in the Spatial Ability Category (with Picture Completion and Block Design).

Glasser and Zimmerman (1967), in discussing the WISC, note that the Object Assembly subtest calls for adequate perception, visual motor coordination, and simple assembly skills. In order to be successful on the subtest, there must be some visual anticipation of part-whole relationships and flexibility in working towards a goal that may be unknown at first.

Glasser and Zimmerman (1967) note that Object Assembly measures the ability to assemble material drawn from life into a meaningful whole; like Block Design, the subtest calls for the ability to see spatial relationships, although a difference exists: in the Block Design subtest, the blocks must be assembled to match a pattern; in the Object Assembly subtest, the child must figure out the overall configuration of what he or she is constructing.

The present author feels that there are several ways to view what the Object Assembly subtest measures. A major feature of the subtest is its assessment of the child's ability to integrate components of a visual problem to yield an overall solution. In addition, the task involves concrete materials, things that can be seen, touched and manipulated motorically, as opposed to the kind of "puzzle" represented by, for example, the Similarities subtest.

Hence the Object Assembly subtest involves visual processes and, moreover, visual synthetic or integrative ones, in which the examinee is presented with a set of separate parts which she or he must integrate into a total image or Gestalt.

The task is facilitated for the examinee by virtue of an initial demonstration and by the examiner providing verbal labels for the first two items of the subtest. These labels may be used by the examinee along with the pieces of the item to generate images of what these two items might look like when constructed.

Another aspect of this task reflected in the examinee's performance is his or her motor coordination or manual dexterity in manipulating the parts of each item. In this regard, it should be noted that the materials from which the WISC–III Object Assembly items are made are thinner and lighter than their counterparts on the WISC–R. This means that any tremor or incoordination the examinee has will be quite evident in his or her efforts to carefully place the parts of each item.

A final aspect reflected in performance on this task is that of the examinee's flexibility in approaching the problem situation. The task may be viewed as involving the examinee setting forth a hypothesis about the proper relationship between or among the parts, then proceeding to test this hypothesis, receiving feedback about the correctness of the hypothesis, then modifying or entirely discarding the hypothesis in working towards the correct solution. Flexibility or rigidity of the examinee's thinking or problem solving may be seen in the way the child deals with an item when his or her solution is evidently incorrect.

Flexibility is in evidence when the individual appears able to relinquish a given approach and to adopt a new one, to try a piece in a different connection, or to rotate a particular piece spatially, thus allowing the examinee more likelihood of achieving a possible correct juxtaposition among parts. Rigidity of approach is in evidence when the child seems to omit various possibilities in trying to determine a correct juxtaposition, or when the examinee continues to place the same pieces together despite her or his realization that the juxtaposition is incorrect.

Thus the Object Assembly subtest measures the examinee's visual integrative skills and visual memory for objects; his or her fine motor coordination abilities; her or his ability to move from discrete and separate bits of information towards an integration of this information into some overall pattern or configuration; and his or her general flexibility or rigidity of problem-solving strategies when dealing with essentially recognizable objects.

In terms of what the Object Assembly subtest measures, during subtest administration, the examiner may periodically remember that this subtest provides a sample of the examinee's Performance IQ, perceptual organization (Wechsler, 1991), spatial ability (Bannatyne, 1974), and fluid intelligence (Horn, 1985; Kaufman, 1990).

Research Pertaining to the Object Assembly Subtest

Research studies using the WISC–R with various learning disabled (e.g., Fischer et al., 1985; Reilly et al., 1985; Zingale & Smith, 1978), emotionally or behaviorally disturbed (e.g., Clarizio & Bernard, 1981; Dean, 1977; Henry & Wittman, 1981), and mentally retarded (e.g., Kaufman & Van Hagen, 1977; Reilly et al., 1985) have found that the Object Assembly subtest is the easiest or among the easiest for these populations.

In their consensus rankings of subtest means for the 10 regular WISC–R subtests across a number of studies, Kaufman et al. (1990) report that the Object Assembly subtest ranks first for learning disabled and emotionally or behaviorally disturbed children and ranks second for mentally retarded children.

Share et al. (1987) reported an investigation of 925 children who were studied from ages 3 to 11. Of those children in the sample who displayed both reading and spelling retardation, the children revealed poor verbal subtest performance on the WISC–R in comparison to non-retarded learners, but those who had both reading and spelling deficits displayed superior functioning on the WISC–R Picture Completion and Object Assembly subtests.

Whipple et al. (1988) report an investigation of sons whose alcoholic fathers had at least one first- or second-degree relative who also suffered from alcoholism. These male children in Whipple et al.'s (1988) sample were found to display an atypical neurocognitive profile: they revealed a reduction in amplitude of the event-related potential during a complex visual discrimination task; and they displayed reduced visuoperceptual perform-ance in their significantly lower scores on the Object Assembly, Block Design, and Picture Completion subtests of the WISC–R.

Overall, research involving the Object Assembly subtest has demon-strated that it is among the easiest of the WISC–R subtests for learning disabled, emotionally disturbed and mentally retarded children.

Information Processing Aspects of the Object Assembly Subtest

Input on the Object Assembly subtest involves visual and verbal modeled instructions and demonstration to the examinee to integrate components of two-dimensional puzzles of familiar objects into a total construction of the puzzle of the object; input on the subtest itself involves separate pieces of each of five puzzles, two with and three without additional cues of verbal labels for the object.

Cognitive operations for the examinee include visual synthetic reasoning (at times with the assistance of a verbal label); recall of visual patterns and images; reasoning regarding visual part-whole relationships; and motor coordination and integration. Output on the subtest involves variously integrated puzzle constructions.

Observation of the child during this subtest involves noting the examinee's visual search strategies, problem-solving approach, fine motor coordination and dexterity. Information processing deficits which may be evident in performance on this subtest may involve difficulties with the storage of visual Gestalt images or with the process of integrating parts of images in the present to reconstruct the patterns stored in long-term memory. Factors that may complicate the examinee's processing of the items are the verbal labels for the first two but not the last three items, and the lack of any surface line stimuli on item #3.

Statistical Characteristics of the Object Assembly Subtest

The Object Assembly subtest has an average split-half reliability coeffi-cient across all ages of the WISC–III of .69 with reliability coefficients that range from .60 to .76 across the 11 age groups. The Object Assembly subtest has an average test-retest stability coefficient for all ages of .66.

According to Sattler's (1992) categorization, which groups subtests into good, fair, and poor measures of *g*, the Object Assembly subtest is a fair measure of *g*. In the original WISC–III sample, the Object Assembly subtest ranked seventh in its *g* loading, while in the Roid et al. (1993) replication study, the Object Assembly subtest ranks eighth in its *g* loading.

Kamphaus and Platt (1992) report subtest specificities for the WISC–III and indicate the Object Assembly subtest has inadequate specificity for the combined age groups on the WISC–III. Bracken et al. (1993; see Table 16 in the present volume) indicate that the Object Assembly subtest has ample specificity for ages 9, 13 and 15, and inadequate specificity for ages 6–8, 10–12, 14 and 16. Sattler (1992) indicates that the Object Assembly subtest has ample specificity for ages 9, 13 and 15, adequate specificity for age 6, and inadequate specificity for ages 7–8, 10–12, 14 and 16.

Relationships Between the Object Assembly Subtest and Other Aspects of the WISC–III

The Object Assembly subtest correlates .58 with the WISC–III Full Scale IQ, .48 with the Verbal IQ and .60 with the Performance IQ.

The Object Assembly subtest correlates best with Similarities (.42) on the Verbal Scale and with Block Design (.61) on the Performance Scale. The Object Assembly subtest correlates least well with the Coding subtest (.18).

The correlation between the Object Assembly and Block Design subtests likely reflects their loading on the Perceptual Organization factor of which both are components.

From a clinical standpoint, one can view the Object Assembly and Block Design subtests as reflecting complimentary aspects of visual processing: Block Design involves primarily the analysis of visual patterns into their component parts, while Object Assembly involves the integration of separate bits of visual information into an overall pattern or image. One major difference between these two subtests is that the Block Design subtest involves abstract or unfamiliar information while the Object Assembly subtest involves familiar, essentially recognizable forms, and therefore involves visual memory to a greater extent than the Block Design subtest.

Hence, comparison of the examinee's performance on these two subtests can provide an indication of whether the examinee is more competent in visual analysis or synthesis and whether the examinee is more capable when dealing with familiar or abstract materials.

Interpretation of the Handling of the Object Assembly Subtest by the Examinee

There are several general issues to be considered regarding interpretation of the examinee's handling of the Object Assembly subtest. First, the present author has found use of the Object Assembly screen extremely awkward. Hence, in setting up each of the subtest items, the present author asks the child to look away or to close his or her eyes. Individuals may respond to this instruction in different ways, either by simply averting their eyes or, in the case of younger or immature older examinees, by hiding their eyes with their arms or even putting their heads down on the examiner's desk. Finally, the examiner may note whether the examinee attempts to peek or see the materials before the examiner says the child can look, suggesting both the examinee's immaturity and/or the pressure the individual may feel in the test situation.

In terms of the child's actual approach to the task, a first issue for the examiner to note is whether the examinee appears to test out various juxtapositions mentally or in actual trial-and-error behavior and whether the individual appears more thoughtful or impulsive in his or her approach to the task.

A second issue is that of the examinee's ability to persist in working on the items, whether the child is successful or not. In this regard, some examinees will obtain partial credit because they may correctly juxtapose two pieces, recognize this and leave these pieces together even though they may be unable to correctly solve the entire item; other children will put two pieces together correctly and then separate them as though they have not recognized the correctness of their partial solution. The examinee who is able to recognize partial solutions would seem more alert and flexible in dealing with situations that may be too difficult for her or him to handle with complete success.

Another issue is the general strategy utilized by the child, which may be one of several types. One approach may be viewed as essentially holistic, in which the individual appears to grasp the entire Gestalt of the object and to proceed to fit the pieces together in a somewhat fluid and natural manner; a second possibility is a part-oriented approach in which the child utilizes a trial-and-error strategy to fit one piece to another and gradually to build up the entire Gestalt in this way. One would infer that these styles of cognition would also characterize the examinee's approach to other cognitive tasks involving visual part-whole relationships.

A related issue is that of the general flexibility of the child's problem-solving style. The Object Assembly subtest requires that the examinee be able to perceive the same piece of the various puzzles as having form qualities *or* line qualities, or as involving surface detail *as well as* shape qualities.

The child can either shift his or her perceptions as needed and approach the task flexibly or else be inflexible in her or his approach, and see any part only in terms of form, or only in one spatial position. The individual's performance on all of these dimensions provide information as to his or her flexibility and capacity to look at a situation from a variety of perspectives.

Another observation that can often be made in the child's handling of this subtest is the examinee who omits pieces of the object. The individual may comment that "these pieces don't fit," which the examiner may view as an indication of the examinee's inclination to fit situations to his or her own view and to discard information inconsistent with the child's own perceptions or hypotheses about the way things should be.

A final general observation should be in the way the examinee fits the pieces of the puzzle together. Thus the child may put the pieces together loosely and carelessly, or very carefully. Both in observing the examinee's performance as well as in seeing how carefully the pieces are juxtaposed to one another, the examiner can note the child's fine motor coordination and whether the examinee has any tremor or incoordination. In addition, the examiner is able to observe the standards the child or adolescent applies to her or his own fine motor coordinated performance.

Regarding the examinee's handling of failure on the Object Assembly subtest, because of the discreteness and the quality of the items, unless the child quickly concludes he or she is no good at puzzles, there is usually little negative carry-over from one item to the next. However, examinees who are vulnerable to failure may react with increasing frustration and anger, resulting in their becoming more distressed, in their giving up more quickly or even flipping or tossing the object parts as an expression of their frustration.

In dealing with the examinee who is experiencing frustration with the Object Assembly subtest and consistent with the gradient model discussed earlier, the examiner can choose among three alternatives on a dimension of increasing examiner activity: empathize with the child's frustration ("Some of these are kinda hard."); offer the individual a choice ("Do you want to keep working on this one or stop?"); or actively encourage the examinee to continue ("Why don't you keep on working and see if you can get it?"). Under these circumstances, the author recommends that the examiner be less directive rather than more directive.

COMPREHENSION

What the Comprehension Subtest Measures

Wechsler (1958) notes that what function this subtest serves is difficult to say, but it might be considered a test of common sense. Success on the subtest appears to depend on the possession of a certain amount of practical information as well as a general ability to evaluate one's past experience. Wechsler

(1958) also notes that one of the most gratifying aspects of the subtest is the rich clinical data it furnishes about the subject. Responses on the subtest provide valuable diagnostically relevant information regarding the subject and almost invariably convey something about his or her social and cultural background.

According to Wechsler (1991), the Comprehension subtest is a component of the Verbal Comprehension factor (with Information, Similarities and Vocabulary).

Sattler (1992) states that the Comprehension subtest requires the child to explain situations, actions or activities that relate to events which are familiar to most children. Success on the subtest depends on the child's possession of practical information as well as the child's ability to draw on previous experience. The child's responses may reflect her or his knowledge of conventional standards of behavior, the degree of the child's cultural opportunities, and the extent of development of the child's conscience or moral sense.

Sattler (1992) also notes that success on the subtest suggests that the child has social judgment, common sense, and a grasp of social convention.

Kaufman (1979a, 1990) notes that the Comprehension subtest reflects common sense (cause-effect relationships), verbal reasoning, and verbal expression. The subtest's unique ability involves measurement of the ability to demonstrate practical information, the evaluation and use of past experiences, and knowledge of conventional standards of behavior, social maturity and judgment.

Kaufman (1979a, 1990) notes that factors which influence performance on the subtest include: cultural opportunities in the child's home, development of conscience or moral sense, and negativism.

According to the Fluid-Crystallized categorization of intellectual tasks (Horn, 1985; Kaufman, 1990), the Comprehension subtest reflects Crystallized Intelligence (with Information, Vocabulary, and Similarities).

According to Bannatyne's (1974) categorization, the Comprehension subtest is included in the Verbal Conceptualization Category (with Similarities and Vocabulary).

Glasser and Zimmerman (1967), in discussing the WISC, note that the Comprehension subtest attempts to determine the level of a child's ability to use practical judgment in everyday social actions; the extent to which social acculturation has taken place; and the degree to which a maintaining conscience or moral sense has developed. Glasser and Zimmerman (1967) note that success on this subtest probably depends a great deal on the child's possession of practical information as well as on his or her ability to evaluate and utilize past experience in socially acceptable ways.

Glasser and Zimmerman (1967) note that the utilization of practical information in adaptive ways is a function of the child's ability to think logically, which in turn reflects the child's emotional state. Hence, the child's mode of approach to solving the problems in the subtest reflect his or her emotional balance, which may be revealed in the child's ability to avoid offering impulsive, antisocial or bizarre responses.

Glasser and Zimmerman (1967) also note that the child's being able to provide socially appropriate responses in the subtest does not mean that the individual will not display inappropriate behavior in his or her real-life adjustment, but being able to give suitable responses to the subtest does indicate the child's understanding of an expected social role.

In the present author's view, there are a number of ways to interpret what the Comprehension subtest measures. First, the subtest may be seen as assessing the child or adolescent's verbal knowledge of what is appropriate social behavior and the underlying rationale for a variety of kinds of social behavior or other things the examinee might observe in her or his surrounding environment.

Thus, the Comprehension subtest reflects the examinee's ability to state the socially conventional way to deal with a number of situations, but also the subtest reveals the child's ability to go beyond mere appearances to articulate a deeper basis or reason for things that occur. Items 1, 2, 4, 5, and 8 of the subtest require the examinee to indicate what to *do* in a given situation; the remaining subtest items require the child or adolescent to provide an *explanation* or *rationale* for why certain things occur or are done.

Thus, the initial items on the Comprehension subtest, intended for young children for whom action is more typical, focus on appropriate behavioral responses in a variety of situations. The remainder of the subtest items focus on the examinee's ability to explain or articulate the rationale for various aspects of the environment or experience that the child may or may not have noticed or thought about.

It is also possible to divide the Comprehension subtest items according to the topic or cognitive requirement of the items. Thus, items 1, 2, 3, 8, and 10 deal with danger and/or aggression. Items 4, 5, 7, 8, 13, 16, and 18 involve rules, principles, or transgression, while items 3, 6, 9, 10, 11, 12, 14, 15, and 17 involve reasoning.

At least one other way of considering the Comprehension subtest is that, in responding to the items, the examinee is called upon to verbalize relatively lengthy, somewhat complex, verbal utterances that describe appropriate action or explain the rationale for social behavior. In doing so, the examinee demonstrates the degree to which he or she already has available, or is capable of generating, verbal explanations of various kinds of social behavior. Since one may infer that what the examinee says aloud she or he could also say subvocally, this subtest can provide an index of the examinee's ability to carry out an internal dialogue—to explain social events to him- or herself and possibly to give her- or himself subvocal commands or instructions.

In terms of what the Comprehension subtest measures, during the administration of the subtest, the examiner may periodically remember that this subtest provides a sample of the examinee's Verbal IQ, verbal comprehension (Wechsler, 1991), verbal conceptualization ability (Bannatyne, 1974), and crystallized intelligence (Horn, 1985; Kaufman, 1990).

Research Pertaining to the Comprehension Subtest

A number of research investigations using the WISC–R with various learning disabled (e.g., Clarizio & Bernard, 1981; Henry & Wittman, 1981; Reilly et al., 1985) and emotionally or behaviorally disturbed (e.g., Fischer et al., 1985; Ollendick, 1979) children have reported that the Comprehension subtest falls in the middle range of difficulty for these populations. Investigations of mentally retarded children using the WISC–R (e.g., Clarizio & Bernard, 1981; Henry & Wittman, 1981) have found that the Comprehension subtest is of variable difficulty for this population.

In their consensus ratings of subtest means for the 10 regular WISC–R subtests across a number of studies, Kaufman et al. (1990) report that the Comprehension subtest ranks fourth for learning disabled children, fifth for emotionally or behaviorally disturbed children, and third for mentally retarded children.

A number of research investigations dealing with the administration and scoring of the Wechsler scales have reported frequent errors on the scoring of the Comprehension subtest (e.g., Slate & Chick, 1989; Slate & Jones, 1990), suggesting that examiners should use extra caution when scoring this subtest.

Research focusing on the Comprehension subtest of any of the Wechsler scales has usually also examined the Picture Arrangement subtest, as these two subtests have traditionally been interpreted in relation to one another (Holt, 1968). There have been a number of research studies over the years which have examined these two subtests on the WISC (e.g., Krippner, 1964; Lipsitz et al., 1993), the WAIS or WAIS–R (e.g., Browning & Quinlan, 1985; Nobo & Evans, 1986; Sipps et al., 1987) and with the WISC–R (e.g., Browning & Quinlan, 1985; Reiff & Gerber, 1990).

These studies have investigated the validity of the proposition that the Comprehension subtest (often with the Picture Arrangement subtest) reflects the individual's social understanding, sensitivity, or social intelligence. Investigations have reported mixed support for this hypothesized relationship. For example, Browning and Quinlan (1985), in studying adolescents and young adult psychiatric inpatients, found a significant correlation between an "ego development rating" on each subject's Sentence Completion Test protocol and the subject's WISC, WAIS or WAIS–R Comprehension subtest score (but not the subject's Picture Arrangement subtest score).

Krippner (1964), using the WISC and the Vineland Social Maturity Scale, found a significant correlation between scores on the WISC Comprehension subtest and the Vineland Social Age score for 53 elementary school-aged boys, but they did not find a significant relationship between the Picture Arrangement subtest and any other measure.

Sipps et al. (1987) administered the CPI and the WAIS–R Comprehension, Picture Arrangement, and Vocabulary subtests to 84 subjects and found that several CPI scales were related to the WAIS–R "social intelligence" subtests of Comprehension and Picture Arrangement.

Lipsitz et al. (1993) examined associations between WISC and WAIS subtest scores on several subtests from these tests. The subtests included the Comprehension and Picture Arrangement subtests, and the sample included 124 at-risk subjects from a longitudinal study of the offspring of parents with schizophrenia and major affective disorder. The comparison group included 113 normal subjects.

The investigation explored the correlation between these subtest scores and clinician ratings of these subjects' social competence and hostility. Although some support was obtained regarding the relationship between Comprehension subtest scores and these ratings for normal subjects, overall, the authors concluded that the results did not support the assumption that the Comprehension or Picture Arrangement subtests are sensitive to children's social functioning.

Nobo and Evans (1986) administered several WAIS–R subtests including the Comprehension and Picture Arrangement subtests and five personality measures (e.g., The MMPI Social Introversion Scale) to a sample of 37 college undergraduates. These authors found a median correlation of −.06 between the Picture Arrangement or Comprehension subtest scores and the personality measures, leading the authors to conclude that one should use caution in drawing personality inferences from these WAIS–R subtests until appropriate validity data have been obtained.

Overall, research regarding the Comprehension subtest indicates that this subtest falls in the middle range of difficulty among the WISC–R subtests for groups of learning disabled, emotionally disturbed or mentally retarded children. Additionally, the subtest is one of those which are more difficult to score reliably. Although there is some research evidence to suggest that the Comprehension subtest may provide an indication of an individual's social awareness or sensitivity, it appears most reasonable not to use the score from the Comprehension (or the Picture Arrangement) subtest to draw inferences about an individual's social intelligence, or the individual's actual ability to relate effectively in social situations.

Information Processing Aspects of the Comprehension Subtest

Input on the Comprehension subtest involves verbal presentation of the subtest items as they are stated by the examiner. Internal cognitive operations for the examinee involve the analysis of the auditory input, abstraction of the meaning of the questions, memory search where this is appropriate, verbal reasoning and judgment, and formulation of an appropriate response. Output on the subtest is in the form of a verbal response which either states an appropriate action in a particular situation or provides the rationale for an event or action described in the examiner's question.

Observation of the child or adolescent during this subtest involves noting the length of time it takes the examinee to formulate his or her response and the linguistic structure of the child's response.

Information processing deficits that may be reflected in performance on the Comprehension subtest would be in various aspects of the examinee's language performance, either in difficulty hearing or comprehending the meaning of the questions, or else in the verbal expressive aspects of the child's language functioning.

Statistical Characteristics of the Comprehension Subtest

The Comprehension subtest has an average split-half reliability coefficient across all ages of the WISC–III of .77 with reliability coefficients that range from .72 to .85 across the 11 age groups. The Comprehension subtest has an average test-retest stability coefficient for all ages of .73.

According to Sattler's (1992) categorization, which groups subtests into good, fair, and poor measures of *g,* the Comprehension subtest is a good measure of *g.* In both the original WISC–III sample as well as in the Roid et al. (1993) replication study, the Comprehension subtest ranked sixth in its *g* loading.

Kamphaus and Platt (1992) report subtest specificities for the WISC–III and indicate the Comprehension subtest has adequate specificity for the combined age groups on the WISC–III. Bracken et al. (1993; see Table 16 in the present volume) and Sattler (1992) both report that the Comprehension subtest has ample specificity for ages 6 and 8–11, adequate specificity for age 12, and inadequate specificity for ages 7 and 13–16.

Relationships Between the Comprehension Subtest and Other Aspects of the WISC–III

The Comprehension subtest correlates .64 with the WISC–III Full Scale IQ, .67 with the Verbal IQ and .49 with the Performance IQ.

The Comprehension subtest correlates best with Vocabulary (.64) on the Verbal Scale and with Block Design (.40) on the Performance Scale. The Comprehension subtest correlates least well with the Mazes subtest (.05).

The correlation between the Comprehension and Vocabulary subtests may reflect the relatively high loading on *g* shared by both of these subtests, and their correlation may also reflect their loading on the Verbal Comprehension factor of which both are components.

From a clinical standpoint, the Comprehension subtest has traditionally been viewed in relation to the Picture Arrangement subtest (Holt, 1968) with these two subtests presumably reflecting different but interrelated aspects of social intelligence. However, much of the research on the validity of this view (see section on "Research Pertinent to the Comprehension Subtest") has indicated that it is not supportable by empirical evidence. Hence, it seems most reasonable to view these two subtests as reflecting the examinee's ability to demonstrate different kinds of thinking that largely reflect general intelligence. It does not appear reasonable to conclude that the child's functioning on either of these subtests, or both together, will have a meaningful predictive relationship to the individual's actual empathy, social intelligence, or social behavior.

Interpretation of the Handling of the Comprehension Subtest by the Examinee

The Comprehension subtest is one of the few subtests on the WISC–III (Similarities and Vocabulary are the other two) where the examinee's responses can or should involve complete sentences of more than several words in length. Hence, the examiner has an opportunity to observe the nature of the child or adolescent's sentence structure or grammatical construction in responding to a verbal item.

The child who is characteristically nonverbal, either by constitution or because of exposure to poor verbal models, may have difficulty with the Comprehension subtest not only because he or she does not know the answers but because of her or his characteristic nonverbal style. (The specific additional questioning on items #2, 6, 7, 11, 12, 15, 17 and 18 is to compensate for this tendency among certain examinees.) Hence, the examiner should note and thoughtfully approach the individual who tends to give a minimum of information when asked, and who may also retreat with further questioning.

Because the discontinuation criterion on the Comprehension subtest is three consecutive failures and since the child can earn two, one, or no credits on each item, many examinees have an erratic profile of successes and failures on this subtest; even young children can advance to the upper subtest items, gaining full, partial or no credit on various items.

However, because of the nature of the Comprehension questions, there is ordinarily little clear feedback to the child as to whether his or her answers are correct or not (unless the examinee states that she or he does not know a particular answer). Hence, the child is usually not specifically aware of how well or poorly he or she is doing, and therefore, the examinee's reaction to failure on this subtest is usually not an issue.

There are several Comprehension subtest items that may stimulate emotional reactions on the part of the examinee. Although Wechsler (1991) attempted to remove or modify any clinically relevant or emotionally provocative items from the WISC–III (Kaufman, 1993), at least several of the items, notably #s 1, 2, 3, 8, and possibly 10, deal with danger or aggression. Further, many of the items (e.g., #s 4, 5, 7, 8, 13, 16, and 18) deal with rules or potential transgression of rule systems. Since many examinees who are being evaluated have been in conflict with various authority figures, such as teachers, parents or police, these items may or may not evoke particular emotional reactions on the part of the child. Hence, the examiner should be aware of the potential of many Comprehension subtest items to stimulate anxiety in the examinee and disrupt his or her response to a particular item or subsequent items.

While any of the items can of course stimulate personal associations on the part of the child and lead to the examinee revealing information about his or her own experience or relationships within her or his family, these kinds of responses are more likely to be stimulated by the first eight items. Items 9 through 18 are more remote from the child's direct experience, and, except for item #16, these latter items are less likely to elicit personal associations from the examinee.

Important aspects of the individual's handling of the Comprehension subtest thus include the nature of the examinee's extended verbal expression; the child's reaction to a variety of items which may provoke his or her anxiety or remind the examinee of rule and authority relationships which may be problematic; and the individual's ability to articulate appropriate behavior, or to reason about the rationale for a variety of conventional actions.

SUPPLEMENTARY SUBTESTS

SYMBOL SEARCH

What the Symbol Search Subtest Measures

The Symbol Search subtest is a supplementary subtest that was newly devised specifically for the WISC–III, and hence there is no discussion of this subtest in Wechsler (1958) who was at that time discussing the WAIS.

According to Wechsler (1991), the Symbol Search subtest involves series of paired groups of symbols being presented to the examinee; each item pair consists of a target group and a search group. The child must scan the two groups and indicate whether or not one of the target symbols appears in the search group.

The development of the Symbol Search subtest was based on reviews of the literature regarding the WISC–R third factor and appears to have been intended to extend the memory and attentional facets of this factor (Wechsler, 1991). The underpinnings of the subtest included controlled-attention research (Shiffrin & Schneider, 1977) and research dealing with memory-scanning abilities (Sternberg, 1966).

The Symbol Search subtest is a component of a new fourth factor, Processing Speed (with Coding), which emerged in the various factor analyses carried out as part of the development of the WISC–III (Wechsler, 1991).

Sattler (1992) states that Symbol Search requires the child to look at a target symbol or symbols and determine whether the symbol(s) is (are) present in an array of similar symbols. He notes the task involves perceptual discrimination, speed and accuracy, attention and concentration, short-term memory, and cognitive flexibility (in the child's need to shift quickly from one array to the next) with visual-motor coordination playing a minor role in terms of the child's drawing a slash for each item.

Part A of the subtest (for children ages 6–7) requires the child to examine one target figure and then determine whether this figure appears in a three-item array. Part B (for children ages 8–16) requires the child to examine a two-figure target and then determine whether either of these two figures appears in a five-item array. Hence Sattler (1992) notes that Part B is more complex than Part A.

Sattler (1992) also notes that most of the symbols used in this subtest are difficult to encode verbally, although some of the symbols may be verbally labelled by the examinee, and he states that research is needed to determine whether children actually do encode these symbols verbally and whether such encoding facilitates performance on the subtest.

Sattler (1992) also states that the speed and accuracy with which the child performs the task provide a measure of the child's intellectual capacity; he notes that one can conceptualize the subtest as involving visual discrimination and visuoperceptual scanning.

Since the Symbol Search subtest was developed for the WISC–III, Kaufman's writings on the WISC–R (1979a) and on the WAIS–R (1990) do not include his views of this subtest and what characteristics of the child's intellectual functioning the subtest measures.

Again, since the Symbol Search subtest was devised for the WISC–III, it does not appear in past Fluid-Crystallized categorizations of intellectual tasks (Horn, 1985; Kaufman, 1990). However, the present author would include this subtest in the Speed category (with Coding).

According to Bannatyne's (1974) categorization, the Symbol Search subtest would not be included in any of the four groups of Wechsler subtest scores.

Similarly, since the subtest was devised for the WISC–III, there is no discussion of this subtest in Glasser and Zimmerman's (1967) discussion of the WISC.

The present author views the Symbol Search subtest as measuring the child's ability for speeded visual information processing with some linguistic component in the task (since the examinee has to determine whether a visual target does or does not meet a specific criterion) and some motor coordination aspect (in terms of the examinee locating and executing the slash mark).

The subtest relies heavily on visual perceptual processes, the child's ability to focus his or her visual apparatus on a target, retain this image for a brief period and then carry out a perceptual search and match between the target symbol (or symbols) and the array. This process in turn may reflect the speed, accuracy and consistency with which the child or adolescent can focus, scan and refocus visually, as well as the examinee's visual short-term memory.

The subtest should also be sensitive to the examinee's ability to concentrate her or his attention and not be distracted easily. Evidence for this view is suggested by the factor analyses reported by Wechsler (1991), where the subtest does have a loading of .48 on the Freedom from Distractibility factor for children ages 6–7 while loadings on this factor for the remainder of the age groups are much lower. This at least suggests that for the young child, the task is sensitive to his or her ability to maintain focus on the task. It might also be noted that distractibility on the Symbol Search subtest may involve visual, not auditory, distractibility as is reflected on other Freedom from Distractibility subtests.

The present author feels that both Symbol Search Part A and Part B involve the above-noted components of the task: examining a visual target, then scanning an array of symbols to determine whether one, or one of two, target symbols appears in the search group. However, Part B represents a greater cognitive strain (Bruner, Goodnow, & Austin, 1956) for the examinee, in that he or she must process two target symbols and hold them in mind or refocus on them while examining the search group.

Both parts of the Symbol Search subtest also require the examinee to focus her or his attention on sets of external stimuli (as opposed to the Digit Span or Arithmetic subtests, for example, which require the child to receive external information and then focus on it while it is held in consciousness). Both parts of the Symbol Search subtest also require that the examinee be able to sustain his or her effort in a redundant task for a relatively extended period of time.

It should be noted that the subtest also requires the individual to deal with the most unfamiliar or unusual stimuli in the entire WISC–III. Virtually all of the other subtests involve basically familiar materials (e.g., Information, Object Assembly). Those that do not (e.g., Block Design and Mazes) have similar item content throughout the subtest (i.e., the designs or mazes become increasingly complex, but the item content remains essentially unchanged). The Symbol Search subtest, however, contains stimuli that are basically unfamiliar to the child, and these stimuli change to some extent throughout the subtest.

This means that the examinee must adapt to the novelty of the subtest initially and be able to establish a strategy for handling this novel task. The child must then be able to maintain her or his focus on the strategy even as the specific stimuli being processed change over the course of the task. And this must be done rapidly in view of the time limit of the subtest.

Although the task only requires that the examinee respond by marking a YES or NO box to indicate his or her decision on each item, the present author would note that this task does involve a shift from visual to linguistic functioning, which may also tap the child's ability to shift frames of reference — from visual to linguistic — rapidly, and this may present a challenge for linguistically impaired or vulnerable examinees (Doll & Boren, 1993; Phelps, Leguori, Nisewaner, & Parker, 1993).

Lastly, it should be noted that although Wechsler (1991) does not describe the rationale for the design or selection of the specific symbols, the symbols can be thought of as being symmetrical or asymmetrical or, like some letters of the alphabet, as facing left or right. In addition, the symbols vary in the degree to which they are comprised of vertical, horizontal, angular or curvilinear lines, which are processed differently by the brain (Farnham-Diggory, 1972).

It is well established that perceptual reversals and spatial rotations are common among learning- and reading disabled children (Farnham-Diggory,

1972). To the extent that the examinee encounters items that *face* to the right or left, or has to deal with items that include vertical, horizontal, angular or curvilinear lines, she or he may reverse items perceptually or become confused by item directionality. The child may have difficulty with particular items or become flustered by the entire task and have difficulty establishing or maintaining a strategy for dealing with the task.

Hence, one would infer that these aspects of the visual processing of the Symbol Search subtest provide a source of variance for examinees with deficits in visual information processing, and might lead to their slowed or deficient performance on this subtest.

Lastly, in view of a primary aspect of this subtest, which appears to include visual analysis of (letter-like) symbols and comparing them to an array of other symbols, performance on the subtest may have implications for the child's ability to develop or to have difficulty with the development of reading and writing skills.

Interpretation of the above noted phenomena may be complicated by virtue of the fact that children with special education needs were not excluded from the WISC–III standardization sample (Wechsler, 1991) and hence differences between learning disabled examinees and the normative group may not always be obvious. However, exploration of the author's hypotheses may be pursued by research into the specific performances of learning disabled children on the Symbol Search subtest.

In terms of what the Symbol Search subtest measures, while administering the subtest, the examiner may periodically remember that this subtest provides a sample of the examinee's Performance IQ and processing speed (Wechsler, 1991).

Research Pertaining to the Symbol Search Subtest

Since the WISC–III is a new test, there is relatively little published research focusing on the Symbol Search subtest per se. Prifitera and Dersh (1993) explored WISC–III subtest patterns among normal, learning disabled, and ADHD samples, and found that Symbol Search was among the four lowest subtest scores for the learning disabled sample, while for the ADHD sample, the Symbol Search subtest score fell within the average range.

Schwean, Saklofske, Yackulic, and Quinn (1993), in their investigation of the WISC–III performance of ADHD children, found that there was no difference in children's Symbol Search subtest performance on or off methylphenidate, but did find that for their entire sample of ADHD children, performance on the Symbol Search subtest (along with Information, Coding,

Picture Arrangement, Arithmetic, and Digit Span) was significantly below the WISC–III standardization sample.

Doll and Boren (1993), in their investigation of the performance of severely language-impaired students on the WISC–III, found that Symbol Search subtest performance (M = 5.72, SD = 2.94) was the lowest of the students' scores on the Performance scale and was more similar to the students' very significantly impaired performance on the Verbal scale.

Thus, research findings with the Symbol Search subtest suggest that children with language or learning disabilities perform more poorly on this subtest than do children without such impairment, while there are inconsistent findings regarding the performance of ADHD children on the subtest. Certainly there will be continuing investigations of the performance of variously defined groups of children on the Symbol Search subtest, and this may clarify the underlying features of the subtest as well as implications of the subtest for children's intellectual or academic functioning.

Information Processing Aspects of the Symbol Search Subtest

For the Symbol Search subtest, input to the examinee is in the form of visual information (the target and search groups) with verbal and modeling instructions to determine whether a target symbol (composed of a single element, or one of two elements) does or does not appear in an array of other symbols. Internal cognitive operations include visual analysis/discrimination of symbols; scanning and comparison/matching of a target symbol with a series of other symbols; and a decision as to whether or not the target symbol appears or does not appear in the group of search symbols. Output involves the marking of a YES or NO box to indicate the examinee's decision.

Observation of the child or adolescent during this subtest involves noting whether the examinee understands the task readily or with difficulty; the individual's physical/visual orientation to the task including the relationship between the examinee and the test form; the degree of impulsivity or reflectivity and persistence or impersistence evident in the child's performance; if the examinee is left-handed, whether this affects his or her visual focusing and tracking; whether the individual uses a pointer finger to focus on the item he or she is processing; and the nature of the child's pencil grip and use of the pencil to mark his or her answers. Additionally, the examiner should note whether the examinee stops at the end of the first page of items and needs to be reminded to continue.

Information processing deficits that might be reflected in performance on the Symbol Search subtest would include deficits in visual analysis or discrimination, visual scanning as well as deficits in visual concentration, impulse control, persistence or fine motor coordination, or difficulties the examinee may have in switching from visual- to verbal-dominated cognitive processing.

Statistical Characteristics of the Symbol Search Subtest

The Symbol Search subtest has an average split-half reliability coefficient across all ages of the WISC–III of .76 with reliability coefficients that range from .69 to .82 across the 11 age groups (although at some ages retesting was not done). The Symbol Search subtest has an average test-retest stability coefficient for all ages of .74.

According to Sattler's (1992) categorization, which groups subtests into good, fair, and poor measures of *g,* the Symbol Search subtests is a fair measure of *g.* In the original WISC–III sample, the Symbol Search subtest ranks ninth among all WISC–III subtests in its *g* loading, while in the Roid et al. (1993) replication study, the Symbol Search subtest ranks tenth among all WISC–III subtests in its *g* loading.

Kamphaus and Platt (1992) report subtest specificities for the WISC–III and indicate that the Symbol Search subtest has adequate specificity for the combined age groups on the WISC–III. Bracken et al. (1993; see Table 16 in the present volume) and Sattler (1992) indicate that the Symbol Search subtest has ample specificity at ages 7 and 10–16 and inadequate specificity at ages 6 and 8–9.

Relationships Between the Symbol Search Subtest and Other Aspects of the WISC-III

The Symbol Search subtest correlates .56 with the WISC–III Full Scale IQ, .44 with the Verbal IQ and .58 with the Performance IQ.

The Symbol Search subtest displays a range of moderate correlations with the other WISC–III subtests. It correlates best with Arithmetic (.41) on the Verbal Scale and with Coding (.53) and Block Design (.45) on the Performance Scale. The Symbol Search subtest correlates least well with the Digit Span subtest (.28).

The correlation between the Symbol Search and Coding subtests may reflect the significant degree of visual processing and the performance of a visual processing task under timed conditions involved in both subtests, which thus supports the grouping of these two subtests in the Processing Speed factor.

From a clinical standpoint, the Symbol Search subtest may be viewed in relation to the Coding subtest. Both subtests involve high degrees of visual information processing. Significantly, neither task involves the processing of readily recognizable stimuli, such as the Picture Completion or Object Assembly subtests. Both tasks deal with symbolic, rather than interpersonally relevant, stimuli.

In contrast to the Coding subtest, where verbal labelling and mediation of the task is possible (Sattler, 1992), using verbal mediational strategies on the Symbol Search subtest appears more difficult. Additionally, the Coding subtest generally involves simpler visual processing of the stimuli. The examinee's task is primarily to copy (and/or memorize) the symbols in order to associate one symbol with another.

The Coding subtest involves only five symbols on Coding A and nine symbols on Coding B. In contrast, the Symbol Search subtest involves a large number of complex symbol configurations to be visually analyzed. Hence the two subtests permit varying degrees of emphasis on pure visual processing (Symbol Search) or on utilization of a short-term associative learning process (Coding).

The child's performance on these two subtests may be examined to determine on which subtest the examinee performed better, and the examiner may consider that the individual's performance reflects his or her greater adequacy when dealing with a task that requires largely visual processing (Symbol Search), or one that permits verbal encoding, possible associative learning and a more extensive fine motor coordinated output (Coding).

Insofar as one must administer the Symbol Search subtest in order to evaluate the four-factor structure of the WISC–III, the present author recommends that the Symbol Search subtest routinely be administered when the WISC–III is given.

Interpretation of the Handling of the Symbol Search Subtest by the Examinee

As with the Coding subtest, the first issue to note is whether the examinee is right-handed or left-handed since non-righthandedness is more common among a number of atypical populations (Kinsbourne, 1989; see section on Coding Subtest).

In addition to the child's handedness, the examiner should note whether and how well the examinee uses his or her other hand to hold the page down, although this behavior is less vital on this subtest than on the Coding subtest because the task demands differ.

In terms of the task performance itself, the examiner should note whether the individual focuses visually on each item or whether the examinee uses her or his hand to point to each item or part thereof. If the child does point to the item being processed, this suggests that he or she may be attempting to compensate for problems in focusing on the visual processing task.

The examiner should also make note of whether the child is able to work consistently on the task, or whether she or he periodically stops, or stops at the end of a page. These behaviors suggest the difficulty the examinee has with sustained focus and application of effort on a given task and would have implications for the child's attention on independent tasks in a classroom setting.

Another aspect of the examinee's handling of this task which should be observed is the control or lack of control displayed in the child's marking his or her answers. These marks can be small and well-controlled, or large, expansive and poorly controlled, providing some indication of the individual's more general motor (and possibly impulse) control.

One other issue to note is the child who corrects her or his performance on an item. While this suggests that the examinee may be impulsive in dealing with a task requiring decision making, it also indicates the individual's capacity for self-awareness and the capacity for altering his or her response or behavior.

DIGIT SPAN

What the Digit Span Subtest Measures

Wechsler (1958) notes that "[P]erhaps no test has been so widely used in scales of intelligence as that of Memory Span for Digits" (p. 70). He notes the popularity of this task is based on the fact that it is easy to administer, easy to score, and specific as to the type of ability it measures. However, he also notes that as a test of general intelligence, it is among the poorest, and generally, whether for digits forward or backward, it correlates poorly with other tests of intelligence.

Wechsler (1958) notes that particular difficulty with the repetition of digits forward or backward in adults occurs in cases of organic disease, mental retardation or mental disturbance. When not associated with organic defects, low scores on this task can be due to anxiety or inattention, but difficulty in repeating digits, particularly in reverse order, correlates with lack of ability in performing tasks which require concentrated effort.

According to Wechsler (1991), the Digit Span subtest is a component of the Freedom from Distractibility factor (with Arithmetic).

Sattler (1992) states that the Digit Span subtest requires the child to repeat series of digits said aloud by the examiner with two trials at each of several levels. The subtest consists of two parts: Digits Forward, containing series from two to nine digits in length; and Digits Backward, containing series from two to eight digits in length.

Sattler (1992) states that Digit Span is a measure of the child's auditory attention and short-term memory and that performance on the subtest may be affected by the child's ability to relax. The task assesses the individual's ability to recall several elements that are not logically related, and since the child must repeat the items in proper sequence, the task also involves sequencing ability.

Sattler (1992) states that Digits Forward primarily involves simple rote learning and memory, while Digits Backward requires a transformation of the input prior to responding. Good performance on Digits Backward, which requires more complex processing than Digits Forward, may indicate cognitive flexibility, tolerance for stress and good capacity for concentration.

Sattler (1992) notes that because of the differences between the two tasks, it is useful to consider the two separately. He feels Digits Forward involves primarily sequential processing, while Digits Backward involves both planning ability and sequential processing. Furthermore, Digits Backward may involve the ability to form mental images and the ability to scan an internal visual display formed from an auditory stimulus.

Kaufman (1979a, 1990) notes that the Digit Span subtest reflects the individual's ability for auditory sequencing, encoding information for further processing (Digits Backward), facility with numbers, mental alertness, and sequential or left-brain processing.

Kaufman (1979a, 1990) notes that factors which influence performance on the subtest include: attention span, the ability to receive stimuli passively, anxiety, distractibility, flexibility, the presence of a learning disability, and negativism (in regard to Digit Span Backward). The subtest's unique ability involves measurement of immediate rote recall and reversibility in thinking (Digits Backward).

According to the Fluid-Crystallized categorization of intellectual tasks (Horn, 1985; Kaufman, 1990), the Digit Span subtest reflects Fluid Intelligence (with Picture Completion, Picture Arrangement, Block Design, Object Assembly, and Similarities) and Retrieval (with Information and Arithmetic).

According to Bannatyne's (1974) categorization, the Digit Span subtest is included in the Sequential Ability Category (with Arithmetic and Coding).

Glasser and Zimmerman (1967), in discussing the WISC, note that Digit Span attempts to measure immediate auditory recall or immediate auditory memory (attention) span. They note that if the child understands grouping operations, can maintain a state of mental alertness, and suspend irrelevant thought processes during the task, he or she should perform well on the task. They also note that being able to repeat more digits backwards than forward may indicate a sudden "catching on" to the task or a stubbornness on the part of the child who rejects the "too easy" task of repeating the digits forward but is challenged by the need to reverse the digits.

As suggested by Gardner (1981) and by the separate norms provided for Digits Forward and Digits Backward by Wechsler (1991), the present author views the Digit Span subtest as involving at least two kinds of separate but interrelated cognitive abilities: the first involves short-term auditory sequential memory, while the second involves more complex internal mental operations. Hence, the two parts of the subtest may be considered separately.

Adequate performance on the Digits Forward portion of the subtest requires a fundamental capacity of the examinee to be able to store information in short-term memory for a brief period of time without losing the information from that store, and the individual must be able to retrieve the information after a brief delay (the length of time it takes the examiner to complete the presentation of the entire series of digits).

This portion of the task usually involves only auditory memory, which in this case assesses the examinee's ability to take in serially ordered numerical information from another person, retain the information, and repeat it. In order to perform adequately, the child must be able to focus her or his attention on the digits being presented. To facilitate this focusing of attention, the examinee must be able to inhibit other stimuli from within (e.g., random thoughts or bodily sensations) and from without (e.g., visual or auditory stimuli other than the digits being presented).

The second part of the Digit Span subtest, in which the child is required to repeat the digits backwards, requires more complex processing of the information presented. In this latter case, the examinee is likely to utilize one of two possible strategies, one relying on the auditory mode, the second involving a shift from the auditory to the visual mode. In the first strategy, the individual attempts to retain the string of digits in auditory memory and then to reauditorize the string of digits backwards. An examinee using this approach may subvocalize the string forward, then pick off the last digit, say this aloud, then subvocally repeat the remainder of the digits forward, pick off the last one and say it aloud, and so forth. The child who approaches the task this way is one who relies almost exclusively on her or his auditory processing without using any visual strategy.

The other possible strategy, and one which is likely more common, is that as soon as the number of digits presented goes above three or four, the examinee realizes that the auditory strategy is inadequate and attempts to shift to a visual strategy. In this case, as the digits are presented, the child attempts to transpose the verbally presented series of digits into a visual array, which the examinee then attempts to scan mentally and to read off backwards.

Overall, then, the Digit Span subtest measures short-term auditory memory and the examinee's ability to focus her or his immediate attention, and to resist or inhibit internal or external distracting stimuli. Additionally, the subtest provides information regarding the child's ability to generate facilitative information processing strategies, to deal with some degree of stimulus overload of the auditory system, and to deal with moderately complex mental tasks that may require transposition of auditory information into visual information.

In terms of what the Digit Span subtest measures, during the administration of this subtest, the examiner may periodically recall that the subtest provides a sample of the examinee's freedom from distractibility (Wechsler, 1991), fluid intelligence and retrieval ability (Horn, 1985; Kaufman, 1990), sequential ability (Bannatyne, 1974), and that the subtest is one component of the ACID profile (Ackerman et al., 1976, 1977).

Research Pertaining to the Digit Span Subtest

Although the Digit Span subtest is a supplementary subtest which is not always administered when the Wechsler is given, a number of research studies on the WISC–R with various normal (e.g., Kaufman, 1975; Reschly, 1978), learning disabled (e.g., Kaufman & Mclean, 1986), emotionally handicapped (e.g., Peterson & Hart, 1979), and mentally retarded populations (e.g., Van Hagen & Kaufman, 1975) have included the Digit Span subtest in their investigations. In view of the subtest's inclusion in the ACID profile, it is often the case that Digit Span is one of the more difficult subtests for a variety of learning disabled children.

The Digit Span subtest is one of the three subtests which were identified as comprising a freedom from distractibility factor on the WISC (Wechsler, 1949) and appeared in all three age groups studied in Cohen's (1959) factor analysis of the WISC standardization sample. However, the composition of the freedom from distractibility factor on the WISC varied from age group to age group.

When Kaufman (1975) factor analyzed the WISC–R standardization sample, he found that Digit Span (along with Arithmetic) loaded substantially on this factor at all age levels, suggesting that, in contrast to the WISC, the freedom from distractibility factor was stable from age to age on the WISC–R. Utilizing hierarchical factor-analytic techniques, Vance, Wallbrown and Freemont (1978) found evidence for a distractibility factor composed of Arithmetic and Digit Span with mentally retarded children, and Blaha and Vance (1979) observed such an Arithmetic-Digit Span distractibility factor with a learning disabled population.

Kaufman et al. (1990) note that of the 31 studies they summarize, meaningful distractibility factors emerged in 21 of the studies. In most of these investigations, this distractibility, or third, factor consisted of two or all three of the WISC–R freedom from distractibility triad of Arithmetic, Coding, and Digit Span subtests.

In discussing the implications for clinical practice of their review of studies on the freedom from distractibility factor with the WISC–R, Kaufman et al. (1990) note that the freedom from distractibility factor should only be explored if one of the component subtests (i.e., Arithmetic, Coding, or Digit Span) deviates significantly from the mean of its respective scale. In addition, the three freedom from distractibility subtests should form a coherent unit (i.e., not differ significantly from one another) in order to justify using this factor to explain the examinee's test performance.

As the reader is aware, with the WISC–III, the freedom from distractibility factor includes only the Arithmetic and Digit Span subtests, while the Coding subtest has now been grouped with the Symbol Search subtest to form a fourth factor called Processing Speed.

In terms of investigations which have focused on the Digit Span subtest, Talley (1986) compared scores on the Rey Auditory Verbal Learning Test (RAVLT) to WISC–R Digit Span scores for 153 white learning disabled students. Using statistical controls for age and IQ, regression analyses found no significant relationship between the RAVLT and longest digits forward span, longest digits backward span, or total Digit Span raw score. However, factor analysis of the RAVLT and the Digit Span scores yielded three factors, which were interpreted to represent a long-term memory factor, a short-term memory factor involving high coding demands, and a short-term memory factor involving low coding demands.

A study by Schofield and Ashman (1986) divided 323 fifth and sixth graders into low-average, high-average, and superior-ability groups on the basis of WISC–R scores, and they were administered measures of sequential processing, simultaneous processing and planning. These authors concluded that Digit Span Forward and Digit Span Backward did not measure a unitary ability. Rather, Forward Digit Span was felt to reflect a serial processing ability, while Backward Digit Span reflected planning ability.

With the WISC–III, Prifitera and Dersh (1993), investigating WISC–III subtest patterns among normal, learning disabled, and ADHD children, report that for the two clinical groups they studied, lowest scores were obtained on the Digit Span, Arithmetic, Coding, and Symbol Search subtests. Schwean et al. (1993), in their investigation of the WISC–III performance of ADHD children, report that nine of the WISC–III subtest scores of the ADHD sample were different from the WISC–III normative sample, including significantly lower scores on the subtests of Information, Coding, Picture Arrangement, Symbol Search, and Digit Span.

In addition, the Digit Span subtest is one of the four subtests in the ACID profile (Arithmetic, Coding, Information, and Digit Span) (Ackerman et al., 1977). Prifitera and Dersh (1993) report that the full ACID pattern occurs infrequently in the standardization population (1.1%) while the pattern appears much more frequently in the learning disabled group (5.1%) and the ADHD group (12.3%) they studied.

Hence, a number of investigations indicate that the Digit Span subtest is sensitive to the ability of examinees to focus their attention and to retain numerical information for brief periods of time, whether the subtest is viewed as part of a freedom from distractibility factor with the Arithmetic subtest or seen independently. It appears that Digit Span Forward and Digit Span Backward measure related but separate kinds of cognitive processing, and that when administered, this subtest is one of the more difficult subtests for learning disabled and ADHD children.

Information Processing Aspects of the Digit Span Subtest

For the Digit Span subtest, input to the child involves auditory verbal lists of numbers along with verbal instructions to repeat the items as presented or in backward sequence. Cognitive operations on Digits Forward involve focusing of attention and short-term auditory recall. Output is a direct repetition of the auditory verbal input list. On Digits Backward, cognitive operations involve attention, short-term auditory recall, and possible recoding of auditory verbal into visual information. Output on this portion of the subtest involves repetition of the original list of digits in reverse order.

Observation of the child or adolescent during this subtest entails noting the examinee's physical orientation to the examiner during the task presentation (e.g., whether the child focuses on the examiner or looks away; whether the individual is physically active or calm, since physical activity may produce competing or distracting stimuli; and whether the examinee appears to be engaging in any strategy-generating behavior (e.g., gaze aversion, revocalization during Digits Backward).

Information processing deficits that might be reflected in performance on the Digit Span subtest would include generalized attentional deficits, deficits in auditory sequencing or auditory-sequential memory, deficits in short-term recall, difficulties in generating or utilizing cognitive problem-solving strategies when faced with information overload, or difficulties in shifting from simple to complex, or auditory to visual, cognitive processing.

Statistical Characteristics of the Digit Span Subtest

The Digit Span subtest has an average split-half reliability coefficient across all ages of the WISC–III of .85 with reliability coefficients that range from .79 to .91 across the 11 age groups. The Digit Span subtest has an average test-retest stability coefficient for all ages of .73.

According to Sattler's (1992) categorization, which groups subtests into good, fair, and poor measures of *g*, the Digit Span subtest is a fair measure of *g*. In the original WISC–III sample and in the Roid et al. (1993) replication study, the Digit Span subtest ranks eleventh among all WISC–III subtests in its loading on *g*.

Kamphaus and Platt (1992) report subtest specificities for the WISC–III and indicate that the Digit Span subtest has ample specificity for the combined age groups on the WISC–III. Bracken et al. (1993; see Table 16 in the present volume) and Sattler (1992) indicate that the Digit Span subtest has ample specificity for all ages of the WISC–III.

Relationships Between the Digit Span Subtest and Other Aspects of the WISC–III

The Digit Span subtest correlates .43 with the WISC–III Full Scale IQ, .42 with the Verbal IQ and .35 with the Performance IQ.

The Digit Span subtest displays a range of low correlations with the other WISC–III subtests. It correlates best with Arithmetic (.43) on the Verbal Scale and with Block Design (.32) on the Performance Scale. The Digit Span subtest correlates least well with the Mazes subtest (.14).

The correlation between the Digit Span and Arithmetic subtests may reflect the degree to which both of these subtests involve the ability to focus attention and to resist distraction, thus providing justification for their inclusion in the Freedom from Distractibility factor.

From a clinical standpoint, the Digit Span subtest may be viewed in relation to the Arithmetic subtest. As well, the Digits Forward and Digits Backward may be seen as parallelling the relationship between the Arithmetic and Digit Span subtests themselves.

The relationship between the Arithmetic and Digit Span subtests has been discussed above (see "Relationship Between Arithmetic Subtest and Other Aspects of the WISC–III"). Basically, the Digits Forward portion of the subtest requires that the examinee listen to a series of verbally presented numbers, then repeat these, a task which appears to primarily require the individual's focused or relaxed auditory attention. In contrast to this, the Arithmetic subtest requires that the child listen to a verbal string, abstract from the verbal string an essential arithmetic problem, solve the problem, and offer an answer to it, a far more complex cognitive task which requires that the examinee be much more active in processing the information presented.

Similarly, the Digits Backward portion of the Digit Span subtest, in contrast to the more passive attention involved in Digits Forward, requires the child to work out a strategy for repeating the digits backwards. This can either involve a reauditorization or a visualization strategy (see section above on "What the Digit Span Subtest Measures"). Regardless of which approach the examinee uses, Digits Backward, like the Arithmetic subtest, is a more complicated task than Digits Forward, requiring more active and flexible cognition and the generating and/or shifting of cognitive strategies on the part of the individual.

Hence, in evaluating the examinee's performance on Digit Span, the examiner may note the child's scaled score, which relates her or his perform-ance to the standardization population, but the examiner may also note the relationship between the examinee's Arithmetic and Digit Span subtest performances. Indeed, if these subtest scores are similar, they may be consid-ered as part of a unitary Freedom from Distractibility factor. However, if the two subtests are significantly different from one another, one would con-clude that they do not reflect a unitary phenomenon or factor and they would be interpreted in relation to one another, but separately.

To determine whether these two subtests are significantly different from one another, Table B.4. Wechsler (1991, p. 265) indicates that a difference of 3.59 is significant at the .05 level. Hence, if the Digit Span and Arithmetic subtest scaled scores differ by as much as 4 units (3 or more if the examiner wishes to use a conservative criterion), the examiner would conclude that they do not reflect a unitary factor and the two subtests would be interpreted separately.

Overall, then, the Digit Span subtest may be viewed as a measure of attentional and short-term memory abilities which can provide additional information about the examinee when seen in relation to the Arithmetic subtest. Insofar as it is necessary to administer the Digit Span subtest as well as the Arithmetic subtest if one wishes to evaluate the WISC–III four-factor structure, the present author recommends that the Digit Span subtest routinely be administered.

Interpretation of the Handling of the Digit Span Subtest by the Examinee

The major aspects of the examinee's handling of the Digit Span subtest include her or his physical activity during the subtest and the individual's strategy for dealing with the task. Thus, the examiner should observe, when the subtest is introduced and the items presented, if the child focuses on the task, whether he or she looks at the examiner or gazes off in some other direction, and if the examinee is fidgety or calm.

Aside from the level of physical activity and basic orientation to the examiner and the task, the examiner may also assess the individual's strategy for processing the digits themselves. Common strategies the examiner may encounter include efforts on the part of the child to code the digits as numbers. Thus, the examinee might reply to a first item of 482 by saying, "four hundred and eighty-two." The child will usually find this strategy unsuccessful as soon as the item involves four digits. However, other strategies that group or chunk the information into smaller bits may occur and these will be more adequate over a range of items.

The major implication of the child's attempting *any* strategy is that she or he is displaying a kind of resourcefulness; that is, the examinee does not simply approach a task impulsively, but is able to think about him- or herself confronted with a task and is attempting to develop a general approach to facilitate handling the problem. The part of the subtest where strategies, if used, become most obvious is on the Digits Backward portion of the subtest. In this case, the examiner may observe any of several strategies employed by the child. The individual may actually quietly vocalize the series forward and then pick off the last digit in sequence, continually repeating this oscillation between saying the digits forward and then separating the last one or two digits to meet the demands of the task.

A second version of this strategy involves the examinee's saying the digits forward to her- or himself silently and only vocalizing the last digit. In either of these approaches, it appears that the child is attempting to rely on auditory vocal strategies, which implies that he or she is inclined to utilize language-mediated approaches for dealing with sequential recall tasks.

A third alternative involves the child or adolescent's attempt to recast the auditory information into a mental image or array and to then read off the digits from right to left, a strategy that is usually indicated by the examinee's gaze. This last strategy is an indication of the child's effort, not necessarily a successful one, to shift from auditory to visual modes, or to utilize more varied and flexible strategies for dealing with information processing tasks.

In interpreting the child's subtest performance itself, the examiner may consult Table B.6. (Wechsler, 1991, p. 267) and Table B.7. (Wechsler, 1991, p. 268). These tables provide separate percentages of longest forward and backward digit spans by age for the standardization population, and the cumulative percentages of difference between the longest digits forward and digits backward spans by age for the standardization population. The tables also provide the mean and standard deviation for forward and backward spans for each age, the median forward and backward spans for each age; and the mean, standard deviation, and median for longest forward minus longest backward span for each age in the standardization population.

The availability of these tables permits the examiner to undertake a more refined analysis of the child's performance on the Digit Span subtest. Viewed from the perspective of the hierarchical model discussed earlier (see section on "Models in Psychology"), the examiner may conceive of the overall Digit Span subtest score as the apex of the hierarchy with the Digits Forward and Digits Backward representing lower levels of the hierarchy, and involving the different cognitive processes discussed above.

In terms of the Digit Span subtest, the relationship between the Digits Forward and Backward enable the examiner to assess the child's ability to pay attention to auditory information (Digits Forward) and to carry out somewhat more complex cognitive operations on this same kind of information (Digits Backward). If the Digits Forward are low in themselves, this suggests that the child has clear difficulty with even a simple, direct and minimally demanding auditory attentional task.

If the examinee's Digits Forward is much better than her or his Digits Backward, the examiner may infer that the examinee is able to attend, but that she or he has difficulty when confronted by a more demanding cognitive task: the child either lacks or cannot develop strategies for processing information held in consciousness; the individual cannot concentrate well on internal operations; or the examinee cannot transpose auditory information into visual images.

If the child's performance on Digits Backward is as good or, as infrequently occurs, better than her or his Digits Forward, this may reflect the examinee's having developed increased motivation or having developed an effective strategy to handle the backward task.

Aside from specific strategies used by the examinee to deal with the subtest, the examiner should also record the specific responses the child gives to each item, whether it is the correct response, a request to have the item repeated, an "I don't know" response, or an incorrect response.

Analysis of the examinee's incorrect responses can indicate whether the response was nearly correct or was markedly incorrect, and whether the error involved a failure in sequencing the numbers in the item, which Rudel and Denkla (1974) note occurring in patients with signs of left frontal lobe dysfunction, or involved the child's creating a set of digits in her or his response completely unrelated to the actual item.

MAZES

What the Mazes Subtest Measures

Wechsler (1958), who was writing about the WAIS, did not discuss the Mazes subtest, which had appeared in the WISC (Wechsler, 1949).

According to Wechsler (1991), the Mazes subtest is a supplementary subtest which is not used in the calculation of the WISC–III Performance IQ when the five standard Performance Scale subtests have been administered. Mazes is the only subtest which is not included in any of the four factors on the test.

Sattler (1992) states that the Mazes subtest requires the child to solve paper-and-pencil mazes that differ in complexity. He notes that to perform successfully on this subtest, the child must: attend to the subtest directions, which instruct the examinee to locate a route from the entrance to the exit without entering blind alleys or crossing lines and keeping the pencil on the paper; and execute the task, which involves recalling and following the instructions, displaying visual-motor coordination, and resisting the effect of any implied need to work quickly.

Sattler (1992) states that the Mazes subtest appears to measure the child's planning and perceptual organizational abilities. In order to succeed, the child must have visual-motor control combined with motoric speed and accuracy.

Kaufman (1979a) notes that the Mazes subtest reflects integrated brain functioning, paper-and-pencil skill, planning ability, nonverbal reasoning, and visual-motor coordination. Kaufman (1979a) notes that factors which influence performance on the subtest include: the ability to respond when uncertain, past experience in solving mazes, and working under time pressure. The subtest's unique ability involves measurement of the child's ability to follow a visual pattern and his or her ability to use foresight.

According to the Fluid-Crystallized categorization of intellectual tasks (Horn, 1985; Kaufman, 1990), the Mazes subtest is excluded from the categorization.

According to Bannatyne's (1974) categorization, the Mazes subtest is not included in any of the four groups of Wechsler subtest scores.

Glasser and Zimmerman (1967), in discussing the WISC, note that the Mazes subtest calls for planning and foresight, pencil control and hence visual-motor coordination, and speed combined with accuracy.

The present author views the Mazes subtest as involving several basic abilities. The first entails an ability for visual part/whole analysis, in which the examinee must be aware of an overall pattern, and be able to work from within this framework, part by part, to achieve a final goal. Thus, the ability to deal with the various items shifts depending on: (1) the child's visual span, her or his ability to visually grasp a given maze in toto until the size and complexity of the maze requires the examinee to adopt a more specifically part-focused strategy; and (2) the individual's ability, when needed, to inhibit motor action (drawing the actual line) in order to carry out a visual trial-and-error exploration of the maze on which the examinee will base his or her pencil moves.

Thus, for the younger child, the Mazes subtest assesses the examinee's visual span. As the mazes become more complicated, too complex for a rapid visual scanning to allow the individual to see quickly the correct pathway, the child must be able to inhibit her or his action while planning his or her next move. This in turn involves the examinee's utilization of a problem-solving strategy in which she or he coordinates visual exploration, ideational planning, and motor inhibition. Additionally, the Mazes subtest requires a linear visual or spatial form of thinking, in which the child or adolescent must be able to move rapidly in linear or sequential fashion through a set of alternative paths. Insofar as the subtest requires problem-solving behavior of the examinee, the subtest lacks social cues (such as Picture Arrangement) which might facilitate or interfere with the child's problem-solving efforts.

In terms of what the Mazes subtest measures, during subtest administration, the examiner may periodically recall that the subtest provides a sample of the examinee's performance abilities (and can contribute to the child's Performance IQ if one of the standard performance subtests is invalidated or cannot be given). Otherwise, the Mazes subtest provides a sample of the examinee's visual thinking, planning, and problem-solving abilities as well as his or her visual-motor coordination and control.

Research Pertaining to the Mazes Subtest

There has been little research focused specifically on the Mazes subtest. In Prifitera and Dersh's (1993) investigation of WISC–III subtest patterns among normal, learning disabled, and ADHD samples, scores on the Mazes subtest fell within the normal range for ADHD children (M = 10.05) and essentially within the normal range for learning disabled children (M = 9.78). In the Schwean et al. (1993) investigation of the WISC–III performance of ADHD children, the sample obtained scores above the WISC–III standardization sample on three subtests, including the Mazes subtest. In Doll and Doren's (1993) investigation of the performance of severely language-impaired students on the WISC–III, the Mazes subtest score was the second highest for the sample for the entire WISC–III and the second highest subtest score on the Performance Scale (M = 8.46), at least suggesting that this subtest places less demand on linguistic skills than most other WISC–III subtests.

One study which included the Mazes subtest as a specific component of its research plan investigated the nature of plans and control of behavior among boys with and without learning disabilities at two age periods (Saneda and Serafica, 1991). The learning disabled (LD) and non-learning disabled (NLD) students at the two age periods were compared on plan execution as measured by a planning task (i.e., creating a poster), and a test of knowledge of the planning process, as well as several formal tests which included the WISC–R Mazes subtest.

For the total sample, the correlation between planning knowledge (i.e., knowledge of the issues involved in generating a plan) and scores on the Mazes subtest was .29 (p < .006). The groups of LD and NLD differed from one another on plan execution whether this was measured on a planning task or on standardized tests, suggesting that LD children exhibit a deficit in planning ability, which is also reflected in their actual behavior when called upon to execute a plan. These findings may also be interpreted as providing some degree of construct validation for the Mazes subtest—i.e., that the subtest does reflect a child's knowledge, understanding of, and ability to implement a planning process.

Overall, research involving the Mazes subtest suggests it is one subtest on which children with deficits in attention or language performance (e.g., ADHD or language-impaired children) may perform more adequately than they do on other WISC–R or WISC–III tasks.

Information Processing Aspects of the Mazes Subtest

For the Mazes subtest, input to the child involves visual information plus verbal instructions and demonstration for the examinee to find his or her way out of a variably complex two-dimensional design. Cognitive operations for the individual involve planning, visual and spatial scanning, motor inhibition, decision making, and motor coordination. Output on the subtest involves the tracing of a line from a beginning point to a predefined goal within specific instructional constraints.

Observation of the child or adolescent during this subtest entails noting the examinee's visual search/scanning strategies, the child's reflective or impulsive response tempo, her or his pencil grip and the degree of control or dyscontrol displayed by the examinee in tracing the line.

Information processing deficits that might be reflected in performance on the Mazes subtest would include difficulties in visual part-whole analysis, visual sequential or spatial processing or organization, motor coordination, or difficulties with impulsivity and self-regulation.

Statistical Characteristics of the Mazes Subtest

The Mazes subtest has an average split-half reliability coefficient across all ages of the WISC–III of .70 with reliability coefficients that range from .61 to .80 across the 11 age groups. The Mazes subtest has an average test-retest stability coefficient for all ages of .57.

According to Sattler's (1992) categorization, which groups subtests into good, fair, and poor measures of *g*, the Mazes subtest is a poor measure of *g*. In both the original WISC–III sample and in the Roid et al. (1993) replication study, the Mazes subtest ranks thirteenth among all WISC–III subtests in its *g* loading.

Kamphaus and Platt (1992) report subtest specificities for the WISC–III and indicate that the Mazes subtest has ample specificity for the combined age groups on the WISC–III. Bracken et al. (1993; see Table 16 in the present volume) and Sattler (1992) indicate that the Mazes subtest has ample specificity for ages 6–14 and 16, while the subtest has inadequate specificity for age 15.

Relationships Between the Mazes Subtest and Other Aspects of the WISC–III

The Mazes subtest correlates .31 with the WISC–III Full Scale IQ, .23 with the Verbal IQ, and .35 with the Performance IQ.

The Mazes subtest displays a range of low correlations with the other WISC–III subtests. It correlates best with Arithmetic (.22) on the Verbal Scale, and with Block Design (.31) on the Performance Scale. The Mazes subtest correlates least well with the Digit Span subtest (.14).

The correlation between the Mazes and Block Design subtests may reflect the fact that both of these subtests involve perceptual organizational abilities on the part of the examinee.

From a clinical perspective, it would be possible to view the Mazes subtest as a linear visual and spatial task that involves the child's planning his or her behavior to achieve a particular criterion goal. However, the Mazes subtest lacks social cues or interpersonal content. It thus might be compared to other subtests on the WISC–III that involve auditory or visual information, and with subtests that do or do not involve social cues. Hence the examinee's score on Mazes might be compared to her or his score on Coding (a linear/sequential task that includes linguistic symbols); the Picture Arrangement subtest (a visual sequential task that includes social cues); or the Digit Span subtest (a sequential task that involves auditory rather than visual information).

Interpretation of the Handling of the Mazes Subtest by the Examinee

One of the major issues regarding the child's handling of the Mazes subtest involves the very young examinee who appears unable to grasp the basic concept of a maze. This individual seems unable or unwilling to draw a line within the pathway at all, instead crossing walls to reach the outside of the maze. Such a performance on the part of the child raises the possibility of a marked intellectual deficit in the examinee.

Another issue in the individual's handling of the Mazes subtest involves his or her reaction to the increasing size and complexity of the mazes (also see sections on the examinee's handling of the Block Design and Object Assembly subtests). Some children comment on the increasing challenge as the mazes become larger and more complex, and these examinees may simply give up rather than attempt to apply themselves to the task. This response suggests that the child may react to difficult task situations by retreating rather than with a mobilization of effort to face the problem.

The care and accuracy of the child's pencil control and her or his coordination may also be noted during this subtest, since some anxious or compulsive examinees may worry about staying in the very center of the pathway, while more impulsive and undercontrolled individuals may carelessly overshoot or cut corners in their drawing of a line through the maze.

Chapter Thirteen

FRAMEWORKS FOR THE INTERPRETATION OF THE WISC-III

This chapter will discuss several basic conceptual approaches, or frameworks, for interpreting the data obtained from the WISC–III administration. These approaches are the factor-analytic approach (Wechsler, 1991; Sattler, 1992); the recategorization approach suggested by Bannatyne (1968, 1971, 1974); the Fluid-Crystallized model based on Horn's views (Horn, 1985, 1988; Horn & Hofer, 1992; Kaufman, 1990); the ACID profile (Ackerman et al., 1976, 1977); and Kaufman's approach to profile analysis (Kaufman, 1979a, 1990; Reynolds & Kaufman, 1985).

WECHSLER'S FACTOR-ANALYTIC APPROACH

The manual for the Wechsler Intelligence Scale for Children-Third Edition (Wechsler, 1991) provides data and discussion regarding the development, standardization and statistical properties of the WISC–III.

Based on past research with the WISC–R (e.g., Kaufman, 1975), Wechsler (1991) adopts a factor-analytic approach to conceptualizing the structure of the WISC–III and what the test measures. Sattler (1990) describes factor analysis as a mathematical technique which is used to analyze the intercorrelations of a group of tests (or other variables) that have been administered to a large number of individuals.

Factor analysis is based on the assumption that intercorrelations among a group of scores can be explained by an underlying factor or set of factors that are fewer in number than the original set of scores. Sattler (1990) notes that a factor represents an element which a group of interrelated tests have in common or share with one another. The results of a factor analysis indicate the extent to which each test loads on, or is correlated with, one or more of the factors which have been identified.

Sattler (1990) states that in the field of intelligence, factor analysis might be used to determine the number of different mental abilities which account for interrelationships among tests in a battery with a prime purpose of the factor analysis being to simplify understanding of the behavior in question by reducing the variables considered to the smallest number.

Sattler (1990) points out that most factor analysis programs, currently almost always carried out by computer, operate to extract first that factor which accounts for the largest proportion of variance in the data set, then the factor which accounts for the largest proportion of the remaining variance, and so on, until all the variance in the data set has been accounted for.

While Hale (1991) notes that factor analysis has been the primary tool for investigating the structure of intelligence, he points out that the factor-analytic approach continues to generate controversy since the method does not refer to a single technique but to a number of different ones, and the results obtained by a factor analysis depend upon the factoring method which has been chosen and utilized. Baron (1987) has also criticized factor analysis while Carroll (1988) has offered a defense of the use of the factor-analytic method.

The manual for the WISC–III (Wechsler, 1991) notes that numerous factor-analytic methods were applied to the standardization data, with both exploratory and confirmatory analyses being performed, and with the results of a variety of extraction and rotation methods being compared and contrasted. These various analyses were carried out on the total sample of 2200 subjects as well as on four age-group subsamples: ages 6–7 (n = 400), ages 8–10 (n = 600), ages 11–13 (n = 600), and ages 14–16 (n = 600).

Wechsler (1991) cites Gorsuch (1983) who suggests that factor solutions should be evaluated not only by empirical criteria but also according to a criterion of "psychological meaningfulness," and hence Wechsler (1991) discusses the factor-analytic results on the WISC–III in the light of previous literature on the WISC–R as well as the model of global intelligence developed by Wechsler (1974).

Based on examination of factor models ranging from one to five, Wechsler (1991) concluded that the examination and comparison of the various models converged to strongly suggest a four-factor solution for the WISC–III with two major factors and two smaller supplementary factors.

The two major factors were those of Verbal Comprehension and Perceptual Organization, which have been found in numerous past factor analyses of the WISC–R (Blaha & Vance, 1979; Carlson, Reynolds, & Gutkin, 1983; Kaufman, 1975; Peterson & Hart, 1979).

The Verbal Comprehension factor found in the WISC–III factor analysis consists of four subtests: Information, Similarities, Vocabulary and Comprehension. The Perceptual Organization factor also consists of four subtests: Picture Completion, Picture Arrangement, Block Design and Object Assembly.

The third factor obtained in the analysis of the WISC–III differs slightly from that obtained with analyses of the WISC–R. On the WISC–R, the third factor consisted of the Arithmetic, Digit Span, and Coding subtests. However, on the WISC–III the third factor consists of only the Arithmetic and Digit

Span subtests, although this factor continues to be labelled Freedom from Distractibility just as it was on the WISC–R.

On the WISC–III, the Coding subtest now loads on a newly determined fourth factor, along with the new Symbol Search subtest, and this fourth factor is labelled the Processing Speed factor.

Thus, Wechsler's (1991) factor-analytic framework for viewing the WISC–III groups the subtests into four factors (see Table 3).

As noted above (see section on WISC–III Internal Validity), in contrast to the factor-analytic results reported by Wechsler (1991), Sattler (1992) carried out his own maximum-likelihood factor analysis of the standardization group for each age group and for the total sample using 2, 3 and 4 factor models. Sattler's (1992) results suggested to him that a three-factor, rather than a four-factor, model fit the data best.

Although the specific pattern of factor-analytic results reported by Sattler (1992) are complex, with his reporting that the model is somewhat weak at ages 6 and 15, he found that Verbal Comprehension accounted for 25% of the variance in the sample, Perceptual Organization accounted for 16% of the variance, and Processing Speed accounted for 10% of the variance. Thus, in Sattler's view, there was no evidence for Wechsler's third, or Freedom from Distractibility, factor, and he concluded that this third factor on the WISC–III should be disregarded until there is further evidence to support its use.

Sattler (1992) concluded that the Verbal Comprehension factor appears to measure a variable common to most Verbal Scale subtests. For the total sample, Vocabulary, Information, Comprehension and Similarities have the highest loadings on this factor; Arithmetic has a moderate loading on the factor while Digit Span has a minimal loading. Sattler (1992) notes that three Performance Scale subtests—Picture Completion, Picture Arrangement, and Block Design—also have some loading on this factor.

Sattler (1992) notes that the Perceptual Organization factor measures a variable common to several Performance Scale subtests. For the total sample, Block Design and Object Assembly have high loadings on the factor; Picture Completion has a moderate loading; and Mazes, Picture Arrangement and Symbol Search have minimal loadings on the factor.

Sattler's (1992) third factor, Processing Speed, reflects the ability to concentrate and attend while processing information by scanning an array. For the total sample this factor includes the Coding and Symbol Search subtests. Thus, Sattler states that his factor-analytic results indicate that the factor structure of the WISC–III closely agrees with the actual organization of the test.

Roid et al. (1993) conducted an independent study to explore the factor structure of the WISC–III, noting that the WISC–III manual had reported both exploratory and confirmatory factor analyses demonstrating that the

WISC–III contained two major factors and two smaller supplementary factors, with this four-factor model having been confirmed in the standardization sample, as well as in samples of a clinical population, a high ability group, and a low ability group.

Roid et al. (1993) note that other researchers have already examined the nature of the third and fourth factors. Kamphaus (1993) had expressed the need for caution in interpretation of these factors, while Sattler (1992) had concluded that the Freedom from Distractibility factor was not found consistently in the data. Roid et al. suggested that Sattler's (1992) use of a 1.0 eigenvalue criterion in his factor analyses across groups in the WISC–III standardization sample was an imprecise method for specifying the number of factors in the WISC–III, and proposed and justified their statistical approach to an analysis of the WISC–III data.

Roid et al. (1993) report an investigation involving the testing of 1,118 children which had been carried out as part of the standardization of the Wechsler Individual Achievement Test (WIAT; The Psychological Corporation, 1992a). The children were administered both the WISC–III and the WIAT to obtain a sample of subjects which was independent of the WISC–III normative data upon which the original WISC–III factor analyses had been based. This sample involved a stratified random sampling plan that used ethnicity/race, parent education level, geographic region, and gender as stratification variables.

Roid et al. (1993) applied both exploratory and confirmatory factor-analytic methods to the new WISC–III data. They found that two major factors and two smaller supplementary factors were again obtained for the WISC–III. They state that the use of a conventional eigenvalue rule as suggested by Sattler (1992) and his conclusion that three factors best explains the WISC–III is too conservative. Roid et al. thus contend that four factors provide the most psychologically meaningful solution for the WISC–III. Their first two major factors are Verbal Comprehension and Perceptual Organization, which account for approximately 54% of the variance in the final solution.

Roid et al. (1993) state that factor three, consisting of Arithmetic and Digit Span, includes approximately 6% of the variance and is labelled Freedom from Distractibility, while the fourth factor, including Coding and Symbol Search, accounts for about 8% of the variance and is labelled Processing Speed.

Roid et al. (1993) carried out a series of analyses to examine and compare a series of different models for the data (e.g., a one general factor model; a three-factor model; a five-factor model). The greatest improvement in contrasting models was from a one-factor to a two-factor model, and the next greatest improvement was from a two-factor to a four-factor model.

Although Roid et al. (1993) found the possible existence of "singleton" factors (those that involved a single subtest such as Comprehension, Arithmetic or Digit Span), they conclude that consideration of singleton factors would not improve the fit of any model to the data. Hence the overall conclusion of Roid et al. is that the results of their exploratory and confirmatory factor analyses of the 13 subtests of the WISC–III provides evidence for the existence of the same four factors which were reported by Wechsler (1991).

Kamphaus, Benson, Hutchinson, and Platt (1994) report an investigation of the WISC–III standardization data in which three different factor models were tested to determine which fit the data best. Kamphaus et al. compared Wechsler's original two-factor model (Wechsler, 1958, 1974), Kaufman's (1979a) three-factor model, and Wechsler's (1991) WISC–III four-factor model. Kamphaus et al. report that, statistically, none of the models fit the data very well except for the three- and four-factor models at ages 6 and 9. However, the four-factor model did fit the model better than the other models for all age groups. Since there is no psychological theory to support the four-factor model, Kamphaus et al. recommend that further theoretical and empirical investigations are required to clarify the meaning of the third and fourth factors.

However, if one adopts a factor-analytic framework for understanding the WISC–III, there are two possible perspectives from which one can choose. Wechsler (1991) concludes that a four-factor solution including Verbal Comprehension, Perceptual Organization, Freedom from Distractibility and Processing Speed best accounts for the variance in the data set. In contrast, Sattler (1992) concludes that a three-factor model is most appropriate. He states that Verbal Comprehension, Perceptual Organization and Processing Speed explain the data best, and that evidence is lacking at this time to support the existence of a Freedom from Distractibility factor.

It should be noted that Sattler's (1992) Verbal Comprehension factor is identical to Wechsler's Verbal Comprehension factor, and in both cases the four subtests are: Information, Similarities, Vocabulary and Comprehension. However, Sattler's (1992) Perceptual Organization factor excludes Picture Arrangement, which is part of Wechsler's (1991) Perceptual Organization factor, since Sattler feels Picture Arrangement has a minimal loading on the Perceptual Organization factor. Hence, Sattler's (1992) Perceptual Organization factor includes Picture Completion, Block Design, and Object Assembly. For both Wechsler (1991) and Sattler (1992), the Processing Speed factor contains Coding and Symbol Search.

As noted above in the present author's discussion of the belief system of the clinician as a critical variable in the clinical enterprise, one can choose to accept Wechsler's (1991) factor analytic conclusions and proceed to use a four-factor model for the interpretation of WISC–III data. On the other hand, if one is more conservative, one may accept Sattler's (1992) thorough but independent and alternative conclusions about factors on the WISC–III. If the findings with respect to the third factor on the WISC–R are any indication, the controversy about a three- or four-factor interpretation of the WISC–III will continue for some time.

However, if one is using a factor-analytic framework, whether one chooses a four-factor or a three-factor model, the interpretation of the child's WISC–III profile involves examination of the examinee's performance on the factors. The factor structure becomes the scaffolding upon which interpretation of the individual's test performance is based, and it is from within this framework that the examiner conceptualizes the child's intellectual performance. The factor structure also becomes the scheme from within which the examiner develops her or his report of the test results.

THE ACID PROFILE

Among the many efforts to identify particular patterns of subtest performance on the Wechsler scales that are characteristic of certain populations of individuals, one approach that has shown some consistency involves that of the so-called ACID profile (e.g., Ackerman et al., 1976, 1977) which refers to a pattern of low scores on the four WISC or WISC–R subtests of Arithmetic, Coding, Information and Digit Span; the acronym ACID refers to this grouping of subtests.

In an early investigation of learning disabled children, Ackerman, Peters, and Dykman (1971) reported the finding that learning disabled children obtained lower scores than controls on the subtests of Information, Digit Span, Arithmetic and Similarities. Subsequent investigations have found evidence to support the ACID profile construct of lowered scores on the Arithmetic, Coding, Information and Digit Span subtests among samples of learning disabled children (e.g., Ackerman et al., 1976, 1977); reading disabled children (Petrauskas & Rourke, 1979); and children with attention-deficit disorder with hyperactivity (Dykman, Ackerman, & Oglesby, 1980).

Sandoval, Sassenrath, and Penaloza (1988), in an investigation which compared the similarity of WISC–R and WAIS–R scores of 30 learning disabled male and female adolescents between ages 16 and 17, noted that differential performance on the ACID subtests (Arithmetic, Coding, Information, and Digit Span) was evident on both test instruments. The ACID subtests comprised the four most difficult WISC–R subtests for the sample and were among the five most difficult WAIS–R subtests for the sample.

Kaufman et al. (1990) summarize a selection of studies conducted with learning disabled, emotionally and behaviorally disturbed, and mentally retarded children. The rank orderings of subtest difficulty for learning disabled and emotionally disturbed children indicated that Coding, Information, and Arithmetic, three of the four ACID subtests, were usually the most difficult for these children (Digit Span was not always administered).

In contrast to the above discussion, however, Kavale and Forness (1984), in their meta-analysis of Wechsler scale profiles and recategorizations, report that their findings indicate only an approximate one-half standard deviation suppression of subtest scores on the ACID profile among learning disabled samples, which translates into a scaled score equivalent of 8.66.

Since a difference of at least three points from the expected subtest mean of 10 would be necessary for the ACID profile to be a meaningful diagnostic indicator, a suppression of barely 1.5 points would not qualify as sufficient evidence to permit an examiner to make a differential diagnosis based on the ACID profile. Thus Kavale and Forness (1984, 1994) conclude that WISC LD profiles, including the ACID profile, do not demonstrate either significant or distinctive groupings for reliably separating LD and normal children.

In their effort to examine the ACID profile on the WISC–III, Prifitera and Dersh (1993) note that Joschko and Rourke (1985) reported that only 6% of a sample of 3,500 reading disabled children had the ACID profile. But Prifitera and Dersh (1993) note that Joschko and Rourke appear to be the only researchers to report the actual percentage of individuals in a learning disabled sample that display the ACID profile. Prifitera and Dersh (1993) attribute the lack of research in the area of the ACID profile to Kaufman's (1979a) observation that analysis of this grouping of subtests is speculative at best when the frequency of occurrence of the ACID profile among normal individuals is unknown.

In an attempt to explore base rates of several WISC–III subtest patterns including the ACID profile, Prifitera and Dersh (1993) determined the percentages of children with various subtest patterns for samples of children with learning disabilities and with attention-deficit hyperactivity disorder, and compared these to the percentages of these patterns which occurred in the WISC–III standardization population. The samples Prifitera and Dersh (1993) describe were all tested as part of the development and validation of the WISC–III (Wechsler, 1991). For the purpose of their investigation, children with IQs below 70 were excluded from each of the samples they studied.

The learning disability (LD) sample consisted of 99 children aged 6 to 14 (M = 10.3 years) including 21% females and 79% males, and 94% Whites, 3% Blacks, 2% Hispanics, and 1% Asians. The subjects displayed a variety of learning disabilities including developmental reading disorders, reading and writing disorders, combined learning disorders and unspecified learning disabilities.

The ADHD sample consisted of 65 children aged 7 to 16 (M = 10.2 years) with a primary diagnosis of attention-deficit hyperactivity disorder (ADHD). This sample consisted of 11% females and 89% males with 98% whites and 2% Asians.

The third sample used by Prifitera and Dersh (1993) was the WISC–III standardization sample, consisting of 2,158 children between the ages of 6 and 16 with 190 to 200 children in each age group. Since children receiving special services were not excluded from the standardization sample, 7% of this sample consisted of children with various kinds of handicapping conditions (see Table 9 for WISC–III subtest scores of the three samples).

Prifitera and Dersh (1993) report the percentage of individuals in the learning disability (LD) sample who display the full and partial ACID profile; the percentage of individuals in a separate attention-deficit hyperactivity disorder (ADHD) sample who display the full and partial ACID profile; and they compare the percentage of occurrence of the full and partial profile in these LD and ADHD samples to the rate of occurrence of the full and partial ACID profile in the WISC–III standardization sample (see Table 10).

Prifitera and Dersh (1993) first calculated the percentage of children in each sample who displayed the ACID profile. Subjects were considered to display this profile when their scaled scores on all four of the ACID subtests were equal to or less than the lowest scaled score on any one of the remaining subtests excluding Mazes and Symbol Search. The latter two subtests were excluded because in prior research on the ACID profile with the WISC–R, the Mazes subtest had often not been administered, and because the WISC–R did not contain the Symbol Search subtest.

Prifitera and Dersh (1993) found that for both the LD and ADHD groups, the lowest subtest scores were obtained on the Digit Span, Arithmetic, Coding, and Symbol Search subtests (see Table 9). However, the Information subtest was not one of the lowest four or five subtests for either the LD or ADHD group, which is not consistent with the standard ACID profile, nor with past research on the ACID profile (e.g., Sandoval et al., 1988).

Comparison of the frequency of the ACID pattern in the WISC–III standardization sample and the two clinical samples indicates that the full ACID pattern, with all four of the ACID subtests being the lowest in the subject's protocol, occurs rarely in the general population (1.1%). This pattern occurs at much higher rates in the LD sample (5.1%) and in the ADHD sample (12.3%), with the differences among these percentages being significant at the .01 level. Prifitera and Dersh (1993) note that although Joschko and Rourke (1985) utilized different criteria to define the ACID profile, the two investigations found similar rates of occurrence of the profile in their samples (5.1% and 6%).

Table 9
MEANS OF THE SUBTEST SCALED SCORES FOR THE
STANDARDIZATION, LD, AND ADHD SAMPLES

| | Sample | | |
Subtest	Standardization (N = 2,158)	Learning Disabled (n = 99)	ADHD (n = 65)
Picture Completion	10.11	10.99	11.98
Information	10.18	9.49	9.75
Coding	10.06	8.05	7.83
Similarities	10.08	9.76	9.48
Picture Arrangement	10.05	10.00	9.63
Arithmetic	10.12	7.87	9.31
Block Design	10.02	9.66	11.14
Vocabulary	10.03	9.06	10.57
Object Assembly	10.04	10.51	11.29
Comprehension	10.10	9.41	10.15
Symbol Search	10.05	8.52	9.09
Digit Span	10.11	8.12	8.43
Mazes	10.07	9.78	10.05
Mean	10.08	9.32	9.90

Note. Reprinted by permission of the journal, the copyright holder, and A. Prifitera from A. Prifitera & J. Dersh, "Base Rates of WISC–III Diagnostic Subtest Patterns Among Normal, Learning-Disabled, and ADHD Samples," *Journal of Psychoeducational Assessment, Monograph Series, Advances in Psychoeducational Assessment, Wechsler Intelligence Scale for Children: Third Edition,* 1993, p. 48. [Wechsler Intelligence Scale for Children – Third Edition. Copyright © 1990 by the Psychological Corporation. Reproduced by permission. All rights reserved. "WISC–III" and "Wechsler Intelligence Scale for Children" and the "WISC–III logo" are registered trademarks of The Psychological Corporation. Their use herein does in no way indicate endorsement of this product by The Psychological Corporation.]

Similarly, the partial ACID pattern, with three of the ACID subtests being the lowest in the child's protocol, is also rare in the general population (5.7%) but more common among the LD sample (21.2%) and the ADHD sample (29.2%), with the difference among these percentages being significant at the .01 level.

In view of the fact that Wechsler's (1991) factor analysis of the WISC–III standardization data grouped the Symbol Search subtest with the Coding subtest (which is one of the ACID subtests) in a Processing Speed factor, Prifitera and Dersh (1993) added the Symbol Search subtest to the four ACID subtests to create a new composite, which they labelled ACIDS. The authors compared the percentages of individuals with the ACIDS profile among their LD and ADHD samples to the percentage of children in the WISC–III standardization sample who display this five subtest profile (see Table 11).

Table 10

CUMULATIVE PERCENTAGES OF THE STANDARDIZATION, LD, AND ADHD SAMPLES AT VARIOUS LEVELS OF THE ACID PROFILE

Number of ACID Subtests Lowest	Sample		
	Standardization	Learning Disabled	ADHD
4	1.1	5.1	12.3
3	5.7	21.2	29.2
2	19.5	36.4	53.8
1	46.9	64.6	78.5

Note. Reprinted by permission of the journal, the copyright holder, and A. Prifitera from A. Prifitera & J. Dersh, "Base Rates of WISC–III Diagnostic Subtest Patterns among Normal, Learning-Disabled, and ADHD Samples," *Journal of Psychoeducational Assessment, Monograph Series, Advances in Psychoeducational Assessment, Wechsler Intelligence Scale for Children: Third Edition,* 1993, p. 49. [Wechsler Intelligence Scale for Children—Third Edition. Copyright © 1990 by the Psychological Corporation. Reproduced by permission. All rights reserved. "WISC–III" and "Wechsler Intelligence Scale for Children" and the "WISC–III logo" are registered trademarks of The Psychological Corporation. Their use herein does in no way indicate endorsement of this product by The Psychological Corporation.]

Prifitera and Dersh (1993) report that the full ACIDS profile is also rare among the general population (.6%), while it occurs much more commonly among the LD sample (4.0%), and among the ADHD sample (6.2%), with the differences among these percentages being significant at the .01 level. The partial ACIDS profile, with four of five subtests being the lowest, occurs infrequently among the standardization population (3.1%) but more often among the LD sample (14.1%) and the ADHD sample (21.5%).

Prifitera and Dersh (1993) conclude that their study provides evidence for specific patterns of cognitive deficit in LD and ADHD children. Children who have been identified as having a learning disability or an attention-deficit disorder display relatively poor performance on subtests that reflect attention, short-term memory, and processing speed. The findings of Prifitera and Dersh (1993) demonstrate that the ACID and ACIDS patterns occur with much greater frequency among clinical groups than in the normal population.

Prifitera and Dersh (1993) note that, utilizing a Bayesian approach, the examiner could employ the baserate information they provide in order to determine the conditional probability that a particular child belongs to the LD or ADHD clinical group given that she or he has a particular number of the ACID or ACIDS subtests as his or her lowest subtest scores. However, the

Table 11
CUMULATIVE PERCENTAGES OF THE STANDARDIZATION, LD, AND ADHD SAMPLES AT VARIOUS LEVELS OF THE ACIDS PROFILE

Number of ACIDS Subtests Lowest	Sample		
	Standardization	Learning Disabled	ADHD
5	.6	4.0	6.2
4	3.1	14.1	21.5
3	10.9	28.3	44.6
2	26.9	48.5	58.5
1	52.2	70.7	81.5

Note. Reprinted by permission of the journal, the copyright holder, and A. Prifitera from A. Prifitera & J. Dersh, "Base Rates of WISC–III Diagnostic Subtest Patterns Among Normal, Learning-Disabled, and ADHD Samples," *Journal of Psychoeducational Assessment, Monograph Series, Advances in Psychoeducational Assessment, Wechsler Intelligence Scale for Children: Third Edition,* 1993, p. 50. [Wechsler Intelligence Scale for Children – Third Edition. Copyright © 1990 by the Psychological Corporation. Reproduced by permission. All rights reserved. "WISC–III" and "Wechsler Intelligence Scale for Children" and the "WISC–III logo" are registered trademarks of The Psychological Corporation. Their use herein does in no way indicate endorsement of this product by The Psychological Corporation.]

authors note a number of cautions in using such an approach for diagnosing a child based on her or his WISC–III test performance. These include the fact that not all children in the clinical groups displayed the ACID pattern, and some normal children may display the ACID or ACIDS pattern. Hence, the examiner must be concerned about false positives or false negatives in the population of children he or she tests.

In addition, children in other clinical groups may display a similar profile of cognitive abilities to those of children who have been diagnosed as having a learning disability or an attention-deficit disorder. Thus, for example, Longman, Inglis, and Lawson (1991) found that children diagnosed as behavior disordered displayed the same cognitive patterns as did a sample of LD children.

The present author does not recommend use of the profile as Prifitera and Dersh (1993) suggest because the examiner may not know the baserate of learning disability in the population of children he or she is dealing with. Secondly, the present author does not believe in using the WISC–III by itself for making a diagnosis of learning disability. In order to determine whether or not a child has a learning disability, the author feels it is necessary to utilize the WISC–III (and/or other measures of general cognitive ability) to assess the child's general intellectual ability, and then to utilize one or more measures of the child's actual academic achievement and to compare the relationship between the child's general intellectual abilities and his or her academic achievement.

There are disagreements in terms of whether simple discrepancy scores or regression methods are more appropriate for determining learning disability status among children (Braden & Weiss, 1988; Wilson & Cone, 1984). Braden and Weiss (1988) note that the magnitude of simple difference discrepancies covaries with IQ level while regression discrepancies do not display a relationship to IQ level. They note that regression methods are thus superior to simple difference methods for determining learning disability eligibility, although they would not recommend either method as the sole criterion for learning disability placement.

In view of the realization that learning disabled children are quite varied (Gaddes, 1985), rather than attempting to utilize the ACID or ACIDS profile to diagnose a child as learning disabled as suggested by Prifitera and Dersh (1993), the present author believes it is far more reasonable for the examiner to note whether a child's WISC–III test protocol reveals the ACID or ACIDS profile, but to then use this information along with other aspects of the examinee's test protocol and performance, and with other tests as appropriate, to determine the individual's learning disability or attention-deficit status rather than seeking to make this determination from some aspect of the child's WISC–III performance in isolation.

BANNATYNE'S CONCEPT OF RECATEGORIZATION OF WECHSLER SCALED SCORES

Bannatyne (1968) noted that dividing the WISC performance of dyslexic children into Verbal and Performance IQs did not facilitate meaningful psychological analysis of the data. Instead, he found it more useful to divide the subtest scores into three categories for reanalysis: a Spatial category including the subtests of Picture Completion, Block Design and Object Assembly; a Conceptual category including the subtests of Vocabulary, Similarities and Comprehension; and a Sequential category including the subtests of Digit Span, Coding and Picture Arrangement. In each of these categories, he assumed an average score of 10 on each subtest so that the total for each of the three categories equalled 30 points.

In his examination of "genetic" dyslexics, Bannatyne (1971) reported that these disabled readers had their highest scores in the Spatial category, intermediate scores in the Conceptual category, and their lowest scores in the Sequential category.

Although Bannatyne's (1968, 1971) definitions of these categories are not always clear, subtests in the Spatial category require the ability to manipulate objects (and parts of objects) either directly or symbolically in multidimensional space without sequencing. Bannatyne (1971) states that the subtests in the Conceptual category involve items that can be answered at least in part by manipulating spatial images conceptually. Rugel (1974) suggests that subtests in the Conceptual category require abilities which are more closely related to language functioning. Rugel (1974) also notes that subtests in the Sequential category require the ability to retain sequences of auditory and visual stimuli in short-term memory. A fourth category which Bannatyne (1971) also added was that of Acquired Knowledge, which reflected the child's educational attainment.

In Bannatyne's (1968) original formulation, the Sequential category included the Digit Span, Coding and Picture Arrangement subtests. Rugel (1974) analyzed 25 published and unpublished studies of WISC subtest scores of disabled readers in terms of the usefulness of recategorization of the scores. This involved calculation of the overall scaled scores for the three categories and then the ranking of the categories from highest to lowest.

Rugel (1974) found that in the 22 populations of disabled readers where complete recategorization of the scores was possible, the Spatial category received the highest rank 18 times, the intermediate rank four times and the lowest rank not at all. The Conceptual category received the highest rank four times, the intermediate rank fourteen times and the lowest rank four times. The Sequential category received the highest rank zero times, the intermediate rank four times and the lowest rank 18 times. Rugel (1974) concluded that his results thus agreed with Bannatyne's findings with genetic dyslexics.

In his comparison of disabled and normal readers, Rugel (1974) found that in the Sequential category, disabled readers demonstrated a clear deficit as compared to normal readers. However, while disabled readers performed more poorly than normal readers on the Digit Span and Coding subtests, on the Picture Arrangement subtest, the scores of disabled readers were not significantly below those of normal readers. On the other hand, on the Arithmetic subtest, which was not included in Bannatyne's (1968) original scheme, disabled readers were significantly lower than normal readers.

In response to Rugel's (1974) article, Bannatyne (1974) noted Rugel's observation that the WISC Picture Arrangement subtest was "wrongly included" in the Sequential category. Bannatyne (1974) noted that the Arithmetic subtest is an oral subtest which requires the child to remember several spoken words or sentences and hence contained a large element of auditory vocal sequential memory which also depends on attentional processes. Bannatyne (1974) thus revised the Sequential category of his WISC recategorization scheme to include Digit Span, Coding and Arithmetic instead of Digit Span, Coding and Picture Arrangement.

Since then, a number of researchers have applied Bannatyne's recategorization approach to WISC–R data (e.g., Decker & Corley, 1984; Gutkin, 1979; Smith, Coleman, Dokecki & Davis, 1977a, 1977b; Vance & Singer, 1979). These investigations have found that reading- and learning disabled children demonstrate their greatest strength in spatial ability (Picture Completion, Object Assembly and Block Design). This is followed by their abilities in verbal conceptualization (Similarities, Vocabulary and Comprehension), which is followed by their performance in sequencing ability (Arithmetic, Digit Span and Coding). They have also been found to display a limited fund of acquired knowledge (Information, Arithmetic and Vocabulary; e.g., Decker & Corley, 1984).

In terms of the diagnostic usefulness of the recategorization approach, Clarizio and Bernard (1981) found that Bannatyne's category system was not able to discriminate between learning disabled, emotionally disturbed, mentally retarded, and non-handicapped children. Similarly, Henry and Wittman (1981) found that the categories did not discriminate between learning disabled and emotionally disturbed children.

Kavale and Forness (1984) reported a meta-analysis to arrive at a quantitative synthesis of the results of 94 studies on the WISC, WISC–R and WPPSI. This meta-analytic procedure involves translating the results of different studies into a common metric, that of "effect size." This statistic represents a standard mean difference in which the mean score for the learning disabled group is subtracted from the mean score for the normal group (or that of the test's standard values), and then this difference is divided by the standard deviation of the normal group (or of the test's standard values).

In their consideration of studies involving Bannatyne's original recategorization scheme, Kavale and Forness (1984) found a significant difference for Spatial and Conceptual > Sequential, while in his revised scheme, they found a significant difference involving Spatial and Conceptual > Sequential and Acquired Knowledge. Hence their findings were consistent with Bannatyne's finding of Spatial > Conceptual > Sequential.

Summarizing a variety of intraindividual comparisons, then, Kavale and Forness (1984) concluded that the LD group performed most poorly in areas requiring memory and attention, while they performed best in tasks involving verbal comprehension, perceptual organization, synthesis and reasoning.

Although the effect size data thus indicated some patterns of strength and weakness on various WISC recategorizations including Bannatyne's, when these performances were translated into scaled-score equivalents, the LD group performed only about a half point above the subtest mean of 10 in areas of strength. Similarly, the LD group performed only a point and one-half below average performance in the areas where they were weak. When compared to the deviation of + or − 3 which is needed for significance, none of the recategorized scores showed any areas to be a significant strength or weakness for the LD group (Kavale & Forness, 1984, 1994).

In addition, all of the obtained scaled scores place the LD group within the average range. Hence, although the LD group displayed slightly significant differences in their recategorized scores, these differences from the performance of normals or the standardization population would not be distinctive enough to be useful for differential diagnosis of a learning disability (Kavale & Forness, 1984, 1994).

Also raising questions about the usefulness of the Bannatyne approach, Gutkin (1979) noted the difficulty in generalizing the typical Bannatyne learning disability profile to Mexican-American learning disabled children. Although Gutkin (1979) found the Spatial > Conceptual > Sequencing profile for white learning disabled children, he found a Spatial > Sequencing > Conceptual group profile for Hispanics.

Similarly, McShane and Plas (1982) recategorized the WISC–R subtest scores of 192 learning disabled Navajo Indian children according to Bannatyne's (1974) system. They found that as a group, the subjects failed to demonstrate the Spatial > Conceptual > Sequential pattern predicted by Bannatyne and they noted the need for caution in utilizing this approach with learning disabled minority children.

Zarske and Moore (1982) reported an investigation of 142 Indian children who had been tested with the WISC, WISC–R or WPPSI. These authors found evidence for a Wechsler Scale performance pattern among Indian children that differed from the pattern found in normal and non-Indian learning disabled groups. Zarske and Moore (1982) found their subjects to have spatial abilities more well developed than sequencing abilities, which were superior to the subjects' conceptual and acquired knowledge performances. The authors observed differences in recategorization patterns between those Indian children who had been raised in a traditional fashion and those who were more Anglo-acculturated, and they discussed factors that might be related to these differential patterns.

Smith et al. (1977b) administered the WISC–R to 208 school-verified learning disabled children and recategorized the obtained subtest scores according to Bannatyne's (1974) system. These authors found that the mean Spatial score was significantly greater than the mean Conceptual score, which in turn exceeded the Sequential and Acquired Knowledge scores.

Smith et al. (1977b) also divided their total sample into high and low IQ subgroups to determine if the Spatial > Conceptual > Sequential pattern was affected by, or was independent of, intellectual level. Although sub-groups of relatively high and low IQ individuals displayed similar patterns of recategorized scores, the recategorization relationships did not hold true for the 26 children in the sample who had obtained Full Scale IQs of 75 or less.

Prifitera and Dersh (1993) note that Smith et al. (1977b) had reported the percentage of children in their sample who individually demonstrated the Bannatyne learning disability profile. Smith et al. (1977b) found that 43% of their sample revealed the Spatial > Conceptual > Sequential pattern, which was significantly more than the 17% that would have been expected by chance. In his investigation, Gutkin (1979) found that 30% of his sample of 53 learning disabled children displayed the Bannatyne profile.

Prifitera and Dersh (1993) compared the WISC–III subtest patterns of three samples: a learning disabled sample; an attention-deficit hyperactivity disorder sample; and the WISC–III standardization sample. In observing the percentages of children in each of their three samples with the Bannatyne profile, Prifitera and Dersh (1993) note, "subjects were considered positive for the profile when their summed scaled score on the Spatial subtests was greater than their summed scaled score on the Verbal Conceptualization subtests, which, in turn, was greater than their summed scaled score on the Sequential subtests" (Prifitera & Dersh, 1993, p. 47).

Prifitera and Dersh (1993) found that in the standardization sample, scores on the four Bannatyne categories were essentially equal. Both the LD and ADHD clinical groups displayed the predicted Bannatyne pattern with highest scores on Spatial subtests, intermediate scores on Verbal Conceptu-alization subtests, and with lowest scores on Sequential subtests. However, in the LD sample, the pattern of the four Bannatyne groups was Spatial > Verbal Conceptualization > Acquired Knowledge > Sequential, while in the ADHD sample, the pattern was Spatial > Verbal Conceptualization > Acquired Knowledge > Sequential (see Table 12).

Prifitera and Dersh (1993) found that the base rate of the Bannatyne pattern (Spatial > Verbal Conceptualization > Sequential) was 13.59% in the standardization population. In contrast, the pattern was found among 33.33% of LD children, and among 47.06% of ADHD children, with these differ-ences being significant at the .01 level. The authors point out that the percentage of LD children they observed with the pattern fell in between the 30% reported by Gutkin (1979) and the 43% reported by Smith et al. (1977b).

The above discussion indicates that although the WISC–R pattern of Spatial > Conceptual > Sequential subtests has often been found among learning disabled children, it is not a universal finding, and the pattern may not be found among various minority or other cultural subgroups within the United States. Even if the pattern does occur at a higher rate among

Table 12
MEANS OF THE IQ, INDEX, AND BANNATYNE SCORES
AND THE SUM OF INDICES THREE AND FOUR FOR THE
STANDARDIZATION, LD, AND ADHD SAMPLES

	Sample		
	Standardization (N = 2,158)	Learning Disabled (n = 99)	ADHD (n = 65)
Verbal IQ	100.94	95.25	99.54
Performance IQ	100.87	99.42	102.91
Full Scale IQ	100.84	96.76	101.03
Verbal Compreh. Index	100.92	97.25	100.29
Perceptual Organ. Index	101.00	102.42	106.80
Free. from Distr. Index	101.59	89.66	94.60
Processing Speed Index	101.35	92.05	93.08
Index 3 & 4 Subtests (Sum)	40.34	32.56	34.66
Bannatyne Scores[a]			
Spatial	30.17	31.15	34.42
Verbal Conceptual	30.21	28.23	30.20
Sequential	30.29	24.04	25.57
Acquired Knowledge	30.33	26.42	29.63

[a]Bannatyne scores were calculated by summing the scaled scores in each category.
Note. Reprinted by permission of the journal, the copyright holder, and A. Prifitera from A. Prifitera & J. Dersh, "Base Rates of WISC–III Diagnostic Subtest Patterns Among Normal, Learning-Disabled, and ADHD Samples," *Journal of Psychoeducational Assessment, Monograph Series, Advances in Psychoeducational Assessment, Wechsler Intelligence Scale for Children: Third Edition,* 1993, p. 49. [Wechsler Intelligence Scale for Children—Third Edition. Copyright © 1990 by the Psychological Corporation. Reproduced by permission. All rights reserved. "WISC–III" and "Wechsler Intelligence Scale for Children" and the "WISC–III logo" are registered trademarks of The Psychological Corporation. Their use herein does in no way indicate endorsement of this product by The Psychological Corporation.]

groups of learning disabled as compared to normal children, it does not necessarily occur among every learning disabled child. In addition, because the actual performance of learning disabled children appears to vary by only a small amount from the normative or comparison group, the finding of the Bannatyne pattern is not definitive for diagnosing a learning disability in a child.

Instead, it may be more reasonable to assume that the pattern, if observed, may provide helpful information about a given child's style of information processing and learning, regardless of whether the child is, or is diagnosed as, learning disabled. Thus the clinician may examine a given child's WISC–

III profile for the presence or absence of this profile and utilize the resulting information as one more aspect of his or her conceptualization of the child's mode of functioning without attempting to base a definitive or diagnostic conclusion on the presence or absence of the Spatial > Conceptual > Sequential pattern.

HORN'S FLUID-CRYSTALLIZED MODEL

Approximately 50 years ago, in discussing adult intelligence, Cattell (1943) stated that "[A]dult mental capacity is of two kinds, the chief character-istics of which may be best connoted by the use of the terms "fluid" and "crystallized" (p. 178). Cattell (1943) noted that fluid ability "has the charac-ter of a purely general ability to discriminate and perceive relations between any fundaments, new or old" (p. 178), and this ability increases until adolescence, then slowly declines. He noted that crystallized ability, on the other hand, "consists of discriminatory habits long established in a particu-lar field, originally through the operation of fluid ability, but no longer requiring insightful perception for their successful operation" (Cattell, 1943, p. 178).

Cattell (1943) also believed that intelligence tests at all ages reflect the combined effects of fluid and crystallized abilities, although fluid abilities are more prominent in childhood, while crystallized abilities predominate in adult life.

Developing, expanding and refining Cattell's ideas, Horn (1968, 1977, 1978, 1985; Horn & Hofer, 1992) has written extensively for the last quarter century regarding his ideas on the nature of intelligence. Horn (1985, 1988; Horn & Hofer, 1992) states that although the many capacities of humans that are viewed as reflecting intelligence might involve a unitary principle of general intelligence as suggested by Spearman's (1923, 1927) concept of *g*, this is extremely improbable. He notes instead that what is labelled intelli-gence involves a variety of phenomena, or a number of different abilities, with differing construct validities, differing genetic and environmental underpinnings, and with separable developmental trajectories over the course of the life span.

Although two of the dimensions Horn focuses on appeared to represent what Cattell (1941, 1943, 1957) had described as fluid and crystallized intelligence, Horn (1985, 1988) notes that many factor analytic investigations of human abilities (e.g., Cattell, 1971; Horn, 1972) indicate a consensus on the way to describe human abilities, and that the concepts of fluid and crystallized ability are insufficient to characterize human intelligence.

Horn and Hofer (1992) note that evidence from factor-analytic investiga-tions indicates that human ability can be described at two levels of organization.

The first of these is that of primary mental abilities (PMA), based on the concepts developed by Thurstone (1938, 1947). In his research, Thurstone had determined that a model involving at least nine factors was required to describe most of the variance obtained with tests designed to measure intelligence.

Although numerous subsequent studies replicated Thurstone's findings (Carroll, 1989), they also led to an expansion of the number of presumed primary mental abilities, which in turn led to an effort to determine a smaller number of basic cognitive processes to explain what is considered human intelligence.

The theory proposed by Horn (1985; Horn & Hofer, 1992), which is labelled Gf-Gc theory and refers to the fluid-crystallized model of intelligence, provides a second level of organization of human abilities. This Gf-Gc theory is based on factor analyses of the abilities reflected in Thurstone's PMA system (Thurstone, 1938, 1947) and is thus a second-order system, or a system of factors among factors in a hierarchical structure. Horn and Hofer (1992) note that results of various factor-analytic investigations indicate that the PMA system can be organized in terms of nine broad dimensions, those comprising the Gf-Gc theory, and these are able to parsimoniously describe the performance that characterize human intelligence.

Broad Reasoning or Fluid Intelligence: G*f*

Horn and Hofer (1992) note that if there is one single feature that characterizes essentially all human intellectual capacity, then Gf certainly has to be considered as a prominent indicator of that feature. But, Horn and Hofer (1992) point out, there does not appear to be any such single feature. Rather, fluid intelligence is only one part of a number of abilities that comprise intelligent behavior.

In distinguishing between fluid and crystallized intelligence, Horn (1985) notes that Gc depends on and reflects individual differences in learning through acculturation, while Gf depends on and reflects individual variation in what he refers to as casual learning, learning that is not largely shaped by the process of acculturation. Horn (1985) sees Gc as a principal outgrowth of acculturation, while feeling that G*f,* in contrast, reflects independent thinking brought on partly by avoiding, or being excluded from, the acculturative process.

Thus, Horn (1988) notes that the abilities of fluid intelligence do not reflect the system of acculturation to the same extent as do the abilities of Gc. And tasks that tap fluid intellectual abilities do not require one to bring forth knowledge as much as they require the individual to demonstrate problem-solving abilities in the immediate testing situation, to deal with "novel" tasks. Fluid intelligence thus involves the capacities of the person to perceive relationships among stimulus patterns, to draw inferences from relationships, and to understand implications. The first-order abilities that most adequately indicate this factor include induction, figural flexibility, integration, and, in conjunction with crystallized intelligence, the ability to reason logically or arithmetically (Horn, 1988).

Fluid intelligence is thus an index of several kinds of reasoning, abstracting, and problem-solving ability, when these capacities have been acquired or developed through personal experience outside a specific acculturation process. The reasoning involved in fluid intelligence entails a variety of cognitive processes, including identification of relationships among events, drawing inferences, comprehending implications, forming and recognizing concepts, and executing inductive, deductive, conjunctive and disjunctive reasoning (Horn, 1988; Horn & Hofer, 1992).

Horn (1988) lists a variety of tasks that assess fluid intelligence. These include, for example, concept formation, in which the individual must determine a rule that indicates why a drawing of colored squares or circles is an instance of a concept; or the effectiveness of using problem-solving strategies, in which the individual is taught strategies for dealing with certain problems and must then apply what she or he has been taught to a set of new problems.

Horn (1988) also notes a variety of tests which indicate Gf rather than either Gc or what he labels Gq, quantitative thinking, another component of the Gf-Gc model. Such tests as "Verbal Analogies Reasoning," in which the person must deal with items such as: "Now is to Here as __?__ is to There"; "Problem Definition," in which the individual is given a problem and information possibly relevant to its solution, and he or she must decide the relevance or necessity of the various pieces of information; and "Numerical Calculation," in which the problems require reasoning rather than simply mathematical knowledge, all reflect Gf to the extent that the test items require novel reasoning as opposed to knowledge of the individual's culture.

On the WISC–III, the subtests felt to reflect fluid intelligence include Picture Completion, Picture Arrangement, Block Design, Object Assembly, Similarities, and Digit Span.

Knowledge or Crystallized Intelligence: Gc

Crystallized intelligence in the individual is indicated by a number of behaviors that point to the breadth of a person's knowledge, his or her experience, sophistication, judgment, communication skills, understanding of conventions, and the individual's capacity for reasonable thinking (Horn, 1988).

Operationally defined, this factor is measured through such abilities as verbal comprehension, concept awareness and concept formation, as well as logical, numerical, and general reasoning. Horn (1988) notes that tests used to measure these abilities include vocabulary, esoteric analogies, remote associations, mathematical reasoning, and practical judgment, while the measured factor is an index of the degree to which the individual has incorporated, through the systematic impact of acculturation, the essential knowledge that may be viewed as the intelligence of a particular culture.

Horn (1988) lists tasks that reflect assessment of the component abilities involved in G*c*. These include "Verbal Knowledge," in which the individual is required to demonstrate stored verbal information; "Following Instructions," where the person must be able to follow written or spoken instructions; and "Information about the Humanities, Social and Physical Sciences, Business and Culture in General," which involves assessment of the individual's factual knowledge in these areas. Horn (1988) notes other abilities which are indicative of G*c* but which are also related to other second-order abilities, such as "Verbal Analogies Reasoning" and "Assessing Everyday Arguments and Evidence," which require the individual to decide if the conclusion of a presented argument is warranted or if the reasoning is cogent.

Thus, although G*c* appears to involve emphasis on stored factual knowledge and information about a specific culture, reasoning is also a part of this ability, particularly if the reasoning is a component of established knowledge of the culture or if the logical thinking involved depends heavily on cultural knowledge, and G*c* represents much of what most people mean when they use the term "intelligence."

The subtests on the WISC–III felt to reflect G*c* include Information, Similarities, Vocabulary, and Comprehension.

Other Second-Order Abilities in the G*f*-G*c* Model

Broad Visual Intelligence: Gv. This ability is in evidence in tasks where the individual must fluently and accurately but not necessarily rapidly perceive spatial configurations, form spatial images, interpret how objects change as they move through space, and form correct perspectives of objects in relation to one another. Extremes of this ability are apparent in high levels of painting, sculpture, and photography.

Broad Auditory Intelligence: Ga. Stankov and Horn (1980) developed a number of tests to measure intellectual abilities with auditory rather than visual problems and concluded that there might be something called auditory intelligence, such as might be displayed by great musicians. This led to their delineation of this ability, which involves a capacity for "chunking" streams of sound stimulation or auditory input, keeping the chunks in one's awareness, and anticipating an auditory form that can develop out of such streams of sound.

Short-Term Acquisition and Retrieval: SAR. The processes involved in this ability, which have been the focus of research on cognition and information processing (e.g., Craik, 1977), include stages of immediate memory — primary, secondary, and tertiary — or else indicate the functions of immediate working memory. These processes involve becoming aware of information, discriminating between different pieces of information, and retaining awareness and discrimination of material for brief periods of time while utilizing it to perform other cognitive operations. The emphasis in *SAR* is on apprehension and retention of information as opposed to the application of these capacities in the service of other cognitive operations.

Long-Term Storage and Retrieval: TSR. This ability involves fluency and breadth of the individual's capacity for retrieving information which has been stored in memory minutes, hours, weeks, months, and years before it is recalled. It is also indicated by what Horn (1988) refers to as secondary or tertiary memory, in which recall and recognition is over periods as brief as two to five minutes. Horn (1988) also points out that it can be difficult to distinguish *TSR* from *SAR,* and Kaufman (1990) has grouped these two forms of memory together in the "Retrieval Category" of the Horn and McCardle model of WAIS–R tasks (which includes Information, Arithmetic, and Digit Span).

Speed in Dealing with Intellectual Problems: Gs and CDS. Noting a variety of past studies (e.g., Horn, 1978, 1981), Horn (1985; Horn & Hofer, 1992) concludes that speed of thinking and power of thinking are not highly correlated, and he notes two speediness components of intellectual functioning. Horn (1988) speaks of Gs as "Attentive Speediness" as a quickness in identifying or distinguishing between elements of a (visual) stimulus pattern, particularly when the task involves measurement of the individual's performance under pressure to maintain her or his focused attention. Horn and Hofer (1992) speak of this ability as involved in almost all intellectual tasks, but measured in purest form in the rapid scanning and responding in intellectually non-demanding tasks where most people would respond correctly if the task were not highly speeded. The second speediness ability, *CDS,* refers to a quickness in deciding on answers, reflecting how quickly a person produces answers, whether correct or incorrect, to problems of moderate difficulty.

Quantitative Thinking: Gq. Horn (1988) notes that although this broad ability has not been distinguished from Gf and Gc in much research on the structure of intellectual abilities, he believes that individual differences in quantitative thinking, involving a person's skills and understanding of mathematics, are distributed independently of individual variation in fluid and crystallized intelligence as well as from other second-order intellectual abilities.

Other Aspects of Horn's Theory

In his discussion, Horn (1985, 1988) reviews the results of various studies and lines of reasoning that reflect structural, developmental and genetic evidence regarding his theoretical viewpoint. He notes that various components of intellectual performance display different paths of development, with different aspects of cognition reaching their peaks at differing points in childhood and young adulthood. In addition, he notes it is likely that the different abilities are determined by differing genetic and environmental determinants.

Based on the discussion and the various aspects of G*f* and G*c* Horn (1985) deals with, he proposes a "remodeled model" of his theory. The characteristics of this recent model may be viewed as hierarchically organized (see section on "Models in Psychology"). Sattler (1992) states that Horn's recent theoretical proposal is a model involving a four-level hierarchy. Horn (1985) appears to describe developmental changes in the structure and function of the individual's intellect as the individual moves from infancy to adulthood.

From one perspective, the individual progresses through a "developmental hierarchy," which goes from infancy, to childhood, then to youth and ultimately to adulthood. At the same time, the person progresses through an "information processing hierarchy," which moves from sensory reception at first, through associative processing of information, then to perceptual organization and ultimately to "relation education" at the highest level.

Within the boundaries defined by these parallel hierarchies, the individual moves from sensorimotor circular activities through awareness, reaction time and the ability to deal with novelty through deep processing of information and the ultimate achievement of "intensional-extensional knowledge".

The contents of Horn's (1985) hierarchical structure include the operation of auditory and visual sensory detectors during infancy; the development of short- and long-term acquisition and retrieval of information during childhood; the appearance of patterns of correct decision speed, clerical speed, broad visualization and broad auditory thinking during youth; and ultimately, at the level of deep processing of information in adulthood, fluid and crystallized thinking abilities.

Despite the fact that Horn's focus has primarily been on the development and decline of intelligence during adulthood and into old age (e.g., Horn,

1982; Horn & Donaldson, 1976), it would be possible to apply the concepts of fluid and crystallized intelligence to the intellectual functioning of children. To the extent that one wished to use this Gf-Gc, or fluid-crystallized, model for conceptualizing the child's handling of the WISC–III, this would involve a division of WISC–III subtests into categories reflecting Horn's (1985, 1988; Horn & Hofer, 1992) theoretical viewpoint.

According to the conceptual model presented by Horn (1985; Kaufman, 1990), intellectual processes as reflected on the Wechsler Scales would involve grouping the Wechsler subtests into four separate groups. Crystallized intelligence would be measured by the subtests of Information, Vocabulary, Comprehension, and Similarities. Fluid Intelligence would be measured by the subtests of Picture Completion, Picture Arrangement, Block Design, Object Assembly, Similarities, and Digit Span.

In addition, Horn's model (Kaufman, 1990) also includes a "Retrieval" category, measured by the subtests of Information, Arithmetic, and Digit Span; and a "Speed" category, measured by the subtest of Digit Symbol. On the WISC–III, the "Speed" category would theoretically be measured by the Coding and Symbol Search subtests.

However, to the extent that the examiner wishes to utilize this framework for interpreting the child's WISC–III protocol, the examinee's performance on those subtests felt to reflect crystallized intelligence would be contrasted with the individual's performance on those subtests felt to reflect fluid intelligence. By examining the child's intellectual functioning from this perspective, it would be possible to conclude whether she or he displays more competence in crystallized or fluid intellectual processes.

If one utilizes a Gf-Gc framework, then the child's handling of crystallized versus fluid intellectual tasks on the WISC–III becomes the structure around which one organizes observations and interpretations of the examinee's intellectual performance and around which the examiner develops his or her report of the test findings.

It should be noted that the WISC–III subtests which reflect crystallized intelligence are the same as those which are included in Wechsler's (1991) factor analytically based verbal comprehension factor. The subtests which presumably reflect fluid intelligence include the subtests on the Perceptual Organization factor plus Similarities and Digit Span. Hence there is actually great similarity between the Wechsler (1991) factor analytic and the fluid-crystallized approaches to the data.

KAUFMAN'S PROFILE ANALYSIS

Kaufman has published extensively on a wide variety of aspects of cognitive and intellectual functioning in individuals across the life span (e.g.,

Kaufman, 1979a, 1982, 1990; Kaufman & Kaufman, 1983). Although he has discussed many issues relevant to test interpretation, such as factor analysis of the WISC–R standardization population (Kaufman, 1975) and verbal-performance discrepancies on the WISC–R (Kaufman, 1976a), his name has become virtually synonymous with the concept of profile analysis (Kaufman, 1979a, 1990), an approach which now forms the foundation of the interpretive scheme presented in the WISC–III manual (Bracken, 1993).

Kaufman (1979a, 1990) has described his philosophy of "intelligent testing" as resting on several basic assumptions: that the focus of any assessment is the examinee rather than the test; that the goal of any examiner is to be better than the test used; that intelligence tests measure what an examinee has learned; that the tasks composing intelligence tests are only illustrative samples of a person's total repertoire of behavior; that intelligence tests assess mental functioning under fixed experimental conditions; that tests (like the WISC–III) are not just administered individually but must also be interpreted individually by a flexible and clever, detective-like examiner; and that intelligence tests are best used to generate hypotheses of potential help to the person and are improperly used when the results lead to a harmful outcome.

Within the context of his overall approach to testing, Kaufman (1976b, 1979a; Reynolds & Kaufman, 1985) contrasts his view of profile analysis to that of normative assessment of a child's performance on the Wechsler scales. According to this view, a normative approach to evaluation of a child's Wechsler protocol makes the assumption that *g* is the primary determinant of the child's Full Scale IQ and that various factors (e.g., verbal comprehension) underlie the child or adolescent's performances on the factorially based subtest groupings.

Viewed from the perspective of a normative interpretation of a child's intellectual test performance, once the Verbal, Performance, and Full Scale IQs have been calculated, the examiner is able to make some statement regarding the child's level of intellectual functioning relative to his or her age peers (Reynolds & Kaufman, 1985).

In his earlier writings, Kaufman (Kaufman, 1982; Reynolds & Kaufman, 1985) notes that a normative framework also makes the assumption that variations in a child's subtest scores reflect chance measurement error. However, Reynolds and Kaufman (1985) emphasize the fact that available statistical procedures permit clinicians to test the assumptions of the normative approach. If fluctuations between the verbal and performance scales, or among subtests, are statistically significant, then "ipsative" or intraindividual evaluation of the child's performance takes over and what Kaufman (1979a) refers to as clinical "detective work" predominates.

When utilizing an ipsative approach rather than using the standardization sample as the basis for comparison, the child's own average level of performance becomes the normative basis to which the child's scores are compared. The first step in this procedure is to examine the difference between the child's Verbal and Performance IQs to determine if use of the child's Full Scale IQ is justified.

The child's Full Scale IQ can only be considered as representative of his or her general intellectual ability if the Verbal and Performance IQs do not differ significantly from one another. If these two IQs do differ significantly from one another, this indicates that the levels of the child's performance on the Verbal and Performance Scales are sufficiently different to suggest a true difference in the individual's ability to think, reason, or express her- or himself through verbal as opposed to nonverbal behavior.

When Kaufman (1979a) initially articulated his views there was little appreciation of the concept of baserates in a standardization population. Hence, Kaufman (Kaufman, 1976a, 1976b; Kaufman, 1979a; Reynolds & Kaufman, 1985; Kaufman et al., 1990) has often presented data to demonstrate the nature of Verbal-Performance discrepancies in various populations, including the WISC–R standardization sample, as a way to provide a normative framework for the interpretation of observed Verbal-Performance IQ differences.

Reynolds and Kaufman (1985) note that in addition to a concept of statistical significance in evaluating the difference between a Verbal and Performance IQ, one should also consider the frequency of occurrence of a difference of a particular magnitude. Having discovered that Verbal-Performance differences vary as a function of socioeconomic level, Kaufman (Kaufman, 1979a; Reynolds & Kaufman, 1985) provides information summarizing the magnitude of various WISC–R Verbal-Performance discrepancies occurring among several socioeconomic levels within the normal population. These tabled values permit an examiner to evaluate observed Verbal-Performance differences to determine whether a given difference is unusual as well as statistically significant.

Reynolds and Kaufman (1985) point out that in evaluating Verbal-Performance IQ differences, the examiner can and should use a variable criterion to determine the meaning of a particular Verbal-Performance discrepancy, at times concluding that a difference which occurs less than 15% of the time is sufficient, while at other times requiring a difference that occurs less than 5% or 2% of the time in order to draw a conclusion about the child's intellectual functioning.

Reynolds and Kaufman (1985) note the importance of recognizing and considering statistically significant differences between a child's Verbal and Performance IQs as well as the frequency of occurrence of a given Verbal-Performance discrepancy. In this regard, these authors make a distinction between diagnosis and treatment. They note that in those instances where a Verbal-Performance IQ difference is *both* significant and rare, this information can be used to contribute to the examiner's formulation of potential diagnostic hypotheses and can likely lead to strategies of remediation as well. However, where a Verbal-Performance difference is significant but occurs fairly often, such a difference may have only remedial implications.

In addition to considering the discrepancy between a child's Verbal and Performance IQs, Reynolds and Kaufman (1985) also note the importance of examining the degree of subtest scatter evident on a child or adolescent's Wechsler profile, including both the range of subtest scores obtained by the individual as well as the number of subtests deviating from the mean of the child's subtest scores. Taking his usual approach, which proposed that to interpret a given examinee's performance one must know how commonly the finding occurs among normal children, Kaufman (1976b) reported on the degree of subtest scatter which characterized the WISC–R standardization sample.

In establishing normative values for subtest scatter, for each child in the normative sample, Kaufman (1976b) rank ordered the child's scores on the 10 regular subtests from high to low, then subtracted the child's lowest score from his or her highest, resulting in a scaled-score range for each child. The average scaled-score range in the standardization sample was seven points with a standard deviation of 2. This meant that the average examinee's scaled scores might range from 6 to 13 or 7 to 14, and even ranges from 3 to 12 or 8 to 17 could be considered as within normal limits. Reynolds and Kaufman (1985) provide tabled values of these findings to assist examiners in interpreting the degree of unusualness of a particular child's scaled-score range.

Kaufman (1976a) had also analyzed the WISC–R standardization data with regard to the number of subtests which deviated significantly from the mean of all subtests on the same scale. He noted that more than half the children displayed at least one subtest which deviated significantly from the scale mean, and nearly one quarter showed at least three significant deviations from the mean of all subtests. Hence, Reynolds and Kaufman (1985) note the importance of consulting baseline data in the standardization sample before concluding that the scatter in a given examinee's Wechsler profile is an indication of that child's exceptionality.

Although in his earlier writings, Kaufman (1976a; Reynolds & Kaufman, 1985) emphasizes the issue of Verbal-Performance discrepancies, more recently Kaufman (1990) has noted that before analyzing profile fluctuations, it is advisable to begin with a statistical treatment of IQs and scores, and he prefers to start with the most global score, that of the Full Scale IQ, which is the most reliable score in the test.

More recently also, Kaufman et al. (1990) review a large sampling of the vast number of research investigations with the WISC–R and conclude that regardless of the specific factor-analytic technique used, the age or ethnic background of the children tested, and whether the sample consists of children described as normal or as having some exceptionality, two major factors consistently emerge from the various analyses: a verbal comprehension factor and a perceptual organization factor.

Based on the emergence of these robust factors that parallel the verbal and performance scales of the WISC–R, Kaufman et al. (1990) recommend that the clinician respect Wechsler's test design and give much credence to a child or adolescent's Verbal and Performance IQs when interpreting his or her Wechsler protocol. This means that the most likely determinant of a child's score on most verbal subtests is the child's verbal comprehension ability, rather than his or her unique ability on a particular subtest. Similarly, the most probable determinant of an individual's score on most performance subtests is the child's perceptual organization ability rather than a unique subtest-specific skill.

From within this somewhat revised perspective, Kaufman et al. (1990) note that instead of treating each subtest as a measure of an isolated set of skills, each verbal subtest score should be compared to the child's own mean score on the relevant scale. If most of these comparisons indicate that particular subtests do not vary significantly from the child's scale mean, the examiner returns to the basic assumption that fluctuations of subtest scores around the mean reflect chance or error variation and are therefore not useful for test interpretation. Only when an examinee's scaled scores do differ significantly from their respective factor means may the examiner speculate about strengths and weaknesses for the child that are less global than verbal comprehension or perceptual organization.

Thus in order to carry out this profile analysis and determine whether a examinee's performance on any subtest represents a specific strength or weakness for the child, Kaufman (Kaufman, 1979a, 1990; Reynolds & Kaufman, 1985) recommends considering the Verbal and Performance scales separately. In dealing with verbal subtests, the child's mean scaled score on the Verbal Scale should be calculated, and then this mean score is subtracted from each verbal subtest score. Similarly, the child's average Performance Scale score should be determined and then subtracted from each Performance subtest score.

To determine the significance of the differences obtained by this procedure with the WISC–R, Kaufman (1979a) originally recommended the use of a variation of + or − 3 from the child's average scale performance; Kaufman (1990) later revised this number upward to take into consideration the error imposed by making multiple comparisons. Once having used the appropriate numerical criterion to determine that a subtest does vary at a statistically significant level from its scale average, the examiner must then determine that the subtest in question has at least adequate "specificity."

Subtest specificity, which is readily determined as a by-product of factor analysis of a test such as the WISC–R, refers to the amount of variance in a subtest score that is both reliable and unique to that particular subtest; that is, not shared with other subtests in the same scale or shared with all subtests in the Wechsler as common variance. Based on his own research (Kaufman, 1979a), Kaufman determined and presented (Kaufman, 1979a; Reynolds & Kaufman, 1985) the relative proportions of subtest-specific variance on the WISC–R, dividing the subtests into those which have ample, adequate or inadequate specific variance.

Once having determined that a particular subtest varies significantly from the child's mean scale performance and that the subtest in question has at least adequate specific variance, the examiner can conclude that the subtest reflects a significant strength or weakness in the child's intellectual ability structure. However, it is then necessary to determine the appropriate interpretation for this finding.

Kaufman (Kaufman, 1979a; Reynolds & Kaufman, 1985) notes that behavioral observation of the child during testing can influence the interpretation made. In addition, it is important to know what the subtest measures, which can be determined by analyzing the mental operations necessary to perform the tasks involved in the subtest, and by noting the correlates of the subtest as indicated by the research literature.

Reynolds and Kaufman (1985) note that Kaufman (1979a), Lutey (1977), and Sattler (1982) are excellent sources of information on the skills reflected in the various subtests, but they note that the examiner must integrate such information with his or her own observation of the child's test performance. In addition, Reynolds and Kaufman (1985) note it is preferable to look for trends in the child's abilities that appear as strengths or weaknesses, not only on each scale individually, but across both scales of the test.

The above discussion thus provides the essential features of Kaufman's profile analysis, a strategy for test interpretation that he has refined (Kaufman, 1990) and which has become a basic method for thinking about interpretation of the Wechsler scales (Kaufman, 1979a, 1990; Sattler, 1990, 1992), and many concepts reflecting this approach have been incorporated into the manual of the WISC–III (Bracken, 1993; Wechsler, 1991).

Sattler (1990, 1992) provides statements which indicate his view of the primary methods of profile analysis as this technique would be applied to the WISC–R or WISC–III. The elements Sattler includes are as follows: comparison of the child's Verbal and Performance IQs; comparison of each Verbal Scale subtest score with the examinee's mean Verbal Scale score;

comparison of each Performance Scale subtest score with the individual's mean Performance Scale score; comparison of each subtest score with the mean subtest score based on all the subtests which have been administered; comparison of pairs of individual subtest scores; comparison of the factor scores (the three he identified in his factor analysis of the WISC–III); and comparison of subtest scores within each factor with their respective mean factor score.

As with other concepts that have been discussed above (e.g., Bannatyne's recategorization approach), profile analysis has not been received without criticism. In their meta-analysis of approaches to the regrouping of Wechsler scores for the purpose of differential diagnosis of learning disabilities, Kavale and Forness (1984, 1994) discuss WISC patterns such as those proposed by Kaufman (1979a). Kavale and Forness (1984, 1994) note that although most effect sizes for WISC patterns were negative, meaning that the LD group performed less well than the normal or comparison group, these effect sizes were typically small and clustered around a value approximately one-tenth of a standard deviation below the mean.

Kavale and Forness (1984, 1994) note that for the patterns described by Kaufman (1979a), LD children appear to perform better on visual organization tasks, prefer meaningful tasks, perform better when much rather than little expression is required for responding, perform best in right-brain processing tasks, and perform about equally poorly on reasoning and recall tasks. Importantly, however, when these WISC patterns are translated into scaled-score equivalents, they do not exhibit a deviation from the mean of 10 that would be required for significance.

Kavale and Forness (1984, 1994) conclude that the limited variation about the mean of 10 evident when LD children are compared to a normal group indicates LD children display largely average performance on the abilities and operations found in WISC patterns. Hence, they feel that reorganization of WISC subtest scores into patterns is actually of little value for differential diagnosis of learning disabilities.

Mueller, Dennis, and Short (1986) have also expressed criticism of Kaufman's (1979a) concept of profile analysis. Mueller et al. (1986) report a meta-exploration of 119 samples of normal and exceptional children drawn from the available research literature on the WISC–R. The subjects represented six levels of overall intellectual functioning and seven psychoeducational diagnostic categories. These authors applied a variety of multivariate clustering and profile analysis techniques to their data and did find three relatively distinct patterns of performance among subjects. However, the distinctive patterns they observed appeared to vary as a function of overall intelligence level of the subjects rather than their diagnostic group. One pattern observed by Mueller et al. (1986) appears to represent the mean performance of somewhat brighter children, suggesting that these children display a tendency to obtain their highest scores on WISC–R subtests that tap verbal facility, and their lowest scores on subtests that tap the ability to process short-term sequential memory items and/or the ability to attend and concentrate.

A second profile appears to represent the pattern displayed by upper "borderline" to lower "average" children. As a group, these children display strengths similar to the mentally handicapped and weaknesses similar to the intellectually superior. They display relative strength in their ability to interpret and/or organize visually perceived material and to manipulate objects, while they show relative weakness in their ability to process short-term memory items and/or remain undistracted.

The third pattern observed by Mueller et al. (1986) appears to represent the performance of children with low intellect, with IQs ranging from 51 to 82. This last group of samples displayed relative strength on tests that reflect the ability to manipulate objects either in actuality or symbolically, and with relative weakness on tests tapping verbal facility.

Mueller et al. (1986) conclude that their results support those researchers who have argued against the use of WISC–R profile analysis for the classification of children on any other basis than intellect. While distinct WISC–R performance profiles do indeed exist, they are most strongly associated with the individual's global level of intellect and not with any other categorization of the individual, such as learning disability status.

Hale (1991) notes that subtest analysis of the various Wechsler scales has been cyclical in that following the publication of a new or revised version of a Wechsler scale, another series of subtest investigations would be published with the ultimate conclusion being that subtest analysis is relatively useless.

Hale (1991) notes that research results may appear inconsistent, but a careful consideration of these results indicates that the literature is actually quite consistent. He distinguishes between two types of investigations: a *classical validity* study and a *clinical utility* study. In the *classical validity* study, the investigation begins with previously defined groups of children (e.g., reading disabled, conduct disordered) and asks if subtest differences can be found between these two groups, or between a particular group and the standardization population. In a *clinical utility* study, the investigator begins with only the subtest scores of the subjects and asks if knowledge of these subtest results can aid in the prediction or differentiation of some socially significant criterion.

Hale (1991) cites Miller's (1980) contention that although investigators may have found certain WISC–R profiles to be characteristic of particular handicapped groups, reflecting the *classical validity* approach, there has been an inability to demonstrate that these profiles are distinctive enough to allow practitioners to differentiate between handicapped and normal children, indicating the failure of these studies to be meaningful from the *clinical utility* perspective.

Hale (1991) concurs with Miller's view. He notes that in those studies that compared predefined groups (e.g., Ackerman et al., 1971; Dean, 1977; Rugel, 1974; Smith et al., 1977b), significant differences in Wechsler profiles have been found between children classified as handicapped and those classified as normal. However, in those studies that started with Wechsler subtest profiles and then attempted to classify children into diagnostic categories (e.g., Hale, 1979; Hale & Landino, 1981) or studies where reclassification was possible (Tabachnick, 1979; Thompson, 1980), high degrees of diagnostic error were found.

In one study which attempted to use WISC–R differences to reclassify behaviorally disorder and normal boys, Hale and Landino (1981) found that their resultant reclassifications were no better than chance. Similarly, Hale and Saxe (1983) found that knowledge of WISC–R profiles did not help in predicting subjects' academic achievement.

Thus Hale (1991) concludes that his review of the literature suggests that knowledge of a child's subtest profile does not appreciably help the clinician in predicting either academic achievement levels or behavioral difficulties the child might display.

The most technically sophisticated criticisms of ipsatization and profile analysis have been put forth by McDermott, Fantuzzo, and Glutting (1990). These authors note the conflicting positions propounded by Wechsler: that the subtests in the Wechsler scales are, at the same time, measures of a global capacity called intelligence *and* also measures of numerous specific abilities reflected in the independent and conjoint variation of subtests. These views presumably cannot both be true. The specific subtests either contribute to the assessment of global capacity that underlies all subtests or they have some independent significance.

McDermott et al. (1990) note the extensive evidence which indicates that global intelligence is associated with such things as scholastic and occupational success, environmental adaptation, and scientific, cultural, and political thought (e.g., Brody, 1985; Herrnstein & Murray, 1994). McDermott et al. note that it has been assumed that the targeted ability constructs on the Wechsler scales remain the same after ipsatiszation as before. However, McDermott, Fantuzzo, Glutting, Watkins, and Baggaley (1992) analyzed the WISC–R standardization data and found that the interrelationships among subcomponents in the test deteriorate after ipsatization; for the WISC–R, ipsatization results in the loss of nearly 60% of the test's reliable variance.

In assessing the predictive value of ipsatized scores, McDermott et al. (1992) compared conventional norm-based and ipsatized scores in terms of their ability to predict a variety of standardized achievement criteria across a wide range of samples. They found that conventional subtest scores accounted for on average almost 40% of academic performance, while ipsative scores accounted for only between 5.8% to 9.0% of this criterion, which represents a two-thirds to three-quarters drop in predictive efficiency for ipsative measures.

These authors also note that for WISC–R scores across 1-month and 3-year intervals, ipsative scores were significantly less reliable than norm-based scores, which would thus reduce the validity of these scores in relation to external criteria. Further, McDermott et al. (1990) note that once ability scores have been ipsatized, they can no longer be used for comparison across or among different individuals, as ipsatization results in a true change in metric and one can no longer apply parametric statistics to such scores. Finally, McDermott et al. (1990) note that ipsative scores must always sum to zero, which means that if one bases a remedial program on a child's ipsative weakness and improves that performance, the child's ability in some other area will necessarily diminish by an equal amount.

Writing in regard to the interpretation of subtest patterns on the Wechsler scales, McDermott et al. (1990) present a number of criticisms of this approach. First, they note that it is usually assumed that groups of similarly diagnosed subjects represent meaningful and even homogeneous categories. However, the research of McDermott (1981, 1988) indicates that this is an unwarranted assumption.

Second, the authors note, present research fails to preclude the use of Wechsler subtest profiles for *both* the initial selection of groups *and* the subsequent determination of subtest profiles within those groups that will ultimately be used to independently define the groups.

Third, the authors point out that much published research combines available samples that may span broad age ranges, but still assumes homogeneity of measurement error for subtests across those age levels. However, research (e.g., Conger, Conger, Farrell, & Ward, 1979) demonstrates that the accuracy of measurement for the subtests varies significantly across the age span of the test, making this assumption unjustified.

Fourth, the authors note that in the literature on profile analysis of the Wechsler, hypothesis testing, when it is actually carried out, is based on linear modeling of the data. However, subtest profiles are defined by two characteristics: their location on the ability spectrum (upper, central or lower region) and their shape (the pattern of peaks and valleys among subtest scores). Since score values for the same subtest can take on variable weights depending on the configuration of other scores, profiles contain nonlinear as well as linear components. This means that questions addressing profile uniqueness cannot be resolved with conventional statistical methods, which are based on linear combinations of subtest scores.

McDermott et al.'s (1990) fifth point is that claims for the discovery of a unique Wechsler profile is never made against a viable null hypothesis, which is that the profile assumed to be unique is actually common among the normal population. McDermott et al. (1990) note that without clear knowledge of the types and prevalence of particular profile types that occur in the normal population, one cannot know whether a profile discovered in a particular research setting is distinctive or common. In this sense, McDermott et al. (1990) actually present an argument which parallels Kaufman's (1979; Reynolds & Kaufman, 1985) view that one cannot interpret aspects of the WISC–R, such as Verbal-Performance discrepancies, without knowing their prevalence in the normal population.

Addressing this issue, McDermott, Glutting, Jones, Watkins, and Kush (1989) report their investigation of the structure and composition of subtest profile types among the standardization sample for the WISC–R. They found seven core profile types which met the variety of statistical criteria they established and which McDermott et al. (1989) felt represented basic Wechsler intelligence test profiles found among children in the normative population. These authors suggest that concluding a particular profile type is unique to some diagnostic group (as is proposed by profile analysis) is only tenable if it can be shown that the profile is not actually one of the core profile types in the normative population.

Profile analysis of the Wechsler scales, which has been written about and popularized by Kaufman (1979a; Reynolds & Kaufman, 1985; Kaufman, 1990), has been accepted by other authors (e.g., Sattler, 1990, 1992) and has become integrated into the manual of the WISC–III (Wechsler, 1991). Nonetheless, this approach has its significant critics, both in terms of its actual usefulness (e.g., Kavale & Forness, 1984, 1994), as well as in terms of a number of methodological and conceptual errors in its fundamental premises (Hale, 1991; McDermott et al., 1989; McDermott et al., 1990; McDermott et al., 1992). It should be noted that both Kaufman (1979a) and Sattler (1990) do offer caveats to the use of profile analysis, essentially noting that the hypotheses generated through this method should be seen as tentative rather than as verified insights. The present author does not recommend the use of profile analysis, and the examiner who chooses to use this method in her or his interpretation of a Wechsler protocol should do so with the utmost of caution.

Part V
THE PSYCHOLOGICAL REPORT

Chapter Fourteen

THE PSYCHOLOGICAL REPORT: GENERAL ISSUES

School psychologists spend a significant portion of their time in assessment activities (Goldwasser, Myers, Christianson, & Graden, 1983). Lacayo, Sherwood and Morris (1981) surveyed the daily activities of school psychologists and found that report writing occupied 18% of their time and was second only to psychoeducational testing procedures themselves, which occupied 21% of their workday. Martin (1994), reported on a study conducted by Bischoff, Wilczynski, Emeis, and Combs. These authors sent survey questionnaires to 3,000 school psychologists with 1,179 surveys being returned. The primary responsibility for 71% of those returning questionnaires was testing and assessment activities. Hence, report writing, including the reporting of children's intelligence test performance, may be an important aspect of the professional activities of all psychologists but particularly of school psychologists.

The psychological report of an intellectual assessment of a child is intended to serve several purposes: it provides an accurate and integrated view of the child's functioning in one (or more) domain(s) of living; it is intended to offer both objective data (i.e., norm-referenced scores) and psychologically meaningful interpretation of a child's functioning; it is to assist in the determination of whether a child is learning disabled, gifted, or suffering from some information processing deficit; and it is to provide recommendations regarding placement, educational strategies and/or interventions for a child based on his or her psychological test functioning (although the report may also include and be partially based on other data sources in addition to testing per se).

The report of an intellectual assessment may be used in one or more of up to four basic ways: (1) at an interpretive interview or conference when the material is presented verbally; (2) when the report is read by a user; (3) when the report is reread by a user or another professional; (4) when the report is shared with or read by a child's parent or by the child her- or himself.

The above paragraphs state the intended purposes and uses of psychological reports. However, researchers have noted that the results of school psychological test reports are not helpful in decision making; intervention strategies do not follow from the reports; teachers and administrators do not read them; and special educators complain that they cannot readily translate the information contained in reports into IEPs (Zins & Barnett, 1983). Ownby (1990b) notes that consumers of psychological reports complain that reports do not include enough basic data, that they contain jargon, and that they are unclear or imprecisely written.

Sloves et al. (1979) and Matarazzo (1990) both distinguish between psychological assessment and psychological testing, noting that the former involves a comprehensive examination of psychological test data, extensive knowledge of the psychometric characteristics of tests used, broad-based knowledge of psychological theory, and the capacity to integrate the clinical observations occurring during the test situation with information from the client's life history. The goal of psychological assessment is thus broader, while psychological testing may be thought of as one component of an overall assessment.

The psychological evaluation of an individual adult or child therefore requires the psychologist to engage in a wide variety of activities: interpersonal relatedness, sensitive inquiry, astute observation, and the ability to integrate various sources and kinds of information into a set of conclusions about the person who is being evaluated.

The writing of a psychological report based on the assessment of a child thus presents many challenges for the examiner as the task is one involving components of sociology, politics, diplomacy, group dynamics, sales, and art (Applebaum, 1970). Although a report is intended to provide an objective characterization of important aspects of the examinee's functioning, it may nonetheless reflect the biases of the report writer (Zins & Barnett, 1983). Furthermore, a psychological report describes a child at a single point in time based on a relatively small sample of behavior. The relationship between the various components of the report and external criteria may vary widely. And finally, even if the report has been written accurately and according to solid theoretical principles, the report refers to past behavior of the examinee; the information it contains may be out of date as soon as the report is written, and hence the report may not be particularly useful in dealing with the child in the future.

RESEARCH ON REPORT WRITING

A number of aspects of the report-writing process have been investigated in recent years. Studies exploring characteristics of the report writer indicate that such variables as experience as a psychologist, teaching experience, age, sex, marital status, and undergraduate or graduate major have no major influence on the judged quality of the report (Rucker, 1967). And Eberst and

Genshaft (1984) found that there was no difference in the effectiveness of reports written by doctoral versus non-doctoral psychologists.

Perceptions of different types of information included in reports and the organization of reports themselves have also been examined. For example, Bagnato (1980) reported that teachers' comprehension of reports is improved when reports are organized by functional domains, meaning by areas of the child's functioning, rather than simply by test results. Weiner (1985) also investigated teachers' comprehension of different psychological report formats and found that teachers better understood reports that organize information by functional domain (e.g., Reason for Referral, Learning Style), that describe strengths and problems in clear behavioral terms, describe the child's learning style fully, and offer specific and elaborated program recommendations.

Weiner (1987) studied the comprehension of psychological reports by school administrators, elementary school teachers, and secondary school teachers. It was found that all three groups of educators preferred reports in which the structure of the report was highly salient, and where both the child description and the recommendations were elaborated with explanations and examples provided.

Pryzwansky and Hanania (1986) examined the preferences of a sample of school psychologists and school staff for reports utilizing different formats: a traditional "topic organization" format (e.g., Reason for Referral, Behavioral Observations, Test Results) and a "problem organization" format (no standard subheadings, but sections are differentiated by the separate problem areas discovered by the evaluation). These authors found that all professional groups preferred the traditionally organized school psychological report.

The different findings of Weiner (1985, 1987) and Pryzwansky and Hanania (1986) may reflect the fact that Pryzwansky and Hanania's (1986) alternative report format would involve a highly variable organization, and this would result in subjects expressing preference for the traditional and more predictable topical organization; Weiner's (1985) alternative report format represents a more refined and articulated version of the traditional report format.

Salvagno and Teglasi (1987) had a sample of elementary school teachers rate the helpfulness of various types of information in test-based and observation-based reports. They found no difference in the teachers's view of the helpfulness of these different kinds of reports, but found that on both types of reports, teachers consistently rated interpretive material as more helpful than factual or descriptive information.

Weise, Bush, Newman, Benes, and Witt (1986) studied teacher perceptions of psychological reports as a function of the level of jargon used in the reports. These investigators developed three versions of the same report content but utilizing varying degrees of jargon. They evaluated teachers' perceptions of four dimensions of the reports: Usefulness, Understanding and Comprehension, Educational Relevance, and Student Behavioral Characteristics. The level of jargon in the reports influenced only the teachers' perceptions of the understandability of the reports, but did not affect teachers' perceptions of the usefulness, educational relevance, or student behavioral characteristics in the reports.

Ownby (1990a, 1990b) reported studies in which school psychologists and mental health counselors rated statements based on a model which involves explanations of the referents in the psychological report. These subjects rated the statements based on the "expository process model" as significantly more credible and persuasive than equivalent statements that were not based on the model.

Overall, then, research suggests that the perceived quality of psychological reports may not vary meaningfully as a function of the experience or professional degree of the writer. In addition, there is some evidence to suggest that jargon in reports makes it somewhat more difficult for them to be understood. Furthermore, educators at various levels appear to prefer reports that emphasize interpretation, rather than mere description, of test data. Educators also understand reports better when the sections of the report are salient and where both descriptions of the child and recommendations which are made are elaborated with explanations and examples. Finally, school psychologists and mental health workers appear to find report statements more persuasive when they include explanatory links between test data and interpretations, and between what the reader already knows and new information provided by the report.

WRITING THE REPORT

In writing the WISC–III report, as the author stated earlier, it is his view that the examiner should write one report that can be seen by the range of target audiences that are likely to see the report. This means that the report should be able to communicate the results of the assessment in a clear, logical fashion without psychological jargon to any of the various individuals along a continuum of potential readers or listeners.

The examiner should keep in mind the fact that although an evaluation may discover some unexpected finding, there should ordinarily be a logical relationship between the reason for referral and the content of the report. The reason for referral provides the context or meaning for the evaluation, and hence for the report.

In formulating the report, the examiner may conceive of him- or herself as a consultant (Zins & Barnett, 1983) to a system which involves the child, the school, and the child's family. As a psychologist-consultant, the examiner is called upon to assist in answering one or more questions about a child. The question or questions are ordinarily posed in one of several fundamental forms based on the chain of reasoning articulated earlier (see section on "Issues in the Clinical Use of the WISC–III"). One assumes that some adult in the child's world (or at times the child him- or herself) has observed a variation in the child's performance from what would be expected or desired. The question is being posed as to whether the perception is accurate, and if so, what is the cause or basis of this deviation from the expected.

The use of an intellectual (or other) assessment is to determine whether the cause for the child's observed variance-from-expected can be obtained with the assessment device (or devices) chosen. This means that the examiner as psychologist-consultant is attempting to address the implicit question of the child's variation from expectation by using the WISC–III as well as by using her or his own knowledge of psychology, child development and learning to come up with an answer to the question(s), or else to generate further questions that require other strategies of information gathering.

From within this perspective, the examiner can conceptualize the psychological report as the vehicle or mechanism which will allow the knowledge or insight gained in the psychological assessment to be translated into one or more strategies to facilitate the child's interaction with, adaptation to, and gaining support from the school system or other systems as needed.

The examiner should also realize that although a primary target for the report may be the school and the child's trajectory within the school setting, the report findings may have a significant impact on the child and his or her life both within *and* outside of the school. These wider effects on the child are based on the fact that the child's parent(s) will obtain the results of the assessment; and the parent(s) and possibly the child may come to perceive the child differently as a function of the labelling or placement process which will follow the assessment.

Chapter Fifteen

THE PSYCHOLOGICAL REPORT: FRAMEWORK AND DESIGN FEATURES

FRAMEWORKS FOR THE REPORT

The author recommends that the examiner approach the writing of the psychological report from within the perspective of two of the models described earlier, the gradient and the hierarchy. In terms of the relevance of the gradient model to the writing of the report, the examiner should keep in mind the fact that the statements he or she makes in the report can be conceptualized as existing on a gradient or continuum. The basic dimensions that would pertain to these statements are those of their supportability and stability. By this the author means that one can conceive of a gradient varying from one pole involving statements whose truth value is quite high and which would likely be made if the child were retested in a week or month or by another examiner, to the other pole involving statements whose truth value is much less certain, and which might not be made if the child were retested in a week or month or by another examiner.

This means that in writing the psychological report, the examiner needs to evaluate the statements included in the report according to the above criteria. As she or he writes the report, the examiner needs to continually assess the various statements made by noting where the statement falls on the continua-of-truth value or certainty of the statement and the likelihood that the observation is a stable one. Insofar as the psychological report is a construction based on the test data, the examiner needs to realize that the concept of reliability does not pertain only to subtest, IQ or factor scores themselves but to the report based on those test scores.

While, typically, examiners write test reports soon after the referred child has been tested (and thus the examiner remembers the examinee and the test interaction), the examiner needs to ask her- or himself how the report might be written if it was written two weeks or a month after the child had been tested, when the examiner no longer recalled the specifics of the individual's test session behavior. This would indicate the need for the examiner to record at the time of testing any specific observations of the examinee that are felt to be relevant, and would be presumed to be stable enough qualities of the child's behavior to be pertinent if the report were to be written some time after the individual had been seen.

If the examiner were to write the report of a child's intellectual assessment a month after the testing, he or she could utilize the written behavioral observations which had been recorded at the time of testing. Since the GATSB (Glutting & Oakland, 1993) does consider the concept of stability of the child's test behavior, this might be one reason to use the GATSB as part of testing.

From the perspective of the other model relevant to the writing of the report, the hierarchy, the model is relevant in three ways: first, in terms of the organization of the report itself; second, in terms of the way in which various parts of the report are written; and third, in terms of the hierarchical structure of the school to which the report will relate.

In terms of the report itself, the author proposes that the examiner can conceptualize the test results as distributed hierarchically (see Figure 5). This means that the apex of the hierarchy (Level 1) involves discussion of the child's overall functioning, including the individual's WISC–III Full Scale IQ, and her or his Verbal and Performance IQs. The next level of the hierarchy (Level 2) represents the division of the child's functioning into a verbal scale and a performance scale and involves a more detailed discussion of the child's functioning in each of these realms of thinking, reasoning and problem solving. This level of analysis includes and is based on the factor-analytic approach to the child's test protocol (Wechsler, 1991; Sattler, 1992).

The third level of the hierarchy (Level 3) involves discussion of the various subtest groupings or patterns of subtest scores, i.e., the ACID profile (Ackerman et al., 1976); Bannatyne's (1974) recategorization of subtest scores into spatial, verbal conceptual, sequential, and acquired knowledge categories; and Horn's concepts of fluid and crystallized intellectual abilities (Horn, 1985; Kaufman, 1990).

The fourth level of the hierarchy (Level 4) involves the examination and discussion of the fluctuations of individual subtest scores around the child's own average performance, either on the entire WISC–III, or separately for the verbal and performance scales. This is the level of intraindividual comparison as proposed by Kaufman (1979a, 1990; Reynolds & Kaufman, 1985).

In terms of the relevance of a hierarchical model to writing the various segments of the report, this refers to the need for the examiner to link his or her observations of the test data with conclusions about the child's broader functioning. Ownby (1990a, 1990b) and Ownby and Wallbrown (1986) have described a model, the "expository process model," for use in writing psychological reports. This model is based on the use of "middle level

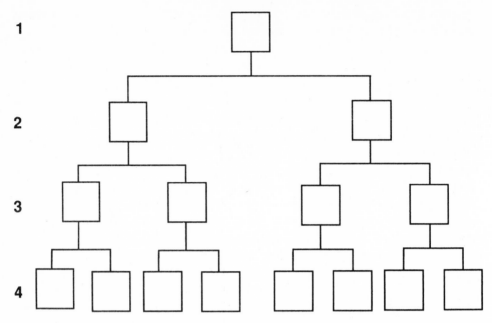

Figure 5. A Hierarchy as Related to Report Writing. (See text for explanation.)

theoretical constructs" or MLCs (Applebaum, 1970) as a means of providing links between data and interpretations.

Ownby (1990b) and Ownby and Wallbrown (1986) integrated Applebaum's (1970) MLC concept with a psycholinguistic approach in their model. They proposed that psychologists in writing reports should use what Clark and Clark (1977) called the "given-new contract." This concept requires that each statement in a report consist of a *given,* which is information that is already known to both the writer and reader, and a *new,* which provides the reader with new information about the *given.* Based on their analysis, Ownby and Wallbrown (1986) proposed that statements in reports should involve logical sequences moving from basic data to an MLC to a conclusion and a recommendation.

The expository process model thus proposes that anything written in a report should involve a "shared referent," information that both the writer and reader understand. Hence what is written in a report should be written so that it is easily understood by the reader, and explanations of the child's functioning and behavior should be provided in a way understandable to the most unsophisticated reader. This model also requires that the report consist of sequences of elements beginning with basic data, moving through MLCs to conclusions and recommendations. Ownby (1990b) reports a test of this model which found that school psychologists rated statements based on the model as significantly more credible and persuasive than non-model statements.

The present author does not specifically subscribe to the expository process model. However, he does concur with the idea of a linkage between the basic data of the test, in IQ scores, factor scores or individual subtest scores, and any interpretations made. In addition, the author believes that the information written in a psychological report should be understandable to any reader of the report.

This aspect of report writing involves a three-level hierarchy: the first level involves the clinical reasoning about the basic data of the testing; the second level involves the report writer devising a clear and simple explanation of the data, or translation of the concepts used into readily understandable ideas; and the third level involves presenting these ideas in the report, either with appropriate explanations or in such terms that any reader can comprehend them.

The reasoning about or interpretation of the data in a child's WISC–III protocol requires what Gambrill (1993) refers to as critical thinking. According to Gambrill (1993), *decision making,* whether implicit or explicit, is at the core of all clinical work. Decisions are made at many levels of clinical activity and complexity and can be conceptualized within the hierarchical model discussed in this volume (see section on "Models in Psychology" and Figures 3 and 5).

The decisions made ordinarily involve choices among various pathways of thought or action at various levels of a hierarchical set of possibilities or domains. Critical thinking abilities are important as they can assist the clinician in choosing wisely among options. This kind of thinking involves the examination by the clinician of her or his assumptions, goals, and the evidence available and is focused on deciding what to believe or what to do in a given situation (Dewey, 1933). The process of critical thinking involves a dialogue with oneself or others in which different points of view are considered and evaluated, and it demands a reflective, analytic mode of thinking, whether one is listening to another person or oneself (Dewey, 1971).

The application of critical thinking and reasoning is of course vitally relevant to the interpretation of a child's WISC–III protocol. The process requires that the examiner approach the task in an orderly and logical fashion; that the examiner recognize he or she is generating one or more hypotheses to parsimoniously explain and integrate the test data; and that the examiner realize she or he is basing his or her interpretative approaches on a particular model comprised of certain cognitive strategies, assumptions, and beliefs.

If one attempts to utilize critical thinking in the interpretation of a child's test protocol, some guidelines should be kept in mind. First, one should be able to evaluate arguments, realizing that the conclusions drawn about the child from testing represent an argument. The examiner needs to consider whether her or his argument is logical and whether the conclusions can be validly based on the data available. Second, the examiner needs to try to avoid "informal fallacies," or mistakes in the reasoning process itself (Gambrill, 1993). This may be best accomplished by continually reviewing one's thinking processes, attempting to determine if one's assumptions are true, if different conclusions within one's thinking are consistent with one another, and if there are alternative interpretations that may be more reasonable than the one the examiner is using.

A third aspect of critical thinking relevant to test interpretation is using language effectively. The terms one uses should be clearly understood and understandable, with clear referents for the examiner, the reader or the potential listener.

A fourth component of critical thinking involves the examiner's recognition and monitoring of affective influences on his or her reasoning. This means the examiner should realize that her or his like or dislike of a child may affect the way the data is evaluated or the conclusions drawn (see section on "Characteristics of the Examiner and Her or His Role"), and the clinician should make every effort to avoid or reduce this kind of error in his or her thinking.

A fifth feature of critical thinking involves the realization that cognitive biases can interfere with evaluating information and reaching accurate conclusions. These biases have been referred to as *heuristics* or rules of thumb (Gambrill, 1993) that may assist with rapid processing of information, but which may also result in incorrect reasoning as well. Cognitive biases include such things as *anchoring,* the failure to adjust one's thinking to accommodate new information; *confirmatory strategies,* the selective attention to information that confirms one's already held hypothesis; *information salience,* giving more weight to concrete or salient information than to less obvious aspects of the data; and *overconfidence,* having excessive confidence in one's initial judgment (Weist, Finney, & Ollendick, 1992).

Thus it is important for the examiner to attempt to utilize critical thinking both during test administration itself and in the evaluation and interpretation of the data which results from the testing of a child. Such an approach is most likely to lead to the fairest assessment of a child and her or his intellectual functioning.

In terms of the third aspect of the relevance of the hierarchical model, the examiner can conceive of various levels of the school system with which the child interacts. At the base of this hierarchical perspective of the child's school would be the child's classroom teacher or teachers, while above this level would be the Multidisciplinary Team, and above the team would be other members of the administration, such as directors of special services, assistant principals or principals. To the extent possible, the report may consider the various perspectives of these individuals, although the examiner simply may not be able to address the precise concerns of all of these people.

For example, the classroom teacher, who likely initiated the evaluation in the first place, may be motivated to find out why a particular child is either not learning or is not responsive to the teacher's efforts at instruction and/or control of the child. The teacher will have initiated the referral as a way to obtain help for his or her specific in-class efforts to accomplish the task of teaching. Clearly, the report and its recommendations should contribute to the classroom teacher's understanding of the child, address the teacher's referral question, and provide strategies that may facilitate the teacher's approach to dealing with the referred child.

Individuals on the Multidisciplinary Team may reflect varying degrees of a desire to help the specific child being evaluated. However, these individuals may also be dealing with the bureaucratic and legal pressures to conform to certain regulations when evaluating a child under the law (e.g., State of Rhode Island, 1992). Hence, their motives may be to "process" the evaluation material, come to a bureaucratic decision regarding the child, develop an *Individualized Educational Plan,* and thus fulfill the school's legal requirement to the child and family. To the extent possible, knowing that the psychological report will be used as part of the Multidisciplinary Team's bureaucratic process, the examiner may consider the information the team requires and attempt to provide that information in the report.

It is important to realize that Multidisciplinary Teams themselves operate as other interpersonal groups and systems. This means that these teams develop a decision-making style to accommodate their task and the specific members of the team. With an awareness of the nature of the decision-making process within the team, the examiner may need to triage her or his own evaluations and to advocate for particular services for a given child. This advocacy process may occur verbally during team meetings or may be conveyed to the team through the psychological report itself.

To the extent that, based on the results of the psychological report and/or other evaluations, the child will be determined eligible for special services, the psychological report may include information and/or recommendations that might be specifically useful to a resource teacher when he or she is working with the referred child.

In regard to this hierarchical view of the school environment, the examiner needs to determine how she or he defines his or her role, which involves to what extent the examiner advocates for the child's needs, identifies with the school and attempts to "process" the child, or attempts to negotiate a course that seeks the best fit or compromise between the child's particular needs and the school's available resources. In making this point, the author is fully aware of the various pressures which may operate on the examiner in her or his functioning, including the examiner's own economic position, self-perception, and beliefs about his or her role in regard to children she or he evaluates.

As noted above, the examiner also needs to realize that the psychological evaluation of a child exists within multiple contexts or systems within which the child lives. One of these systems is the school, which may be the primary focus of the psychological evaluation of the child.

However, in addition to school, a second system of which the child is a member is her or his family (Fine & Carlson, 1992). From a systemic viewpoint, there are a number of ways that one can conceptualize the family (e.g., Fraser, 1982; Nichols, 1984; Stanton, 1981). The family can also be considered to be hierarchically organized, with the parent or parents at the apex, various intrafamilial subsystems beneath this, and with the child (or siblings) at the base.

From within this systemic perspective of the family, one can consider the psychological report as having impact on various levels of the hierarchy. First would be the meaning to the parent or parents of being informed of the level and nature of their child's intellectual functioning. Related to this would be the understanding they may have of the short-term meaning and implications of this classification—i.e., that their child is gifted, above average, average, below average, mentally retarded, or learning disabled— and will thus obtain special services or not.

Second would be the understanding they may have of the longer-term implications of their child's intellectual level—e.g., that the child can succeed in school or not, how far the child may be able to go in school, and what implications the child's level of intellectual functioning may have for his or her ultimate vocational aspirations.

Third would be the impact on the child her- or himself of the results of the evaluation findings, in terms of the way the parents relate to the child, and the way the child may come to define him- or herself, as capable, average or in some way handicapped. Lastly, the examiner may also consider the meaning of any of these issues—e.g., the referred child's "IQ"—if or as the child's siblings find out about the evaluation results.

Another consideration in the writing of the report is the style of the report. It is highly unlikely that extensive detail within the report will be retained as an effective guide for anyone who reads or hears the report, unless they feel it is so insightful or helpful that they recode it (write notes on it) or make a copy for themselves to re-refer to at various points in their dealing with the child. Therefore, for the examiner's report to have impact and be remembered, the hierarchical model may again be relevant. From this view, one would begin sections of the report with general or abstract statements, then follow these with more detailed elucidation of those statements, or with concrete examples that illustrate the point being made. With this organization of presented material, the reader may lose the more detailed information from memory but may still retain the abstract or general statement. In addition, however, this approach involves a redundancy of information, which provides different codes to enable the reader to retain the material which has been presented.

In this regard, it is also important for the examiner to at least take some step from the conclusions of the report to include tactics or strategies for the reader of the report to utilize in dealing with the child; these statements, in the form of strategic recommendations, can be retained as simple rule systems that can guide the teacher in his or her interaction with the referred child.

One more aspect of the writing of the report which is relevant is the tense in which the report is written. The examiner has two choices: writing the report (or all of it other than the behavioral observations) in the present tense or in the past tense. The present author believes that writing a report in the present tense is likely to make it more vivid and current for the reader, and if it is assumed that a teacher may reread the report several weeks, months, or even a year after it was written, the report may convey information about the way the child is presumed to be at the point in time when the report is being consulted.

Thus in writing the report, the examiner should maintain an awareness of the multiple audiences that may see, hear or read the psychological report; realize that the findings of the report will have an impact on the school, the child, and the child's family; and keep in mind that the more effectively the report is organized, the more influence it is likely to have.

DESIGN FEATURES OF THE REPORT

Insofar as the psychological report involves the transmission of information from the examiner to an audience, the issue involved is one of design of an information flow. Hence in thinking about the psychological report, the examiner should consider the report from a design perspective and determine what features of a report will facilitate the transmission of information from the examiner to the audience.

One aspect of this question is the selection of a consistent report format for the presentation or communication of test results. The value of using the same report structure consistently is that examiners typically work in relatively few settings and therefore generally deal with a finite number of recipients of their reports. Using the same report structure facilitates the use of the report by the users, as they will be able to learn where information is contained in the examiner's report.

To facilitate this further, however, the author recommends that the report be designed in a way that enhances information flow. This means, for example, that the report can be designed in a fashion which places information in the report in a logical location according to an organizational model which makes intuitive sense and thus is likely congruent with the thinking of the typical reader of the psychological report.

The present author has adopted a temporal and contextual organization in his own conceptualization of the report structure; that is, past time in terms of what led up to the evaluation; test findings; the presentation, evaluation and interpretation of these findings; and recommendations for the future. The context of the report is the reason for referral, the child's place in school and within a family, and the characteristics of the evaluation itself (i.e., the physical setting of the evaluation and the examiner's style of test administration).

The examiner can also use an outline procedure to set off the various parts of the report in order to facilitate the reader's locating particular information on first reading or if he or she wishes/needs to return to some part of the report at a future date. The present author recommends division of the psychological report into more sections than is typically suggested for such reports (Sattler, 1990).

In addition, the present author assumes that many if not most examiners will be using a computer/word processor to write reports if they do not use a computer program to generate entire reports. It is therefore possible, and recommended, that the examiner highlight (boldface, set off in italics or color code) those particular elements of the report that should be emphasized. The author assumes that there are certain parts of the report that carry crucial meaning, while other parts provide a context for this essential information. Although the examiner should attempt to write the entire report to include the most meaningful distillation of the assessment, the examiner may also highlight those parts of the report which are felt to carry the most important meaning for the reader. If the examiner dictates his or her report, it would be necessary to decide how to instruct the typist to highlight/boldface certain items in the report.

As noted above, when writing a report, the examiner needs to consider the concept of target audience. This can range from the least sophisticated reader/listener, the child him- or herself, to the most sophisticated reader/listener, a professional colleague. Although this conceptualization would permit a gradient of report types to be generated (e.g., the *WISC-III Writer*

[Psychological Corporation, 1994] produces a professional report and a parent report), it is the present author's view that a single report should be written that can be seen by any reader. This facilitates openness with clients and provides a monitor function for the examiner: if the examiner is writing a report that the child's parent(s) or the child may someday see, the examiner is more likely to write the report in a sympathetic and empathic way than if the examiner feels he or she is writing a report *about* someone that the person will never see.

Finally, the author conceptualizes the report format which is presented here as an ideal model for an intellectual assessment (and modifiable but applicable to other kinds of assessment as well). If the examiner is a trainee who is testing one or two children a month, it may be an intriguing experience to use this model in its entirety. If one is a private practitioner who tests children two or three times a week, this report format may also be quite appropriate.

But if one is a school psychologist under great pressure to test children whose names appear on a seemingly unending list of new referrals, testing may be quite arduous, and this model may appear simply too time consuming or demanding to consider. It is the author's intent to provide his view of an ideal model while realizing that the examiner may adapt the model and shorten it as desired.

Chapter Sixteen

WRITING THE PSYCHOLOGICAL REPORT

USE OF THE TEST ANALYSIS WORKSHEET

Before the actual writing of the psychological report, the examiner must analyze, decode and organize the data contained in the child's WISC–III protocol. The present author has designed a "Test Analysis Worksheet" (see Table 13) to facilitate the examiner's analysis of the data on the WISC–III in a way which is consistent with the report she or he will create. In general, the examiner may fill in those specific parts of the form he or she intends to use in the analysis of the child's test protocol.

The worksheet is organized to be used from top to bottom and is divided into four sections, numbered (1) through (4). At the top of the worksheet is space to record the name of the child who has been evaluated, her or his date of birth, the date of the examination, and the child's age.

In using the "Test Analysis Worksheet" in relation to the WISC–III test form, the examiner would complete the upper left portion of the WISC–III test form on the WISC–III record form itself. This means that after completing the testing of the child with the WISC–III, the examiner would transfer all subtest raw scores to their appropriate locations on the front of the test booklet. The determination of the scaled score for each subtest's raw score is obtained from Wechsler (1991, Table A.1., pp. 217–249).

At this point, the sums of scaled scores for the Verbal, Performance and Full Scale IQs and for the four factors can be transferred to the upper-left portion of the "Test Analysis Worksheet" form [sections (1) and (2); e.g., FSSS, VSS, PSS, VCSS, etc.]. The individual subtest scaled scores may also be transferred to the lower portion of section (4) of the worksheet. (Note that the form is designed so that verbal subtest scores are recorded together on the left-hand side of the form, while performance subtest scores are recorded together on the right-hand side of the form.)

The examiner can proceed to obtain the Verbal, Performance, and Full Scale IQs and the factor scores, percentiles, and confidence intervals from Wechsler (1991, Tables A.2. through A.7., pp. 251–257). The verbal classifications for the various scores may be obtained from Wechsler (1991, Table 2.8., p. 32) or from Table 5 in the present volume. The examiner can then proceed to carry out the calculations which he or she chooses in sections (2), (3), and (4) of the worksheet.

Table 13
TEST ANALYSIS WORKSHEET

Name: _____ DOB: _____ DOE: _____ Age: _____

(1) FSSS = ____ FSIQ = ____ %ile ____ %CI = ____ Classification = ____
    VSS = ____ VIQ = ____ %ile ____ %CI = ____ Classification = ____
    PSS = ____ PIQ = ____ %ile ____ %CI = ____ Classification = ____

(2) VCSS = ____ VCI = ____ %ile ____ %CI = ____ Classification = ____
    POSS = ____ POI = ____ %ile ____ %CI = ____ Classification = ____
    FDSS = ____ FDI = ____ %ile ____ %CI = ____ Classification = ____
    PSSS = ____ PSI = ____ %ile ____ %CI = ____ Classification = ____

VIQ/VCI ____ DSd ____ AR – DS = ____ VCI ____ – FDI ____ = ____
–PIQ/POI = ____   CD – SS = ____ POI ____ – PSI ____ = ____

____ % ____ V/VCI:H – L = ____ P/POI:H – L = ____ F:H – L = ____

(3)
ACID(S):AR ____ CD ____ IN ____ DS ____ (SS) ____ = <lo SM ____ VO ____ CO ____ PC ____ PA ____ BD ____ OA ____

PATTERN:SPA: PC ____ VERCON: SM ____ SEQ: AR ____ ACKNO: IN ____ Order: ____
             BD ____   VO ____   DS ____   AR ____
             OA ____   CO ____   CD ____   VO ____
             Tot ____   Tot ____   Tot ____   Tot ____
             Av ____   Av ____   Av ____   Av ____

FLU–CRYS: FLU:SM ____ DS ____ PC ____ PA ____ BD ____ OA ____ CRYS:IN ____ SM ____ VO ____ CO ____
          Tot FLU = ____ Av FLU = ____   Tot CRYS = ____ Av CRYS = ____

• • • • •

(4) INDEX: Tot Index = ____ VCI ____ POI ____ FDI ____ PSI ____   (M)
           Av Index = ____   – ____

PROFILE: INv SMv ARf VOv COv (DS)f PCp CDs PAp BDp OAp (SS)s
AvV/VCI = ____ – ____ – ____ – ____ – ____ – ____ – ____ – ____ – ____ – ____ – ____ – ____ – ____
AvP/POI = ____ – ____ – ____ – ____ – ____ – ____ – ____ – ____ – ____ – ____ – ____ – ____ – ____
AvFS   = ____

Section (1) provides space for the recording of the sum of scaled scores for the Full Scale (FSSS), the Verbal Scale (VSS), and the Performance Scale (PSS), as well as space for the IQ equivalent, percentile rank, confidence interval (the author recommends using the 95% confidence interval), and verbal classification for each of these three scores.

Section (2) provides space for the sum of scaled scores for the four Index scores: VCSS for Verbal Comprehension; POSS for Perceptual Organization; FDSS for Freedom from Distractibility; and PSSS for Processing Speed. For each of these scores, space is provided to record the relevant Index, the percentile score, confidence interval, and verbal classification for that Index.

Section (2) also includes a variety of prompts for further analyzing the WISC–III protocol. This section includes a prompt, VIQ/VCI−PIQ/POI, to subtract the Performance IQ from the Verbal IQ or the Verbal Comprehension Index from the Perceptual Organization Index (the important issue is the size and significance of the difference between these two IQs or Indices, so the direction of difference does not matter). Beneath the subtraction is a space to record if the difference is significant and the percentage of occurrence of a difference this size in the standardization population.

To determine the significance of the obtained Verbal-Performance IQ or Verbal Comprehension-Perceptual Organization Index discrepancy, the examiner can refer to Wechsler (1991, Table B.1., p. 261); or Table 14, "Differences Between WISC–III IQ and Index Scores Required for Significance By Age," based on Naglieri (1993); or the examiner may use a Verbal-Performance rule-of-thumb discrepancy of 20 or more points as significant (*WISC-III Writer* [Psychological Corporation, 1994]). The frequency of occurrence of a particular Verbal-Performance discrepancy can be obtained from Wechsler (1991, Table B.2., p. 262).

Section (2) also includes a prompt regarding the Digit Span subtest: DSd, representing the Difference Between Digits Forward and Digits Backward. This prompt has a line next to it for the score and a line next to that to record the cumulative percentage of the obtained score in the standardization population.

From the viewpoint of the hierachical model discussed earlier (see section on "Models in Psychology"), one may conceptualize the total Digit Span score as the apex of a hierarchy, with the Digits Forward and Digits Backward representing two component abilities (below the apex in the hierarchy). Before concluding that the Digit Span subtest represents a relatively coherent ability for the child being tested, the examiner should determine whether the difference between Digits Forward and Backward is significant or insignificant (see Wechsler, 1991, Table B.7., p. 268, "Cumulative Percentages of Difference Between Longest Digits Forward and Digits Backward Spans by

Table 14
DIFFERENCES BETWEEN WISC-III IQ AND INDEX SCORES REQUIRED FOR SIGNIFICANCE BY AGE

Age (Years)	p	VIQ–PIQ	VC–PO	VC–FD	VC–PS	PO–FD	PO–PS	FD–PS
6	.05	16.2	17.2	19.0	21.4	19.0	21.4	22.9
	.01	19.3	20.4	22.6	25.5	22.6	25.5	27.2
7	.05	17.1	17.6	20.2	21.8	20.6	22.1	24.3
	.01	20.4	21.0	24.1	25.9	24.5	26.4	28.9
8	.05	15.1	16.2	17.1	18.5	19.8	21.0	21.8
	.01	18.0	19.2	20.4	22.1	23.6	25.0	25.9
9	.05	16.2	16.7	19.8	19.0	21.0	20.2	22.9
	.01	19.3	19.8	23.6	22.6	25.0	24.1	27.2
10	.05	15.1	16.2	18.1	19.0	19.8	20.6	22.1
	.01	18.0	19.2	21.5	22.6	23.6	24.5	26.4
11	.05	15.6	16.7	17.2	17.6	19.4	19.8	20.2
	.01	18.6	19.8	20.4	21.0	23.1	23.6	24.1
12	.05	15.1	15.1	17.6	17.1	19.4	19.0	21.0
	.01	18.0	18.0	21.0	20.4	23.1	22.6	25.0
13	.05	16.2	16.2	17.6	20.2	18.5	21.0	22.1
	.01	19.2	19.3	21.0	24.1	22.1	25.0	26.4
14	.05	16.2	16.2	17.6	19.4	20.2	21.8	22.9
	.01	19.2	19.2	21.0	23.1	24.1	25.9	27.2
15	.05	12.8	14.0	15.1	15.1	16.2	16.2	17.2
	.01	15.2	16.7	18.0	18.0	19.3	19.3	20.4
16	.05	14.6	16.2	16.2	15.6	18.1	17.6	17.6
	.01	17.3	19.2	19.2	18.6	21.5	21.0	21.0
6–16	.05	15.5	16.2	17.6	18.7	19.1	20.1	21.3
	.01	18.5	19.3	21.0	22.3	22.8	24.0	25.4

Key: VIQ = Verbal IQ; PIQ = Performance IQ; VC = Verbal Comprehension index; PO = Perceptual Organization index; FD = Freedom from Distractibility index; PS = Processing Speed index.

Note. Reprinted by permission of the publisher and J. A. Naglieri from J. A. Naglieri, "Pairwise and Ipsative Comparisons of WISC-III IQ and Index Scores," Psychological Assessment, 1993, 5, p. 114. Copyright 1993 by the American Psychological Association, Inc.

Age Group"). Although the discussion in Wechsler regarding this table (Wechsler, 1991, p. 177) is not clear, the present author assumes that this table provides raw scores for the standardization sample, and that Digits Forward or Digits Backward refer to the examinee's success on at least one trial of a given length.

In evaluating the significance of the difference between the longest Digits Forward and Digits Backward Spans, the author recommends using the figure nearest 10% of the population for each age (e.g., for 6- and 10-year-old children, 6 percent of the subjects had a difference between Longest Digits Forward and Digits Backward Span of 5; for 7- and 12-year-old children, 10% of the subjects had a difference between Longest Digits Forward and Digits Backward Span of 4) as indicating a significant difference between these spans. If the child displays a difference between Forward and Backward Spans of this magnitude, the present author would conclude that the elements comprising the Digit Span subtest are inconsistent; hence the components of the Freedom from Distractibility factor are not coherent and the factor should not be interpreted.

Section (2) also includes a prompt, AR - DS, to remind the examiner to check the size of the difference between the Arithmetic and Digit Span subtests. Even if the difference between Digit Span Forward and Backward is not significant, if the difference between the Arithmetic and Digit Span subtests is significant (3.00 or 4.00 [Wechsler, 1991, p. 265] depending on whether the examiner wishes to use a conservative criterion or not), the examiner would also conclude that these two subtests do not form a coherent factor and should not be interpreted as the Freedom from Distractibility factor.

If, however, the Digit Span Forward and Backward Spans and the Arithmetic and Digit Span subtests are not different from one another, the examiner can proceed to the next prompt, VCI - FDI to determine the relationship between the child's Verbal Comprehension and Freedom from Distractibility factors. The examiner may determine if these factors are significantly different from one another by consulting Wechsler (1991, Table B.1., p. 261) or Table 14 in the present volume, "Differences Between WISC–III IQ and Index Scores Required for Significance by Age," based on Naglieri (1993).

Parallelling the sequence for the FDI factor, section (2) also includes a prompt, CD - SS, to remind the examiner to evaluate the discrepancy between the Coding and Symbol Search subtests. If this difference is significant (4.00 scaled-score units or more [Wechsler, 1991, Table B.1., p. 265]), these two subtests should not be combined into the Processing Speed factor and the factor should not be interpreted separately. If the Coding and Symbol Search subtests are not significantly different from one another, they can be considered to form a coherent factor and then the examiner can proceed to the next prompt, POI - PSI, to determine the relationship between the examinee's Perceptual Organization and Processing Speed factors. The significance of the difference between these two factors can be evaluated by consulting Wechsler (1991, Table B.1., p. 261) or Table 14 in the present volume, "Differences Between WISC–III IQ and Index Scores Required for Significance by Age," based on Naglieri (1993).

Section (2) also includes prompts to examine the degree of scatter within the WISC–III Verbal (V/VCI: H - L), Performance (P/POI: H - L), and Full Scales (F: H - L). For the Verbal and Performance scales, the examiner may use either the IQ or Index scores. In each case, the examiner would subtract the lowest scaled score from the highest scaled score. These differences can then be compared to the listed values in Wechsler (1991, Table B.5., p. 266) to determine the usualness or unusualness of the degree of intersubtest scatter which is evident in the scale being considered.

The author recommends a degree of scatter within any group of subtests (e.g., 5 Verbal or 10 subtests) obtained by approximately 10–15% of the standardization population (e.g., 8.4% of the normative population displayed 8 scaled-score units of scatter when 5 Verbal subtests were considered, and 16.3% of the normative population displayed 7 scaled-score units of scatter when 5 Verbal subtests were considered) as indicative of a significant degree of scatter for the examinee. Space is provided to the right of each of the scatter indicies (e.g., V/VCI: H - L) to record the percentage chosen by the examiner or the significance of that result.

Section (3) of the "Test Analysis Worksheet" provides prompts for the analysis of the examinee's WISC–III data from the perspectives of three sets of subtest patterns: the ACID or ACIDS profile [ACID(S)] (Prifitera & Dersh, 1993); Bannatyne's (1974) recategorization approach [PATTERN]; and Horn's (1985, 1988; Horn & Hofer, 1992) Fluid-Crystallized categorization of intellectual tasks [FLU–CRYS].

According to the ACID or ACIDS approach, the subtests included in the ACID (or ACIDS) profile are listed to the left of the = <lo sign. Scores on these subtests can be compared to those on the right side of the = <lo sign, which include the remaining subtests on the WISC–III except for the Mazes subtest. The child or adolescent has the full ACID profile if the scaled score on each of the four ACID subtests is equal to or less than the lowest scaled score on any one of the remaining subtests excluding Mazes and Symbol Search. The examinee has the full ACIDS profile if the scaled score on each of the five ACIDS subtests is equal to or less than the lowest scaled score on any one of the remaining WISC–III subtests excluding Mazes. One can also note if the child has a partial ACID or ACIDS profile if some but not all of the relevant scaled scores fit this definition. The examiner can compare the

child's performance (whether the child has the full or partial ACID or ACIDS profile or neither) to the base rates of occurrence of these profiles found in the standardization sample by consulting Tables 10 and 11.

According to the Bannatyne recategorization approach to Wechsler scores, the examiner can fill in the subtest scores for the Spatial, Verbal Conceptualization, Sequential, and Acquired Knowledge categories where indicated on the "Test Analysis Worksheet." These subtest scores in each category are summed, and the average scaled score for each category is calculated. The totals for each category, or the average scaled score for each category, may then be compared.

The examiner can record the order of the groups of recategorized scores next to the "Order" prompt. The child is considered to have the Bannatyne profile if his or her scores emerge with Spatial > Verbal Conceptual > Sequential. The examiner can consult Table 12, "Means of the IQ, Index, and Bannatyne Scores and the Sum of Indices Three and Four for the Standardization, LD and ADHD Samples," to note the scores obtained by the standardization sample as well as by a learning disabled and an ADHD sample on the Bannatyne recategorized scores.

The examiner can also observe whether the examinee has any other pattern of scores and where in the pattern of Bannatyne recategorized scores the child's Acquired Knowledge score falls. In addition, the examiner should note, even if the child has the Bannatyne pattern, the size of the differences between the various components of the pattern since if the differences are small, the nature of the examinee's pattern of intellectual performance would not have any meaningful implications for her or his academic instruction.

The last part of section (3) involves prompts regarding the concept of Fluid and Crystallized intelligence. Although, according to this approach, the subtests of the WISC–III could be divided into those reflecting fluid and crystallized intelligence, retrieval, and speed (Kaufman, 1990), the present author has chosen to focus only on dividing the subtests of the WISC–III into those that reflect fluid, or more culture-free, intellectual abilities and those that reflect crystallized, or more culture-bound, intellectual abilities. In terms of the WISC–III, the fluid abilities involve those that are included in Wechsler's (1991) Perceptual Organization factor plus the subtests of Similarities and Digit Span, while the crystallized abilities are those that are included in Wechsler's (1991) Verbal Comprehension factor.

The examiner can sum the scaled scores on the Fluid Intelligence subtests, then obtain the average scaled score for these subtests. The clinician can then sum the scaled scores on the Crystallized Intelligence subtests and obtain the average scaled score of these subtests. The examiner can then compare the child's average scaled scores on Fluid and Crystallized subtests and determine whether the examinee displays any noteworthy advantage for either type of intellectual performance.

The present author would also note a slightly different approach to evaluating the examinee's functioning on the constructs of fluid and crystallized intelligence. It is the author's view that the clearest representations of these two different forms of thinking are in four of the WISC–III subtests. It is felt that the Information and Vocabulary subtests most clearly reflect the individual's assimilated knowledge of the United States culture, both in specific facts and in knowing the dominant language of that culture. It is felt that the clearest reflections of the child's ability to utilize problem-solving strategies for dealing with novel tasks emerge in her or his handling of the Block Design and Object Assembly subtests. Hence the examiner may also compare the individual's performances on these four subtests, two representing G*f* and two representing G*c,* to estimate the child's relative abilities for these different kinds of thinking.

Section (4) is devoted to the concept of an intraindividual, or ipsative, approach to the WISC–III. Hence section (4) provides a prompt regarding the calculation of the examinee's total and average Index scores and also provides prompts to indicate the subtraction of each Index score from the average of all the Index scores. If either the Freedom from Distractibility factor or the Processing Speed factor is felt to be unusable, the author does not recommend using an ipsative approach regarding the four factors. If the examiner chooses to obtain the average of three factors and calculate the variation of each factor from the average, there are no tabled values in Wechsler (1991) or Naglieri (1993) that permit determination of the significance of the result.

If all four Index scores are usable, the examiner can subtract the examinee's Average Index score from each of the child's Index scores if the examiner wishes to utilize an ipsative approach (Naglieri, 1993) in the evaluation of the individual's functioning on the four factors of the WISC–III. Determination of the significance of variation of the Index scores around their mean score would be obtained from Table 15, "Ipsative Differences Required for Significance When Comparing Each Index With the Average of the Four Index Scores," based on Naglieri (1993), since Wechsler (1991) does not provide tables on these comparisons.

Although the lower portion of section (4) is set up to deal with Kaufman's (1979a, 1990; Reynolds & Kaufman, 1985) intraindividual, or profile, analysis approach, this section can also be used in terms of a normative approach to the child's test performance. According to the normative approach, the examiner would simply note those subtests that are at least one standard deviation or more scaled-score units above or below the standardization mean of 10 for each subtest.

Table 15

**IPSATIVE DIFFERENCES REQUIRED FOR SIGNIFICANCE
WHEN COMPARING EACH INDEX WITH THE
AVERAGE OF THE FOUR INDEX SCORES**

Age (Years)	Group p	VC	PO	FD	PS
6	.05	10.36	10.36	11.64	13.33
	.01	12.57	12.57	14.13	16.18
7	.05	10.56	10.89	12.68	13.75
	.01	12.83	13.22	15.40	16.69
8	.05	8.64	10.80	11.45	12.33
	.01	10.49	13.12	13.89	14.97
9	.05	9.61	10.64	12.74	12.19
	.01	11.66	12.92	15.47	14.80
10	.05	9.08	10.52	11.78	12.37
	.01	11.03	12.77	14.30	15.01
11	.05	8.89	10.68	11.02	11.33
	.01	10.79	12.97	13.38	13.75
12	.05	8.43	9.97	11.59	11.29
	.01	10.24	12.10	14.07	13.71
13	.05	9.47	10.18	11.18	12.92
	.01	11.50	12.36	13.57	15.68
14	.05	8.79	10.92	11.85	12.98
	.01	10.67	13.26	14.39	15.76
15	.05	7.84	8.70	9.47	9.47
	.01	9.52	10.56	11.49	11.49
16	.05	8.53	10.05	10.05	9.70
	.01	10.36	12.20	12.20	11.77
6–16	.05	9.14	10.36	11.45	12.05
	.01	11.10	12.58	13.90	14.63

Key: VC = Verbal Comprehension; PO = Perceptual Organization; FD = Freedom from Distractibility; PS = Processing Speed.

Note. Reprinted by permission of the publisher and J. A. Naglieri from J. A. Naglieri, "Pairwise and Ipsative Comparisons of WISC–III IQ and Index Scores," *Psychological Assessment, 5,* 1993, p. 115. Copyright 1993 by the American Psychological Association, Inc.

The examiner can set a criterion of three scaled-score units above or below the mean (i.e., scaled scores of 13 or above, or 7 or below). When any subtest score on the child's protocol reaches the criterion level the examiner has set, the examiner would conclude that this subtest represents a strength or weakness for the child in comparison to the standardization population.

In section (4) on the "Test Analysis Worksheet," beneath each subtest that meets this criterion the examiner would note an S or W to describe that subtest for the child.

If the examiner uses section (4) of the "Test Analysis Worksheet" to implement Kaufman's (1979a, 1990; Reynolds & Kaufman, 1985) intraindividual, or profile, analysis, this section of the worksheet provides prompts and space to record the average scaled score for the Verbal, Performance and Full Scale scores and also provides space to record the subtest score for each subtest which has been administered to the child.

The form is organized so that all the verbal subtests are together and all the performance subtests are together, rather than organizing the subtests according to their sequence of administration on the WISC–III. Each subtest is listed with an abbreviated title and a lowercase letter to indicate the subtest's factor membership (v = Verbal Comprehension; f = Freedom from Distractibility; p = Perceptual Organization; s = Processing Speed). Although the Mazes subtest is listed, it is not a member of any factor.

The examiner may use this section of the worksheet to subtract the relevant mean (of either the Verbal, Performance or Full Scale) from each subtest score. The significance of the variation of individual subtest scores from the relevant mean can be evaluated by referring to Wechsler (1991, Table B.3., pp. 263–264). If one or more scores emerge as apparent strengths or weaknesses, they must first be evaluated to determine if the subtest in question has sufficient specificity at the age level being considered. This can be done by referring to Sattler (1992, Table I-12, p. 1049) or Table 16, "WISC–III Subtest Specificities," in the present volume based on Bracken et al. (1993). If the subtest in question does in fact have at least adequate specificity, the examiner may conclude that the subtest represents a strength or weakness within the child's own cognitive profile of abilities, and the subtest may be marked with an S or W to indicate this.

In determining whether to use the child's average score on *all* the subtests or the child's average score on the Verbal and the Performance parts of the scale separately, the examiner would note the VIQ/VCI–PIQ/POI difference that she or he calculated in section (2).

If there is a significant difference between these two IQ or Index scores, the examiner would conclude that the Verbal and Performance scales must be considered separately. In this case, the examiner would calculate the child's mean performance on the verbal subtests and determine the variation of the verbal subtests from that mean. And similarly, the examiner would determine the child's mean performance on the nonverbal subtests and determine the variation of the child's handling of the performance subtests as compared to that mean. Significance levels for these comparisons may be determined by consulting Wechsler (1991, Table B.3., p. 263).

Table 16

WISC-III SUBTEST SPECIFICITIES

Subtests	Ages with Ample Specificity	Ages with Adequate Specificity	Ages with Inadequate Specificity
Information	11	8–10, 12–16	6–7
Similarities	6, 14	11–12, 15–16	7–10, 13
Arithmetic	6–7, 10, 13, 15	16	8–9, 11–12, 14
Vocabulary	6, 11	7–8, 12–16	9–10
Comprehension	6, 8–11	12	7, 13–16
Digit Span	6–16	—	—
Picture Completion	6–11, 13–14, 16	—	12
Coding	6–16	—	—
Picture Arrangement	6–16	—	—
Block Design	6–16	—	—
Object Assembly	9, 13, 15	—	6–8, 10–12, 14, 16
Symbol Search	7, 10–16	—	6, 8–9
Mazes	6–14, 16	—	15

Note. Subtests labeled "ample specificity" have specific variance that reflects 25% or more of the subtest's total variance and exceeds the subtest's error variance. Subtests labeled "adequate specificity" have specific variance that is between 15% and 24% of the subtest's total variance and exceeds the subtest's error variance. Subtests with "inadequate specificity" have specific variance that either is less than 15% of the subtest's total variance or is equal to or less than the subtest's error variance.

Note. Reprinted by permission of the publisher and B. A. Bracken from B. A. Bracken, R. S. McCallum and R. M. Crain, "WISC-III Subtest Reliabilities and Specificities: Interpretive Aids," *Journal of Psychoeducational Assessment, Monograph Series, Advances in Psychoeducational Assessment, Wechsler Intelligence Scale for Children: Third Edition,* 1993, p. 31. Copyright 1993 by the *Journal of Psychoeducational Assessment.*

If there is no significant difference between the child's Verbal and Performance IQs or VCI and POI, then the examinee's functioning on all 10, 12 or 13 subtests which have been administered may be considered together. In this case, the examiner may calculate the mean of all the subtests administered and use that number to determine significant variation among the child's handling of the individual WISC–III subtests. Significance levels for these comparisons may be determined by consulting Wechsler (1991, Table B.3., pp. 263–264).

An alternative approach to determining the significance of the difference between a single subtest score and the mean of several subtests, or between two verbal, two performance, or a verbal and a performance subtest, involves the use of rules of thumb (Kaufman, 1990). According to this approach, the examiner may use simple rules of thumb to determine significant variation in a test profile rather than having to consult tables in the test manual which provide precise values for subtest comparisons. If one wishes to use such a rule-of-thumb approach, the present author suggests the following rules.

In view of the concept presented by Naglieri (1993), that in making numerous comparisons after the data has been examined the experimentwise error rate is inflated, the author has chosen rules of thumb that are conservative, so that the numbers chosen to determine the significance of various comparisons are larger than those tabled in Wechsler (1991, Table B.3., pp. 263–264).

To determine if a single subtest score varies significantly (at the .05 level) from the mean of 5 or 6 verbal subtests, or 5 or 6 performance subtests, the difference between the single subtest and the mean of the subtests being considered should be at least 4.00. To determine if a single subtest score varies significantly (at the .05 level) from the mean of 10 subtests (5 verbal and 5 performance), 12 subtests (6 verbal and 6 performance), or 13 subtests (6 verbal and 7 performance), the difference between the single subtest and the mean of the subtests being considered should be at least 5.00.

To determine if the difference between any two verbal subtests is significant (at the .05 level), the difference between the two subtests should be at least 4.00. To determine if the difference between any two performance subtests, or between any verbal and any performance subtest, is significant (at the .05 level), the difference between the two subtests being considered should be at least 5.00.

If the examiner chooses to, she or he can use section (4) of the "Test Analysis Worksheet" to calculate variation of any subtest in the Verbal Comprehension or Perceptual Organization factor from the mean of that factor. Thus section (4) includes prompts labelled "AvV/VCI," "AvP/POI," and "AvFS." The examiner may use this section to record *either* the average Verbal subtest score *or* the average Verbal Comprehension Index subtest score, the average Performance subtest score *or* the average Perceptual Organization Index subtest score, and the average Full Scale subtest score. The examiner may thus compare each of the examinee's subtests on the VCI with the average of all the subtests on the VCI, and the examiner may compare each of the examinee's subtests on the POI with the average of all the subtests on the POI.

Significance levels for these comparisons may be determined by consulting Wechsler (1991, Table B.3., p. 264). Alternatively, according to the rule-of-thumb approach, to determine if a single subtest score varies significantly from the mean of the verbal comprehension subtests, or from the mean of the perceptual organization subtests, the difference between the single subtest score and the mean being considered (of either the four verbal comprehension subtests or the four perceptual organization subtests) should be at least 4.00.

SECTIONS OF THE REPORT

In *The Clinical Use and Interpretation of the Wechsler Intelligence Scale for Children-Revised* (Cooper, 1982), the author provided a number of possible models for the psychological report. At this time, the author would recommend one format for the psychological report, the "Psychological Evaluation" format (see Table 17). This format is recommended for a psychological report that deals with an evaluation focused on the child's intellectual functioning. If the WISC–III has been administered with another test (e.g., the WRAT-3; Wilkinson, 1993) or as part of a total battery of tests, which also addresses the child's personality organization or neuropsychological functioning, the format would need to be modified to some extent.

The report should contain the following sections:

1) identifying data: the child's name, date of birth, date of evaluation, age, school, and grade level.
2) the reason for referral.
3) background on the child.
4) past testing.
5) test(s) utilized.
6) test situation and behavioral observations.
7) medication status.
8) reliability and validity statement.
9) test results (WISC–III subtest scores).
10) overall intellectual functioning.
11) verbal functioning.
12) nonverbal functioning.

Table 17
THE PSYCHOLOGICAL EVALUATION FORMAT

Name: DOB:
DOE: Age:
School: Grade:

Reason for Referral:

Background:

Past Testing:

Test(s) Utilized:

Test Situation and Behavioral Observations:

Medication Status:

Reliability and Validity Statement:

Test Results:

Verbal Subtests	SS	*Performance Subtests*	SS
Information		Picture Completion	
Similarities		Coding	
Arithmetic		Picture Arrangement	
Vocabulary		Block Design	
Comprehension		Object Assembly	
(Digit Span)		(Symbol Search)	
		(Mazes)	

Overall Intellectual Functioning:

Verbal Functioning:

Nonverbal Functioning:

Subtest Patterns:

Intraindividual Analysis:

Post-test Feedback:

Summary:

Recommendations:

Signature:

13) subtest patterns.
14) intraindividual analysis.
15) post-test feedback.
16) summary.
17) recommendations.
18) signature and date of signature.

When a copy of the report is to be given to the parent(s) of the child who has been referred for evaluation, the parent may also be given an "Explanation of the WISC–III" form (see Table 18), which provides an explanation to the parent(s) of the basic ideas of the WISC–III and its interpretation.

In the following section, the author will discuss each section of the psychological report.

The top section of the psychological report should include the basic identifying information regarding the child. This information includes the child's name, date of birth, the date of the evaluation and the child's age, school and grade level.

The *Reason for Referral* should involve a statement of why and by whom the child was referred. This provides the context for the evaluation, determines the major focus of the evaluation, and will pose the essential question(s) that the examiner seeks to answer in the subsequent parts of the report. As one of the questions the examiner should ask the child at the beginning of testing (see section on "Pre- and Post-WISC–III Questions"), the child should be asked why she or he is being seen for testing. This provides some indication of the examinee's awareness of him- or herself in relation to school or general adjustment and indicates the individual's ability to see the testing in relation to her or his broader life functioning.

The *Background* section should include information obtained from the child's school record, other informants, or information obtained directly from the examinee through the pre-test questions the examiner may ask (see section on "Pre- and Post-WISC–III Questions"). Information the examiner may describe in this section includes who the child lives with, any physical or medical concerns the individual may have, and any information about the examinee's family, developmental background (e.g., trauma, the child being bilingual), or academic history or situation, such as the examinee receiving resource help, that is relevant to the current testing.

The *Past Testing* section should summarize any past testing the child has had. The examiner may include IQ scores here if he or she wishes, but the examiner may also simply indicate by verbal label the relevant classification of the examinee's past test scores and any other relevant information from the prior testing.

The *Test(s) Utilized* section should include a listing of the specific test or tests which have been administered to the child or adolescent, as well as any questionnaires or forms the examinee's parent(s) or teacher(s) have completed describing the child.

The *Test Situation and Behavioral Observations* section should include a description of the test situation, the examiner and his or her style of test administration, and the child and her or his test behavior. The examiner should describe the physical setting where testing occurs, whether this is in a quiet, private office, or in some part of a somewhat noisy school building.

The examiner should also describe him- or herself in terms of age, sex

Table 18
EXPLANATION OF THE WISC-III

The WISC-III is a test which was made for use with children between the ages of 6 and 16. The idea of the test is to find out about the way a child thinks and figures things out when he or she is dealing with words or when the child is dealing with things that she or he can see and touch. When the test was made up, it was given to 1100 boys and 1100 girls of different ages and races, who lived in all different parts of the country and whose parent(s) had different amounts of schooling. The idea was to see how all these different children did on the test.

The way your child did on the WISC-III was compared to the way children his or her own age did on the test from out of this large group of children across the whole country. The test results show and talk about how your child compares to other children her or his age from all across the country in handling these kinds of problems.

The WISC-III is made up of five short verbal tests and five short performance tests and three extra tests. Each of these short tests has a number of questions or items on it of the same kind. Scores on the WISC-III can be given as what is called subtest scores (each short test), IQ scores, factor scores (groups of short tests), or percentile scores. For the Full Scale IQ score, the highest score a child can get is 160, and the lowest score a child can get is 40. At each age, half of all the children taking the test would get a score below 100, and half of all the children at that age would get a score over 100. IQ scores between 90 and 109 are all average. The percentile score tells the percent of children your child's age that his or her score was better than. For example, if your child's score was at the 50th percentile, it means that her or his score was better than about 50 out of 100, or about 50%, of the children his or her age.

How your child did on the WISC-III was looked at in three ways. First, how he or she did on verbal tests, where she or he had to answer questions the examiner asked, gives a Verbal IQ. Second, how he or she did on performance tests, where he or she had to put together puzzles or figure things out without using words, gives a Performance IQ. Finally, by putting together how your child did on these five verbal and five performance tests, the result is a Full Scale IQ, which tells how your child did overall in thinking and figuring out different kinds of problems. These different scores tell us how well your child is able to do in handling the things he or she has to do and learn in school.

How your child did on the test may also have been looked at in other ways, for example, by looking at how she or he did on a few short tests that seem to go together, or by comparing how he or she did on each short test in comparison to how she or he did on all the short tests together, or his or her own average.

By looking carefully at how your child did on the WISC-III, it will help the school figure out the best way to help your child learn the things she or he needs to learn, so he or she will be able to do well in school. The results of this test usually stay about the same for a long time, but your child may be tested again in two to three years.

and race, and also note whether the examiner's style involved an emphasis on questions and reinforcement or not. The examiner should also describe the examinee and his or her test behavior. In terms of the gradient model which has been utilized throughout this book, there are three possible strategies for describing examinee behavior during testing (see section on "Behavioral Observations of the Examinee").

However, the child should be described physically first, noting at least the child's age, sex, stature, racial/ethnic background (the child may be asked what label he or she uses for this characteristic), developmental/pubertal status, any obvious handicapping conditions, whether the examinee wears glasses or hearing aids, and the child's speech and language. Next, the examiner should describe the individual's test behavior using either the examiner's own observational framework, the aspects of test behavior suggested in Table 7, "Aspects of the Child and Child Behavior to be Observed During Testing," or using the framework in the "Child Test Behavior Observation Form" (see Table 8), or reporting the results of the GATSB if that has been used.

The *Medication Status* section should include a statement of whether or not the child was taking any regular medication at the time of testing, how long before testing the child took medication if known, and whether the medication may have had any effect on the child's test performance (see section on "Medication and Psychological Testing").

The *Reliability and Validity Statement* section should include a discussion of whether the test results are felt to be a reliable estimate of the child's intellectual functioning and, if so, for how long these results are felt to be valid. Although Wechsler IQ scores have generally been found to be stable over time (Wechsler, 1991), Bauman (1991) has questioned the stability of WISC–R scores with learning disabled children. On the other hand, Elliott and Boeve (1987) report an investigation on the three-year stability of WISC–R IQs for a balanced sample of Anglo, black, and Mexican-American handicapped children. These authors found that over the three-year test-retest period, Verbal IQs decreased by an average of 2 points, while Performance IQs increased by an average of almost 3 points. Although the results were statistically significant, the authors concluded that the influence of three years of time on the intelligence test performance of this sample was clinically insignificant.

It is thus common to consider test results as valid for approximately two to three years from the date of testing, and typically children receiving special educational services are required to be reevaluated every three years. As justification for the examiner's statement in this section regarding the reliability and validity of test results, he or she may use her or his own observations, or the GATSB.

One way this section may be phrased is as follows: In view of this child's behavior during testing, her (or his) performance is felt to provide a reliable estimate of her (or his) current intellectual functioning, which means that if tested a week ago or a week from now, the results would be about the same. These results can be used for two (or three) years from the date of this testing to make decisions regarding this child's intellectual functioning and academic needs. Beyond (date), he or she should be retested.

If the examiner concludes that the child's test behavior was highly variable or inappropriate, or varied significantly from the normative population, the examiner may state that, due to the examinee's test behavior or other characteristics, the results are not felt to provide a reliable or valid estimate of the individual's current intellectual functioning, or that the findings represent a very conservative estimate of the examinee's actual ability, and either should not be used for decision making or academic planning, or else should be used cautiously.

The *Test Results* section should include the WISC–III subtest scores as well as the scores of any other tests that may have been administered. This section should display the Verbal and Performance subtests separately, listing each subtest which has been administered with its associated scaled score, and with supplementary subtests in parentheses.

The *Overall Intellectual Functioning* section should begin with a statement to remind the reader or listener that no measure of intelligence is perfectly accurate. This section of the report should include the listing of the child's performance on the Verbal Scale, the Performance Scale, and the Full Scale. Within this and the next two sections of the report, the emphasis should be on comparison of the child to the WISC–III normative population. It would be within this section of the report that italicization or highlighting of particular information, e.g., of the child's IQs, IQ ranges or percentile ranks, would be indicated.

Kaufman (1990) recommends reporting the Full Scale IQ with a band of error around it to make sure that the IQ is seen as a range of scores rather than a specific number (Kaufman, 1990, p. 421). Sattler (1990) similarly notes that whenever an IQ is reported, a precision range for that IQ, which is a function of the standard error of measurement and the confidence level, should also be stated.

Sattler (1990) provides an explanation of the confidence interval and describes its calculation. However, Wechsler (1991) includes the 90% and 95% confidence intervals with the IQ and Index score equivalents of sums of scaled scores (Wechsler, 1991, Table A.2.–A.7., pp. 251–257) so the examiner need not calculate these him- or herself. Kaufman (1990) and Sattler (1990) provide discussions of some of the technical aspects of the confidence interval, which the interested reader may wish to consider.

If the examiner chooses to report the Full Scale IQ as Kaufman (1990) and Sattler (1990) recommend, then certainly the appropriate confidence interval of the obtained score should also be presented. However, instead of proceeding as Kaufman (1990) and Sattler (1990) describe, an alternate approach for the examiner to consider is as follows: Rather than reporting the Full Scale IQ as a single numerical score, *the examiner may report only the percentile rank of the child's Full Scale IQ score; the verbal label of the IQ classification within which the child's Full Scale IQ falls; and the confidence interval within which the child's true Full Scale IQ score is likely to fall.*

The purpose of this strategy is to reduce or avoid the focus by the listener or reader on a single IQ score, but instead to indicate that the score is only an estimate of a quality of the child which is characterized by variability and error and cannot be measured with certainty. Insofar as one considers the examiner's role as one of child advocacy, this strategy can serve to deemphasize the identification of the child with a single IQ score, but establishes the perception of the child as functioning within a particular range of intellectual performances.

The Verbal and Performance IQs, when reported in this section, may also be listed in the same way as the Full Scale IQ: with a verbal label of the classification within which each falls, a percentile rank for the score, and a confidence interval which is likely to contain the true Verbal or Performance IQ score.

The *WISC-III Writer* (Psychological Corporation, 1994) notes that at times, the VCI is a better estimate of the child's verbal reasoning abilities than the VIQ, and that the POI is a better estimate of the examinee's nonverbal reasoning skills than the PIQ. The reason for this is that the VIQ includes the Arithmetic subtest, while the VCI does not and the PIQ includes the Coding subtest and the POI does not.

The Arithmetic subtest correlates only .62 with VIQ (the other verbal subtests correlate from .67 to .78 with VIQ), and the Arithmetic subtest loads on the Freedom from Distractibility factor. Kaufman et al. (1990), reporting on the WISC–R, note that in a large number of studies of learning disabled, emotionally disturbed, and mentally retarded individuals, Arithmetic has been among the most difficult subtests for emotionally disturbed and learning disabled children. Thus, for some examinees, particularly those in special education, the Arithmetic subtest may be a significant weakness for the child and result in an underestimate of his or her verbal reasoning abilities.

Similarly, the Coding subtest correlates only .32 with PIQ (the other performance subtests correlate from .49 to .65 with PIQ), and the Coding subtest loads on the Processing Speed factor. Kaufman et al. (1990), reporting on the WISC–R, note that in a large number of studies of variously handicapped children, Coding has been among the most difficult subtests for emotionally disturbed and learning disabled individuals. Hence, for some children, the Coding subtest may be a significant weakness and thus result in an underestimate of the child's nonverbal reasoning skills.

While the examiner may choose to approach this section of the report as the *WISC-III Writer* (Psychological Corporation, 1994) does, by substituting the VCI for the VIQ or the POI for the PIQ when indicated, the present author does not recommend this strategy. The primary reason for this is that the psychological report must communicate to a number of different individuals. The more complex the structure of the report, and the more exceptions or alternate ways the report is written, the less competently it will serve the purpose of communication. Hence the present author recommends reporting VIQ, PIQ and FSIQ (or percentiles and confidence intervals) in this section of the report.

In terms of the reporting of the IQ scores at this level, the purpose is to provide the reader with an overview of the child's intellectual functioning and to determine whether or not the Full Scale IQ is an appropriate representation of the individual's overall intellectual abilities (Kaufman, 1979a, 1990). Hence there should be a clear statement of whether or not the child's Verbal and Performance IQs scores are significantly different from one another.

If the examinee's Verbal and Performance IQ scores do not differ significantly, the Full Scale IQ (or confidence interval range) can be considered to be a meaningful representation of the child's overall verbal and nonverbal reasoning abilities. If, on the other hand, the child's Verbal and Performance IQs are significantly different from one another, then the Full Scale IQ (or confidence interval range) would not be considered to meaningfully characterize the child's overall verbal and nonverbal reasoning skills.

This section of the report should thus include a statement regarding this conclusion. The examiner may say something to the effect that, "Jane's Verbal and Performance IQs are not significantly different from one another. This means that she handles verbal and nonverbal reasoning tasks with essentially similar competence, and thus her Full Scale IQ range provides a meaningful representation of her overall intellectual functioning."

If there is a significant difference between the child's Verbal and Performance IQs, the examiner may say something such as, "Andrew's Verbal and Performance IQs differ by 21 points and are thus significantly different from one another. This indicates that he displays a true difference in his handling of verbal and nonverbal reasoning tasks, and thus his Full Scale IQ range cannot be considered to be a meaningful representation of his overall intellectual functioning."

Since Wechsler (1991; Table B.2., p. 262) also provides data regarding the cumulative frequency of occurrence of various VIQ–PIQ discrepancies, the examiner may also state whether the obtained VIQ–PIQ discrepancy is common or uncommon in addition to being statistically significant (Reyonds & Kaufman, 1985). Although the more extreme the verbal-performance discrepancy, the more certain one can be that the difference is meaningful, using a marked discrepancy to draw conclusions about the examinee's cerebral integrity is not warranted.

For example, Moffitt and Silva (1987) examined children from an unselected birth cohort who had WISC–R VIQ–PIQ discrepancies that placed them beyond the ninetieth percentile. These authors found little evidence to indicate that these children displayed greater frequencies of perinatal difficulties, early childhood neurological abnormalities, health problems of neurological significance, or concussion than children without such VIQ–PIQ discrepancies. Moffitt and Silva (1987) thus concluded that cautious interpretation is called for regarding VIQ–PIQ discrepancies in a non-neurological setting.

Also within this section of the report, the examiner may compare present test results with the findings of past testing and, where necessary, attempt to explain any significant changes in the child's test scores. Major sources of marked changes in children's test scores aside from head trauma (e.g., Klonoff & Low, 1974) may involve practice effects (Sattler, 1992; Wechsler, 1991); testing a child with a newly normed version of a test (Flynn, 1987); or the effects of psychological events in the life of the examinee (Plante, Goldfarb, & Wadley, 1993).

Also within this section of the report, the examiner may note the degree of intersubtest scatter, or variation, which characterizes the child's overall WISC–III performance. Kaufman (1976b; Kaufman et al., 1990; Reynolds & Kaufman, 1985) has discussed this and noted the extensive intraindividual variation that was evident among children in the WISC–R normative sample. The WISC–III manual provides a table (Wechsler, 1991, Table B.5., p. 266) which indicates the cumulative percentages of intersubtest scatter within various scales in the standardization sample.

For the entire scale, when 10, 12, or 13 subtests have been administered, the average difference between lowest and highest subtest scaled scores is from seven-and-a-half to eight-and-a-half units, with a standard deviation of over two. Hence, a spread of up to 11 points across the subtests administered would not be unusual. The examiner considering this scatter within the child's profile needs to be aware of this before drawing any conclusions about the significance of an apparently large spread of subtest scores.

Although there are no specific norms in the Wechsler (1991) manual regarding intrasubtest scatter, examinees do display differing degrees of unevenness in their test performance with this reflected in consistent or inconsistent scores of 0, 1, or 2 on subtest items, or in varying patterns of success and failure on the various subtests, and the examiner may make note of this phenomenon regarding a given examinee and include this in the discussion of the child's overall or verbal and nonverbal abilities.

After discussing the child's overall intellectual functioning, the examiner would proceed to discuss the examinee's verbal and nonverbal abilities separately, using the four-factor structure proposed by Wechsler (1991) as a framework, and stating that the next two sections of the report will discuss the examinee's "test results in terms of the major factors or clusters of subtests that best explain his (or her) performance."

In proceeding to discuss the test results from within the four-factor framework, based on the extensive research support for the verbal comprehension and perceptual organization factors on the Wechsler scales (e.g., Hale, 1991; Kaufman et al., 1990), it is assumed that the VCI and POI of WISC–III can be interpreted. Whether the examiner also can discuss the child's performance on the FDI and PSI factors as well will depend on whether these factors appear coherent (i.e., their component subtests do not differ significantly from one another).

The *Verbal Functioning* section should include a discussion of the child's performance on the Verbal Scale subtests. The author recommends that this discussion include the following topics: the child's level of functioning on the VCI, including her or his percentile rank and his or her performance on the various VCI subtests; mention of the degree of intersubtest (and/or intrasubtest) scatter within the VCI and the implications of this scatter; discussion of whether the FDI is interpretable or not, and if the FDI is found to be interpretable, the relationship of the FDI to the standardization sample, and the relationship between the VCI and FDI; and an overall statement regarding the child's verbal skills and any implications of the examinee's Verbal Scale performance for his or her school functioning or instruction.

The examiner also may wish to mention any subtest(s) on the Verbal Scale which represent significant strengths or weaknesses for the child relative to the standardization sample (i.e., subtest scores of 13 or above, or 7 or below). Included in this section as well would be any discussion regarding the child's test behavior on the verbal scale (the examiner may use the data he or she recorded on the "Child Test Behavior Observation Form" during test administration if that form was used).

Discussion of the child's VCI reflects his or her abilities relative to the standardization population and thus indicates the examinee's general abilities for processing verbal information: attending to, receiving, storing, comprehending, reasoning about and being able to communicate information about the world through the use of a verbal code or linguistic symbol system when compared to the standardization sample.

The discussion of the degree of intersubtest scatter that characterizes the child's VCI would be based on Wechsler (1991, Table B.5., p. 266). In view of the variability found in the normative population (e.g., the mean difference between the lowest and highest VCI scaled scores for the standardization sample was almost four points with a standard deviation of almost two), a spread of as much as six points on the VCI would not be unusual.

Thus the examiner needs to be cautious in his or her interpretation of the intersubtest scatter which may be evident in the child's protocol. However, if the examinee displays a seven-point scatter among the VCI subtests (obtained by only about 9% of the standardization population), the examiner may conclude that there is a significant degree of unevenness in the individual's handling of different verbal tasks; that the examinee may have higher level capacity than is reflected in his or her overall score, and that variability of functioning would likely characterize the child's in-school learning and performance when dealing with most verbal tasks.

In addition, the examiner may note any verbal strengths or weaknesses displayed by the child in comparison to the normative sample—i.e., those subtests on which the child obtained scaled scores of 13 or above, or 7 or below. This approach, in contrast to Kaufman's ipsative approach (1979a, 1990), is consistent with the concept of the WISC–III providing information about a child's intellectual performance in relation to a normative population.

The examiner would also mention the Freedom from Distractibility factor, noting whether, based on the consistency of its constituents, the factor is interpretable or not. The Freedom from Distractibility factor on the WISC–R, as noted above, has been interpreted in a variety of ways (e.g., Kaufman, 1979a; Kaufman et al., 1990; Woodcock, 1990). The present author would assume that the WISC–III FDI represents the capacity of the child to focus his or her attention, to receive, retain, and execute variously complex operations on numerical or numerical and verbal information. The factor may reflect either resistance to, or vulnerability to, inattention, distractibility or anxiety.

If the FDI is felt to be interpretable, the examiner can note its relationship to the standardization sample and its relationship to the VCI, whether the FDI falls at the same level as the child's VCI or whether the FDI represents a significant strength or weakness for the examinee. The relationship between the VCI and FDI would have been evaluated during the completion of section (2) of the "Test Analysis Worksheet."

If the FDI has been determined to not be interpretable, the examiner may consider the Arithmetic and Digit Span subtests individually in terms of their relationship to the standardization sample. The examiner may comment on whether the Arithmetic subtest is a strength or weakness for the child relative to the normative sample if its scaled score is 13 or above or 7 or below. Similarly, the examiner may identify the Digit Span subtest as a strength or weakness for the examinee relative to the normative group if its scaled score is 13 or above or 7 or below and Digits Forward and Backward are not significantly different from one another.

Finally, the examiner may include a statement in this section regarding the learning or instructional implications of the child's verbal abilities.

The *Nonverbal Functioning* section should include a discussion of the child's accomplishment on the Performance Scale subtests. The author recommends that this discussion include the following topics: the child's level of functioning on the POI, including her or his percentile rank and his or her performance on the various POI subtests; mention of the degree of intersubtest (and/or intrasubtest) scatter within the POI and the implications of this scatter; discussion of whether the PSI is interpretable or not, and if the PSI is found to be interpretable, the relationship of the PSI to the standardization sample, and the relationship between the POI and PSI; and an overall statement regarding the child's nonverbal skills and any implications of the examinee's Performance Scale functioning for his or her school performance or instruction.

The examiner also may wish to mention any subtest(s) on the Performance Scale which represent significant strengths or weaknesses for the child relative to the standardization sample (i.e., subtest scores of 13 or above, or 7 or below). Included in this section as well would be any discussion regarding the child's test behavior on the Performance Scale (the examiner may use the data he or she recorded on the "Child Test Behavior Observation Form" during test administration if that form was used).

Discussion of the child's POI reflects his or her abilities relative to the standardization population and thus indicates the examinee's general abilities for processing nonverbal information: attending to, comprehending, reasoning about and manipulating various kinds of visual, spatial and tangible information or materials to solve problems within a time constraint.

The discussion of the degree of intersubtest scatter characterizing the examinee's POI would be based on Wechsler (1991, Table B.5., p. 266). Considering the variability found in the normative population (e.g., the mean difference between the lowest and highest POI scaled scores for the standardization sample was almost five points with a standard deviation of almost two-and-a-half), a spread as large as seven points on the POI would not be unusual.

Thus, while the examiner needs to be cautious in interpreting the intersubtest scatter which may be apparent in the child's protocol, if the examinee displays a nine-point scatter on the POI (evidenced by approximately 8% of the standardization population), the examiner may conclude that there is a significant degree of variation in the child's handling of different nonverbal tasks; that the individual may have higher-level potential than is reflected in his or her overall score, and that unevenness of performance would likely characterize the child's in-school functioning when dealing with tasks involving visual or spatial materials.

In addition, the examiner may note any nonverbal strengths or weaknesses displayed by the child in comparison to the normative sample—i.e., those subtests on which the child obtained scaled scores of 13 or above, or 7 or below. This approach, in contrast to Kaufman's ipsative approach (1979a, 1990), is consistent with the concept of the WISC–III providing information about a child's intellectual performance in relation to a normative sample.

The examiner would also mention the Processing Speed factor, noting whether, based on the consistency of its components, the factor is interpretable or not. The Processing Speed factor has been described by Sattler (1992) as reflecting the ability to use a high level of attention and concentration when processing information rapidly by scanning an array. The present author views the Processing Speed factor as reflecting the individual's ability to rapidly process visual symbols by either comparison or associative learning, with the addition of decision speed and motor speed components also involved in the individual's performance.

If the PSI is felt to be interpretable, the examiner can note its relationship to the standardization sample and its relationship to the POI, whether the PSI falls at the same level as the child's POI, or whether the PSI represents a significant strength or weakness for the examinee. The relationship between the POI and PSI would have been evaluated during the completion of section (2) of the "Test Analysis Worksheet."

If the PSI has been determined to not be interpretable, the examiner may consider the Coding and Symbol Search subtests individually in relation to the normative sample. The examiner may then comment on whether either the Coding or Symbol Search subtest is a strength or weakness for the child relative to the standardization sample if the scaled score for either subtest is 13 or above or 7 or below.

Finally, the examiner may include a statement in this section regarding the learning or instructional implications of the child's nonverbal abilities.

The *Subtest Patterns* section provides an opportunity for the examiner to offer one or more additional perspectives on the child's intellectual functioning. These multiple viewpoints on the child's cognitive performance can be conceived of as different ways to chunk the data obtained in the assessment. These various perspectives may be entirely consistent with one another, or they may highlight different features of the child's intellectual functioning, and enable one or another teacher to approach the child in a helpful way.

This section should include a discussion of the child's performance when viewed from the perspectives of the ACID or ACIDS profile, the Bannatyne recategorization of subtests, and the Fluid-Crystallized categorization of subtests.

The ACID and ACIDS Profile

The focus of the ACID profile approach to the Wechsler (see discussion in "Frameworks for the Interpretation of the WISC–III") has been on using this pattern of subtest scores to identify learning disabled children. Prifitera and Dersh (1993) present base rates on the ACID and ACIDS profiles among a learning disability sample, an ADHD sample and the WISC–III standardization sample (see Tables 10 and 11), and they provide a method based on Bayesian calculation formulae to determine the probability of a child having either ADHD or a learning disability based on the presence of the ACID or ACIDS profile in his or her WISC–III protocol.

While the present author does not recommend use of the ACID or ACIDS profile as a criterion for the diagnosis of a learning disability, in view of the findings of the frequency of this pattern among children with academic difficulties (Kaufman et al., 1990), it is felt worthwhile for the examiner to note the presence and/or degree of this pattern in the child's test protocol.

Thus in this section of the report, the examiner may describe the degree to which the child displays the ACID or ACIDS configuration in his or her test performance. The observation of the child's performance on this constellation of subtests might be noted by stating, "The ACID (or ACIDS) profile refers to the finding that children with a learning or reading disability or ADHD often perform more poorly on a specific group of four (or five) WISC–III subtests than they do on the remaining non-ACID subtests. On these subtests (Arithmetic, Coding, Information, Digit Span [and Symbol Search]), Sally performed more poorly than she did on the remaining subtests. This indicates that in her cognitive functioning, she is relatively less capable on tasks requiring short-term focusing of attention, possibly rapid learning, and the storage and retention of information than she is in other kinds of reasoning processes. Only about 1% of the children in the standardization sample revealed this pattern of test performance."

Since four of the five ACIDS subtests appear as components of the Freedom from Distractibility and the Processing Speed factors, the child's performance on these attentional, short-term focusing and processing tasks may have been noted in the Verbal and Nonverbal Functioning sections of the report. If so, the comment on the ACID or ACIDS profile will provide additional support to the observations made earlier.

The Bannatyne Recategorization Pattern

As with other efforts to delineate diagnostically significant subtest patterns on the Wechsler scales, the Bannatyne recategorization approach has resulted in mixed findings (e.g., Smith et al., 1977a, 1977b; Gutkin, 1979; Kavale & Forness, 1984, 1994; Prifitera & Dersh, 1993 [also see Table 12 reprinted from Prifitera & Dersh, 1993]).

It is also true that the four Bannatyne categories parallel and to some extent overlap with the four factors which are derived from the WISC–III. Thus Bannatyne's Spatial category contains three of the four subtests in Wechsler's POI; Bannatyne's Verbal Conceptualization category includes three of the four subtests in Wechsler's VCI; Bannatyne's Sequential category includes three subtests which comprised the WISC–R Freedom from Distractibility factor (Kaufman, 1979a) and includes three of the four subtests which comprise Wechsler's (1991) FDI and PSI; and Bannatyne's Acquired Knowledge category includes two subtests from Wechsler's VCI.

Nonetheless, the present author believes that examination of the child's test performance to determine whether she or he displays a Bannatyne pattern is straightforward and can provide an additional perspective on the nature of the child's intellectual functioning, without the examiner attempting to rely on the presence or absence of this pattern to conclude that a child has or does not have a reading or learning disability.

Thus, within this section of the report, the examiner can include the observations of the child's pattern of subtest scores according to Bannatyne's recategorization. This comment may be phrased in the following way. "Bannatyne and others have noted a frequently occurring pattern of subtest scores among reading- and learning disabled children. According to this pattern, the child performs most adequately on subtests involving spatial reasoning, less well on verbal conceptualization tasks, and least well on subtests requiring sequential processing. Steven displays such a pattern on his WISC–III, performing best on subtests which require visual and spatial analysis (e.g., Block Design); performing somewhat less well on subtests involving verbal and categorical reasoning (e.g., Similarities); and performing least adequately on subtests sensitive to the recall and processing of sequentially organized material (e.g., Digit Span). These findings suggest that Steven is most comfortable and most competent when he is dealing with tasks that involve spatial and pictorial perception while he is least capable when required to deal with sequentially ordered information."

The Fluid-Crystallized Categorization

Although the Fluid-Crystallized categorization of subtests has been dealt with extensively in terms of the nature of adult development, functioning, and decline (Horn, 1981, 1982, 1985; Horn & Hofer, 1992; Kaufman, 1990), there has been less discussion of these concepts as they might apply specifically to children and the Wechsler Intelligence Scales for Children.

In addition, examination of the subtests which would be included in the Crystallized Intelligence category (Information, Similarities, Vocabulary, and Comprehension) and the Fluid Intelligence category (Similarities, Digit Span, Picture Completion, Picture Arrangement, Block Design, and Object Assembly) indicate that these two categorizations are essentially the VCI and the POI, with Similarities and Digit Span being added to the latter.

Perhaps because of the fundamental similarity of this view of the WISC–III to Wechsler's factor-analytic approach, there has been no attempt to obtain normative data on the degree to which children in the WISC–III standardization sample display a preference for Fluid or Crystallized Intelligence on the WISC–III.

While it appears unlikely that examining the child's WISC–III protocol from within this framework will provide markedly different information about the child, this view offers a different *perspective* on the child's cognition. Fluid intelligence involves the individual's adaptive abilities for dealing with new learning situations and reflects intellectual *processes* and *strategies* the child may employ. In contrast, Crystallized intelligence reflects assimilated knowledge, dealing with overlearned material, and thus is related to mental *products* and *contents* (Guilford, 1967).

Therefore, examination of the child's Fluid versus Crystallized intellectual abilities alters the examiner's perceptual framework. It should enable the examiner to think of the examinee as being more proficient in relatively culture-free kinds of cognition, or as being more capable in those cognitive abilities which are highly dependent for their development on exposure to a given culture (Sattler, 1990).

Comments in regard to the examinee's performance when viewed from this perspective might be as follows: "Authors such as Horn have noted that the Wechsler scales may be divided into subtests reflecting Fluid Intelligence, or the individual's abilities for dealing with new or novel learning tasks, and Crystallized Intelligence, which reflects assimilated or overlearned knowledge related to a particular culture. When Jack's test results are viewed from this perspective, it appears that he performs at approximately the same level whether he is called upon to utilize more novel problem solving strategies, or whether he is required to recall more culturally bound and overlearned material."

The *Intraindividual Analysis* section should include a discussion of the child's test performance in which the child him- or herself, rather than the standardization population, becomes the frame of reference. The examiner may discuss the variation among the four factors (VCI, FDI, POI, and PSI) around their average; or the examiner may discuss the variation of individual subtest scores within the child's WISC–III profile around any of the child's own average scale performances (Kaufman, 1979a, 1990; Reynolds & Kaufman, 1985; Sattler, 1992).

The variation of the four indices around their mean may have been calculated when the examiner completed section (4) of the "Test Analysis Worksheet." The determination of significant variation among the four factors would be based on Naglieri (1993) or Table 15 in the present volume. If one is to utilize this "ipsative" approach for assessing the WISC–III Index scores, it is important to remember that the same arguments and criticisms apply to the Index scores as would apply to subtest scores (Naglieri, 1993).

If one were to include a comment on the child's variation in Index scores from within this ipsative perspective, the examiner might say something such as: "Authors such as Kaufman have suggested analyzing a child's WISC–III by using the child's own average performance instead of the standardization sample as frame of reference. When viewed this way, Paul demonstrates a significant strength on the Verbal Comprehension Index while he displays a significant weakness on the Processing Speed Index. His other Index scores do not show any marked difference from Paul's own average performance. This means that compared to his own typical performance, which is below average compared to others his age, Paul does better on tasks involving verbal reasoning and understanding, while he does less well on tasks requiring rapid visual scanning and short-term visual learning."

If one is to utilize Kaufman's profile analysis approach, the first step in this procedure is to determine whether there is a significant difference between the child's Verbal and Performance IQs. If there is no significant difference between these two IQ scores, the examiner can treat all of the subtest scores in terms of their variation around a single average score reflecting all the subtests which have been administered.

If there is a significant discrepancy between the child's Verbal and Performance IQs, the examiner must conclude that verbal and nonverbal reasoning abilities are actually different for the child being considered, and variation must be examined *within* each scale separately. The difference between each subtest and the relevant mean (overall or within scale) is determined, and if the difference is statistically significant (see Wechsler, 1991, Table B.3., pp. 263–264), and if the subtest has sufficient specificity (see Sattler, 1992, Table I-12, p. 1049; also see Table 16 in the present volume based on Bracken et al., 1993), the examiner can conclude that the particular subtest represents a significant strength or weakness for the child. Sattler (1992) has presented a listing of the various possibilities to consider if one is executing a profile analysis.

As Kaufman (1979a; Reynolds & Kaufman, 1985) and Sattler (1990) have noted, the findings obtained with profile analysis lead to hypotheses which must be confirmed or disconfirmed by other aspects of a test battery, or by virtue of other sources of information about the child; the findings of profile analysis do not result in definitive conclusions about the examinee's functioning.

This section of the report would thus contain the delineation of the child's intellectual strengths and weaknesses from an intraindividual perspective. It is important to note as various critics of profile analysis have (e.g., McDermott et al., 1990) that this framework requires that if the individual has any particular cognitive strengths, she or he must also have weaknesses; that the assumptions about the Wechsler and what it measures change when one shifts to an intraindividual framework; that the long-term stability of individual subtest scores may be insufficient to support such an interpretive strategy; and that ipsatization of scores results in a loss of ability to accurately predict standardized achievement criteria.

The *Post-Test Feedback* section should state whether, after testing had been completed, the examiner asked the examinee if he or she wished to discuss her or his test performance; and if the child chose to, how the individual perceived her or his own performance, what feedback or recommendations were provided by the examiner, and how the child responded to the feedback or recommendations her- or himself, and in terms of the child's anticipation of parent or family response.

The *Summary* section of the report should include a summary of the most salient and pertinent findings of the testing, and may include the most important findings from any of the above sections of the report, or only include what the examiner feels would be most relevant to anyone wanting a concise statement of the major test findings. However, this section should include a specific response regarding the referral question (which should have been addressed in earlier sections of the report) and should also include a statement regarding the child's more effective learning or information processing style and any implications this may have for the child's educational experience.

The *Recommendations* section should include any recommendations based on the test findings or observations of the examinee during testing. First, the examiner should determine, based on the current testing, whether or not any further assessment of the child is indicated. This further assessment may involve additional testing, such as personality, neuropsychological, career, or achievement testing, but it might also involve medical or neuro-logical evaluation if the examiner observed behaviors suggestive of these problems or if, for example, a medication evaluation and trial appears warranted.

Second, the examiner should note whether retesting of the child's intellec-tual functioning is indicated. Although if an examinee is involved in special services, this retesting would be mandated, the examiner may recommend retesting at a slightly different time to coincide, for example, with the individual changing schools in a year from an elementary to a middle school, and the examiner wishes to code the examinee's life trajectory with a planned re-evaluation at a particular point in time.

Third, the examiner should include any recommendation for the child's academic placement. The gradient model is relevant here in terms of the need for more extensive recommendations depending on the degree to which the examinee's functioning deviates from the norm. Thus, if the individual displays increasingly above average abilities in his or her profile, this might lead to recommendations for academic enrichment opportunities for the individual. To the degree that the examinee displays an increasing degree of deficit in her or his intellectual performance, the examiner would recommend increasing support services to assist the child.

Fourth, based on the findings in the sections on verbal and nonverbal functioning, subtest patterns, and individual subtest analysis, the examiner may abstract a set of instructional strategies for use by the classroom or resource teacher. The models of the hierarchy and gradient may frame the examiner's thinking in this regard. The hierarchical model implies that the examiner may focus his or her recommendations on different levels of the hierarchical concept of the test the author has discussed—i.e., Full Scale or general intelligence at the apex, moving down through verbal and perform-ance abilities, groupings of subtests, or specific subtests. In general, the author believes it is wiser to provide instructional recommendations at middle to upper levels of the hierarchy than at the specific subtest level of the hierarchy.

This means that the examiner would do better to aim his or her recom-mendations at groupings of intellectual tasks such as verbal or nonverbal skills; spatial performance, or verbal conceptual performance rather than in terms of putting together puzzles, or noticing details of pictures. Some aspects of the WISC–III, of course, refer to both general and specific abilities. For example, the child with low average verbal skills should be encouraged to develop his or her vocabulary and general fund of information, and the examiner may have recommendations that will address this aspect of the child's functioning.

To the extent that one uses the hierarchy as a model for thinking about recommendations, it would of course be possible to provide recommendations at different levels of the hierarchy, offering both general conceptual views of dealing with the child as well as one or more specific and concrete suggestions to assist the teacher who would prefer recommendations for specific behaviors rather than more abstract strategies.

The gradient model refers to a slightly different view of the child's functional ability. For the child who displays widespread difficulties in independent problem solving, the examiner would recommend teacher or instructional behaviors at the low end of the gradient, involving small steps, extensive teacher support, and little opportunity for the child to make mistakes. For the child who displays greater intellectual competence and independence, the examiner may recommend less teacher support and greater emphasis on the child's independent intellectual performance and problem-solving activities.

In addition, to the extent that the child displays greater concreteness in his or her thinking, the examiner may note that reinforcement strategies within the school may be more effective if they are concrete rather than abstract or symbolic. The more abstract the child's thinking, the more she or he would be expected to be capable of responding to symbolic reinforcers, such as praise or statements regarding his or her problem-solving skills.

Fifth, the examiner may make any recommendations which would pertain to the parent(s) or family of the child who has been evaluated. These recommendations should reflect the examiner's realization that the findings of the evaluation may alter the parent(s)' perception of, and behavior toward, the child who has been evaluated. This may involve changes in parental expectation for the child, changes in the child's being in regular class or resource classes, and hence losing friendships, and the child's change in his or her own self-perception and self-esteem. The examiner may thus make recommendations for psychological intervention for the child or family system if this is felt indicated.

The *Signature* section of the report should include the examiner's name, professional degree, and state license number if the examiner wishes. If the testing has been done by a trainee or supervisee of the examiner, the names and degrees of both the trainee or supervisee and the supervising individual should be included.

A SAMPLE EVALUATION REPORT

To illustrate the use of the "Test Analysis Worksheet" and to provide a sample Psychological Evaluation Report, the author has included the completed "Test Analysis Worksheet" (see Table 19) and the Psychological Evaluation Report (see Table 20) written regarding an almost eight-year-old

Table 19
MARIA'S TEST ANALYSIS WORKSHEET

Name: Maria   DOB: 7/15/84   DOE: 6/1/92   Age: _____

(1)

				%CI		%ile	Classification
FSSS = 100	FSIQ	= 100	94–106	= 95	50		= Average
VSS = 51	VIQ	= 101	95–107	= 95	53		= Average
PSS = 49	PIQ	= 99	91–107	= 95	47		= Average

(2)

				%CI		%ile	Classification
VCSS = 42	VCI	= 103	96–110	= 95	58		= Average
POSS = 34	POI	= 91	84–100	= 95	27		= Average
FDSS = 21	FDI	= 104	94–113	= 95	61		= Average
PSSS = [25]	PSI	= [114]	[102–122]	= 95	[82]		= [Hi Aver]

VIQ/VCI 101   VCI 103 – FDI 104 = –1   ns
–PIQ/POI 99   POI – PSI = _____
ns   3   ns   5   .05
% 91   DSd 3   AR – DS = 3   CD – SS = 5

27.5   V/VCI:H – L = 6   19.1   P/POI:H – L = 4   69.4   F:H – L = 4   39.7

(3)

ACID(S):AR 9   CD 15   IN 14   DS 12   (SS) 10 = <lo   SM 8   VO 9   CO 11   PC 6   PA 9   BD 10   OA 9

PATTERN:SPA:	VERCON:	SEQ:	ACKNO:	Order:
PC 6	SM 8	AR 9	IN 14	SEQ 12
BD 10	VO 9	DS 12	AR 9	ACK 10.7
OA 9	CO 11	CD 15	VO 9	VER 9.3
Tot 25	Tot 28	Tot 36	Tot 32	SPA 8.3
Av 8.3	Av 9.3	Av 12	Av 10.7	Av 10.7

FLU-CRYS: FLU:SM 8   DS 8   PC 6   PA 9   BD 10   OA 9   VO 9   CO 11
Tot FLU = 54   Av FLU = 9   CRYS:IN 14   SM 8   VO 9   CO 11
Tot CRYS = 42   Av CRYS = 10.5

(4) INDEX: Tot Index = _____ NA _____ VCI _____ POI _____ FDI _____ PSI _____

Av Index = _____ (M)

• • • • •

PROFILE:

	INv	SMv	ARf	VOv	COv	(DS)f	CDs	PCp	PAp	BDp	OAp	(SS)s
	14	8	9	9	11	12	15	6	9	10	9	10
AvV/VCI = 10.2	10.2	10.2	10.2	10.2	10.2		9.8	9.8	9.8	9.8	9.8	
9.8	3.8	2.2	1.2	1.2	.8		5.2	3.8	.8	.2	.8	
AvP/POI = 9.8							S	W				
AvFS = 10												

girl who was referred for intellectual evaluation as part of her school Special Services assessment.

As can be noted on Table 19, section (1) deals with Maria's Full Scale, Verbal, and Performance Scaled Scores, IQs, percentiles, confidence intervals, and verbal classifications. Section (2) deals with the analysis of Maria's four Index scores and records the Index score, percentile, confidence interval and verbal classification for each of these scores. Although Maria's Freedom from Distractibility Index was usable (the difference between Digits Forward and Backward, and the difference between the AR and DS subtests was not significant), the Processing Speed Index (enclosed in brackets) was felt unusable because the difference between the CD and SS subtests was 5 scaled-score units, which is significant at the .05 level.

To evaluate the difference between Maria's verbal and nonverbal abilities, her VIQ and PIQ were compared and found to not differ significantly. To evaluate the scatter in Maria's test protocol, the examiner used the VCI and POI subtests rather than the VIQ and PIQ subtests. The degree of scatter evident in the VCI and POI subtests and the overall WISC–III was not significant.

Section (3) deals with the analysis of Maria's test results from the perspectives of the ACID profile, the Bannatyne pattern, and the Fluid-Crystallized Intelligence approach.

Section (4) deals with intraindividual analysis of Maria's protocol. Since not all four of her Index scores were useable, the author did not carry out an ipsative analysis on the Index scores.

In the profile analysis of individual subtest scores which was carried out, the Verbal and Performance scales were evaluated separately. Although the Information subtest score was above average, because at age 6–7, Information has inadequate specificity (see Table 16), this subtest was not interpreted as a strength for Maria in the Psychological Evaluation Report.

PROVIDING VERBAL FEEDBACK ON TEST RESULTS

Consistent with the systems approach that has been discussed throughout this book (see section on "Models in Psychology" and Figure 4), the assessment of the child has been viewed as occurring within the context of multiple systems which include the school and the child's family.

In conceptualizing the transmission of information obtained in the evaluation to relevant aspects of the systems within which the child exists, it is important to consider strategies for conveying the information to each component of the system: the school, the child's parent(s), and the child her- or himself. As has been discussed earlier (see "Application of the Model to the Intellectual Assessment of Children and Adolescents"), some immediate

Table 20
SAMPLE PSYCHOLOGICAL EVALUATION REPORT

Name: Maria   DOB: 7/15/84
DOE: 6/1/92   Age: 7.10
School: Central   Grade: 2

Reason for Referral: Maria was tested as part of her current Special Services evaluation, which had been initiated by her teacher. Maria was unable to say why she was being evaluated, and the examiner explained that this was because it seemed she was having some trouble in reading and arithmetic and we wanted to find out how to help her do better.

Background: Maria's teacher described her as daydreaming a lot although she is not overly active. She is below grade level in reading and math, with her reading comprehension varying on different days. Maria's fine motor control was described as "not bad," and it was noted that she gets along well with her peers. Maria's teacher said Maria's mother describes her at home as the same as in school: she is slow at tasks, daydreams, is disorganized, and it takes her forever to do anything.

Past Testing: There were no records regarding any past testing of Maria.

Test Utilized: Wechsler Intelligence Scale for Children-III (WISC–III) Guide to the Assessment of Test Session Behavior (GATSB).

Test Situation and Behavioral Observations: Maria was seen for testing on one occasion. Testing took place in a small, quiet room off her school library. Maria came by herself from her classroom to the testing room. The examiner is a 50-year-old Caucasian male who utilized minimal additional questioning with Maria, with little feedback or reinforcement offered during testing itself. Maria is a solidly built, almost eight-year-old, right-handed Hispanic girl of average height and weight with a somewhat dreamy expression. During testing, Maria was cooperative and attentive, but generally worked quite slowly on tasks. She was noted to display a motor tremulousness and some slightly odd motor movements during testing.

Medication Status: Maria reported that she does not take any daily medication.

Reliability and Validity Statement: Based on Maria's general effort and motivation during testing (GATSB T score = 47, within the normal range), it is felt that the present results are a reliable estimate of her current functioning, which means that if tested a week before or after the current testing, the results would be about the same. These findings are felt to be valid for educational planning purposes until approximately the beginning of 1995 when Maria should be reevaluated.

Test Results:

Verbal Subtests	SS	Performance Subtests	SS
Information	14	Picture Completion	6
Similarities	8	Coding	15
Arithmetic	9	Picture Arrangement	9
Vocabulary	9	Block Design	10
Comprehension	11	Object Assembly	9
(Digit Span)	(12)	(Symbol Search)	(10)

Overall Intellectual Functioning: It should be noted that any measure of a child's IQ is not perfectly accurate but provides estimates of the child's abilities. On the WISC–III, Maria's Verbal IQ falls in the average range, better than about 53% of children her age, and there is a 95% chance that her true Verbal IQ falls between 95 and 107. Her Performance IQ falls in the average range, at better than about 47% of children her age, with a 95% chance that her true Performance IQ falls between 91 and 107. Since her Verbal and Performance IQs are not very different from one another, it is reasonable to say that Maria's Full Scale or overall IQ is in the average range, at better than 50% of children her age, with a 95% chance that her true Full Scale IQ falls in the range of 94 to 106.

Based on these findings, Maria handles verbal and nonverbal reasoning tasks with basically similar skill. In addition, she handled the different tasks on the WISC–III at basically the same level, suggesting that she is able to deal with a variety of kinds of intellectual material with about the same level of success. Moreover, she is able to deal with any single kind of task (for example, information questions) consistently as well. In the next sections, Maria's verbal and nonverbal reasoning abilities will be discussed separately, in terms of the major factors or clusters of subtests that best explain her test performance.

Verbal Functioning: On the Verbal Comprehension Index, a cluster of four verbal subtests (Information, Similarities, Vocabulary, and Comprehension), Maria is functioning in the average range of ability, at better than approximately 58% of children her age. She displays a normal degree of unevenness in her handling these different tasks, and she displays relatively little unevenness within any particular area (e.g., answering information questions). This suggests that she is fairly consistent in her handling of a group of tasks which all reflect her abilities for verbal understanding, recall, and reasoning.

A second factor which emerges for Maria on the Verbal scale is that of Freedom from Distractibility, comprised of the Arithmetic and Digit Span subtests. Her performance on this cluster falls in the average range, at better than 61% of children her age. This means that despite her teacher's and mother's report, Maria is generally able to focus her attention and resist distraction better than most children her age. Her functioning on both the Verbal Comprehension and the Freedom from Distractibility Indices are in the average range, and her ability to attend is thus neither a strength nor weakness for her as compared to her general verbal skills. Maria's behavior during the verbal portion of the WISC–III was dreamy, yet she was attentive and reflective throughout. These findings indicate that Maria is able to learn verbally coded information consistently within the average range and that no specific strategies directed to her verbal skills appear warranted.

Nonverbal Functioning: On the Perceptual Organization Index, a cluster of four performance subtests (Picture Completion, Picture Arrangement, Block Design, and Object Assembly), Maria is functioning in the average range of ability, at better than approximately 27% of children her age. She displays a normal degree of unevenness in her handling of these different tasks, although she displays a moderate degree of unevenness within any particular area (e.g., reproducing designs with blocks). This suggests that she is fairly consistent in her handling of a group of tasks which all reflect her abilities for nonverbal reasoning when she must analyze visual information into its components, integrate parts into wholes or organize material into logical sequences.

A second factor on the Performance scale is that of Processing Speed. This is not interpretable for Maria since she performed differently on the two subtests which make up this factor (Coding and Symbol Search) even though she did well on both subtests. This suggests that Maria is able to handle visual search and learning tasks adequately, but may handle different tasks of this sort with different levels of success. Maria's behavior during the performance portion of the WISC–III was marked by a slow and careful although flexible approach to tasks. These findings indicate that she is able to deal with visual and spatial information fairly consistently within the average range and that no specific strategies directed to her nonverbal skills appear indicated.

Subtest Patterns: The ACID profile refers to the finding that children with a learning or reading disability or ADHD often perform more poorly on a specific group of four subtests (Arithmetic, Coding, Information, and Digit Span) than they do on the remaining six WISC–III subtests. When Maria's WISC–III results are examined from this viewpoint, it is noted that she does not display the ACID profile; in fact, she handles the ACID subtests better than the remaining subtests, indicating that she performs quite adequately on tasks of attention, long- and short-term recall, and concentration.

Bannatyne and others have noted a frequently occurring pattern of subtest scores among reading- and learning disabled children in which the child's subtest scores show the pattern of Spatial subtests > Verbal Conceptual subtests > Sequential subtests. If Maria's WISC–III is viewed this way, she does not display the Bannatyne pattern, and instead is most capable in dealing with sequentially ordered material (e.g., Digit Span) and does least well with spatial material (e.g., Picture Completion).

Lastly, according to authors such as Horn, tests such as the WISC–III may be divided into those subtests which reflect fluid intelligence, or the child's abilities for dealing with new or novel learning tasks; and those which reflect crystallized intelligence, or the child's assimilated and overlearned knowledge related to a particular culture. When Maria's test results are looked at this way, it appears that she does equally well whether she is called upon for more novel problem solving (e.g., Block Design) or is required to recall more overlearned material (e.g., Vocabulary).

Overall, then, examination of Maria's WISC–III performance from several additional perspectives suggests that she does not display a noteworthy weakness in attention or short-term learning; she handles sequential information quite well; and she handles tasks requiring novel approaches or overlearned responses at about the same level.

Intraindividual Analysis: Authors such as Kaufman have suggested analyzing a child's WISC–III by using the child's own average performance instead of the standardization sample as a frame of reference. Since not all four of Maria's Indices were useable, it is not appropriate to compare her performances on the four factors. If one examines her individual subtests to determine her own strengths and weaknesses, Maria shows a strength on the Coding subtest, indicating she is quite capable on a task requiring rapid scanning, transposition of information, and possibly short-term learning. She displays a weakness on the Picture Completion subtest, which reflects her ability to focus her visual attention, remember how common objects look, and notice what part is missing from them. Maria's performances on these subtests suggest that she may do better with short-term visual learning, but have problems with long-term visual recall, which might interfere with her reading. Although she did well on the Information subtest, at her age this subtest lacks enough unique meaning to permit it to be interpreted as a strength.

Post-Test Feedback: Maria was interested in how she had done on the WISC–III and was told that she seemed to handle the different things differently, some very well and others not so well, but that mostly she seemed to do just as well as other children her age and sometimes better. Her tremor was mentioned and she was asked to have her mother take her to the doctor to check on that. She was told that the results would be talked about with her teachers and with her mother to see what things we could do to help her with reading and arithmetic.

Summary: Maria is a quiet, cooperative, almost eight-year-old who is functioning in the overall average range with similar verbal and nonverbal reasoning abilities. She does well with sequential information, displays relative difficulty with spatial reasoning, and performs about equally well whether called on for problem solving or the recall of overlearned materials. Present testing does not provide a clear understanding of her reading or math difficulties.

Recommendations: (1) Maria should be referred for medical evaluation regarding her tremor; (2) Specific diagnostic evaluation of her reading and math skills may assist in determining a remedial plan for her; (3) Based on her difficulty with visual recall, increased practice with letter-sound associations might help her improve her reading performance; (4) In view of her quite adequate performance on sequential tasks, teachers should not make an issue of her seeming slowness or dreamy behavioral style; possibly a reinforcement program can be devised which will motivate her to increase her behavioral tempo somewhat; (5) Retesting is indicated for Maria at the beginning of 1995. No other specific recommendations are indicated for Maria or her family at this time.

Shawn Cooper, Ph.D., M.P.H.

feedback regarding the child's test performance may be provided to the examinee at the time of testing. The information gathered in the evaluation may be shared with school personnel through the Psychological Report, when this is presented at a conference or read by a user.

The evaluation findings can be communicated to the child's parent(s) and to the child by permitting them to read the Psychological Report (with an "Explanation of the WISC–III" form; Table 18). Also, however, test results may be provided by the examiner in a specific feedback or interpretive interview with the child's parent(s) and/or the child.

Such an interview should be divided into several basic phases: (1) "setting" the meeting; (2) establishing the context for the discussion of test results; (3) providing the specific information regarding the child's test performance; and (4) providing an opportunity for discussion about the findings and their short-term, and possibly longer-term, implications for the child.

The first phase involves "setting" the meeting. This involves the examiner explaining that the purpose of the meeting (which may include one or both parents, and possibly the examinee) is to discuss the findings of the evaluation of the child. This phase should also include an explanation of the original purpose for which the testing was determined to be indicated, for example, that the child had been having difficulty with his or her academic performance, and intellectual assessment was felt to be one way to determine the source of the difficulty.

The second phase of this interview is devoted to establishing the context for discussing the test results themselves. First, the examiner would provide an explanation of intelligence as conceived of within the framework of the WISC–III. Thus, the examiner would explain that there are different ideas as to what it is that allows children to learn and solve the problems they face in school. A widely accepted view is that something called "intelligence," reasoning, or thinking ability is important in children's ability to handle schoolwork.

It can be explained that the test that was given to the examinee measures what we think of as intelligence, or the broad ability to think and to solve different kinds of problems. This test, the Wechsler Intelligence Scale for Children-Third Edition, involves tasks that require the child to use or understand words or language as well as basic mathematical reasoning, and tasks that require the child to work with materials that can be seen, touched, or manipulated to solve problems. These two different kinds of tasks show how the child solves problems when he or she must use words, or when she or he must use materials that can be seen and touched.

In the second aspect of describing the context for the test, the examiner should point out that when the test was being developed, it was given to a number of boys and girls between 6 and 16 from all across the country to see how all these children did on the test. This group of children became the standard group, or standardization sample, and then, when any child is given the test, that child's performance is compared to all the children in the standard group. So when we figure out how a child did on the test, it is by comparing his or her results to this standard group.

The examiner may explain that the test is divided into small tests called subtests. The ones using words are called verbal subtests, and the ones using materials like blocks are called performance subtests. How the child does on the verbal subtests results in a Verbal IQ. How the child does on the performance subtests results in a Performance IQ. These two groups of subtests can usually be combined to result in a Full Scale, or overall, IQ. These different IQs show how the child does in these different kinds of reasoning and problem solving as compared to the children in the standard group.

The examiner should also note that no measure of anything is perfect, and that for different reasons, we sometimes can be mistaken when we try to measure anything, including intelligence, so the results of this test might not be perfectly accurate in measuring this child's intelligence.

The examiner may ask the parent(s) how they believe the child did compared to other children, better, the same or not as well, as this will provide some guideline for the examiner regarding any disparity that might exist between parental expectation and how the child actually did on the test. The examiner should then proceed to present the specific test results regarding the child who has been evaluated, either reading or discussing and explaining the various sections of the report. If the examiner had provided some feedback to the examinee at the time of testing, that feedback may be confirmed, corrected if it was not accurate, or amplified if the examiner wishes to. It is important for the examiner to avoid providing information, for example, specific test questions or answers, to the parent(s) or child that might reduce the validity of the WISC–III.

Once the material in the report has been presented, the results may be related to the original reason for the testing, and the implications these findings may have for the child's learning ability, learning style, or recommendations for the child's academic program can be discussed. At this point the examiner should be prepared to answer any questions the parent(s) or child may have about the child's test performance. The examiner should be aware of the fact that the parent(s) may have questions or concerns they may be unable to express, for example, if the child's performance was below average and the parent(s) are concerned about the child's ability to achieve in life or function independently as an adult. If there are suggestions for the parent(s) that follow from the test findings, for example, trying to encourage the child to express him- or herself verbally, these may also be presented during this interview.

The examiner may also note that if there are continuing concerns about the examinee's learning or academic performance, the child may be tested again at some future time in two to three years. The examiner may give the parent(s) a copy of the Psychological Report along with the "Explanation of the WISC–III" form. If the child has not been included in the interpretive interview, the examiner may discuss with the parent(s) whether and/or how the findings may be shared with the child.

The above-noted approach would thus complete the process which was initiated when the child was first selected as being in need of psychological assessment, and more specifically, intellectual assessment with the WISC–III.

Part VI
SPECIAL TOPICS

Chapter Seventeen

BIAS AND THE WECHSLER SCALES

The following discussion of bias regarding the Wechsler scales draws primarily from Reynolds and Kaiser (1990) and Hale (1991). Reynolds and Kaiser (1990) note that the issue of test bias in intellectual or aptitude assessment has been of concern for some time, and these authors list several of the basic objections put forth regarding the use of standardized educational or psychological tests with minorities. These concerns can be grouped in terms of test construction, the testing experience itself, and the outcomes of testing.

In terms of test construction, critics have said that many commonly used aptitude and educational tests have inappropriate content, which refers to the view that minority children have not been exposed to the materials involved in the test items, while white middle-class children have been. It is also suggested that inappropriate standardization samples have been used in test development in that minority children have been underrepresented in the collection of normative data on the tests. It is then argued that because of these factors, such tests may measure different psychological constructs for majority and minority children.

In terms of the testing itself, it is proposed that examiner and language bias adversely affects the minority child's test performance. This refers to the fact that most examiners are white and typically speak English as their native language; this may intimidate minority children, create communication problems during testing, and result in lowered test scores for minority children.

In terms of the outcomes of testing, it is argued that there is differential predictive validity for minority and majority children, meaning that tests may accurately predict a variety of outcomes for white middle-class children, but fail to predict any relevant criteria at an acceptable level for minority children. Finally, it is suggested that the above factors result in inequitable social consequences, referring to the disproportionate placement of minority group members in low level educational tracks due to the biases which exist in the design, construction, and administration of commonly used aptitude and achievement tests.

Hale (1991) describes two events in recent history that have resulted in a renewed interest being focused on the issue of test bias: (a) the passage of

Public Law 94-142, the Education for All Handicapped Children Act of 1975, which required the evaluation of handicapped children with non-biased assessment procedures; and (b) two court cases (*Larry P.* v. *Wilson Riles*, and *Parents in Action on Special Education* v. *Hannon*), which involved opposing court decisions regarding the use of IQ scores in the determination of educable mental retardation as a handicapping condition in the case of minority children.

Oakland and Parmelee (1985), Sattler (1990), and Hale (1991) all review these court decisions. In the *Larry P.* v. *Wilson Riles* decision of 1979, Judge Peckham ruled that: (a) California schools could not utilize, permit the use of, or approve the use of any standardized intelligence test for the identification of black educable mentally retarded children or permit their placement into educable mentally retarded classes without obtaining the approval of his court; (b) the overrepresentation of blacks in educable mentally retarded classes was to be eliminated; and (c) the harm done to blacks who had been misclassified as educable mentally retarded was to be remedied, and the discrimination caused by using the IQ concept could not be allowed to recur.

In addition, this decision stated that every black child in educable mentally retarded placement was to be reevaluated, but without the use of standardized intelligence tests, which were felt to be biased against black children.

In contrast to this decision, in 1980 in the case of *Parents in Action on Special Education* v. *Hannon*, Judge Grady determined that the same tests as had been considered biased in the *Larry P.* case were not biased with respect to minority status children in Chicago public schools. Hence, these two court decisions involved fundamentally opposing conclusions regarding the question of bias in intellectual test instruments and their use.

In his effort to clarify the concept of bias in psychological testing, Hale (1991) states that both of these judges failed to properly distinguish between the ability of the tests to *discriminate* between groups of individuals on the one hand, and whether those tests are *biased* against those same groups of individuals on the other hand. Hale (1991) points out that intelligence tests were designed specifically to discriminate between children who are able to succeed scholastically and those who are not.

If, as the research literature suggests, minority group children are less successful academically than majority group children in traditional school environments, then IQ measures should reflect this fact. If intelligence tests are performing as they should, minority group children should have lower IQs as a group than majority children. And if IQ scores are utilized in the decision to place children in special programs, then proportionally more minority group children will be found in special educational programs.

Hale (1991) notes that the ability of an IQ test, such as the Wechsler, to discriminate between children or groups of children is a necessary function of the test. Bias, however, refers to the *unequal* measurement of the construct of intelligence in *different* groups, and this would involve improper performance of the test instrument.

Reynolds and Kaiser (1990), in their discussion of the definition of test bias, state that test bias refers in a global way to a systematic error in the estimation of some "true" value for a group of individuals. These authors note that the critical concept is "systematic" error, since all measurement contains some degree of error variance which, however, is presumed to be randomly distributed. Reynolds and Kaiser (1990) also distinguish between two terms often used in research on test bias: single-group validity and differential validity. Single-group validity refers to the case when a test is valid for one group but not for another, while differential validity refers to a situation where a test is valid for all groups concerned, but the degree of validity varies as a function of group membership.

Hale (1991) and Reynolds and Kaiser (1990) note that bias in an intelligence test can be examined by investigating the degree to which the test displays similar or differential validity across different groups. If the test does not demonstrate the same validity for different groups, then it can be said to be biased. Validity is essentially of three types: content, construct, and criterion. And an intelligence test can be considered biased if it displays differential validity in any one of the three areas—content, construct, or criterion—either for or against one or more groups.

RESEARCH FINDINGS

Bias in Content Validity

One contention in terms of bias in intelligence tests such as the Wechsler scales is that items for these tests are drawn from white middle-class culture and hence may be of differential difficulty for minority children and white children. The most common way to assess this question is by having "experts" examine the items to determine whether they are biased or not. However, the evidence suggests that such expert judgments are themselves unreliable (Sandoval & Millie, 1980) and invalid (Sandoval, 1979). Thus, empirical evaluation of item analysis does not support subjective judgments of item bias.

In one study dealing with the content validity of the WISC–R, Jensen and Figueroa (1975) investigated black-white differences in performance on the WISC–R digit-span subtest, and although differences were found in subtest performance, Jensen and Figueroa (1975) concluded that their results did not indicate any content bias in the subtest.

Reynolds (1980) matched 270 black children with 270 white children from the WISC–R standardization sample on the basis of gender and WISC–R Full Scale IQ and examined black-white differences in performance on each of the subtests to determine which, if any, subtests were disproportionately difficult for blacks or whites. Blacks performed better than whites on the subtests of Digit Span and Coding, while whites exceeded blacks on the subtests of Comprehension, Object Assembly and Mazes. There was also some trend for blacks to perform better than whites on the Arithmetic subtest, and whites to perform at a higher level than blacks on the Picture Arrangement subtest.

These results indicate the existence of bias in several of the WISC–R subtests, but Reynolds and Kaiser (1990) note that the actual differences between the performances of blacks and whites were very small (only .10 to .15 standard deviations), and the amount of variance in performance associated with ethnic group membership was less than 5% in each case.

Item difficulties were examined for the WISC (Miele, 1979) and the WISC–R (Oakland & Feigenbaum, 1979; Sandoval, 1979), and these studies reported that item difficulties on these tests were not ordered differently for blacks and whites, which provides evidence for the similarity of content validity for blacks and whites on these intelligence tests.

Thus, Reynolds and Kaiser (1990) conclude that based on a large number of studies using different methodologies, it appears that content bias in well-designed, standardized tests occurs irregularly, and the variance in group score differences on mental tests associated with ethnic group membership when content bias has been found is relatively small.

Bias in Construct Validity

Reynolds and Kaiser (1990) note that there is no single method for the precise determination of the construct validity of an educational or psychological test. Hence, they note, the definition of bias in construct validity requires a broad statement that can be researched from a number of viewpoints and with a variety of research methods. The definition they put forth states that bias exists in regard to construct validity when a test is shown to measure different hypothetical traits for one group as contrasted to another group, or to measure the same trait in different groups, but with differing degrees of precision.

Hale (1991), Reynolds and Kaiser (1990), and Kaufman (1990) all discuss factor analysis (Anastasi, 1988) as a technique that is a useful and popular method for the empirical investigation of construct validity. Factor analysis is a procedure that identifies clusters of test items or of subtests within a psychological test that correlate highly with one another, and less highly or not at all with other items or subtests.

As Hale (1991) has noted, factor analysis does not refer to a single mathematical technique, and the results obtained depend upon the factoring method utilized. However, in view of the wide use of the WISC (Wechsler, 1949) and the WISC–R (Wechsler, 1974) with school age children, the factor structure of these tests across race has been extensively studied for a variety of normal and referral populations.

As one part of his comprehensive analysis of test bias on the WISC, Miele (1979) compared the first principal component factor across race for blacks and whites at the preschool, first-, third-, and fifth-grade levels. This first principal component factor, often viewed as a measure of general intelligence, did not differ significantly across race at any age level. These results with the WISC indicate that when score differences on this test occurred between racial groups, these differences reflected whatever was common to all variables that made up the test, not to some moderator variable that was specific to one group or the other. In other words, the test had adequate construct validity for both black and white children.

Reschly (1978) compared the factor structures of the WISC–R for four racial groups: whites, blacks, Mexican-Americans, and Native American Papagos. Similar to the findings reported with the WISC (Silverstein, 1973), Reschly (1978) found that the two-factor solutions (reflecting the verbal-performance distinction) were highly similar for all four groups. The groups were quite similar in terms of the proportion of variance accounted for by a general intelligence factor, and the Verbal-Performance scale distinction appeared equally appropriate for all four racial groups. Reschly (1978) concluded that the interpretation of the WISC–R Full Scale IQ as a measure of general intellectual ability was thus equally appropriate for whites, blacks, Mexican-Americans, and Native American Papagos.

Vance and Wallbrown (1978) factor analyzed the the intercorrelation matrix of the WISC–R subtests for a group of 150 black children who had been referred to a community agency for psychological assessment. The ability hierarchy they obtained included a relatively weak general factor reflecting positive loadings on all the WISC–R subtests. They also found a bifurcation between the verbal and performance subtests, with the former defining a verbal-educational factor, and the latter defining a spatial-perceptual factor. These findings suggested that the basic ability dimensions for referred black children were the same as for referred whites and normal children in the standardization population.

Oakland and Feigenbaum (1979) assessed test bias on the WISC–R by carrying out a number of statistical procedures (e.g., internal consistency, item difficulty analyses) on the WISC–R and Bender Gestalt Test data of 436 elementary school white, black, and Mexican-American children. On the WISC–R, although group differences were most discernible for age, sex, family structure and race, the authors concluded that the results of their factor analysis did not reflect bias with respect to construct validity for these three racial-ethnic groups.

Dean (1980) compared the underlying factor structure of the WISC–R for 109 Anglo and 123 Mexican-American children ranging from 8 to 15 years of age. Test results were analyzed separately for each group, and three factors emerged for each ethnic group; these factors corresponded closely to the factors usually obtained with the WISC–R. The coefficients of congruence between the factors for the two groups were above .80, which indicated a high degree of similarity in the constructs being measured by the WISC–R in the two ethnic groups.

Gutkin and Reynolds (1981) investigated the factorial similarity across race for the WISC–R by carrying out separate principal-factor analyses for the white and black children from the WISC–R standardization sample. Similarities in the magnitude of unique variances for each subtest and the factor pattern of the subtests were assessed with coefficients of congruence. Similarities in the strength of each factor across race were evaluated by comparing the portion of total variance accounted for by common factor variance, and the percentage of common factor variance accounted for by each factor. On every measure considered, the white and black groups were found to be highly similar to one another. Gutkin and Reynolds (1981) concluded that the WISC–R factor structure was basically invariant for black and white children and that no evidence of either single-group or differential construct validity could be found.

Reynolds and Harding (1983) note that in studies of test bias, a variety of methods of measuring factorial similarity have been utilized in evaluating the cross-group similarity of factor-analytic results. They compared six methods of factor comparison regarding the WISC–R for blacks and whites and found that, regardless of the method of comparison used, the factor structure of the WISC–R for blacks and for whites was determined to be invariant, which would justify similar interpretation of performance on the test for whites and blacks.

Dean (1979) reported a comparison of three-factor WISC–R solutions across race for whites and Mexican-Americans who had been referred due to learning problems in the regular classroom. Dean (1979) reported coefficients of congruence between corresponding factors of .84 for verbal comprehension, .89 for perceptual organization, and .88 for freedom from distractibility. Although these coefficients of congruence are slightly below the .90 level usually needed to indicate equivalent factors, these results do demonstrate a high degree of factorial similarity for Anglos and Mexican-Americans.

Gutkin and Reynolds (1980) compared two- and three-factor principal factor solutions to the WISC–R across race for referred Anglo and Chicano children. These factor solutions were also compared with those for normal, Anglo, Chicano, black, and Papago students as reported by Reschly (1978), and with those for the WISC–R standardization sample. In their original study, Gutkin and Reynolds' (1980) findings indicated a substantial congruence across race for both the two- and three-factor solutions. When they compared their solutions with those obtained by Reschly (1978) for normal white, black, Mexican-American, and Papago children, and with results obtained with the WISC–R standardization sample, coefficients of congruence were all above .90. Their basic conclusion was that there was a consistency of factor-analytic results across race.

Taylor and Ziegler (1987) reported an investigation in which the WISC–R was administered to 189 black, 184 Hispanic, and 187 white non-referred children. The subtest scores were factor analyzed and the first principal factor was extracted. Comparison of the magnitude and pattern of factor loadings were similar for the three ethnic groups, leading the authors to conclude that a similar general intellectual factor is measured when the WISC–R is used with children of different ethnic groups.

The conclusion drawn by Reynolds and Kaiser (1990) is that construct validity investigations of a large number of psychometric assessment instruments (including the WISC and WISC–R) have been carried out with a variety of minority and white children of both sexes, and no consistent evidence of bias in construct validity has been found. This leads to the conclusion that aptitude tests operate in essentially the same manner across race and sex, and that tests measure the same constructs with equal accuracy for blacks, whites, Mexican-Americans, and other American minority group members, of either sex.

Bias in Predictive or Criterion-Related Validity

Hale (1991) cites Reynolds (1982) as noting that in relation to test bias, criterion-related validity is the most crucial type for a test. Reynolds and Kaiser (1990) state that finding an agreed-upon definition of bias in predictive validity is a difficult task. They propose a modified version of the definition put forth by Cleary, Humphreys, Kendrick, and Wesman (1975). This definition, which has been generally accepted although with some criticism, essentially states that a test is considered biased with respect to predictive validity if the inference drawn which is based on the test score is not made with the smallest possible random error, or if there is a constant error in an inference or prediction as a function of membership in a particular group (Reynolds & Kaiser, 1990).

Reynolds and Kaiser (1990) note that the evaluation of bias according to the above definition, which is considered the regression definition, is straightforward. When one is dealing with simple regression, predictions take the form of $Y_i = aX_i + b$, where a is the regression coefficient and b is a constant. When one graphs this equation to form a regression line, a represents the slope of the regression line and b represents the Y intercept.

Insofar as the definition of bias Reynolds and Kaiser (1990) use requires that errors in prediction be independent of group membership, the regression line formed for any pair of variables must be the same for each group for whom predictions are to be made. Whenever either the slope or the intercept differs significantly across groups, there will be a bias in prediction if one attempts to use a regression equation based on the data for the combined groups. On the other hand, whenever the regression equations for two (or more) groups are equivalent, then prediction will be the same for all groups, and if they are combined, there will be no bias in prediction based on the common regression line. This condition is referred to as homogeneity of regression across groups, simultaneous regression, or fairness in prediction.

Reschly and Sabers (1979) evaluated the validity of WISC–R IQs in the prediction of performance on the reading and math subtests of the Metropolitan Achievement Test for whites, blacks, Mexican-Americans, and Native American Papagos. The Reschly and Sabers' (1979) comparison of regression systems did find bias in the prediction of the various achievement scores. However, the bias resulted in generally significant underprediction of white performance when a common regression equation was utilized. Achievement test performance of the Native American Papago group demonstrated the greatest amount of overprediction of all the non-white groups.

Reschly and Reschly (1979) investigated the predictive validity of WISC–R factor scores with samples of white, black, Mexican-American, and Native American Papago children. The correlations of the WISC–R and achievement measures (teacher ratings and Metropolitan Achievement Test performance) were significant except for the Native American Papago group. Reschly and Reschly (1979) concluded that their data confirmed the relatively strong relationship of WISC–R scores to achievement for most non-Anglo as well as Anglo groups.

Reynolds and Gutkin (1980) investigated the predictive validity of the WISC–R for 174 Chicano and 94 Anglo children who had been referred for psychological services. Regression lines for the prediction of academic achievement were compared across the two races through the Pothoff analysis, which simultaneously tests slope and intercept values. Only the regression equation between the WISC–R Performance IQ and arithmetic achievement differed for the Anglo and Chicano groups, with the difference in the two equations being due to an intercept bias that resulted in the overprediction of achievement for the Mexican-American children. Reynolds and Gutkin (1980) concluded that the results generally supported the predictive validity of the WISC–R across race with the referral sample studied.

Thus, Reynolds and Kaiser (1990) conclude that with respect to predictive validity bias (regarding the WISC and WISC–R), the evidence suggests conclusions similar to those regarding bias in content and construct validity: there is no strong evidence to support contentions of the existence of differential or single-group validity. Bias appears to occur infrequently and without any observable pattern. When bias does occur, it appears to consistently favor low socioeconomic, disadvantaged ethnic minority children.

Reynolds and Kaufman (1985), Kaufman et al. (1990), and Sattler (1990) have also discussed the issue of test bias with the Wechsler scales. These various authors generally conclude that the WISC–R displays many features of lack of bias. Yet, Kaufman et al. (1990), citing Flaugher's (1978) discussion of the intricacies of the test bias issue, note that even though the studies they describe can be viewed as supportive of the notion that the WISC–R has some unbiased qualities, they do not intend to suggest that the issue is anywhere near resolved or closed.

TEST BIAS AND THE WISC-III

With respect to the WISC–III, research on bias is just beginning to emerge. Weiss, Prifitera, and Roid (1993) report an investigation of predictive bias with the WISC–III regarding the variables of ethnicity and gender. These authors note that in the development of the WISC–III, there were many efforts taken to ensure test fairness. The sampling plan for the WISC–III normative group emphasized exact minority representation at each year of age and for males and females; the stimulus materials utilized were carefully balanced for both gender and ethnic references; the development of items utilized content review by bias panels; and item selection included statistical analyses of differential item performance across ethnic and gender groups.

The Weiss et al. (1993) investigation involved two samples. The first sample consisted of 700 children aged 6 to 16 years (median = 11) which was selected to represent the U.S. population percentages of children aged 6 to 16 according to ethnicity, gender, and parental education level. The sample included 74.7% whites, 14.7% blacks, and 10.6% Hispanics, evenly divided by gender within ethnic group.

Each child in the sample was administered the WISC–III and one of a variety of achievement tests (e.g., Comprehensive Test of Basic Skills, Form U; California Achievement Test, Form E). Analyses on this sample were conducted using Reading, Writing, and Math Normal Curve Equivalent (NCE) scores which are normalized transformations of national percentile scores.

The second sample consisted of 1,000 children between 6 and 16 years inclusive (median = 12) which was selected to represent the U.S. population percentages of children aged 6 to 16 according to ethnicity, gender, and parental education. This sample included 79.9% whites, 10.8% blacks, and 9.3% Hispanics, evenly divided by gender within ethnic group. Each child in this sample was administered the WISC–III, and in addition, teacher-assigned grades between 0 and 100 in Reading, Math, and English were obtained for each child in this sample.

The relationship between WISC–III FSIQ and each measure of achievement was then evaluated by use of Pothoff's formula 1, which permits a simultaneous comparison of regression slopes and intercepts across groups. The resulting F values for the simultaneous comparisons of slopes and intercepts for the first sample (comparing Black/White, Hispanic/White, and Female/Male groups' Reading, Writing and Math NCE scores) were nonsignificant for all nine comparisons. For the second sample, comparison of the slopes and intercepts (with Black/White, Hispanic/White, and Female/Male groups' teacher-assigned English, Math, and Reading grades) resulted in eight of nine comparisons being nonsignificant.

The one significant difference involved a differential prediction for males and females; for children with the same IQ, females tend to score 3.1 grade points higher in English than males and 1.5 points higher than would be predicted by the common regression lines. The authors also report correlations of each achievement measure with FSIQ by gender and ethnic group, and all correlations were significant for the White, Black, male and female groups.

Weiss et al. (1993) note several potential limitations in their study, including achievement tests and grades being only two possible methods for evaluating achievement; and the effect on the regression equations of combining different achievement tests. However, they conclude that the findings of their investigation are consistent with previous studies with the WISC and WISC–R that have demonstrated that these instruments generally predict academic achievement fairly across ethnic and gender groups when the criteria are either group-administered achievement test scores or teacher-assigned grades.

Hence this investigation, which utilized two large samples which were matched to the 1988 census for ethnicity, gender, and socioeconomic status, extends past findings on test fairness and the absence of differential prediction to the WISC–III. Consistent with previous research, the results of this study suggest that differential prediction across ethnic groups does not occur when a variety of achievement measures are predicted from WISC–III Full Scale IQ scores.

The present author would take the view that the issue of test bias with the WISC–III, as with other issues humans deal with, may ultimately reflect the belief systems of the individuals involved. While a significant amount of evidence has been adduced to demonstrate the lack of bias of the Wechsler scales, it would not seem reasonable to conclude that the issue is resolved. It may be that the core beliefs and values of a system, such as American society, are reflected in various ways, some more subtle or obvious than others, throughout the system. And the question of test bias with intelligence tests is one such issue.

The examiner using the WISC–III may be able to believe that the WISC–III is fairly free of extreme bias in the measurement of intellectual performance in both majority and minority individuals. Yet the examiner should keep in mind all of the concerns expressed by those who maintain the unfairness of such tests in evaluating the abilities of minority individuals, and exercise both caution and thoughtfulness when administering and interpreting the WISC–III in the assessment of the intellectual functioning of any member of a minority group.

Chapter Eighteen

MEDICATION AND PSYCHOLOGICAL TESTING

At the present time, there is a national debate within the profession of psychology regarding whether or not psychologists should seek, or will be able to obtain, privileges to prescribe psychotropic medication for their patients (Brentar & McNamara, 1991a, 1991b; DeNelsky, 1991). Regardless of how this debate ultimately is resolved, psychologists are currently often involved in the testing of children or adolescents who are or have been taking medication at the time of testing.

There are at least two major concerns that may be considered in terms of psychological testing and various kinds of psychotropic medication. The first issue involves whether medication an examinee may be taking at the time of testing significantly affects her or his test functioning. The second is whether, on the basis of the child or adolescent's test performance, a medication trial should be recommended by the examiner.

To address the second issue first, it is the present author's view that testing involves the sampling of a subset of behaviors from the universe of total behaviors that characterize the examinee's functioning. The broader the subset of behaviors sampled during testing, the more likely the test sample is to reflect the individual's overall repertoire of behavior, and the more likely that conclusions drawn about the examinee from his or her test functioning will accurately characterize the person's broader adaptation.

There is certainly evidence that, for example, learning disabled and ADHD children perform less well on certain subtests or groups of subtests of the WISC–III than children in the standardization sample (e.g., Prifitera & Dersh, 1993; Schwean et al., 1993). However, the present author does not believe that a recommendation for a medication trial for a child should be based on only one sample of the child's behavior. Such a recommendation may include an evaluation of the child's profile of scores on the WISC–III, but should also include other sources of information about the examinee, such as his or her behavior during testing; the examinee's performance on other tests and interviews; parental reports (e.g., the Child Behavior Checklist [Achenbach, 1991a]); and teacher reports (e.g., Child Behavior Checklist Teacher's Report Form [Achenbach, 1991b]); or a comprehensive evaluation of the examinee's attentional performance (e.g., Loney, 1986).

In terms of the first issue — i.e., the effect of medication on an examinee's test functioning—it is the present author's view that the examiner must act as an independent evaluator of the examinee, even if the child is under the care of a pediatrician, a psychiatrist, or another physician. By independently observing the child or adolescent's functioning, and by gathering relevant information from or about the examinee, the examiner may be able to advocate for the child's welfare in other ways than simply by providing a careful and accurate assessment of the individual's intellectual functioning.

This means that the examiner should attempt to observe and evaluate any and all aspects of the examinee's functioning possible. If the child is taking medication at the time of assessment, this becomes one more factor which the examiner should make note of, in terms of any examinee behaviors which might reflect the effects, either positive or negative, of medication on the individual's functioning. If the examiner observes some behavior of the examinee which may reflect positive medication effects, the examiner should consider this in his or her evaluation of the test data. In addition, if the examiner concludes that the child's functioning does or may reflect an adverse effect of medication, the examiner should be prepared to pursue this further, through consultation with the examinee, her or his parent, or the physician who has prescribed the medication.

CHILD PSYCHOPHARMACOLOGY

The use of psychotropic medications for the treatment of childhood psychological or behavioral disorders began in the late 1930s when Bradley (1937) first described the use of Benzedrine with behaviorally disordered children. Approximately 15 years later, following the introduction of such antipsychotics as chlorpromazine (Thorazine) and thioridazine (Mellaril), other drugs began to be used for the control of childhood behavior disorders (Cepeda, 1989).

Most of the early focus of psychotropic drug treatment with children involved patients who displayed undercontrolled behavior in restlessness, anxiety, or hyperactivity. Aside from the amphetamines, antianxiety medications such as hydroxyzine (Atarax), and later, the tricyclic antidepressants such as imipramine (Tofranil), and more recently antimania drugs such as Lithium and anticonvulsants such as Tegretol (Green, 1991) have been used in the psychopharmacological treatment of children (Cepeda, 1989).

The field of child psychopharmacology has always focused on the treatment of symptoms, and while many child behaviors that reflect a particular diagnosis do respond to medication, the underlying disease process is not directly treated by the prescribed medication. In contrast to the psychopharmacological treatment of adult-onset mental illness such as schizophrenia or bipolar disorder, no treatment-responsive symptoms appear unique to particular diagnoses among children (Cepeda, 1989).

In terms of the evolution of child psychopharmacology, in 1973, a special issue of the *Psychopharmacology Bulletin* (National Institute of Mental Health, 1973) devoted to pharmacotherapy of children reviewed research on disorders of childhood that appeared amenable to pharmacological treatment, summarized the needs in the field of childhood psychopharmacology, and provided both recommended assessments and rating scales that had been found useful in clinical research. This publication, which was updated more recently (National Institute of Mental Health, 1985), facilitated a more uniform set of strategies for research in the field of childhood psychopharmacology.

In addition, developments in this field were further facilitated by the publication of the *Diagnostic and Statistical Manual of Mental Disorders*, 3rd edition (DSM–III; American Psychiatric Association, 1980) which provided research-grade diagnostic criteria that could be used by investigators in their identification of patients for inclusion in research studies. The subsequent diagnostic manual (DSM–III–R; American Psychiatric Association, 1987) assisted with the further refinement of the accurate diagnosis of children, and the most recently published diagnostic manual (DSM–IV; American Psychiatric Association, 1994) should continue to facilitate research on the use of various forms of psychopharmacological treatment with clearly and consensually diagnosed children and adolescents.

Hence the field of child psychopharmacology has developed more refined and focused methods for investigating the use of psychotropic medications with children and adolescents. The development of more precise methods for the diagnosis of childhood disorders as well as the ability to more accurately measure the pharmacokinetics and effects of various medications in patients should result in further improvements in the psychopharmacological treatment of children and adolescents in the future.

UNTOWARD OR SIDE EFFECTS OF MEDICATION

One of the most fundamental concepts regarding medication usage is that of titration of dose, which parallels the gradient model which has been discussed throughout this book. According to this concept, although psychotropic medication is presumably prescribed in relation to the child's weight, in fact, the physician ordinarily begins with a low dose which is gradually titrated, or adjusted, until one of several possible outcomes is encountered (Green, 1991):

1) Totally adequate symptom control is established;
2) The upper limit of the recommended dose (or higher level if usually accepted) has been reached;
3) Untoward (side) effects that preclude further increases in dose have appeared;
4) After a measurable improvement in the target symptoms, a plateau in improvement or a worsening of symptoms occurs when the dose is increased further.

Green (1991) points out that all drugs, including placebos, have "untoward," or side, effects, which are often just as predictable as a drug's intended therapeutic effect. It is useful to think of untoward effects as the "unwanted" effects for the particular patient and the specific purpose for which the medication is being prescribed (Green, 1991). While many side effects are related to dose or serum level, others may not be. Thus, untoward effects may occur almost immediately (e.g., an acute dystonic reaction) or they may not occur for years (e.g., tardive dyskinesia), and at times the untoward effect of a particular drug may vary according to the age or diagnosis of the individual.

The ability of the psychologist to be aware of some of the possible untoward effects of medications may allow her or him to recognize if medication is affecting a child or adolescent's test performance, but also allows the examiner to alert a parent if the medication is having an effect that the child may not realize is potentially a medication side effect.

The reason for this is that the ability to understand untoward effects and to verbalize unusual sensations varies not only among individual children but also varies developmentally. Thus, younger children typically spontaneously report untoward effects less often than older children (Green, 1991). Hence, the younger the child, the more important it becomes for caretakers, or psychological examiners, to attempt to determine if the child may be experiencing such untoward effects which might indicate the need to alter or discontinue particular dosages or medications.

The following discussion involves an attempt to review some of the issues that an examiner should be aware of in regard to his or her intellectual assessment of children and adolescents who may be using prescribed medication at the time of testing. The groups of drugs which will be discussed include stimulant, antipsychotic, antidepressant, antimania, and antianxiety medications. This section is based largely on the writings of Cepeda (1989), Green (1991), Brown and Borden (1989), and Barkley (1989) as well as the author's own views.

Stimulant Drugs

Psychostimulants are the class of drugs that produce excitation of the central nervous system. The most commonly prescribed of this class of drugs are the dextroamphetamines, methylphenidate, and pemoline, each of which is widely used in treating behavioral and learning problems among children and adolescents (Barkley, 1989; Brown & Borden, 1989).

Dextroamphetamine sulfate (Dexedrine) is usually administered in tablet form two or three times daily, although it may also be administered as a sustained-release (S–R) capsule once per day. The onset of behavioral effects occurs within an hour of administration and peak effects typically occur from one to four hours after drug administration.

Methylphenidate (Ritalin) is given to approximately two thirds of all children who have an attention-deficit disorder and who are treated with stimulants (Brown & Borden, 1989). Methylphenidate is typically administered to the child in two divided doses during the course of the day (before leaving for school and during the lunch hour), although this medication also comes in sustained-release form. Although an improvement in target symptoms can be seen in as few as 20 minutes (Green, 1991), the clinical effects of methylphenidate have been found to dissipate approximately four hours after administration (Brown & Borden, 1989).

Magnesium pemoline (Cylert) results in central nervous system changes similar to those produced by the other stimulants, although it is structurally different from them. The major advantage of this medication over the other stimulants is that only a once-daily administration is necessary. On the other hand, one of the primary drawbacks of magnesium pemoline is its slower onset of effect. While the other stimulants may demonstrate clinical effects within a few hours following a single dose, the beneficial effects of magnesium pemoline may not be observed for several weeks (Brown & Borden, 1989). However, the therapeutic effects of magnesium pemoline during a given day ordinarily last for several hours, and the effects of the medication have been sustained for as long as two weeks following its discontinuation (Conners & Taylor, 1980).

The major effects produced by the stimulants include improvement in sustained attention and impulse control and in reduction of task-irrelevant activity, especially in situations which demand restraint of behavior (Barkley, 1989). As a result of medication, children may become more compliant with parental and teacher commands and often increase their cooperation with others with whom they may have to accomplish a task (Barkley, Karlsson, Strzelecki, & Murphy, 1984; Cunningham, Siegel, & Offord, 1985).

In terms of specific effects on cognition, Barkley (1977) has noted that stimulant drugs consistently improve performance on basic laboratory tasks involving such things as continuous performance tasks, simple reaction time, rote learning, and concept formation. However, with the WISC–III, Schwean et al. (1993) did not find that subtest scores on the WISC–III varied according to whether ADHD children were on or off Methylphenidate.

It has been estimated that between 1 and 2.6% of all elementary school children are prescribed some type of stimulant medication (Bosco & Robin, 1980; Gadow, 1981; Safer & Krager, 1983). There appears to be general agreement that the primary indications for stimulant drug therapy involve hyperactivity and short attention span (Rapoport, 1983). These characteristics of the child are often symptoms of the diagnosis of attention-deficit hyperactivity disorder (American Psychiatric Association, 1987, 1994), although they may in fact reflect other conditions or diagnoses.

Approximately 75% of children treated with stimulants will show a positive response, although these responses will vary from mild to marked improvement in target symptoms (Barkley, 1977; Green, 1991). In addition, some children will respond unfavorably to one stimulant but will respond favorably to another (Green, 1991) and, in fact, the effects of medication appear to be individually unique (Rapport, DuPaul, Stoner, & Jones, 1986).

In terms of contraindications to the use of stimulant medications, Green (1991) notes that stimulants may cause stereotypies, tics, and psychosis *de novo* in individuals who are sensitive or if the medication is given in high enough doses. Green (1991) also notes that these medications are relatively contraindicated in children and adolescents with a history of schizophrenia or other psychoses, pervasive developmental disorders, or borderline personality organization, as stimulants appear to worsen these conditions in many cases.

As far as the side effects the examiner should be aware of when testing a child who is known to be on a stimulant medication, ones that might be elicited with basic questioning include insomnia, nausea, abdominal pain or cramps, headache, thirst, vomiting, lability of mood, irritability, sadness, or weepiness (Green, 1991). Some of these are symptoms which could occur at the time of testing and thus interfere with the examinee's ability to handle the testing. If the child or adolescent reports any of these symptoms, this does not mean they are necessarily side effects, but the examiner may ask if such symptoms began with the initiation of medication and, if so, further exploration of their origin with the child, her or his parent(s), or the prescribing physician may be indicated.

Other behavioral features the examiner should be aware of in testing individuals on stimulants include rebound effects. These refer to an appearance of the same symptoms for which the medication has been prescribed, i.e., symptoms of attention-deficit disorder, and in some cases, the rebound phenomena, which may occur about 5 hours after the last of dose of stimulant, may exceed the levels at which the symptoms were evident prior to stimulant administration.

A final consideration in regard to stimulant medication is that of the relationship of these medications to tics and Tourette's disorder. There is disagreement among experts as to whether stimulants should be given to children or adolescents who display tics or Tourette's disorder (Shapiro & Shapiro, 1989) or who have a family history of tics (Green, 1991), but Green notes that, at the present time, a conservative approach would consider the stimulants relatively or absolutely contraindicated in treating children who display tics or Tourette's disorder and a reason for caution with a child who has a family history of such phenomena.

The examiner should be alert to any tic behavior on the part of the examinee since this symptom would be a contraindication for prescribing stimulant medication, and in a child who is currently on such medication, it would provide a basis for review of the medication strategy.

Antipsychotic Drugs

In adults or adolescents these drugs, also referred to as neuroleptics or major tranquilizers, are used primarily to treat psychotic symptoms (Cepeda, 1989; Green, 1991). Antipsychotics are thus used in treating such adult disorders as schizophrenia, major depression with psychotic features, bipolar disorders with manic features, and delirium with psychotic features. The features of psychosis which appear most responsive to medication include those symptoms which have an acute onset, such as disorganized thinking, hallucinations, or marked confusion.

In terms of children, the kinds of symptoms seen in adult psychotic disorders are uncommon, and the diagnostic category which encompasses these disorders among children is ordinarily that of pervasive developmental disorders (DSM–IV; American Psychiatric Association, 1994), which reflect the child's impairment in a wide variety of aspects of adaptation including deficits in physical, emotional, and intellectual functioning.

In these childhood disorders, there may be arrests or deviations in the development of language, perception, interpersonal relatedness, and motor function. In autism, the child may display marked resistance to change in his or her environment, echolalic speech patterns, and bizarre verbalizations or motor activity. The child may experience periods of severe anxiety, highly atypical patterns of movement, excessive involvement in fantasy, and at times self-mutilation. It is in dealing with these disorders and their associated symptoms that antipsychotic drugs are utilized in the treatment of childhood psychopathology.

A second group of diagnoses among children where antipsychotics appear to be the drugs of choice include those of chronic motor or vocal tic disorder or Tourette's disorder (Cepeda, 1989; Shapiro & Shapiro, 1989).

Antipsychotics have also been found effective in the treatment of severely aggressive, conduct-disordered children (Green, 1991), although Lithium is also effective in treating such children and appears to have fewer untoward effects than neuroleptic medication.

Lastly, Green (1991) notes that, although there is controversy about the matter, antipsychotics are also used in the treatment of mentally retarded individuals, particularly those who are institutionalized. With this population, antipsychotics reduce the psychomotor agitation, excessive anxiety, irritability, and aggressive behaviors and sleep disturbance evident among these individuals (Cepeda, 1989; Green, 1991).

Antipsychotics can be divided into high-potency and low-potency types, and although they may be equally effective in reducing symptoms when given in equivalent doses, they differ with respect to the frequency and severity of their untoward effects (Green, 1991). Usually, the higher-potency antipsychotics (e.g., thiothixene [Navane] and haloperidol [Haldol]) cause less sedation and fewer autonomic side effects but more extrapyramidal effects, while lower-potency antipsychotics (e.g., chlorpromazine [Thorazine] and thioridazine [Mellaril]) result in greater sedation, more autonomic side effects but fewer extrapyramidal effects (Baldessarini, 1990). In an effort to minimize any cognitive dulling in schoolchildren and in the mentally retarded, who may already have difficulties with cognitive functioning, high-potency and less sedating antipsychotics are ordinarily preferred.

Common untoward effects of antipsychotics include what are called extrapyramidal syndromes (Green, 1991), of which there are several kinds. One of these is called acute dystonic reactions; the period of maximum risk for these reactions is within hours to five days of the beginning of neuroleptic medication (Green, 1991). The symptoms of these dystonic reactions include the sudden onset of spasms of such muscle groups as the neck, mouth or tongue; both eyes may roll up (called an oculogyric crisis) or the child may experience a spasm in which the spine and extremities are bent with a forward convexity. These symptoms may be painful and certainly frightening to the child, but they reportedly respond rapidly to the administration of appropriate medication.

A second extrapyramidal syndrome is parkinsonism, which includes symptoms of tremor, muscular rigidity, drooling, a decrease in facial expressive movements which results in a mask-like expression, and akinesia, or a slowness in initiating movements. The period of maximum risk for the development of parkinsonism is five to 30 days after beginning neuroleptic treatment. These symptoms can also be treated with other medications.

A third untoward extrapyramidal effect due to neuroleptic medication is called akathisia, or motor restlessness (Green, 1991). The period of maximum risk for the development of these symptoms is five to 60 days after the initiation of antipsychotic treatment, although akathisia has been reported to occur soon after an initial dose of neuroleptic medication. The symptoms of this condition include constant restlessness and a feeling of marked tension in the lower extremities, often accompanied by a strong or even irresistible urge to move them. In addition, the person may feel unable to sit still and may engage in foot-tapping or pacing.

A final syndrome to be mentioned is that of tardive dyskinesia, which is the most clinically significant untoward effect associated with neuroleptic treatment. Definitions of this condition and related dyskinesias vary, but Green (1991) notes the research diagnostic criteria of Schooler and Kane (1982) as possibly the most influential. This definition requires that the individual has been exposed to neuroleptics for a total cumulative period of at least three months; that the individual display at least "moderate" abnormal involuntary movements in one or more body areas (e.g., face, lips, jaw, tongue, upper or lower extremities) and at least "mild" movements in two or more body areas; and that there be an absence of other conditions that might produce abnormal movements.

Green (1991) notes that tardive dyskinesia develops while an individual is taking a neuroleptic in contrast to a withdrawal dyskinesia, which occurs when a neuroleptic dose is reduced or when the medication is discontinued altogether. Tardive dyskinesia, which may be severely disabling to the individual and which can also be irreversible, may begin after only a few days, or may not appear until after more than 10 years of treatment with neuroleptics, although it is felt that the risk of developing this disorder increases with the total cumulative dose and duration of neuroleptic treatment. In addition, a withdrawal dyskinesia may develop if medication is reduced or discontinued.

The symptoms of tardive dyskinesia typically involve abnormal movements of the mouth that may look like persistent chewing, lip-smacking or repetitive tongue protrusion (Cepeda, 1989), although involuntary choreoathetoid, combined jerky and writhing, movements reflecting this condition may also affect the torso and extremities (Green, 1991).

Cepeda (1989) notes that if antipsychotic medication is discontinued, the clinical effects may persist for 24 to 36 hours, but that the drug is completely metabolized and cleared from the body within three to four days, and thereafter there would be no clinical effect of the drug.

In his review of studies that have dealt with the effects of neuroleptics on cognition, Cepeda (1989) notes that various studies observe that as the symptoms of aggression, restlessness and impaired concentration improve, the child's performance on learning and academic tasks also improves. Although antipsychotics appear to have some positive impact on autistic children in terms of Wechsler test performance, if these medications are administered to children with other than psychotic diagnoses, the results are either inconclusive or reveal some negative impact of the drugs on test performance.

In terms of the guidelines Cepeda (1989) proposes, he notes that antipsychotic treatment of children with pervasive development disorder, if not resulting in obvious sedation, should not adversely affect the test results on an instrument such as a Wechsler scale. In fact, the medication should improve the child's performance since it may reduce target symptoms, such as hyperactivity, restlessness or aggressivity that would impede the child's test functioning.

Adverse effects of neuroleptic medication on test performance would likely be more obvious just after medication has been initiated since the child may be having a reaction to the medication or need to adjust to the changes brought about by the medication. At reasonable doses, the medication would be a less significant factor after the child has been on the medication for one to two months. If testing is to be used for educational placement or longer-term planning, it should be deferred until the child is on a stable maintenance dose, and if the child is to be tested off neuroleptic medication, a three- or four-day delay after medication discontinuation should be sufficient (Cepeda, 1989).

Antidepressant Drugs

Antidepressant medications were developed to treat a variety of symptoms, referred to as melancholia, which occur as part of major depressive disorders, the depressive component of a bipolar disorder, and sometimes as the depressive features of schizoaffective disorder. The symptoms of these disorders which appear most responsive to antidepressant medication include what are felt to be biological concomitants of depression: crying, decreased appetite and weight loss, diurnal mood variation, initial, middle, and terminal insomnia, decreased libido, and impaired concentration (Cepeda, 1989).

Although psychoanalytic theory, which dominated child clinical work until recently, asserted that depression as a disorder does not exist among children, in the early 1970s, a new position emerged which acknowledged that depression does occur among children, although its manifestations differ from those of adult depression (Kazdin, 1989). This view contended that instead of appearing in dysphoric mood and pervasive loss of interest, childhood depression is "masked" and appears in other symptoms, such as tantrums, irritability, or delinquency.

Research investigations in the last 20 years, however, have focused on and established the fact that the essential features of depression are similar in children, adolescents, and adults, and that the diagnostic criteria developed with adults can be applied directly to the diagnosis of affective disorders in children (Kazdin, 1989).

Many of the medications which have been used to treat adult depression have also been applied to children with mood disorders. Although monoamine oxidase inhibitors (MAOIs; e.g., tranylcypromine sulfate [Parnate] and phenelzine sulfate [Nardil]) have been investigated with children, because of the potentially serious drug interactions and untoward effects of MAOIs, their use with children and adolescents is not usually recommended. In addition, although in recent years there has been the development of selective serotonin reuptake inhibitors such as fluoxetine hydrochloride [Prozac] for treatment of adult depression, these have not been approved for use with younger adolescents or children (Green, 1991).

Most research on the use of antidepressants with children and adolescents until recently has been with the tricyclic antidepressants of imipramine [Tofranil] and amitryptaline [Elavil] (Kazdin, 1989). Although there have been questions raised regarding the methodology in some of the research, the basic findings have been that imipramine and amitriptyline result in decreased symptoms of depression among children (Weller & Weller, 1986). However, studies with adolescents do not find support for the use of tricyclic antidepressants with adolescents (Ryan et al., 1986).

Besides the treatment of depression in children, antidepressant medications have several other uses in child psychopharmacology. For example, in the early 1970s, the tricyclic antidepressant imipramine was used to treat hyperactivity in children, and most studies found that imipramine was as effective as stimulants in treating this disorder (e.g., Quinn & Rapoport, 1975; Rapoport & Mikkelsen, 1978), although stimulants appear to have fewer side effects and have become the drugs of choice for treating attention deficits in children and adolescents (Barkley, 1989).

The antidepressant imipramine has also been used to treat enuresis (Cepeda, 1989), and although medication treatment is successful, relapse rates for psychopharmacological treatment of enuresis suggest that behavioral methods with bell and pad conditioning are the preferred intervention for functional enuresis (Green, 1991).

Imipramine has also been used in the treatment of children with separation anxiety disorder (Cepeda, 1989; Green, 1991). These children may experience fears of leaving home, and hence may refuse to attend school, and such children have been reported to respond to treatment with imipramine, which reduces their anxiety and permits them to separate from home and return to school.

Although Green (1991) notes that imipramine (and other antidepressants) has many untoward effects, some of which are potentially life threatening, Cepeda (1989) notes that there are no dramatic behavioral side effects with antidepressants as there are with antipsychotics. This refers to the fact that although antidepressants may involve risks, such as cardiovascular effects, blood pressure changes, and decreased seizure threshold, these would not be obvious behaviorally.

When tricyclic antidepressants are discontinued after prolonged use, the clinical medication effects ordinarily dissipate after a week to 10 days.

Cepeda (1989) notes that the cognitive effects of single dose administration of antidepressants have been investigated, and it has been found that some antidepressants have more sedating effects than others, with subjective reports of sleepiness peaking between two and three hours after drug ingestion and disappearing by seven hours after ingesting the drug, although these effects would likely not be the same for prolonged antidepressant use.

The effects of antidepressants on cognition have been studied among children being treated for enuresis, hyperactivity, childhood depression, and aggressive behavior (e.g., Brumback & Staton, 1980; Kupietz & Balka, 1976). Cepeda (1989) reports that psychological testing after successful drug treatment usually shows an improvement over pretreatment performance on such measures as the WISC, and Wilson and Staton (1984) reported improved neuropsychological functioning, including improved WISC–R performance, among children treated with antidepressants. Cepeda (1989) notes that in those investigations that compared pre- and post-treatment IQs for children treated for conduct problems or enuresis, no significant improvement was observed in cognitive performance as a function of medication.

Cepeda (1989) suggests the following guidelines for psychological testing in regard to antidepressant medication. If the child to be tested is receiving treatment with a tricyclic antidepressant to ameliorate melancholic symptoms of depression and if testing is to be used for long-term educational planning, it should be delayed until a clinical improvement is seen in the child's depression. Although Cepeda notes the delay might have to be two to three months, the present author feels this is often not feasible under the requirements of short hospital stays and the laws that regulate testing in schools. The examiner would need to proceed with testing but be cognizant of the fact that the child's test performance might be an underestimate of his or her longer-term functioning. Once the child is stabilized on an antidepressant medication, there does not appear to be any evidence to indicate that the child's test performance will be adversely affected by being on a tricyclic antidepressant.

If one is testing a child who is receiving antidepressant medication for problems other than depression, Cepeda (1989) notes that the sedative or anticholinergic effects of medication (e.g., mild fine hand tremor, dry mouth, or blurred vision) might influence testing if the child is evaluated during the first week or two after beginning medication. Hence it would be best, if possible, to delay testing until the child has been on medication for a few weeks. If a child must be seen off antidepressant medication, testing should be delayed until approximately one to two weeks after the discontinuation of medication usage.

Antimanic Drugs

Lithium carbonate [Eskalith, Lithobid] is the primary psychopharmacological treatment for the manic phase of bipolar disorder in adults and is approved by the FDA only for the treatment of manic episodes in bipolar illness and for maintenance therapy for patients over age 12 with a history of mania (Green, 1991). However, in recent years, lithium has been investigated in the treatment of children and adolescents who display undersocialized and aggressive conduct disorders and has been found to provide a successful intervention for such children (Platt, Campbell, Green, & Grega, 1984).

Green (1991) notes that one major problem with the use of lithium is its low therapeutic index, which refers to the fact that lithium toxicity is closely related to its blood serum level, and toxicity may occur at doses which are close to the therapeutic level. Lithium toxicity may appear initially as diarrhea, vomiting, mild ataxia, coarse tremor, drowsiness, slurred speech, or impaired coordination. The untoward effects of lithium which occur early in the course of treatment and which do diminish or disappear during the first weeks of treatment include fine tremor, polydipsia (extreme thirst), polyuria (frequent urination), nausea, headache and gastrointestinal complaints.

Cepeda (1989) notes that in usual therapeutic doses, lithium does not produce CNS-mediated behavioral side effects although he reports a study by Judd, Hubbard, Janowsky, Huey and Takahashi (1977) which found that in normal volunteers, therapeutic levels of lithium did impair performance on the WAIS Digit Symbol subtest.

Because of the lack of research pertaining to the use of lithium with younger individuals, Cepeda (1989) feels that no clear conclusions can be drawn regarding the effects of lithium on children's cognitive performance, although he notes that in contrast to other medications he reviewed, lithium did not demonstrate an improvement in cognitive function which parallelled improvement in clinical status.

Although the specific effects of lithium on children's or adolescents' cognitive functioning or test performance cannot be stated, it would seem reasonable to avoid testing an individual during the first few weeks of lithium treatment if this is possible. Under any circumstances, when testing a child or adolescent who is taking lithium, the examiner should be alert to the above-noted untoward effects since their presence may signal the need for review of the examinee's medication or medical status.

Antianxiety Drugs

Anxiety is a universally experienced phenomenon among both adults and children. Benzodiazepines, the medications used for the symptomatic relief of anxiety, were introduced into clinical practice in the early 1960s, and for the 12 years prior to 1980, they were the most frequently prescribed drugs in the United States (Green, 1991). Greenblatt, Shader, and Abernathy (1983) note that by 1980, the trend toward increasing use of these medications had reversed, possibly reflecting publicity regarding their significant abuse potential.

Concern about the possible abuse of these medications has continued, however, and the American Psychiatric Association convened a Task Force on benzodiazepines which in a summary statement noted that when these drugs are prescribed appropriately, they have relatively mild toxic profiles and a low tendency for abuse (Salzman, 1990). A recent national study on drug dependence prevalence (Anthony, Warner & Kessler, 1994) notes that in the sample in their survey approximately 1 in 13 (7.5%) had a history of dependence on an inhalant or controlled substance (which would include an anxiolytic). Among users of drugs other than tobacco or alcohol, about 15% had become dependent on the drug. This study dealt with individuals from age 15–54, and dependence on anxiolytics (with analgesics and hypnotics) was more prevalent among older groups. Hence the findings point out the general importance of potential dangers of this class of drugs for adolescents and/or children.

Green (1991) notes that benzodiazepine abuse is quite common among alcoholics as well as among cocaine, narcotic, and methadone abusers, as these individuals use anxiolytics to augment the effects of other drugs or to decrease the withdrawal symptoms from other drugs they may use.

The major benzodiazepines include chlordiazepoxide [Librium], diazepam [Valium], and alprazolam [Xanax]. Benzodiazepines are prescribed for older adolescents and adults to relieve generalized or specific anxiety, to treat muscular tension, for sleep disorders, or to treat seizure disorders. However, it is relatively uncommon for these drugs to be used with children, except for brief periods of time, and there is no clinical literature which advocates their use for the treatment of children with diagnoses of anxiety disorder (Cepeda, 1989).

With children, these medications are used primarily for treatment of sleep and seizure disorders, and Green (1991) notes that, at present, the childhood disorders for which the benzodiazepines appear most justified as the drug of choice are sleep terror disorder (pavor nocturnus) and sleepwalking disorder (somnambulism), although even these disorders are not usually treated pharmacologically unless they are extremely severe.

The major contraindication to use of these drugs would involve whether the individual might be predisposed to substance abuse since these drugs have the potential for physical and psychological dependence. In addition, adolescents who are likely to become pregnant or who are known to be pregnant should not be prescribed these medication since they may represent a risk to the developing fetus. In terms of the clinician who uses the systems perspective discussed in this book, the introduction of these medications into a family where adult members might be at risk for substance abuse should be a consideration as well.

Green (1991) notes that the most common untoward effects of benzodiazepines reflect their central nervous system depressant properties. Thus, oversedation, fatigue, drowsiness, ataxia, and confusion which may progress to coma at high doses occur with the benzodiazepines. In addition, "paradoxical reactions" involving marked disinhibition have been reported among children and adolescents using these medications. Symptoms of these reactions include acute excitation, increased anxiety, aggression, insomnia and nightmares.

In general adult psychiatry, benzodiazepines may be used for the management of anxiety disorders (e.g., panic disorder), the short-term relief of anxiety symptoms (e.g., an airplane flight or public speaking engagement), and the short-term treatment of some sleep disorders. These medications are also used for the relief of acute symptoms of alcohol withdrawal. However, at the present time, there are no specific clinical guidelines for treating any childhood anxiety disorders with benzodiazepines. One specific childhood anxiety disorder, that of obsessive-compulsive disorder, is most typically treated pharmacologically with clomipramine hydrochloride [Anafranil], which is an antidepressant (Green, 1991; Milby & Weber, 1991).

Cepeda (1989) notes that there is a paucity of literature on the cognitive and behavioral side effects of these medications with children. He notes one study that evaluated anxiolytic drug effects on the cognitive functioning of children which concluded that at therapeutic doses, the medication had no adverse effect on cognitive performance (Ferguson & Simeon, 1984). Cepeda (1989) also notes that most studies of adults find that at therapeutic doses of these medications, little if any difference can be observed between placebo and active medication groups of subjects.

Cepeda (1989) concludes that at high doses of anxiolytics, the sedative effect of the medication will impair cognitive performance. However, as with the antimanic drugs, there are insufficient research data to comment on the effects of these medications in regard to routine psychological testing. The present author would note that insofar as these medications reduce subjective anxiety, they might facilitate the performance of a highly test-anxious examinee, although if the dosage is too high, sedation might interfere with the speed of the individual's information processing, perhaps particularly affecting his or her handling of the WISC–III performance subtests. If the child is to be free of anxiolytic medication effects for testing, Cepeda (1989) notes that a delay of one day after the last dose should be sufficient.

CONCLUDING COMMENT

The information in this chapter attempts to provide some guidelines for the examiner to utilize when she or he is testing a child who is, or has recently been on, some kind of psychotropic medication. The guidelines should be used in conjunction with knowledge of what medication a child is or has been taking, the purpose of the medication, and how long the child has been on the medication.

Whether the reader of this book someday is able to prescribe medication for her or his child and adolescent patients or not, the purpose of this section has been to provide the examiner with a broadened perspective on the testing situation. Many children who are tested psychologically are taking prescribed medication. It is important for the examiner to realize and remember that all medications have untoward, or side, effects. The examiner is in a position to observe: (1) whether these medication effects have any apparent impact on the examinee's test performance; (2) whether these medications might be producing some untoward effect that neither the child nor her or his parent is aware of; and (3) to determine the nature of the child's own awareness and understanding of medication he or she may be taking.

This last issue relates to the acculturation of children in terms of their perceptions of ingesting chemicals as a way to alter their functioning, which certainly may contribute to the way in which they think of solving problems in their own future lives (Brown & Borden, 1989). Although it has been suggested that the use of medication in the treatment of children may place them at risk for subsequent substance abuse, there is some data to refute this concern (Blouin, Bornstein, & Trites, 1978; Henker, Whalen, Bugenthal, & Barker, 1981; Loney, Kramer, & Milich, 1981).

Nonetheless, it is the present author's view that the examiner must assess the entire field in which the child operates. This should include the child's own capacity for functioning, the child's family system, the tolerance of the child's school environment, and the contribution medication may make to the child's overall adaptation and development as well as the potential negative side effects the medication may involve for the child. And whether the examiner is evaluating a child who is currently on medication or is considering making a recommendation for an examinee to be on medication, a thoughtful approach reflecting the examiner's own long-term perspective and ability for foresight regarding children and their development should be utilized.

Chapter Nineteen

COMPUTERS AND THE WISC-III

The developments in computer technology in the United States in the last thirty years have had an extraordinary impact on all aspects of American society, on business, the professions, and on the lives of average citizens. In psychology, the first computer-based interpretive systems became available in the early 1960s (Honaker & Fowler, 1990), and since then there have been startling developments in the reduction in size and the increase in speed, power and memory capacity of computers.

The rapid changes in the computer industry have resulted in the widespread availability of computer hardware and software, and this in turn has affected the development of the field of computer-based assessment. The early computer systems involved large, expensive mainframe computers which were adapted to assist in some limited components of the assessment process. These early systems served primarily to provide rapid scoring of test results with brief descriptions of the scores but little more.

As computers became increasingly sophisticated and more readily available, an emphasis on actuarially based interpretation of test scores developed and computers began to be utilized as adjuncts for the entire assessment process. Thus, by the beginning of the 1980s, computer systems had been devised that could not only score or do simple clerical work on tests, but could also administer and provide somewhat sophisticated interpretations for many of the major psychological tests in use as well (Johnson & Williams, 1980).

THE PRESENT STATUS OF COMPUTER-ASSISTED ASSESSMENT

At the present time, with the advent of inexpensive, powerful, and portable microcomputers, it has become possible to use computers in virtually all aspects of practice management (Harrell, 1993), as well as in the administration, scoring, and interpretation of a wide variety of psychological assessment instruments (Honaker & Fowler, 1990; Schlosser & Moreland, 1993). Since the mid-1980s, a number of individuals and small companies, as well as large test publishers, have begun to produce and market an array of assessment software. Newly developed software programs permit the admin-

367

istration and interpretation of traditional paper-and-pencil tests as well as providing for instruments specifically designed for computer administration (e.g., Weiss, 1985).

The Wechsler scales cannot be administered by a computer nor can the initial scoring be accomplished by a computer. But computers are able to quickly and accurately execute a spectrum of tasks with the raw scores which are obtained. At the low end of the spectrum (e.g., *Scoring Assistant for the Wechsler Scales* [Psychological Corporation, 1992b]), these computer-based processes can convert raw scores into scaled scores, factor scores, or IQs and also determine the percentile ranks of any of these scores with respect to the standardization population.

Based on the assumption that the individual's test scores reflect both the person's "true" score and an error component, the computer can calculate confidence intervals for true scores, and evaluate the significance of differences among and between various scores or groups of scores on the individual's profile, to rapidly determine the examinee's cognitive strengths or weaknesses.

Beyond these basic statistical analyses of the test data, programs are available at the high end of the spectrum (e.g., *The WISC-III® Report* [Psychologistics, 1984, 1991]; *WISC-III Writer®* [The Psychological Corporation, 1994]) which generate comprehensive reports describing the examinee's intellectual functioning, and these computerized programs offer the examiner the opportunity to edit the report, so that the final product is an integration of the clinician's observations along with the computer-generated material.

If one compares using versus not using a computer to assist in generating a report regarding the WISC–III, there appear to be three major advantages favoring computer use: (1) the accuracy and reliability of score calculations; (2) the time required for computer-assisted as opposed to examiner-based interpretation of a child or adolescent's WISC–III protocol; and (3) the reliability or repeatability of the report that is generated based on the data.

ETHICAL AND PROFESSIONAL ISSUES REGARDING COMPUTER-ASSISTED ASSESSMENT

The advent of computer technology has had an enormous impact on all aspects of society, and the widespread use of computers in psychology has of course raised a number of ethical and professional questions regarding the place of this technology in the profession of psychology (Honaker & Fowler, 1990).

Ethical questions regarding computer-assisted testing first appeared in the mid-1960s regarding mail-in reporting services for various personality tests since the APA ethical code prohibited the provision of mail-order psychological services to clients. Concerns about these issues ultimately led to the development by the American Psychological Association of a set of interim guidelines for the use of computer-based test interpretation services (American Psychological Association, 1966).

These interim guidelines became obsolete with the increase in availability of personal computers and assessment-related software and services. Hence the Committee on Professional Standards and the Committee on Psychological Tests and Assessment of the American Psychological Association (1986) published a new set of guidelines pertaining to computer-based tests and interpretations.

These guidelines, based on the 1981 version of the American Psychological Association Ethical Principles (APA, 1981), provide recommendations for those who use computer-based tests and interpretations and for those who develop computer-based test services. The guidelines emphasize that the user of computer-based assessment techniques "should be a qualified professional with: (a) knowledge of psychological measurement; (b) a background in the history of the test or inventories being used; (c) experience in the use and familiarity with the research on the tests or inventories, including gender, age, and cultural differences if applicable; and (d) knowledge in the area of intended application" (Committee on Professional Standards and Committee on Psychological Tests and Assessment, 1986, p. 8).

Regarding recommendations specifically for users of computer-based tests and interpretations, the guidelines state that "[C]omputer-generated interpretive reports should be used only in conjunction with professional judgment. The user should judge for each test taker the validity of the computerized test report based on the user's professional knowledge of the total context of testing and the test taker's performance and characteristics" (Committee on Professional Standards and Committee on Psychological Tests and Assessment, 1986, p. 12).

Apropos of ethical considerations with respect to computer-based test interpretations, Butcher (1993) notes several pitfalls to be avoided by the user of computer-based clinical reports. First, such reports can encourage the clinician to passively abdicate total responsibility to the computer. Second, computer-generated evaluations may "mystify" the process of assessment, offering an unwarranted sense of scientific precision, so the clinician may simply accept the computer interpretations without questioning the decision rules or validity research which underlies the computer report. Finally, the clinician's failure to maintain control over computer-generated reports can lead to problems since such reports become part of a client's file and might not be clearly distinguished from a psychologist-generated final report.

Similarly, Eyde (1993) points out that one of the greatest temptations faced by busy practitioners is to disregard the warning on many CBTIs which states that the computer-generated report should not be used as the only source of information about a client.

The ethical issues surrounding the use of computers in report writing touch on the complex matter of defining the professional psychologist. As suggested by Gardner (1983, 1993), some individuals (including psychologists) may conceive of their computers and software programs as components of their own intelligence, as tools that are extensions of their own brain processes, and hence they may be unable to see any difference between a personally- or a computer-generated psychological report. The ethical questions regarding the clinician's responsibility to the patient, and the way in which this responsibility will be shared with, or turned over to, a computer will become a more significant issue as computers become increasingly relied upon in clinical practice.

EXAMINATION OF COMPUTER-INTERPRETIVE PROGRAMS FOR THE WISC-III

Tuttle and Smith (1993) provide a number of guidelines to use when one is choosing the best available software for one's needs. When the author began the process of writing the present book, he felt it would be important to include a section on computer interpretation of the WISC–III. The author decided to contact a sample of several of the major publishers of WISC–III interpretive software, which is in fact consistent with the guidelines proposed by Tuttle and Smith (1993).

The author devised a list of publishers who advertised in the APA Monitor in the early part of 1993, offering computerized interpretive programs for the WISC–III, and the author also contacted The Psychological Corporation regarding any computerized programs for the WISC–III it had available. The author's list included Psychological Assessment Resources, Inc., Psychologistics, Inc., The Psychological Corporation, Psych Support Systems, and MHS.

The author composed a letter which requested information about a publisher's WISC–III computer-based interpretive program(s), asked for one or more sample reports, and posed a number of questions the author felt would be pertinent to assisting readers of this book to select among computerized interpretive programs for the WISC–III. This letter was then sent to the various publishers.

Information was obtained from Dr. Thomas H. Harrell of Psychologistics, Inc. (personal communication, April 27, 1993) regarding their *WISC–III*®

Report program; Dr. Hugh Poyner of The Psychological Corporation (personal communication, April 28, 1993) regarding the *Scoring Assistant for the Wechsler Scales* (personal communication, August 19, 1994) and the *WISC-III® Writer;* and Mr. Richard Grimord of Psychological Assessment Resources, Inc. (personal communication, November 9, 1993) regarding their *Report Writer: Children's Intellectual and Achievement Tests.*

Appendix A.1. indicates the series of questions which were asked of each of the above-noted publishers regarding its WISC–III computerized interpretive program(s). Appendicies A.2., A.3., and A.4. provide verbatim or slightly modified versions of the replies of each respondent regarding each of the questions that were asked.

Examination of these appendices will provide the reader with information about the WISC–III computer-interpretive programs offered by three major publishers and may provide some assistance to the clinician who is considering whether to further explore the option of obtaining a software package to use in writing reports regarding the WISC–III.

DECIDING WHETHER OR NOT TO USE A COMPUTER PROGRAM FOR WISC-III REPORT WRITING

The decision as to whether to purchase and whether or not to utilize a computer program in one's interpretation of the WISC–III will depend on a variety of factors. As has been discussed throughout this book, the author views this decision as a selection by the clinician among paths that she or he will choose to follow.

The issues discussed above regarding computer interpretation of psychological tests are relevant to this decision. If the examiner has grown up with computers, uses computer programs for the interpretation of other psychological tests, sees computers as essential time-saving and convenient devices, and has the financial resources available to purchase a WISC–III interpretive program, then it is likely that the examiner will choose the computer-interpretive pathway.

If the examiner feels less comfortable with computers, has less trust in what machines produce and more trust in her or his own thinking, prefers to deal with clinical data him- or herself, and enjoys the process of testing and interpretation as professional activities, then it is more likely that the examiner will defer obtaining and/or using a computer program for the interpretation of the WISC–III.

The author would add several other comments to this discussion. First of all, the gradient model which has been discussed throughout this book appears relevant to this issue as well. Thus, there seems little doubt that, at present, computers play a vital role in the lives of most people and certainly most psychologists. Further, computers may have an important role to play in certain kinds or aspects of psychological assessment. The question is at what point on a continuum of psychologist function one turns over responsibility to the computer? Does the examiner use the computer as a word processor to type out a report? Does the psychologist use the computer to generate basic calculations on which to base a report that the psychologist then develops? Or does the psychologist merely enter the basic scores of the WISC–III and obtain an essentially fully written report including interpretation of the data, and perhaps recommendations for the individual who has been evaluated?

The present author would add one final note to this discussion. That is, to the extent that one moves in the direction of the increased utilization of computer interpretation of psychological tests, one may lose her or his own abilities to engage in this kind of interpretive activity. In terms of the general curtailment of mental health services that is evident in society at this time, purchasing and utilizing a computer program for WISC–III interpretation may contribute to the replacement of clinicians with computers as a cost-reduction strategy. The clinician who is making a decision to utilize a computer instead of his or her own brain may be casting a vote in this larger issue.

Chapter Twenty

REVIEWS OF THE WISC-III

S ince the publication of the WISC–III, several reviews of the test have been published (e.g., Carroll, 1993; Kaufman, 1993; Post & Mitchell, 1993). Consistent with the concept of the gradient which has been discussed in this book, these reviews appear to vary along a continuum from those that are largely positive in evaluating the WISC–III (e.g., Kaufman, 1993) to those that are significantly more negative (e.g., Carroll, 1993) in their comments about the test.

One of the broadest criticisms regarding the test is that written by Carroll (1993). He focuses on the issue of what latent traits are measured by the subtests of the WISC–III. Carroll reviews and then critiques the factor analyses presented in the WISC–III manual (Wechsler, 1991), since Wechsler (1991) does not discuss the commonalities and specificities of the scales in the various analyses, while Carroll contends that clinical use of a test such as the WISC–III must be based on a knowledge of the specificity of each scale.

Carroll (1993) notes that the factor analyses presented by Wechsler (1991) neglect the fact that the factors, when subjected to oblique simple structural rotations, are correlated, a quality of factors which Carroll (1993) in his own work deals with statistically. He also notes that the WISC–III was actually not designed for a factor-analytic strategy since the various factors it may reflect are not represented by multiple measures, which is necessary to justify a factor-analytic approach to a test.

Carroll (1993) goes on to conclude that based on his evaluation of the test, the factorial structure of the WISC–III shows relatively little improvement over its predecessors, and he questions the computations that lead to the Verbal, Performance, and Full Scale IQs, as well as the computations that lead to the four Index scores, particularly those of Freedom from Distractibility and Processing Speed. Discussing the WISC–III in the context of a more comprehensive view of cognitive abilities, Carroll (1993) notes that with the knowledge available currently, it would have been possible to produce a test similar to the WISC–III but which more adequately reflected the diversity of individuals' cognitive abilities.

In a similar vein, Sternberg (1993) notes that if one compared the rate of technological change in the industry that creates and publishes psychological tests to the rate of technological change in any other industry, testing companies may well come in "dead last." Comparing the WISC–III to a third version of the first electronic digital computer, Sternberg (1993) essentially asserts that the WISC–III represents recycling of old concepts rather than any new invention whatsoever.

Sternberg (1993) notes Gardner's (1983) theory of multiple intelligences as an example of contemporary theorizing about intelligence, and states that the WISC–III does measure some aspects of linguistic, logical-mathematical, and spatial intelligences, but little or nothing of such kinds of intelligence as musical, bodily-kinesthetic, interpersonal or intrapersonal. Citing his own triarchic theory of human intelligence (Sternberg, 1985b), Sternberg (1993) notes that although some of the WISC–III subtests (e.g., Digit Span, Arithmetic, and some Performance subtests) provide measures of working memory, the scale provides poor measures of synthetic-creative and practical contextual abilities, and he asserts that one could do quite well on the WISC–III without a "drop" of creative intelligence.

Sternberg (1993) points out that if one is looking for a test of new constructs in intelligence, or even simply a new test, she or he should look elsewhere. Still, Sternberg (1993) points out that the WISC–III, as other currently used tests, does an excellent job in measuring intelligence as it is traditionally defined in psychometric theory. Further, tests of this sort do provide fairly good predictions of academic performance, and they are also somewhat valid for predicting job performance.

Although noting the value of such tests as the WISC–III because school psychologists are familiar with their administration and interpretation, Sternberg (1993) states their drawbacks: they do not measure what some modern theorists consider to be important aspects of intelligence; the test problems are decontextualized, that is, removed from ordinary problems found in everyday life; and examinees have little opportunity to display the unique qualities that make them who they are.

Edwards and Edwards (1993), on the other hand, express a generally positive view of the WISC–III. They briefly compare the WISC–R and the WISC–III, noting, for example, that 73% of the WISC–R items have been retained for the WISC–III in original or in only slightly modified form (Wechsler, 1991), and that order of subtest administration has changed slightly. They also review such features of the WISC–III as administration time, normative data, subtest floors and ceilings and item gradients, as well as the test's reliability and validity.

Edwards and Edwards (1993) conclude that the WISC–III is a well-constructed and standardized test for the assessment of the intellectual ability of children and adolescents. They note that reliability is satisfactory although repeated administrations in a short period of time would reflect practice effects. They state that the validity of the test also appears satisfactory although they recommend caution in interpreting factor scores, and lastly, they note that use of the WISC–III to plan intervention strategies and/or to diagnose neuropsychological impairment is questionable in view of the lack of research support for the test's treatment validity, and the fact that research does not support the validity of profile analysis.

Post and Mitchell (1993), in their review of the WISC–III, note that the test's updated norms, sound psychometric properties, and modern packaging combine to make it a state-of-the-art intelligence test. A major focus of their review, however, is on the reported decline in students' WISC–III Verbal, Performance, and Full Scale IQs when compared to their previous WISC–R IQ scores. Post and Mitchell (1993) cite several recent studies (e.g., Dumont & Faro, 1993) whose results indicate more substantial declines in students' WISC–III scores compared to their WISC–R scores than those reported in the Wechsler (1991) manual.

Post and Mitchell (1993) note that this marked decline in student scores from WISC–R to WISC–III will have a noteworthy impact on special educators, administrators, parents and children since the significant lowering of test scores will affect the relationship between a child's ability and achievement, will result in many changes in the labelling and classification of children, and will thus result in changes in children's eligibility for resource assistance and access to special programs. Despite these concerns, Post and Mitchell (1993) express a generally positive and supportive view regarding the WISC–III and feel that practitioners will ultimately benefit from endorsing this test during its transition years.

Kaufman's (1993) review of the WISC–III discusses the nature of a variety of changes from the WISC–R to the WISC–III, summarizing the changes and then evaluating the changes which have been made. The changes Kaufman reviews include new items and artwork; elimination of items with clinical content; modifications aimed at improving subtest reliabilities; increased emphasis on speed of responding; new standardization with a more complete definition of ethnicity; inclusion of a comprehensive section on validity; and addition of new supplementary subtest and four-factor system of interpretation.

Of the several changes Kaufman (1993) discusses, three are noteworthy. First, he states that as part of the restructuring of the WISC–III subtests, items with clinical or provocative emotional content were removed or modified. While the advantage of this strategy is that some children might have gotten such items wrong because of their emotional response to the item, this approach seems a disservice to Wechsler's most strongly held views of the Wechsler scales as clinical instruments, able to provide the clinician with unique information about the examinee and his or her response to emotionally stimulating material.

Second, Kaufman (1993) notes that a number of changes in the test were made presumably to enhance subtest reliabilities (e.g., increasing the number of items on several subtests). However, despite the publisher's thoughtful and thorough approach to this issue, these efforts failed to accomplish their goal: the reliability and stability coefficients did not increase. In fact, while split-half reliability coefficients remained constant from the WISC–R to the WISC–III, stability coefficients frequently declined. Thus a majority of WISC–III subtests—three Verbal and four Performance—are below an acceptable cutoff for stability coefficients. The major implication of this observation is that one must use extreme caution when interpreting profile fluctuations.

Third, Kaufman notes that speed of problem solving takes on much greater significance for the WISC–III than for the WISC–R or WAIS–R in that bonus points are now given for rapid, accurate solutions on six Arithmetic problems, and three bonus points per item are provided for the Picture Arrangement subtest. This emphasis on speed, as with the change in item clinical content, is contrary to Wechsler's own approach, as when he revised the WISC and WAIS he wanted to make the Picture Arrangement subtest a task which measured problem-solving ability.

Kaufman (1993) notes that it is hard for an individual to do well on the WISC–III if he or she does not solve problems very quickly, and thus the impact of problem-solving speed on an individual's WISC–III IQ is substantial. This means that children with reflective cognitive styles, children with learning disabilities, and those with even minor coordination problems will all be penalized on highly speeded items.

Despite these and his other concerns, Kaufman (1993) states that overall, the WISC–III is a "technically superior instrument." He feels the test items are attractive and well-constructed, the standardization is nearly perfect, and the manual provides comprehensive data on the test's reliability and validity. The reliability and stability coefficients range from adequate to excellent for the IQ and index scores, while they are less impressive for the subtests, and Kaufman (1993) notes that the low stability coefficients present a significant concern for profile analysis.

Kaufman (1993) also notes that tables for interpreting the WISC–III scores are extremely helpful and well presented. However, he notes that interpretation may be compromised by the publisher's decision to eliminate most of the items with clinical content and to increase greatly the role of speed of responding in determining a child's IQ; even the new subtest and Processing Speed factor focus on speed.

The present author's views of the WISC–III have been included throughout the current volume. The author agrees with some of the conceptual criticisms put forth by Sternberg (1993) in terms of the overall nature of the

WISC–III. Similarly, Kaufman's (1993) comments regarding the stability coefficients are important to note, particularly since they are made by the major advocate of profile analysis, when many others (e.g., Kavale & Forness, 1984, 1994; Naglieri & Das, 1990) have been highly critical of this approach. The issues regarding whether the test can be interpreted as a four-factor instrument or not remains to be determined (Kaufman, 1993; Sattler, 1992).

In addition, the present author is concerned with the reliability and validity of the third and fourth factors (Freedom from Distractibility and Processing Speed) since each of these factors is based on only two subtests. Questions regarding the psychometric properties of these tests themselves, as well as their relationship to external criteria, are likely to be unresolved for years to come, if they are ever actually resolved satisfactorily during the life of the WISC–III.

Although the statistical and psychometric properties of the WISC–III and the presentation of this information in the manual are both impressive, the present author believes that the WISC–III should have been standardized in a variety of settings and with a number of different examiner-examinee seating arrangements. As with the old saying about form following function, this would have allowed clinicians to feel more comfortable in using the test in ways they very likely have in the past and will in the future, regardless of what the WISC–III manual states. In view of the author's concern with spatial relations in clinical situations, he feels that it is inappropriate for the examiner to be required to sit directly across the table from a young child or an adolescent of either sex when the child may have a known or an unknown history of abuse and thus may experience significant interpersonal anxiety in the testing situation.

From the standpoint of use of the WISC–III in a clinical setting with a real examinee, the author feels the WISC–III has many drawbacks. The crackback manual seems far less user friendly than an easel design manual, and the Wechsler manual should have a friction surface for those examiners who would rather keep it on their laps than on the desk. It seems also that the pages in the manual do not lie properly so that they curl and become misaligned when the manual is kept in the test case.

The front page of the test booklet contains space for extensive information, but the author wonders if this is all useful to the examiner. On the upper left of the front of the test booklet, it would have been wiser to recast the subtest scores into the familiar verbal and performance grouping; this would have required little effort on the part of the examiner in transposing raw scores from each subtest to the front of the record form, and then the scores would be in the verbal and performance grouping so familiar to psychologists.

In addition, since the publisher has integrated so much of Kaufman's (1979a, 1990) profile analysis approach into the WISC–III manual, it might have been reasonable to include space for such a strategy on the front of the WISC–III form, perhaps in place of the graph which appears on the lower right of the page.

As noted elsewhere in this book, the author does not believe the inside front cover of the test booklet is a place where data about the examinee is easily recorded. Typically, the examiner would make brief notes about the examinee where the significant behavior occurs and is observed, during each subtest. Hence the form should have been designed to accommodate this strategy if it was intended to provide room for examiner notes on child behavior or functioning.

The specific bit of information the examiner would need during each subtest—i.e., the discontinue criterion—should have been color-coded so the examiner can obtain this information with a quick glance while administering a given subtest. And the discontinue criterion should be on both pages for those subtests (Vocabulary and Comprehension) that span two pages. The visual design of the Arithmetic subtest makes tracking of what item one is on difficult for the examiner. The design would be improved if there was a vertical white space between the two halves of the subtest (Items 1–12 and Items 13–24).

The Object Assembly shield is awkward to use, and the Object Assembly materials are so thin that they make the task more complicated and difficult for some children who want to fit the pieces together carefully.

Nonetheless, the WISC–III has many positive features. The test's careful standardization, the efforts of the publisher to avoid bias in its construction, and the careful attention which was paid to the test's psychometric properties do make it a useful clinical instrument. The use of color on the materials, the enlargement of the stimuli used in the test, and the test's basic design, organizational and administrative continuity with its predecessors also facilitate clinicians' acceptance of the test and their ability to make the WISC–III a cornerstone of their test armamentarium, which it is likely to be for many years to come.

Part VII
CONCLUDING COMMENT

Chapter Twenty-One

CONCLUDING COMMENT

In the present volume, the author has discussed a variety of aspects of the WISC–III which are relevant to the clinical use and interpretation of this instrument. The author has attempted to place the use of the test in a number of contexts, including an ethical framework for the psychological testing of children and adolescents, the historical background and development of the WISC–III, and the test's statistical and psychometric properties.

The author has also attempted to present several concepts which he feels are relevant not only to the use of the WISC–III but to many aspects of clinical work. These concepts, of context, path, and belief, are felt to apply to the activities of psychologists whether they are engaged in the psychological testing of a child, consultation to an organization, or an effort at psychotherapeutic intervention with an individual or family.

The author holds that most human behavior occurs in some context which provides meaning for the behavior, and the examiner using the WISC–III should always be aware of the context within which he or she utilizes the test in the assessment of a given individual. Similarly, the author contends that life is made up of a number of paths that individuals travel. The path may be chosen for or by the individual and once selected, the individual moves along that path through a particular set of experiences toward or to some goal or endpoint. The present volume has attempted to provide a variety of paths for the examiner to consider and to choose from in her or his use of the WISC–III in a clinical setting.

Lastly, the author has attempted to make the point that a great deal of human behavior reflects and is dictated by the belief system of the individual. This concept is most relevant to the WISC–III in terms of the polemics regarding whether the test is or should be interpretable as a four-factor instrument as suggested by Wechsler (1991), or from a three-factor perspective as recommended by Sattler (1992), and whether profile analysis of the WISC–III is appropriate (Kaufman, 1979a, 1990; Sattler, 1992) or inappropriate (Kavale & Forness, 1984, 1994; McDermott et al., 1990). It is the present author's contention that each examiner should be aware of the fact that his or her own belief system and the criteria she or he uses for acting will be critically involved in the decision he or she makes regarding whether to use the three- or four-factor model and whether or not to use profile analysis in the interpretation of the WISC–III.

Beyond this, however, the clinician's belief system will determine the way she or he approaches the decision-making process, whether it is to accept the three- or four-factor model, profile analysis, or to decide on some other aspect of his or her clinical work. Hence, the clinician must always examine the nature of the beliefs that underlie all of her or his clinical decisions.

In addition to the above concepts, the present book has discussed the relevance of several basic models which are felt to be valuable in the use of the WISC–III but also in clinical work more broadly. It is the author's view that these models, the gradient, non-gradient, hierarchy, and system are pertinent conceptual tools whether one is administering the WISC–III or involved in almost any kind of psychological work, whether its intent is assessment, consultation, or treatment. It has been one purpose of the present volume to introduce these conceptual models as they apply to the clinical use of the WISC–III at the same time that the reader may be able to see their value for other aspects of his or her clinical work (e.g., Cooper, 1991).

Perhaps a major model of the current volume has been to analogize testing of the child to a brief term therapy encounter. The purpose of this is to place testing in the context of other clinical activities in which the focus of the interaction is the client him- or herself. Viewed from within this framework, the clinician has a relationship with the child or adolescent being tested, much as with any client that might be seen for counseling or psychotherapy. Hence the testing should be translated into information that is meaningful for the examinee, and the person most able to do this is the examiner, and the most propitious time to do it may be at the time of testing itself. Approached this way, the testing situation, instead of one involving mechanical drudgery, may become one of significant engagement between the examiner and child or adolescent, with an outcome that may immediately translate into a beginning change process for the examinee, which is presumed the ultimate purpose of the assessment enterprise.

Psychological Testing and Public Health

Public health is a discipline which involves a set of strategies aimed at understanding and improving the healthful behavior and health status of populations. There are many aspects to a public health approach, but major features of this view rest on epidemiology, defined as the investigation of the distribution and determinants of disease in human populations (MacMahon & Pugh, 1970). In adopting a public health approach to a problem, the incidence and prevalence of a particular disorder is estimated; the potential or actual causes of the condition are determined and explored; and strategies are devised which will remediate or reduce the factors which increase the disease or its risk in the population of concern.

As the United States moves into the decade of the 1990s, it has become clear that a major risk to the youth of the nation lies in various forms of child maltreatment (Newberger, 1991). These risks involve neglect, as well as physical and sexual abuse of children, and a number of investigations over the last 30 years have documented the prevalence of various kinds of child maltreatment (e.g., Gelles, 1980; Gil, 1970).

Reports of child sexual abuse have shown an over 300% increase during the 1980s (National Center on Child Abuse and Neglect, 1988). Finkelhor (1991) reports that surveys of adults regarding past experience estimate that from 6 to 62 percent of women and from 2 to 15 percent of men have experienced childhood sexual abuse, with the peak ages of vulnerability appearing to be between 9 and 12 although as many as 25 percent of abuse incidents occur before the child is eight years of age.

Estimates indicate that for both children and adolescents these kinds of maltreatment have been on the increase in recent years (Council on Scientific Affairs, American Medical Association, 1993) and it seems likely that they will continue to increase for the foreseeable future. Aside from the adverse effects of childhood abuse experience on the child's subsequent social development and functioning (e.g., Hernandez, Lodico, & DeClemente, 1993; Kendall-Tackett, Williams, & Finkelhor, 1993), the potential for transmission of the human immunodeficiency virus to sexually abused children (Gutman, Herman-Giddens, & McKinney, 1993; Hanson, 1993) makes the early discovery of sexual abuse in children even more critical.

Related to the problem of child maltreatment is the increase in violent and antisocial behavior among youth themselves (Loeber, 1990) which also appears to be increasing in recent history. This means that individuals are engaging in antisocial activity at younger ages, and thus young children are increasingly the perpetrators rather than only the victims of violent behavior.

A number of organizations in the United States share in efforts to deal with these problems since child maltreatment has profound effects on children's present functioning and has major implications for the kinds of adults and parents these young people will become (Kendell-Tackett et al., 1993). The American Psychological Association, particularly divisions dealing with children, youth and families; the American Psychiatric Association; the American Public Health Association; the National Association of Social Workers; the American Academy of Pediatrics; the National Association of School Psychologists; and the American Association for the Prevention of Child Abuse and Neglect are perhaps a few of the major national organizations involved in efforts to deal with the problems of child maltreatment and with the problems of youthful antisocial behavior.

Each of these organizations utilizes its own preferred methods for approaching the problem. One of the major public health strategies used in attempts to combat problems that befall a population is the concept of screening (Mayrent, 1987). This fundamentally involves an effort to locate individuals who are at risk for a particular disorder, or else to discover early in the development of the disorder those individuals who have been exposed to its presumed etiological factor. The strategies used for establishing screening programs have an extensive conceptual base, organizational structure, and set of criteria of their own (Mayrent, 1987; Silber, 1987). However, screening strategies typically involve the determination of an appropriate target population for applying some screening device; the application of that screening method; and the further evaluation or treatment of those individuals who are determined by the screen to have particular risk factors or who suffer from the disorder.

The present volume proposes that this public health perspective should be integrated with the occasion of psychological assessment. The author had hoped that the WISC–III itself could be used as a screening device to determine which examinee had experienced past trauma. In view of the frequent utilization of the Wechsler with child populations (e.g., Archer et al., 1991; Goh et al., 1981), it would be a truly significant contribution if patterns of intellectual test performance could indicate whether a child was currently experiencing a particular trauma or else had undergone significant trauma in her or his past.

In terms of investigations of patterns of intellectual test performance relevant to this question, as reviewed in earlier sections of this book, there have been a variety of efforts over the years to utilize the Wechsler scales to identify or diagnose a number of childhood characteristics, including psychopathological conditions.

Several studies have focused on children's intellectual performance as a function of their psychological condition or factors which might bear on a child's psychological state. For example, Kaplan et al. (1987) report an investigation of the intellectual performance of 41 children (aged 7 to 19) who had at least one parent who had at one time had a diagnosis of major depression.

Among their sample of children, the authors investigated VIQ–PIQ discrepancies, individual subtest scatter, discrepancies between the Freedom from Distractibility factor and the Full Scale IQ, and a pattern which Saccuzzo and Lewandowski (1976) proposed as characteristic of emotional disturbance: the Information subtest score as lowest or second lowest on the verbal scale, and the Similarities subtest score as the highest or second highest verbal subtest.

Kaplan et al. (1987) found that as compared to a control group, children with one or two depressed parents displayed impaired intellectual performance on the WISC–R in terms of subtest variability (having three or more subtests deviating by 3 or more scaled-score points from the child's own mean subtest score) and on the pattern of low Information-high Similarities. The children's intellectual performance was not found to vary as a function of the children's own psychiatric diagnoses. The authors hypothesized that the observed intellectual deficits might be the result of alterations in the quality of parenting provided to these children by their depressed parents.

Hale and Landino (1981) carried out a discriminant function analysis with 11 WISC–R subtest scores of 100 Caucasian males between the ages of 6 and 16 who displayed conduct problems, withdrawal problems, mixed problems and no problems. Using the identified discriminant functions to categorize the children into their appropriate disorder group, one out of every three children was categorized incorrectly, leading Hale and Landino (1981) to conclude that WISC–R subtest scores do not provide a reliable index for classifying children's psychopathological status.

Hodges and Plow (1990) investigated the intellectual functioning of a sample of 76 hospitalized children (50 boys and 26 girls) with an average age of 10, focusing on variation of WISC–R performance as a function of psychiatric diagnosis. The children were diagnosed as having conduct disorder, oppositional disorder, depression, or anxiety disorder (although children could have multiple diagnoses). These authors found a relative deficit in verbal abilities for conduct-disordered children, which parallelled findings that had been previously reported for adolescent delinquents (Culbertson, Feral, and Gabby, 1989; Moffitt, Gabrielli, Mednick, & Schulsinger, 1981). Hodges and Plow (1990) also found that anxiety-disordered children had a significantly lower Full Scale IQ than did children without an anxiety disorder. Children with depression or oppositional disorder did not display significant variations in intellectual performance.

In the further analysis of their data, Hodges and Plow (1990) calculated scores for the anxiety-disordered children on the ACID profile (Prifitera & Dersh, 1993) and on the four Bannatyne categories (Bannatyne, 1974). Hodges and Plow (1990) found significant main effects for Bannatyne's sequencing category and for the ACID profile, indicating that anxiety-disordered children performed more poorly than non-anxiety-disordered children on WISC–R subtests that have traditionally been associated with learning disabilities or attentional problems.

Zimet, Zimet, Farley, and Adler (1994) report their effort to replicate Hodges and Plow's (1990) investigation. Zimet et al. (1994) studied 178 children, average age 9.7 years, who were in either an inpatient or day-hospital setting, and these authors categorized their subjects into the same four diagnostic groups as Hodges and Plow (1990): conduct disorders, oppositional disorders, depressed disorders, and anxiety disorders. Using Multiple Analysis of Variance to analyze each of the four diagnostic groups, Zimet et al. (1994) found no significant differences in intellectual performance for their study sample between children with and those without a particular disorder. These authors concluded that their results confirmed Hale and Landino's (1981) findings that WISC–R scores do not provide a reliable tool for discriminating among emotional disorders in school-age children.

Focusing on the effects of specific psychosocial stressors on children's aptitude and achievement test performance, Plante et al. (1993) report an investigation of the records of 100 children (61 males and 39 females) who had been referred for diagnostic testing to a multidisciplinary child outpatient facility during 1989–1990. The investigators focused on demographic information about their subjects (e.g., history of parental separation/divorce, physical and/or sexual abuse) as well as the children's scores on the Wechsler Intelligence Scale for Children-Revised and the Woodcock-Johnson Test-Revised which had been administered to them. The researchers also used the DSM–III–R (American Psychiatric Association, 1987) Axis IV, the "Severity of Psychosocial Stressors" scale to provide an operational definition of each child's stress, and Axis V, the current "Global Assessment of Functioning" scale as an index of the adequacy of the child's coping abilities.

Plante et al. (1993) report a number of significant findings in their investigation. For example, overall stress as reflected in DSM–III–R Axis IV scores was significantly associated with the Freedom from Distractibility factor of the WISC–R ($r = -.27, p < .01$). The specific stress of physical and/or sexual abuse was significantly associated with the Verbal Comprehension ($r = -.37, p < .01$) and Freedom from Distractibility ($r = -.36, p < .01$) factors. The stress of parental separation or divorce was significantly associated with the Verbal Comprehension ($r = -.30, p < .01$) and the Perceptual Organization ($r = -.21, p < .05$) factors of the WISC–R.

Adequacy of children's coping abilities, as reflected in the DSM–III–R Axis V scores, was significantly associated with the Verbal Comprehension ($r = .26, p < .05$), Perceptual Organization ($r = .41, p < .01$), and Freedom from Distractibility ($r = .40, p < .01$) factors of the WISC–R. Thus both general and specific stressors as well as children's coping abilities were found to correlate significantly with their WISC–R performances.

Hence, although there have been some positive findings regarding the relationship between parental functioning, psychiatric diagnosis, or past trauma and the intellectual functioning of children, there does not appear to be any specific pattern or set of signs reported that would permit an examiner to identify a given child as having had a past traumatic experience, or having a particular psychiatric diagnosis based on the child's Wechsler test performance. And certainly, the criticisms of various kinds of Wechsler pattern and profile analyses (Kavale & Forness, 1984, 1994) indicate that such an approach would be unproductive.

On the other hand, it is possible to conceptualize the event of psychological testing as providing an opportunity for the screening of the child's status on those variables that place children at risk for untoward development. This view places the examiner in the role of a public health professional and makes the focus of any intellectual assessment twofold: (1) the evaluation of the particular child's intellectual functioning; and (2) the consideration of whether the examinee may have been or is being exposed to a significant psychosocial risk, or whether the child is exposing someone else to such a risk.

Intellectual assessment is perhaps the most frequent form of all psychological testing (Archer et al., 1991), which means that the psychological assessment of children and adolescents, or the intellectual evaluation of individuals of this age range, provides a naturally occurring opportunity for a trained mental health professional to interact with a member of the population at risk.

In addition, since not every child in the school-age population is selected for formal individual assessment, any child who is chosen for an intellectual (individual) evaluation may be assumed to have come from a subpopulation, and although one may question the precision of child maltreatment data or the relationship of child maltreatment to other child categorizations (Council on Scientific Affairs, AMA, 1993; Newberger, 1991), it is felt that individuals in these subpopulations (e.g., those displaying learning or behavior problems) may be at higher risk for the factors of child maltreatment than the general population of school-age children.

From within the framework proposed by the present author, then, psychological assessment and/or testing may be viewed as serving two functions: (1) the assessment of the individual child or adolescent who is being evaluated intellectually; and (2) the use of the testing circumstance as an opportunity to determine whether that child or adolescent has been or is being exposed to a major risk factor for his or her future psychological development or whether the child or adolescent being evaluated is subjecting other individuals to a significant risk. In those cases where the screening indicates that the child or adolescent is at risk or is putting others at risk, the examiner must take appropriate action, which would be to report the findings to a suitable person or agency in order to initiate proper action on behalf of the child or adolescent, or on behalf of others being affected by the child.

Relevant to the issues the author is discussing, Batchelor, Dean, Gridley, and Batchelor (1990) report a study whose purpose was to examine the incidence of child sexual abuse reports to school psychologists and the perceived quality of service provided to child victims, and to survey the usage of child sexual abuse prevention and screening programs as adjunctive school services to address the problem of child sexual abuse.

Batchelor et al. (1990) found that of the 171 usable replies to their survey (62 males and 109 females), those respondents who had had prior child sexual abuse training rated their performances significantly higher than those without training in handling such cases. Based on their findings, Batchelor et al. (1990) suggested that in the future, child sexual abuse training should be part of school psychology graduate programs, while practicing school psychologists who lack a background in child sexual abuse should consider learning about this topic in their continuing education.

Also relevant to this issue are the findings of Sorenson and Snow (1991) who describe their research with over 600 cases of alleged child sexual abuse in which the authors were involved as therapists or evaluators. They note that revelations of child sexual abuse appear preponderantly to involve accidental disclosure with some tendency for adolescents as opposed to younger children to purposefully tell; that revelations ordinarily involve a process including denial, tentative disclosure, then active disclosure, often followed by recanting and ultimate reaffirmation. Sorenson and Snow (1991) note that among primary school-age children who purposefully tell, the influence of educational programs, which stressed assertiveness and personal rights, appeared to be dramatic. One can easily see any discussion with a child at the close of psychological assessment as analogous to the educational programs which Sorenson and Snow (1991) describe.

Finally, the Council on Scientific Affairs (American Medical Association, 1993) notes that screening questions have been effective in identifying cases of sexual abuse among males, since adolescent maltreatment often goes undetected, and self-disclosure is one of the primary ways in which such abuse is revealed for adolescents.

The present author would concur with the recommendations of Batchelor et al. (1990) regarding the importance of training in child sexual abuse or other forms of maltreatment for any psychologist who deals with children. The present author would add to this the idea suggested above: apart from evaluating the examinee's cognitive performance, the examiner may consider three issues during any evaluation: (1) the child being evaluated might be a victim or perpetrator of child maltreatment; (2) the examiner can inquire about and/or provide a definition of child maltreatment for the examinee; and (3) the examiner can remind the child of his or her ability to report such life experience and/or the examiner can specifically screen for such experience in the child with a set of more specifically focused questions. In this way, psychological evaluation of a child can serve the dual purposes of focused assessment of the child's cognition as well as the public health function of case finding.

A Final Note on Intellectual Assessment

This volume has focused on the background and clinical use of the WISC–III in the testing of children and adolescents. And certainly the test can make a valuable contribution to the clinician's assessment of children on the dimension of human functioning which is labelled intelligence. However, it is important to note that the WISC–III may be considered to be a device which measures convergent as opposed to divergent thinking (Guilford, 1967), and in addition, the test is constructed on the assumption that g and four Indices based on Wechsler's (1991) factor analysis adequately explain children's intellectual performance.

But there are certainly alternative ways to think about children's intellect and cognition. These wider perspectives (e.g., Gardner, 1983, 1993; Horn & Hofer, 1992) assert that individuals' cognitive abilities include a number of different capacities for relating to their surroundings effectively. Gardner (1983, 1993) suggests that there are multiple intelligences, and he describes seven different ways in which individuals may demonstrate intelligence: linguistic, logical-mathematical, musical, spatial, bodily-kinesthetic, and two forms of personal intelligence — one directed toward other persons and one directed toward the self.

Similarly, Horn (1988; Horn & Hofer, 1992), in addition to discussing fluid and crystallized intelligence, also notes a number of other kinds of abilities within his model of intelligence. These include visual, auditory, and quantitative forms of intelligence among others. Thus it is vital for the psychologist evaluating a child or adolescent's cognitive functioning to keep in mind that there are many additional frameworks for thinking about an individual's cognitive abilities in addition to those provided by the conceptual and definitional view offered by the WISC–III.

Finally, when one is evaluating a child or adolescent, it is critical to consider the concept of creativity and originality (Sternberg, 1988) as this applies to human cognition, remembering as Sternberg (1993) has said, that "one could do quite well on the WISC–III without a drop of creative intelligence, and with just a few drops of common sense" (p. 162). The examiner must thus be able to recognize the uniqueness of a child's approach to the tasks of an evaluation, and the examiner should remember that although an examinee may not obtain points on the WISC–III for a particular response, that response may indicate the child's potential to see the world from her or his own original and unique perspective, and this potential will be crucial for the child and the society. It is the responsibility of the examiner to have and apply this larger, broader, and more flexible perspective on human behavior whenever he or she evaluates a child's intellectual performance.

APPENDICES

Appendix A.1.

QUESTIONS ASKED OF PUBLISHERS REGARDING WISC–III COMPUTER–INTERPRETATIVE PROGRAMS

1) Is your software for the WISC–III only for use with the WISC–III, or does the software also deal with other tests such as the WAIS–R? If so, what other tests does the software apply to?
2) What data, reliability and validity checks have been used by you to establish your software program?
3) What are the specifications of a computer system which is needed to operate the software?
4) How easy/difficult is it to use the software and how long does it take to process an individual evaluation?
5) What are the specific inputs to the program? What is the specific output from the program?
6) Does your report include behavioral or other statements about the client, or does it involve recommendations for instruction or for other specific evaluations for the client?
7) Does your software for the WISC–III relate scoring or interpretation of the WISC–III to the results of any other test (e.g., WRAT–R)? If yes, to what test(s) does your software relate the WISC–III results and how?
8) What is the cost of the software program you offer for use with the Wechsler Intelligence Scale for Children-III? How many assessments will the software process before needing to be replaced? What do you anticipate the cost for your software program will be in 1994?
9) What are the unique features of your report and what advantages would your report have over other software/reports?
10) Why would an individual in a private practice with a small number of evaluations choose your organization's software?
11) Why would an individual in a school setting involving a large number of evaluations choose your organization's software?
12) What warranty and/or support do you provide to the purchaser of your software program? (e.g., an 800 number for questions).
13) Do you anticipate any revisions or new developments in software for the Wechsler-III that your organization will offer within the next year?

Appendix A.2.

RESPONSES FROM PSYCHOLOGISTICS, INC. REGARDING WISC–III COMPUTER-INTERPRETIVE PROGRAMS

1) The WISC–III® Report program is designed for use with the WISC–III® only. A separate program is available for the WAIS–R.

2) With respect to the programming, Psychologistics, Inc. uses industry models for programming to insure internal consistency, appropriate redundancies, and internal error checking in their code. There is also some external error checking of data entries (e.g., subtest scores must be integers between 1 and 19, so the program does not allow entries outside this range). With respect to the scoring and interpretive tasks of the program, program operations are based on Kaufman's and Sattler's analytical and interpretive approaches. Calculations and interpretive statements are derived from Kaufman and Sattler.

3) Psychologistics, Inc.'s WISC–III® program is available for both IBM and Macintosh computer systems. All IBM versions of this software will run on an IBM–PC, AT, System 2 or any compatible computer, providing the computer system uses DOS 2.0 or later version, has at least 128K RAM, one DSDD disk drive and either a second disk drive or a hard disk, and a compatible printer. All IBM version programs are available on 3.5″ or 5″ disks. All Apple versions of this software will run on the Apple II family of computers providing the system uses DOS 3.3, has at least 48K RAM, one 5″ disk drive, and a compatible printer. A second disk drive or hard disk is needed to write reports to text files. Macintosh versions run on any Macintosh computer as recent as a Macintosh Plus with 1 megabyte (1024K) of memory, and require two 800K floppy disks or a hard drive. Macintosh System software 6.0.5 or later must be installed on the start-up disk of the system.

4) Psychologistics, Inc. describes its programs as quite simple to use, and an evaluation may be processed in 2 to 5 minutes, depending on whether or not the examiner enters behavioral observations and how much one thinks about alternative responses.

5) Users input basic demographic information, subtest scaled scores, and IQ scores. Output is organized into a scoring summary and a narrative report.

6) The report allows the user to enter behavioral observations from the testing session, which are summarized in the narrative report. The user can also indicate relevant special characteristics of the child (e.g., sensory disability) and/or exceptional conditions (e.g., behavior problems in the classroom) from a menu in the program. Recommendations for instruction or further evalua-

tion are made, but they are not highly specific as Psychologistics, Inc. believes that only a trained clinician can make specific recommendations based on a broader data base, the circumstances of testing, and the context and purpose of the evaluation.

7) Psychologistics, Inc.'s program does not relate findings to other tests.

8) The cost of the Psychologistics, Inc.'s WISC–III® Report is $295. This is an unlimited use program and they do not anticipate a price change for 1994.

9) Psychologistics, Inc. states that its program provides a balance of relevant calculations for interpretation with an organized and readable narrative report and that no other WISC–III® program provides such a balanced report. Psychologistics, Inc. also believes the content of its report strikes a balance with respect to specificity. The narrative report, as produced by the program, can stand alone or be written to a text file and easily modified by the user. The program follows a clear analytical and interpretive strategy based on the works of Kaufman and Sattler, and with a little reading, one can trace the derivation of any statement in the narrative report. Psychologistics, Inc. notes they are the oldest developer of microcomputer software for psychologists, marketed the first microcomputer-based software program for the Wechsler (in 1981), and offer the only WISC–III® program for the Macintosh at the time they responded to this question.

10) Psychologistics, Inc. has a relatively equal number of individual and agency users. Individual practitioners like the program because it clearly organizes the scores needed for interpretation, and many like the basic report to which they can add specifics, e.g., on additional tests. Agencies choose the program because it enables them to provide a standardized written summary of test results in a time-effective manner, and the narrative report is used without modification in many school systems.

11) See response to item (10).

12) Psychologistics, Inc. replaces defective programs without charge to the user, even if defects are due to postal handling or user misuse. They also provide a full refund for unsatisfied purchasers, and they provide as much telephone support as users need to use the program, but do not provide an 800 number.

13) Psychologistics, Inc. did not have plans for revisions at the time they responded to these questions.

Appendix A.3.

RESPONSES FROM THE PSYCHOLOGICAL CORPORATION REGARDING WISC-III COMPUTER-INTERPRETIVE PROGRAMS

1) Three instruments are addressed by the product: WISC–III, WIAT, and GATSB. Only the first two instruments having scoring provided. The GATSB is considered a supporting measure to be used only in conjunction with another test. WISC stands for *Wechsler Intelligence Scale for Children*, WIAT for *Wechsler Individual Achievement Test*, and GATSB for *Guide to the Assessment of Test Session Behavior*.

2) The scores provided by the program were thoroughly checked against those in the test manuals. There were three rounds of field testing, considerable hand checking, and electronic comparison of scores to the *Scoring Assistant for the Wechsler Scales* [The Psychological Corporation, 1992].

3) IBM compatible 286 or newer running DOS 3.1 or newer, 640K RAM with 540K available, and # MB of free hard disk space. Mouse, color screen and printer not required but recommended. In late 1995, the Macintosh version will require System 7.5 or newer, 4 MB of RAM or more, 2 MB of hard disk space, and at least a 12-inch monitor or notebook display.

4) The essential information is entered on just one screen: name, gender, dates of birth and test, and raw scores. After filling in these fields, an interpretive report can be printed by pressing just two keys. About two minutes is the typical time required for this. Additional time can be spent filling in the on-screen biographical and psychoeducational questionnaires or editing the final report with the built-in word processor.

5) Required: first name, nickname, last name, gender, date of birth, date of test, and subtest raw or scaled scores. Optional: test site, grade, examiner name, examiner title, examiner license. There is a large number of optional background questions pertaining to biographical and psychoeducational information that is mentioned next.

6) The "background questionnaires" are organized into sections of optional information one can enter by checking off answers about the child. These extensive sections address the reasons for referral, home setting, language skills, developmental history, health and medical history, school program experience and behavioral observations. Information entered into the background sections is blended with test score interpretation to tailor and individualize the reports. Recommendations for instruction are provided in the Clinical Review, an optional report.

7) An ability-achievement discrepancy (A–AD) analysis is calculated for the WISC–III and WIAT where expected achievement levels are contrasted to those obtained. Two optional methods of analysis are available: regression and simple-difference. The user can choose the level of significance or specify a minimal critical difference for A–AD analysis.

8) The 1995 price is $249 for a single license to have unlimited scorings. No network license is available.

9) There are many unique features of this program beyond the fact that it is the only scoring and reporting program published by the creators of the WISC–III. A Parent/Guardian Report, a Tables and Graph Report and an Interpretive Report for WISC–III and WIAT alone or in combination can be printed, exported to a word processor, or displayed on-screen for editing within the program. A unique Clinical Review provides suggestions or recommendations for the examiner to consider when interpreting children's test profiles. The extensive Scrapbooks provide cut-and-paste phrases and statements that can be selected to further individualize reports.

10) Accurate, authoritative, fast reporting, convenient, scoring and word processing in one product, economical.

11) Adaptable to conform to schools' policy for the scoring and reporting. Password security maintains confidentiality of data when more than one psychologist must share a single copy of the program on one computer; also see other reasons above.

12) There is a one-year warranty and unlimited software support available, with an 800 number in the United States and a non-800 number in Canada.

13) A Macintosh edition is being made available in late 1995. A *WAIS–III Writer* is planned following the release of the WAIS–III, and a Windows edition of the *WISC–III Writer* is being considered.

Appendix A.4.

RESPONSES FROM PSYCHOLOGICAL ASSESSMENT RESOURCES, INC. REGARDING WISC–III COMPUTER–INTERPRETIVE PROGRAMS

1) At the time Psychological Assessment Resources, Inc. responded to the author's inquiry, they offered one software product called the *Report Writer: Children's Intellectual and Achievement Tests*. This software produces a comprehensive interpretation for:
   WISC–III/WISC–R
   WRAT–R
   PIAT–R
   WPPSI–R
   K–ABC
   Kaufman Test of Educational Achievement
   Stanford-Binet, 4th Edition
   Woodcock-Johnson Achievement Test-R

2) The respondent to the author's questions indicated that only the originating author could comment on what validity checks were built into the software.

3) IBM PC, XT, AT or compatible with 640K, MS–DOS 2.1 or later, and two disk drives—with one drive a hard drive.

4) Psychological Assessment Resources, Inc. stated that once familiar with the data-entry process, the program is very easy to use. *Report-Writer* has on-screen instructions that guide the user through data entry.

5) *Report Writer* accepts raw and scaled scores; interpretation is based on the scaled scores and the VIQ, PIQ, and FSIQ.

6) *Report Writer* gives the user control over statistical analyses—the user sets significance levels, confidence intervals, and optional grade equivalents. WISC–III/WISC–R analysis offers optional subtest combination scores in deviation quotient form for IQ comparison. Analyze [sic] VIQ/PIQ differences, scatter, measurement error, intellectual and developmental disability ranges, and hypotheses for educational intervention.

7) The respondent indicated "See #1."

8) *Report Writer* is priced at $595.

9) The respondent indicated "see catalog copy attached."

10) The software is fast, powerful, and easy to use. It is extremely cost-effective, as Psychological Assessment Resources, Inc. does not charge a per-use fee. Psychological Assessment Resources, Inc. also features toll-free technical support for all their software products.

11) The respondent indicated "For the same reasons as #10."
12) Unlimited toll-free, no-fee technical support. No-risk guarantee.
13) If and when revisions to software are made, customers are promptly notified. Upgrade fees are traditionally very nominal and very fair for the value of new features added.

REFERENCES

Achenbach, T. M. (1991a). *Manual for the Child Behavior Checklist/4–18 and 1991 Profile.* Burlington, VT: University of Vermont Department of Psychiatry.

Achenbach, T. M. (1991b). *Integrative guide for the 1991 CBCL/4–18, YSR, and TRF profiles.* Burlington, VT: University of Vermont Department of Psychiatry.

Ackerman, P. T., Dykman, R. A., & Peters, J. E. (1971). Children with specific learning disabilities: WISC profiles. *Journal of Learning Disabilities, 4,* 33–49.

Ackerman, P. T., Dykman, R. A., & Peters, J. E. (1976). Hierarchical factor patterns on the WISC as related to areas of learning deficit. *Perceptual and Motor Skills, 42,* 381–386.

Ackerman, P. T., Dykman, R. A., & Peters, J. E. (1977). Learning-disabled boys as adolescents: Cognitive factors and achievement. *Journal of the American Academy of Child Psychiatry, 16,* 296–313.

American Association on Mental Retardation. (1992). *Mental retardation: Definition, classification, and systems of supports* (9th ed.). Washington, DC: American Association of Mental Retardation.

American Educational Research Association, American Psychological Association, & National Council on Measurement in Education. (1985). *Standards for educational and psychological testing.* Washington, DC: American Psychological Association.

American Psychiatric Association. (1980). *Diagnostic and statistical manual of mental disorders* (3rd. ed.). Washington, DC: Author.

American Psychiatric Association. (1987). *Diagnostic and statistical manual of mental disorders* (3rd ed. Rev). Washington, DC: Author.

American Psychiatric Association. (1994). *Diagnostic and statistical manual of mental disorders* (4th ed.). Washington, DC: Author.

American Psychological Association. (1966). Interim standards for automated test scoring and interpretation services. *American Psychologist, 22,* 1141.

American Psychological Association. (1981). Ethical principles of psychologists. *American Psychologist, 36*(6), 633–638.

American Psychological Association. (1985). *Standards for educational and psychological testing.* Washington, DC: Author.

American Psychological Association. (1992). Ethical principles of psychologists and code of conduct. *American Psychologist, 47,* 1597–1611.

Anastasi, A. (1988). *Psychological testing* (6th ed.). New York: Macmillan.

Anderson, M., Kaufman, A. S., & Kaufman, N. L. (1976). Use of the WISC–R with a

401

learning disabled population: Some diagnostic implications. *Psychology in the Schools, 13,* 381–386.

Anthony, J. C., Warner, L. A., & Kessler, R. C. (1994). Comparative epidemiology of dependence on tobacco, alcohol, controlled substances, and inhalants: Basic findings from the national comorbidity survey. *Experimental and Clinical Psychopharmacology, 2,* 244–268.

Applebaum, S. A. (1970). Science and persuasion in the psychological test report. *Journal of Consulting and Clinical Psychology, 35,* 349–355.

Arasim, B., & Frankenberger, W. (1989). Assessment procedures by multidisciplinary team members in the assessment of learning disabilities. *Mental Retardation and Learning Disability Bulletin, 17,* 38–50.

Archer, R. P., Maruish, M., Imhof, E. A., & Piotrowski, C. (1991). Psychological test usage with adolescent clients: 1990 survey findings. *Professional Psychology: Research and Practice, 22*(3), 247–252.

Azar, B. (1994). Psychology's input leads to better tests. *The APA Monitor, 25,* 1, 15.

Bagnato, S. J. (1980). The efficacy of diagnostic reports as individualized guides to prescriptive goal planning. *Exceptional Children, 46,* 554–557.

Baldessarini, R. J. (1990). Drugs and the treatment of psychiatric disorders. In A. G. Gilman, T. W. Rall, A. S. Nies & P. Taylor (Eds.), *Goodman and Gilman's the pharmacological basis of therapeutics* (8th ed., pp. 383–435). New York: Pergamon Press.

Bannatyne, A. (1968). Diagnosing learning disabilities and writing remedial prescriptions. *Journal of Learning Disabilities, 1,* 242–249.

Bannatyne, A. (1971). *Language, reading and learning disabilities.* Springfield, Il: Charles C Thomas.

Bannatyne, A. (1974). Diagnosis: A note on recategorization of the WISC scaled scores. *Journal of Learning Disabilities, 7,* 272–274.

Barkley, R. A. (1977). The effects of methylphenidate on various measures of activity level and attention in hyperkinetic children. *Journal of Abnormal Child Psychology, 5,* 351–369.

Barkley, R. A. (1989). Attention-deficit hyperactivity disorder. In E. J. Mash & R. A. Barkley (Eds.), *Treatment of childhood disorders* (pp. 39–72). New York: The Guilford Press.

Barkley, R. A., Karlsson, J., Strzelecki, E., & Murphy, J. (1984). Effects of age and Ritalin dosage on the mother-child interactions of hyperactive children. *Journal of Consulting and Clinical Psychology, 52,* 750–758.

Barlow, D. H. (1988). *Anxiety and its disorders: The nature and treatment of anxiety and panic.* New York: The Guilford Press.

Baron, J. (1987). Tools for studying human intelligence. *Contemporary Psychology, 32,* 135–136.

Batchelor, E. S., Dean, R. S., Gridley, B., & Batchelor, B. (1990). Reports of child sexual abuse in the schools. *Psychology in the Schools, 27,* 131–137.

Bateson, G. (1972). *Steps to an ecology of mind.* New York: Ballantine.

Bateson, G., Jackson, D. D., Haley, J., & Weakland, J. (1956). Toward a theory of schizophrenia. *Behavioral Science, 1,* 251–264.

Bauman, E. (1991). Determinants of WISC–R subtest stability in children with learning difficulties. *Journal of Clinical Psychology, 47,* 430–435.

Beck, A. T., Rush, A. J., Shaw, B. F., & Emery, G. (1979). *Cognitive therapy of depression.* New York: Guilford Press.

Berrien, K. E. (1968). *General and social systems.* New Brunswick, NJ: Rutgers University Press.

Berry, K. K. (1975). Teacher impressions of psychological reports on children. *Journal of Pediatric Psychology, 3,* 11–14.

Bertalanffy, L. von (1968). *General systems theory.* New York: George Braziller.

Binet, A., & Simon, T. (1916). *The development of intelligence in children* (E. S. Kit, trans.). Baltimore: Williams & Wilkins.

Black, R., & Dana, R. (1977). Examiner sex bias and Wechsler Intelligence Scale for Children scores. *Journal of Consulting and Clinical Psychology, 45,* 500.

Blaha, J., & Vance, H. (1979). The hierarchical factor structure of the WISC–R for learning disabled children. *Learning Disabilities Quarterly, 2,* 71–75.

Blouin, A. G. A., Bornstein, R. A., & Trites, R. L. (1978). Teenage alcohol use among hyperactive children: A five-year follow-up study. *Journal of Pediatric Psychology, 3,* 188–194.

Boll, T. J., & Barth, J. T. (1981). *Neuropsychology of brain damage in children.* In S. B. Filskov & T. J. Boll (Eds.), *Handbook of clinical neuropsychology* (pp. 418–452). New York: Wiley.

Boodoo, G. M., Barona, A., & Ochoa, H. (1988, April). *Factor structure of the WISC–R with an Hispanic learning disabled population.* Paper presented at the 1988 Meetings of the National Council on Measurement in Education, New Orleans.

Bosco, J. J., & Robin, S. S. (1980). Hyperkinesis: Prevalence and treatment. In C. K. Whalen & B. Henker (Eds.), *Hyperactive children* (pp. 173–187). New York: Academic Press.

Boulding, K. E. (1968). General systems theory: The skeleton of science. In W. Buckley (Ed.), *Modern systems research for the behavioral scientist* (pp. 3–10). Chicago: Aldine Publishing.

Bracken, B. (1993). Editor's comments. *Journal of Psychoeducational Assessment, Monograph Series, Advances in Psychoeducational Assessment, Wechsler Intelligence Scale for Children: Third edition,* 4–5.

Bracken, B. A., & Fagan, T. K. (1988). Abilities assessed by the K–ABC Mental Processing subtests: The perceptions of practitioners with varying degrees of experience. *Psychology in the Schools, 25,* 22–34.

Bracken, B. A., & Fagan, T. K. (1990). Guest editors' introduction to the conference "Intelligence: Theories and practice." *Journal of Psychoeducational Assessment, 8,* 221–222.

Bracken, B. A., McCallum, S., & Crain, R. M. (1993). WISC–III subtest composite reliabilities and specificities: Interpretive aids. *Journal of Psychoeducational Assessment, Monograph Series, Advances in Psychoeducational Assessment, Wechsler Intelligence Scale for Children: Third Edition,* 22–34.

Bradbury, P., Wright, S. D., Walker, C. E., & Ross, J. M. (1975). Performance on the

WISC as a function of sex of E, sex of S, and age of S. *Journal of Psychology, 90,* 51–55.

Braden, J. P., & Weiss, L. (1988). Effects of simple difference versus regression discrepancy methods: An empirical study. *Journal of School Psychology, 26,* 133–142.

Bradley, F., Hanna, G., & Lucas, M. (1980). The reliability of scoring the WISC–R. *Journal of Consulting and Clinical Psychology, 48,* 530–531.

Bradley, W. (1937). The behavior of children receiving Benzedrine. *American Journal of Psychiatry, 94,* 577–585.

Brakal, S. J., Parry, J., & Weiner, B. A. (1985). *The mentally disabled and the law.* Chicago, Il: American Bar Foundation.

Brannigan, G. (1975). Scoring difficulties on the Wechsler intelligence scales. *Psychology in the Schools, 12,* 313–314.

Brannigan, G. G., & Ash, T. (1977). Social judgment in conceptually impulsive and reflective children. *Psychological Reports, 41,* 466.

Brentar, J., & McNamara, J. R. (1991a). The right to prescribe medication: Considerations for professional psychology. *Professional Psychology: Research and Practice, 22,* 179–187.

Brentar, J., & McNamara, J. R. (1991b). Prescription privileges for psychologists: The next step in its evolution as a profession. *Professional Psychology: Research and Practice, 22,* 194–195.

Bridgeman, B., Strang, H. R., & Buttram, J. (1974). Game versus test instructions for the WISC. *Journal of Educational Measurement, 11,* 285–288.

Brody, N. (1985). The validity of tests of intelligence. In B. Wolman (Ed.), *Handbook of intelligence* (pp. 353–389). New York: John Wiley.

Brown, R. T., & Borden, K. A. (1989). Neuropsychological effects of stimulant medication on children's learning and behavior. In C. R. Reynolds & E. Fletcher-Janzen (Eds.), *Handbook of clinical child neuropsychology* (pp. 443–474). New York: Plenum Press.

Brown, S. W., Hwang, M. T., Baron, M., & Yakimowski, M. E. (1991). Factor analysis of responses to the WISC–R for gifted children. *Psychological Reports, 69*(1), 99–107.

Brown, S. W., & Yakimowski, M. E. (1987). Intelligence scores of gifted students on the WISC–R. *Gifted Child Quarterly, 31*(3), 130–134.

Browning, D. L., & Quinlan, D. M. (1985). Ego development and intelligence in a psychiatric population: Wechsler subtest scores. *Journal of Personality Assessment, 49,* 260–263.

Brumback, R. A., & Staton, R. D. (1980). Neuropsychological study of children during and after remission of endogenous depressive episodes. *Perceptual and Motor Skills, 50,* 1163–1167.

Bruner, J. S., Goodnow, J. J., & Austin, G. A. (1956). *A study of thinking.* New York: John Wiley & Sons.

Buckhalt, J. A. (1990). Attributional comments of experienced and novice examiners during intelligence testing. *Journal of Psychoeducational Assessment, 8,* 478–484.

Budman, S. L., & Gurman, A. S. (1988). *Theory and practice of brief therapy.* New York: Guilford Press.

Butcher, J. N. (1993). Using computer-based clinical reports: Pitfalls to avoid. In B. Schlosser & K. L. Moreland (Eds.), *Taming technology: Issues, strategies and resources for the mental health practitioner* (pp. 92–94). Phoenix, AZ: Division of Independent Practice of the American Psychological Association.

Cadwell, J., & English, F. (1983, April). *The effect of learning disabilities on the factor structure of the WISC-R: A test of factorial invariance.* Paper presented at the meetings of the American Educational Research Association, Montreal.

Campbell, D. T., & Fiske, D. W. (1959). Convergent and discriminant validation by the multitrait-multimethod matrix. *Psychological Bulletin, 56,* 81–105.

Canino, I. A., & Spurlock, J. (1994). *Culturally diverse children and adolescents: Assessment, diagnosis, and treatment.* New York: Guilford Press.

Carlson, L. C., Reynolds, C. R., & Gutkin, T. B. (1983). Consistency of the factorial validity of the WISC–R for upper and lower SES groups. *Journal of School Psychology, 21,* 319–326.

Carroll, J. B. (1988). Cognitive abilities, factors and processes. *Intelligence, 12,* 101–109.

Carroll, J. B. (1989). Factor analysis since Spearman: Where do we stand? What do we know? In R. Kanfer, P. L. Ackerman, & R. Cudeck (Eds.), *Abilities, motivation, and methodology: The Minnesota symposium on learning and individual differences* (pp. 43–67). Hillsdale, NJ: Erlbaum.

Carroll, J. B. (1993). What abilities are measured by the WISC–III? *Journal of Psychoeducational Assessment, Monograph Series, Advances in Psychoeducational Assessment, Wechsler Intelligence Scale for Children: Third Edition,* 134–143.

Cattell, R. B. (1941). Some theoretical issues in adult intelligence testing. *Psychological Bulletin, 38,* 592 (Abstract).

Cattell, R. B. (1957). *Personality and motivation structure and measurement.* Yonkers-on-Hudson, NY: World Book.

Cattell, R. B. (1971). *Abilities: Their structure, growth and action.* Boston: Houghton-Mifflin.

Cepeda, M. L. (1989). Nonstimulant psychotropic medication. In C. R. Reynolds & E. Fletcher-Janzen (Eds.), *Handbook of clinical child neuropsychology* (pp. 475–485). New York: Plenum Press.

Chadwick, O., Rutter, M., Thompson, J., & Shaffer, D. (1981). Intellectual performance and reading skills after localized head injury in childhood. *Journal of Child Psychology and Psychiatry, 22,* 117–139.

Chan, D. W. (1984). Factor analysis of the HK–WISC at 11 age levels between 5 and 15 years. *Journal of Consulting and Clinical Psychology, 52,* 482–483.

Clair, D., & Prendergast, D. (1994). Brief psychotherapy and psychological assessments: Entering a relationship, establishing a focus, and providing feedback. *Professional Psychology: Research and Practice, 25,* 46–49.

Clarizio, H., & Bernard, R. (1981). Recategorized WISC–R scores of learning disabled children and differential diagnosis. *Psychology in the Schools, 18,* 5–12.

Clark, H. H., & Clark, E. V. (1977). *Psychology and language.* New York: Harcourt Brace Jovanovich.

Cleary, T. A., Humphreys, L. G., Kendrick, S. A., & Wesman, A. (1975). Educational uses of tests with disadvantaged students. *American Psychologist, 30,* 15–41.

Cohen, J. (1957). The factorial structure of the WAIS between early adulthood and old age. *Journal of Consulting Psychology, 21,* 283–290.

Cohen, J. (1959). The factorial structure of the WISC at ages 7–16, 10–6, and 13–6. *Journal of Consulting Psychology, 23,* 285–299.

Committee on Professional Standards and Committee on Psychological Tests and Assessment. (1986). *Guidelines for computer-based tests and interpretations.* Washington, DC: American Psychological Association.

Conger, A. J., Conger, J. C., Farrell, A. D., & Ward, D. (1979). What can the WISC–R measure? *Applied Psychological Measurement, 3,* 421–436.

Conner, R., & Woodall, F. (1983). The effects of experience and structured feedback on WISC–R error rates made by student-examiners. *Psychology in the Schools, 20,* 376–379.

Conners, C. K., & Taylor, E. (1980). Pemoline, methylphenidate, and placebo in children with minimal brain dysfunction. *Archives of General Psychiatry, 37,* 922–930.

Connolly, A. J. (1988). *KeyMath, Revised manual.* North Tonawanda, NY: Multi-Health Systems.

Cooper, S. (1982). *The clinical use and interpretation of the Wechsler Intelligence Scale for Children-Revised.* Springfield, Illinois: Charles C Thomas.

Cooper, S. (1991). The gradient in psychotherapy. *Behavior Therapist, 14,* 109–110.

Council on Scientific Affairs, American Medical Association. (1993). Adolescents as victims of family violence. *Journal of the American Medical Association, 270* (15), 1850–1856.

Craik, F. I. M. (1977). Age differences in human memory. In J. E. Birren & K. W. Schaie (Eds.), *Handbook of the psychology of aging.* Princeton, N.J.: Van Nostrand-Reinhold.

Crano, W. D., Denny, D. A., & Campbell, D. T. (1972). Does intelligence cause achievement? A cross-lagged panel analysis. *Journal of Educational Psychology, 63,* 258–275.

Culbertson, F. M., Feral, C. H., & Gabby, S. (1989). Pattern analysis of Wechsler Intelligence Scale for Children-Revised profiles of delinquent boys. *Journal of Clinical Psychology, 45,* 651–660.

Cummins, J. P., & Das, J. P. (1980). Cognitive processing, academic achievement, and WISC–R performance in EMR children. *Journal of Consulting and Clinical Psychology, 48,* 777–779.

Cunningham, C. E., Siegel, L. S., & Offord, D. R. (1985). A developmental dose response analysis of the effects of methylphenidate on the peer interactions of attention deficit disordered boys. *Journal of Child Psychology and Psychiatry, 26,* 955–971.

Das, J. P., Naglieri, J. A., & Kirby, J. R. (1994). *Assessment of cognitive processes: The PASS theory of intelligence.* Boston, MA: Allyn & Bacon.

Davanloo, H. (1978). *Basic principles and techniques in short-term dynamic psychotherapy.* New York: Spectrum.

Dean, R. S. (1977). Patterns of emotional disturbance on the WISC-R. *Journal of Clinical Psychology, 33,* 486–490.

Dean, R. S. (1979, September). *WISC-R factor structure for Anglo and Hispanic children.*

Paper presented to the annual meeting of the American Psychological Association, New York.

Dean, R. S. (1980). Factor structure of the WISC–R with Anglos and Mexican-Americans. *Journal of School Psychology, 18*(3), 234–239.

Decker, S. N., & Corley, R. P. (1984). Bannatyne's "genetic dyslexic" subtype: A validation study. *Psychology in the Schools, 21,* 300–304.

Dekraai, M. B., & Sales, B. D. (1991a). Liability in child therapy and research. *Journal of Consulting and Clinical Psychology, 59,* 953–860.

Dekraai, M. B., & Sales, B. D. (1991b). Legal issues in the conduct of child therapy. In T. R. Krachowill & R. J. Morris (Eds.), *The practice of child therapy* (2nd ed., pp. 441–458). Boston: Allyn & Bacon.

DeNelsky, G. Y. (1991). Prescription privileges for psychologists: The case against. *Professional Psychology: Research and Practice, 22,* 188–193.

Denkowlski, K. M., & Denkowski, G. C. (1982). Client-counselor confidentiality: An update of rationale, legal status, and implications. *The Personnel and Guidance Journal, 60,* 371.

Dewey, J. (1933). *How we think, a restatement of the relation of reflective thinking to the educative process.* New York: Heath Books.

Dewey, J. (1971). *How we think.* Chicago: Henry Regnery.

Dolgin, M. J., & Jay, S. M. (1989). Pain management in children. In E. J. Mash & R. A. Barkley (Eds.), *Treatment of childhood disorders* (pp. 383–404). New York: The Guilford Press.

Doll, B. & Boren, R. (1993). Performance of severely language-impaired students on the WISC–III, language scales, and academic achievement measures. *Journal of Psychoeducational Assessment, Monograph Series, Advances in Psychoeducational Assessment, Wechsler Intelligence Scale for Children: Third Edition,* 77–86.

Dollard, J., & Miller, N. E. (1950). *Personality and psychotherapy.* New York: McGraw-Hill.

Drabman, R. (1985). Graduate training of scientist-practitioner-oriented clinical psychologists: Where we can improve. *Professional Psychology: Research and Practice, 16,* 623–633.

Dudley-Marling, C., Kaufman, N., & Tarver, S. (1981). WISC and WISC-R profiles of learning disabled children: A review. *Learning Disability Quarterly, 4,* 307–319.

Dumont, R., & Faro, C. (1993). The WISC–III: Almost two years old; proceeding with caution—practitioners' concerns. *Communique, 21*(7), 12–15.

Dunn, L. M., & Dunn, L. M. (1981). *Peabody Picture Vocabulary Test, Revised (PPVT-R).* Circle Pines, MN: American Guidance Service.

Dykman, R. A., Ackerman, M. A., & Oglesby, B. A. (1980). Correlates of problem solving in hyperactive, learning disabled and control boys. *Journal of Learning Disabilities, 13,* 23–32.

Eberst, N. D., & Genshaft, J. (1984). Differences in school psychological report writing as a function of doctoral vs. nondoctoral training. *Psychology in the Schools, 21,* 78–82.

Edwards, R., & Edwards, J. L. (1993). The WISC–III: A practitioner perspective. *Journal of Psychoeducational Assessment, Monograph Series, Advances in Psycho-educational Assessment, Wechsler Intelligence Scale for Children: Third Edition,* 144–150.

Elliott, C. D. (1990). *Differential Ability Scales: Administration and scoring manual.* San Antonio, TX: The Psychological Corporation.

Elliott, R. W. (1989). Neuropsychological sequelae of substance abuse by youths. In C. R. Reynolds & E. Fletcher-Janzen (Eds.), *Handbook of clinical child neuropsychology* (pp. 311–331). New York: Plenum Press.

Elliott, S. N., & Boeve, K. (1987). Stability of WISC–R IQs: An investigation of ethnic differences over time. *Educational and Psychological Measurement, 47,* 461–465.

Epstein, S. (1978). Avoidance-approach: The fifth basic conflict. *Journal of Consulting and Clinical Psychology, 46,* 1016–1022.

Epstein, S., & Fenz, W. D. (1962). Theory and experiment on the measurement of approach-avoidance conflict. *Journal of Abnormal and Social Psychology, 64,* 97–112.

Eyde, L. (1993). Tips for clinicians using computer-based test interpretations (CBTIs). In B. Schlosser & K. Moreland (Eds.), *Taming technology: Issues, strategies and resources for the mental health practitioner* (pp. 97–99). Phoenix, AZ: Division of Independent Practice of the American Psychological Association.

Fabes, R. A., McCullers, J. C., & Hom, H. L. (1986). Children's task interest and performance: Immediate versus subsequent effects of rewards. *Personality and Social Psychology Bulletin, 12,* 17–30.

Farley, F. (1990). Type T behavior and families: Introduction and background to a new theory. *The Family Psychologist, 6,* 24–25.

Farnham-Diggory, S. (1972). *Cognitive processes in education: A psychological preparation for teaching and curriculum development.* New York: Harper & Row.

Fennell, E. B., & Bauer, R. M. (1989). Models of inference in evaluating brain-behavior relationships in children. In C. R. Reynolds & E. Fletcher-Janzen (Eds.), *Handbook of clinical child neuropsychology* (pp. 167–177). New York: Plenum Press.

Ferguseon, H. B., & Simeon, J. G. (1984). Evaluating drug effects on children's cognitive functioning. *Progress in Neuropsychopharmacology and Biological Psychiatry, 8,* 683–686.

Fine, M. J. (1992). A systems-ecological perspective on home-school intervention. In M. J. Fine & C. Carlson (Eds.), *The handbook of family-school intervention* (pp. 1–17). Boston: Allyn & Bacon.

Fine, M. J., & Carlson, C. (1992). *The handbook of family-school intervention: A systems perspective.* Boston: Allyn and Bacon.

Finkelhor, D. (1991). Child sexual abuse. In M. L. Rosenberg & M. A. Fenley (Eds.), *Violence in America: A public health approach* (pp. 79–94). New York: Oxford University Press.

Fischer, W. E., Wenck, L. S., Schurr, K. T., & Ellen, A. S. (1985). The moderating influence of gender, intelligence, and specific achievement deficiencies on the Bannatyne WISC–R recategorization. *Journal of Psychoeducational Assessment, 3,* 245–255.

Fish, J. M. (1988). Reinforcement in testing: Research with children and adolescents. *Professional School Psychology, 3,* 203–218.

Flaugher, R. L. (1978). The many definitions of test bias. *American Psychologist, 33,* 671–679.

Flynn, J. R. (1984). The mean IQ of Americans: Massive gains 1932 to 1978. *Psychological Bulletin, 95,* 29–51.

Flynn, J. R. (1987). Massive IQ gains in 14 nations. What IQ tests really measure. *Psychological Bulletin, 101,* 171–191.

Forgays, D. G. (1991). Primary prevention of psychopathology. In M. Hersen, A. E. Kazdin, & A. S. Bellack (Eds.), *The clinical psychology handbook* (2nd ed., pp. 743–761). New York: Pergamon Press.

Frankenberger, W., & Harper, J. (1988). Perceived importance of contributions made by professionals participating in multidisciplinary evaluation teams. *Mental Retardation and Learning Disability Bulletin, 16,* 29–35.

Franklin, M., Stillman, P., Burpeau, M., & Sabers, D. (1982). Examiner error in intelligence testing: Are you a source? *Psychology in the Schools, 19,* 563–569.

Fraser, J. S. (1982). Structural and strategic family therapy: A basis for marriage or grounds for divorce? *Journal of Marital and Family Therapy, 8,* 13–22.

Freud, S. (1966). *The complete introductory lectures on psychoanalysis* (J. Strachey, Trans.). New York: W. W. Norton & Co.

Friedlander, W. J. (1982). A basis of privacy and autonomy in medical practice. *Social Science and Medicine, 16,* 1709–1718.

Gaddes, W. H. (1985). *Learning disabilities and brain function* (2nd ed.). New York: Springer.

Gadow, K. D. (1981). Prevalence of drug treatment for hyperactivity and other childhood behavior disorders. In K. D. Gadow & J. Loney (Eds.), *Psychosocial aspects of drug treatment* (pp. 13–70). Boulder, CO: Westview Press.

Gagne, F. (1985). Giftedness and talent: Reexamining a reexamination of the definitions. *Gifted Child Quarterly, 29,* 103–112.

Gagne, R. M. (1970). *The conditions of learning* (2nd ed.). New York: Holt, Rinehart & Winston.

Galbraith, G., Ott, J., & Johnson, M. C. (1986). The effects of token reinforcement on WISC–R performance of low socioeconomic Hispanic second graders. *Behavioral Assessment, 8,* 191–194.

Gambrill, E. (1993). What critical thinking offers to clinicians and clients. *The Behavior Therapist, 16,* 141–147.

Gardner, H. (1983). *Frames of mind: The theory of multiple intelligences.* New York: Basic Books.

Gardner, H. (1993). *Frames of mind: The theory of multiple intelligences* (10th ann. ed.). New York: Basic Books.

Gardner, R. A. (1981). Digits forward and digits backward as two separate tests: Normative data on 1567 school children. *Journal of Clinical Child Psychology, 10,* 131–135.

Garfield, S., & Kurz, R. (1973). Attitudes toward testing: A survey of directors of internship training. *Journal of Consulting and Clinical Psychology, 40,* 350–355.

Gatewood, C. K. (1987). Effects of varying writing implements on WISC–R coding performance. *Perceptual and Motor Skills, 64*(2), 578.

Gelles, R. J. (1980). Violence in the family: A review of research in the seventies. *Journal of Marriage and Family, 42,* 873–878.

Geschwind, N., & Behan, P. (1982). Left-handedness: Association with immune disease, migraine, and developmental learning disorder. *Proceedings of the National Academy of Science, 79,* 5097–5100.

Gil, D. G. (1970). *Violence against children: Physical child abuse in the United States.* Cambridge: Harvard University Press.

Gjesme, T. (1974). Goal distance in time and its effects on the relations between achievement motives and performance. *Journal of Research in Personality, 8,* 161–171.

Gjesme, T. (1975). Slope of gradients for performance as a function of achievement motive, goal distance in time, and future time orientation. *Journal of Psychology, 91,* 143–160.

Glasser, A. J., & Zimmerman, I. L. (1967). *Clinical interpretation of the Wechsler Intelligence Scale for Children.* New York: Grune & Stratton.

Glutting, J., & Oakland, T. (1993). *Guide to the assessment of test session behavior for the WISC-III and WIAT.* San Antonio: The Psychological Corporation.

Glutting, J. J., Oakland, T., & McDermott, P. A. (1989). Observing child behavior during testing: Constructs, validity, and situational generality. *Journal of School Psychology, 27,* 155–164.

Goh, D., Teslow, C. J., & Fuller, G. B. (1981). The practice of psychological assessment among school psychologists. *Professional Psychology, 12,* 696–706.

Golden, C. J. (1981a). The Luria-Nebraska children's battery: Theory and formulation. In G. W. Hynd & J. E. Obrzut (Eds.), *Neuropsychological assessment and the school-aged child: Issues and procedures.* New York: Grune & Stratton.

Golden, C. J. (1981b). A standardized version of Luria's neuropsychological tests: A quantitative and qualitative approach to neuropsychological evaluation. In S. B. Filskov & T. J. Boll (Eds.), *Handbook of clinical neuropsychology* (pp. 608–644). New York: Wiley.

Golden, C. J., Sawicki, R. F., & Franzen, M. D. (1990). Test construction. In G. Goldstein & M. Hersen (Eds.), *Handbook of Psychological Assessment* (2nd ed., pp. 21–40). New York: Pergamon Press.

Goldstein, F. C., & Levin, H. S. (1984). Intellectual and academic outcome following closed head injury in children and adolescents: Research strategies and empirical findings. *Developmental Neuropsychology, 1,* 195–214.

Goldstein, G. (1990). Comprehensive neuropsychological assessment batteries. In G. Goldstein & M. Hersen (Eds.), *Handbook of psychological assessment* (2nd ed., pp. 197–227). New York: Pergamon Press.

Goldstein, G., & Hersen, M. (1990). Historical perspectives. In G. Goldstein & M. Hersen (Eds.), *Handbook of psychological assessment* (2nd ed., pp. 3–20). New York: Pergamon Press.

Goldwasser, E., Myers, J., Christianson, S., & Graden, J. (1983). The impact of P.L. 94-142 on the practice of school psychology: A national survey. *Psychology in the Schools, 20,* 153–165.

Gorsuch, R. L. (1983). *Factor analysis* (2nd ed.). Hillsdale, NJ: Lawrence Erlbaum.

Graziano, W. G., Varca, P. E., & Levy, J. C. (1982). Race of examiner effects and the validity of intelligence tests. *Review of Educational Research, 52,* 469–498.

Green, W. H. (1991). *Child and adolescent clinical psychopharmacology.* Baltimore: Williams & Wilkins.

Greenblatt, D. J., Shader, R. I., & Abernathy, D. R. (1983). Current status of benzodiazepines (first of two parts). *New England Journal of Medicine, 309,* 354–358.

Groff, M., & Hubble, L. (1982). WISC–R factor scores of younger and older youth with low IQs. *Journal of Consulting and Clinical Psychology, 50*(1), 148–149.

Grossman, H. J. (Ed.). (1983). *Classification in mental retardation.* Washington, DC: American Association on Mental Deficiency.

Grote, C., & Salmon, P. (1986). Spatial complexity and hand usage on the Block Design subtest. *Perceptual and Motor Skills, 62*(1), 59–67.

Guilford, J. P. (1967). *The nature of human intelligence.* New York: McGraw-Hill.

Gutkin, T. B. (1978). Some useful statistics for the interpretation of the WISC–R. *Journal of Consulting and Clinical Psychology, 46,* 1561–1563.

Gutkin, T. B. (1979). Bannatyne patterns of Caucasian and Mexican-American learning-disabled children. *Psychology in the Schools, 16,* 178–183.

Gutkin, T. B., & Reynolds, C. R. (1980). Factorial similarity of the WISC–R for Anglos and Chicanos referred for psychological services. *Journal of School Psychology, 18,* 34–39.

Gutkin, T. B., & Reynolds, C. R. (1981). Factorial similarity of the WISC–R for white and black children from the standardization sample. *Journal of Educational Psychology, 73,* 227–231.

Gutman, L. T., Herman-Giddens, M. E., & McKinney, Jr., R. E. (1993). Pediatric acquired immunodeficiency syndrome. Barriers to recognizing the role of child sexual abuse. *American Journal of Diseases of Children, 14*(7), 775–780.

Haier, R. J., Siegel, B. V., Jr., Neuchterlein, K. H., Hazlet, E., Wu, J. C., Paek, J., Browning, H. L., & Buchsbaum, M. S. (1988). Cortical glucose metabolic rate correlates of abstract reasoning and attention studied with positron emission tomography. *Intelligence, 12,* 199–217.

Hale, R. L. (1979). The utility of WISC–R subtest scores in discriminating among adequate and underachieving children. *Multivariate Behavioral Research, 14,* 245–253.

Hale, R. L. (1991). Intellectual assessment. In M. Hersen, A. E. Kazdin, & A. S. Bellack (Eds.), *The clinical psychology handbook* (2nd ed., pp. 374–405). New York: Pergamon Press.

Hale, R. L., & Landino, S. A. (1981). The utility of WISC–R subtest analysis in discriminating among groups of conduct problem, withdrawn, mixed and nonproblem boys. *Journal of Consulting and Clinical Psychology, 49,* 91–95.

Hale, R. L., & Saxe, J. E. (1983). Profile analysis of the Wechsler Intelligence Scale for Children-Revised. *Journal of Psychoeducational Assessment, 1,* 155–161.

Halstead, W. (1947). *Brain and intelligence: A quantitative study of the frontal lobes.* Chicago: The University of Chicago Press.

Hammill, D. D. (1991). *Detroit Tests of Learning Aptitude* (3rd ed.). Austin, TX: Pro-Ed.

Hanna, G., Bradley, F., & Holen, M. (1981). Estimating major sources of measurement error in individual intelligence scales: Taking our heads out of the sand. *Journal of School Psychology, 19,* 370–376.

Hanson, R. M. (1993). Sexually transmitted diseases and the sexually abused child. *Current Opinion in Pediatrics, 5*(1), 41–49.

Harrell, T. (1993). The Macintosh computer in clinical practice. In B. Schlosser & K. L. Moreland (Eds.), *Taming technology: Issues, strategies and resources for the mental health practitioner* (pp. 11–14). Phoenix, AZ: Division of Independent Practice of the American Psychological Association.

Haynes, J. P., & Howard, R. C. (1986). Stability of WISC–R scores in a juvenile forensic sample. *Journal of Clinical Psychology, 42,* 534–537.

Hendrickson, D. E. (1982). The biological basis of intelligence. In H. J. Eysenck (Ed.), *A model for intelligence* (pp. 151–228). New York: Springer-Verlag.

Henker, B., Whalen, C. K., Bugenthal, D. B., & Barker, C. (1981). Licit and illicit drug patterns in stimulant treated children and their peers. In K. D. Gadow & J. Loney (Eds.), *Psychosocial aspects of drug treatment for hyperactivity* (pp. 443–462). Boulder, CO: Westview.

Henry, S. A., & Wittman, R. D. (1981). Diagnostic implications of Bannatyne's recategorized WISC–R scores for learning disabled children. *Journal of Learning Disabilities 14,* 517–520.

Hernandez, J. T., Lodico, M., & DiClemente, R. J. (1993). The effects of child abuse and race on risk-taking in male adolescents. *Journal of the National Medical Association, 85*(8), 593–597.

Herrnstein, R. J. & Murray, C. (1994). *The bell curve.* New York: The Free Press.

Hetherington, E. M. (1972). Effects of father absence on personality development in adolescent daughters. *Developmental Psychology, 7,* 313–326.

Hishinuma, E. S., & Yamakawa, R. (1993). Construct and criterion-related validity of the WISC–III for exceptional students and those who are "at risk." *Journal of Psychoeducational Assessment, Monograph series, Advances in Psychoeducational Assessment, Wechsler Intelligence Scale for Children: Third edition,* 94–104.

Hodges, K., & Plow, J. (1990). Intellectual ability and achievement in psychiatrically hospitalized children with conduct, anxiety, and affective disorders. *Journal of Consulting and Clinical Psychology, 58,* 589–595.

Holt, R. R. (Ed.). (1968). In D. Rapaport, M. M. Gill, & R. Schafer, *Diagnostic psychological testing* (Rev. ed.). New York: International Universities Press.

Honaker, L. M., & Fowler, R. D. (1990). Computer-assisted psychological assessment. In G. Goldstein & M. Hersen (Eds.), *Handbook of psychological assessment* (pp. 521–546). New York: Pergamon Press.

Horn, J. L. (1968). Organization of abilities and the development of intelligence. *Psychological Review, 75,* 242–259.

Horn, J. L. (1972). The structure of intellect: Primary abilities. In R. M. Dreger (Ed.), *Multivariate personality research.* Baton Rouge, LA: Claitors.

Horn, J. L. (1977). *Intellectual development through the vital years. Final report.* Washington, DC: Army Research Institute.

Horn, J. L. (1978). *Individual differences in cognitive development. Final report.* Bethesda, Maryland: National Science Foundation.

Horn, J. L. (1981). *Age differences in human abilities. Final report.* Bethesda, Maryland: National Institute on Aging.

Horn, J. L. (1982). The aging of human abilities. In B. B. Wolman (Ed.), *Handbook of developmental psychology.* New York: Prentice-Hall.

Horn, J. (1988). Thinking about human abilities. In J. R. Nesselroade & R. B. Cattell (Eds.), *Handbook of multivariate experimental psychology* (2nd ed., pp. 645–685). New York: Plenum Press.

Horn, J. L., & Donaldson, G. (1976). On the myth of intellectual decline in adulthood. *American Psychologist, 31,* 701–719.

Horn, J. L., & Hofer, S. M. (1992). Major abilities and development in the adult period. In R. J. Sternberg & C. A. Berg (Eds.), *Intellectual development* (pp. 44–99). New York: Cambridge University Press.

Irwin, S. (1990). *Drugs of abuse: An introduction to their actions & potential hazards.* Tempe, AZ: D.I.N Publications.

Jastak, S., & Wilkinson, G. S. (1984). *Wide Range Achievement Test-Revised.* Wilmington, DE: Jastak Associates.

Jenkins, J. O., & Ramsey, G. A. (1991). Minorities. In J. Hersen, A. E. Kazdin, & A. S. Bellack (Eds.), *The clinical psychology handbook* (2nd ed., pp. 724–742). New York: Pergamon Press.

Jensen, A. R. (1982). The chronometry of intelligence. In R. J. Sternberg (Ed.), *Recent advances in research on intelligence.* Hillsdale, NJ: Laurence Erlbaum.

Jensen, A. R. (1985). The nature of the black-white difference on various psychometric tests: Spearman's hypothesis. *Behavioral and Brain Sciences, 8,* 193–219.

Jensen, A. R. (1987). The *g* beyond factor analysis. In R. R. Ronning, J. A. Glover, J. C. Conoley, & J. C. Witt (Eds.), *The influence of cognitive psychology on testing* (pp. 87–142). Hillsdale, NJ: Erlbaum.

Jensen, A. R., & Figueroa, R. A. (1975). Forward and backward Digit-Span interaction with race and IQ. *Journal of Educational Psychology, 67,* 882–893.

Jensen, A. R. (1982). The chronometry of intelligence. In R. J. Sternberg (Ed.), *Recent advances in research on intelligence.* Hillsdale, NJ: Laurence Erlbaum.

Jensen, A. R. (1985). Methodological and statistical techniques for the chronometric study of mental abilities. In C. R. Reynolds & V. L. Wilson (Eds.), *Methodological and statistical advances in the study of individual differences* (pp. 51–116). New York: Plenum.

Jensen, A. R. (1987). The *g* beyond factor analysis. In R. R. Ronnin, J. A. Glover, J. C. Conoley, & J. C. Witt (Eds.), *The influence of cognitive psychology on testing* (pp. 87–142). Hillsdale, NJ: Erlbaum.

Johnson, J. H., & Williams, T. A. (1980). Using on-line computer technology in a mental health admitting system. In J. B. Sidowski, J. H. Johnson, & T. A. Williams (Eds.), *Technology in mental health care delivery systems* (pp. 237–249). Norwood, NJ: Ablex.

Joschko, M., & Rourke, B. P. (1985). Neuropsychological subtypes of learning-disabled children who exhibit the ACID pattern on the WISC. In B. P. Rourke (Ed.), *Neuropsychology of learning disabilities: Essentials of subtype analysis* (pp. 65–88). New York: Guilford Press.

Judd, L. L., Hubbard, B., Janowsky, D. S., Huey, L. Y., & Takahashi, K. (1977). The effect of lithium carbonate on the cognitive functions of normal subjects. *Archives of General Psychiatry, 34,* 355–357.

Juliano, J. M., Haddad, F. A., & Carroll, J. L. (1988). Three-year stability of WISC–R factor scores for black and white, female and male children classified as learning disabled. *Journal of School Psychology, 26,* 317–325.

Kames, F. A., & Brown, K. E. (1980). Factor analysis of the WISC–R for the gifted. *Journal of Educational Psychology, 72*(2), 197–199.

Kamphaus, R. W. (1993). *Clinical assessment of children's abilities.* Needham, MA: Allyn & Bacon.

Kamphaus, R. W., Benson, J., Hutchinson, S., & Platt, L. O. (1994). Identification of factor models for the WISC–III. *Educational and Psychological Measurement, 54*(1), 174–186.

Kamphaus, R. W., & Platt, L. O. (1992). Subtest specificities for the WISC–III. *Psychological Reports, 70,* 899–902.

Kaplan, B. J., Beardslee, W. R., & Keller, M. B. (1987). Intellectual competence in children of depressed parents. *Journal of Clinical Child Psychology, 16,* 159–163.

Kaplan, E., Fein, D., Morris, R., & Delis, D. (1991). *Manual for the WAIS–R NI: WAIS–R as a neuropsychological instrument.* San Antonio, TX: The Psychological Corporation.

Kaufman, A. S. (1975). Factor analysis of the WISC–R at 11 age levels between 6½ and 16½ years. *Journal of Consulting and Clinical Psychology, 43,* 135–147.

Kaufman, A. S. (1976a). Verbal-Performance IQ discrepancies on the WISC–R. *Journal of Consulting and Clinical Psychology, 9,* 160–168.

Kaufman, A. S. (1976b). A new approach to the interpretation of test scatter on the WISC–R. *Journal of Learning Disabilities, 9,* 160–168.

Kaufman, A. S. (1979a). *Intelligent testing with the WISC–R.* New York: Wiley.

Kaufman, A. S. (1979b). Cerebral specialization and intelligence testing. *Journal of Research and Development in Education, 12,* 96–107.

Kaufman, A. S. (1979c). WISC–R research: Implications for interpretation. *School Psychology Digest, 8,* 5–27.

Kaufman, A. S. (1982). The impact of WISC–R research for school psychologists. In C. R. Reynolds & T. B. Gutkin (Eds.), *The handbook of school psychology,* (pp. 156–177). New York: Wiley.

Kaufman, A. S. (1990). *Assessing adolescent and adult intelligence.* Boston: Allyn and Bacon.

Kaufman, A. S. (1993). King WISC the third assumes the throne. *Journal of School Psychology, 31,* 345–354.

Kaufman, A. S., & Doppelt, J. E. (1976). Analysis of WISC–R standardization data in terms of the stratification variables. *Child Development, 47,* 165–171.

Kaufman, A. S., & Harrison, P. L. (1986). Intelligence tests and gifted assessment: What are the positives? *Roeper Review, 8,* 154–159.

Kaufman, A. S., Harrison, P. L., & Ittenbach, R. F. (1990). Intelligence testing in the schools. In T. B. Gutkin & C. R. Reynolds (Eds.), *Handbook of school psychology,* (2nd. ed., pp. 289–327). New York: John Wiley & Sons.

Kaufman, A. S., & Kaufman, N. L. (1983). *The Kaufman Assessment Battery for Children (K-ABC)*. Circle Pines, MN: American Guidance Services.

Kaufman, A. S., & McLean, J. E. (1986). K–ABC/WISC–R factor analysis for a learning disabled population. *Journal of Learning Disabilities, 19*(3), 145–153.

Kaufman, A. S., & Van Hagen, J. (1977). Investigation of the WISC–R for use with retarded children: Correlation with the 1972 Stanford-Binet and comparison of WISC and WISC–R profiles. *Psychology in the Schools, 14,* 10–14.

Kavale, K. A., & Forness, S. R. (1984). A meta-analysis of the validity of Wechsler scale profiles and recategorizations: Patterns or parodies? *Learning Disabilities Quarterly, 7,* 136–156.

Kavale, K. A., & Forness, S. R. (1994). Learning disabilities and intelligence: An uneasy alliance. In T. E. Scruggs & M. A. Mastropieri (Eds.), *Advances in learning and behavioral disabilities: Vol. 8,* (pp. 1–64). Greenwich, CT: JAI Press.

Kazdin, A. E. (1989). Childhood depression. In E. J. Mash & R. A. Barkley (Eds.), *Treatment of childhood disorders* (pp. 135–166). New York: The Guilford Press.

Keiffer, D. A., & Goh, D. S. (1981). The effects of individually contracted incentives on intelligence test performance of middle- and low-SES children. *Journal of Clinical Psychology, 37,* 175–179.

Kendall, P. C., Vitousek, K. B., & Kane, M. (1991). Thought and action in psychotherapy: Cognitive-behavioral approaches. In M. Hersen, A. E. Kazdin, & A. S. Bellack (Eds.), *The clinical psychology handbook* (2nd ed., pp. 596–626). New York: Pergamon Press.

Kendall-Tackett, H. A., Williams, L. M., & Finkelhor, D. (1993). Impact of sexual abuse of children: A review and synthesis of recent empirical studies. *Psychological Bulletin, 113,* 164–180.

Keogh, B. K. (1982). Research in learning disabilities: A view of status and need. In J. P. Das, R. F. Mulcahy, & A. E. Wall (Eds.), *Theory and research in learning disabilities* (pp. 27–44). New York: Plenum.

Killian, G. A., Campbell, B. M., & Diston, L. (1986). Block Design elevations on the Wechsler scales: A caveat. *Psychotherapy in Private Practice, 4*(2), 31–32.

Kinsbourne, M. (1989). Mechanisms of development of hemisphere specialization in children. In C. R. Reynolds & E. Fletcher-Janzen (Eds.), *Handbook of clinical child neuropsychology* (pp. 69–85). New York: Plenum Press.

Klerman, G. L., Weissman, M. M., Rounsaville, B. J., & Chevron, E. S. (1984). *Interpersonal psychotherapy of depression.* New York: Basic Books.

Klonoff, H., & Low, M. (1974). Disordered brain function in young children and early adolescents: Neuropsychological and electroencephalographic correlates. In R. M. Reitan & L. A. Davison (Eds.), *Clinical neuropsychology: Current status and applications* (pp. 121–178). Washington, DC: V. H. Winston & Sons.

Koocher, G. P. (Ed.). (1976). *Children's rights and the mental health professions.* New York: Wiley.

Korchin, S. J. (1976). *Modern clinical psychology.* New York: Basic Books.

Krippner, S. (1964). WISC Comprehension and Picture Arrangement subtests as measures of social competence. *Journal of Clinical Psychology, 20,* 366–367.

Krug, S. E. (1993). *Psychware sourcebook* (4th ed.). Champaign, IL: MetriTech.

Kupietz, S. S., & Balka, E. B. (1976). Alterations in the vigilance performance of children receiving amitriptyline and methylphenidate pharmacotherapy. *Psychopharmacology, 50*, 29–33.

Lacayo, N., Sherwood, G., & Morris, J. (1981). Daily activities of school psychologists: A national review. *Psychology in the Schools, 18*, 184–190.

Lipsitz, J. D., Dworkin, R. H., & Erlenmeyer-Kimling, L. (1993). Wechsler Comprehension and Picture Arrangement subtests and social adjustment. *Psychological Assessment, 5*, 430–437.

Loeber, R. (1990). Development and risk factors of juvenile antisocial behavior and delinquency. *Clinical Psychology Review, 10*, 1–41.

Loney, J. (1986). Predicting stimulant drug response among hyperactive children. *Psychiatric Annals, 16*, 16–19.

Loney, J., Kramer, J., & Milich, R. S. (1981). The hyperactive child grows up: Predictors of symptoms, delinquency and achievement at follow-up. In K. D. Gadow & J. Loney (Eds.), *Psychosocial aspects of drug treatment for hyperactivity* (pp. 381–415). Boulder, CO: Westview.

Longman, R. S., Inglis, J., & Lawson, J. S. (1991). WISC–R patterns of cognitive abilities in behavior disordered and learning-disabled children. *Psychological Assessment: A Journal of Consulting and Clinical Psychology, 3*, 239–246.

Losco, J., & Epstein, S. (1977). Relative steepness of approach and avoidance gradients as a function of magnitude and valence of incentive. *Journal of Abnormal and Social Psychology, 43*, 155–178.

Luria, A. R. (1966). *Higher cortical functions in man.* New York: Basic Books.

Luria, A. R. (1973). *The working brain.* New York: Basic Books.

Lutey, C. (1977). *Individual intelligence testing: A manual and sourcebook* (2nd & enlarged ed.). Greeley, CO: Carol L. Lutey.

MacMahon, B., & Pugh, T. F. (1970). *Epidemiology: Principles and methods.* Boston: Little, Brown and Company.

Mann, J. (1973). *Time-limited psychotherapy.* Cambride, MA: Harvard University Press.

Martin, S. (1994, October). School psychologists: Little time for counseling. *The APA Monitor, 27*, 46.

Massman, P. J., Nussbaum, N. L., & Bigler, E. D. (1988). The mediating effect of age on the relationship between Child Behavior Checklist hyperactivity scores and neuropsychological test performance. *Journal of Abnormal Child Psychology, 16*(1), 89–95.

Matarazzo, J. D. (1972). *Wechsler's measurement and appraisal of adult intelligence* (5th ed.). New York: Oxford University Press.

Matarazzo, J. D. (1985). Review of Wechsler Adult Intelligence Scale-Revised. In J. V. Mitchell (Ed.), *The ninth mental measurements yearbook* (pp. 1703–1705). Lincoln, NE: The Buros Institute of Mental Measurements, University of Nebraska.

Matarazzo, J. D. (1990). Psychological assessment versus psychological testing: Validation from Binet to the school, clinic, and courtroom. *American Psychologist, 45*, 999–1017.

Matarazzo, J. D. (1992). Psychological testing and assessment in the 21st century. *American Psychologist, 47,* 1007–1018.

Mayrent, S. L. (Ed.). (1987). In C. H. Hennekens & J. E. Buring. *Epidemiology in medicine.* Boston: Little, Brown and Company.

McArdle, J. J., & Horn, J. L. (1983). *Validation by systems modeling of WAIS abilities.* Bethesda, Maryland: National Institute of Aging.

McDermott, P. A. (1981). Sources of error in the psychoeducational diagnosis of children. *Journal of School Psychology, 19,* 31–44.

McDermott, P. A. (1988). Agreement among diagnosticians or observers: Its importance and determination. *Professional School Psychology, 3,* 225–240.

McDermott, P. A., Fantuzzo, J. W., & Glutting, J. J. (1990) Just say no to subtest analysis: A critique on Wechsler theory and practice. *Journal of Psychoeducational Assessment, 8,* 290–302.

McDermott, P. A., Fantuzzo, J. W., Glutting, J. J., Watkins, M. W., & Baggaley, A. R. (1992). Illusions of meaning in the ipsative assessment of human ability. *Journal of Special Education, 25,* 504–526.

McDermott, P. A., Glutting, J. J., Jones, J. N., Watkins, M. W., & Kush, J. (1989). Core profile types in the WISC–R national sample: Structure, membership, and applications. *Psychological Assessment: A Journal of Consulting and Clinical Psychology, 1*(4), 292–299.

McMann, G. M., Plasket, C. M., Barnett, D. W., & Siler, R. F. (1991). Factor structure of the WISC–R for children of superior intelligence. *Journal of School Psychology, 29*(1), 19–36.

McQueen, W., Meschino, R., Pike, P., & Poelstra, P. (1994). Improving graduate student performance in cognitive assessment: The saga continues. *Professional Psychology: Research and Practice, 25,* 283–287.

McShane, D. A., & Plas, J. M. (1982). Wechsler scale performance patterns of American Indian children. *Psychology in the Schools, 15,* 176–179.

Melamed, B., & Seigel, L. (1975). Reduction of anxiety in children facing hospitalization and surgery. *Journal of Clinical and Consulting Psychology, 43,* 511–521.

Miele, F. (1979). Cultural bias in the WISC. *Intelligence, 3,* 149–164.

Milby, J. B., & Weber, A. (1991). Obsessive compulsive disorders. In T. R. Kratochwill & R. J. Morris (Eds.), *The practice of child therapy* (2nd ed., pp. 9–42). New York: Pergamon Press.

Miller, C., & Chansky, N. (1972). Psychologists' scoring of WISC–R protocols. *Psychology in the Schools, 9,* 114–152.

Miller, C., Chansky, N., & Gredler, G. (1970). Rater agreement on WISC protocols. *Psychology in the Schools, 7,* 190–193.

Miller, G. A., Galanter, E., & Pribram, K. H. (1960). *Plans and the structure of behavior.* New York: Holt, Rinehart & Winston.

Miller, M. M. (1980). On the attempt to find WISC–R profiles for learning and reading disabilities (a response to Vance, Wallbrown, and Blaha). *Journal of Learning Disabilities, 13,* 338–340.

Miller, N. E. (1948). Theory and experiment relating psychoanalytic displacement to stimulus response generalization. *Journal of Abnormal and Social Psychology, 43,* 155–178.

Miller-Jones, D. (1989). Culture and testing. *American Psychologist, 44,* 360–366.

Mishra, S. P. (1984). WISC–R performance patterns of learning-disabled children from Papago culture. *Journal of Clinical Psychology, 40,* 1489–1492.

Moffitt, T. E., Gabrielli, W. F., Mednick, S. A., & Schulsinger, F. (1981). Socioeconomic status, IQ, and delinquency. *Journal of Abnormal Psychology, 90,* 152–156.

Moffitt, T. E., & Silva, P. A. (1987). WISC–R verbal and performance IQ discrepancy in an unselected cohort: Clinical significance and longitudinal stability. *Journal of Consulting and Clinical Psychology, 55,* 768–774.

Morris, R. J. (1993, January). Ethical issues in the assessment and treatment of children and adolescents. *Register Report, 19,* 4–13.

Mueller, H. H., Dennis, S. S., & Short, R. H. (1986). A meta-exploration of WISC–R factor score profiles as a function of diagnosis and intellectual level. *Canadian Journal of School Psychology, 2,* 21–43.

Naglieri, J. A. (1993). Pairwise and ipsative comparisons of WISC–III IQ and index scores. *Psychological Assessment, 5*(1), 113–116.

Naglieri, J. A., & Das, J. P. (1990). Planning, attention, simultaneous and successive (PASS) cognitive processes as a model for intelligence. *Journal of Psychoeducational Assessment, 8,* 303–337.

Naglieri, J. A., & Pfeiffer, S. I. (1983). Reliability and stability of the WISC–R for children with below average IQs. *Educational & Psychological Research, 3,* 203–208.

National Center on Child Abuse and Neglect. (1988). *Study of National Incidence and Prevalence of Child Abuse and Neglect: 1988.* Washington, D.C.: U. S. Government Printing Office.

National Institute of Mental Health. (1973). Pharmacotherapy of children. *Psychopharmacology Bulletin, Special Issue, 9,* 1–195.

National Institute of Mental Health. (1985). Rating scales and assessment instruments for use in pediatric psychopharmacology research. *Psychopharmacology Bulletin, 21,* 713–1125.

National Joint Committee on Learning Disabilities. (1983). Learning disabilities: Issues on definition (Position paper). *Learning Disability Quarterly, 6,* 42–44.

Newberger, E. H. (1991). Child abuse. In M. L. Rosenberg & M. A. Fenley (Eds.), *Violence in America: A public health approach* (pp. 51–78). New York: Oxford University Press.

Nichols, M. (1984). *Family therapy: Concepts & methods.* New York: Gardner Press.

Nihira, K. (1985). Assessment of mentally retarded individuals. In B. B. Wolman (Ed.), *The Handbook of Intelligence.* New York: John Wiley & Sons.

Nobo, J., & Evans, R. G. (1986). The WAIS–R Picture Arrangement and Comprehension subtests as measures of social behavior characteristics. *Journal of Personality Assessment, 50*(1), 90–92.

Oakland, T., & Feigenbaum, D. (1979). Multiple sources of test bias on the WISC–R and the Bender Gestalt Test. *Journal of Consulting and Clinical Psychology, 47,* 968–974.

Oakland, T., & Parmelee, R. (1985). Mental measurement of minority-group children.

In B. B. Wolman (Ed.), *Handbook of intelligence* (pp. 699–736). New York: John Wiley & Sons.

O'Donnell, L., Granier, M. J., & Dersh, J. J. (1991, August). *Does handedness affect children's Coding performance on the WISC-III?* Poster session presented at the annual meeting of the American Psychological Association, San Francisco, CA.

Ollendick, T. H. (1979). Discrepancies between verbal and performance IQs and subtest scatter on the WISC–R for juvenile delinquents. *Psychological Reports, 45,* 968–974.

Osborne, R. T., & Lindsey, J. M. (1967). A longitudinal investigation of change in the factorial composition of intelligence with age in young school children. *Journal of Genetic Psychology, 110,* 49–58.

Otis, A. S., & Lennon, R. T. (1989). *Otis-Lennon School Ability Test, Form I* (6th ed.). San Antonio, TX: The Psychological Corporation.

Ownby, R. L. (1990a). A study of the expository process model in mental health settings. *Journal of Clinical Psychology, 46,* 366–371.

Ownby, R. L. (1990b). A study of the expository process model in school psychological reports. *Psychology in the Schools, 27,* 353–358.

Ownby, R. L., & Wallbrown, F. (1986). Improving report writing in school psychology. In T. Kratochwill (Ed.), *Advances in school psychology,* (Vol. 5, pp. 7–49). Hillsdale, NJ: Erlbaum.

Ownby, R. L., Wallbrown, F., & Brown, D. Y. (1982). Special education teachers' perceptions of reports written by school psychologists. *Perceptual and Motor Skills, 55,* 955–961.

Perlman, M. D., & Kaufman, A. S. (1990). Assessment of child intelligence. In G. Goldstein & M. Hersen (Eds.). *Handbook of psychological assessment,* (2nd ed., pp. 59–78). New York: Pergamon Press.

Peterson, C. R., & Hart, D. H. (1979). Factor structure of the WISC–R for for a clinical-referred population and specific subgroups. *Journal of Consulting and Clinical Psychology, 47,* 643–645.

Petrauskas, R. J., & Rourke, B. P. (1979). Identification of subtypes of retarded readers: A neuropsychological multivariate approach. *Journal of Clinical Neuropsychology, 1,* 17–37.

Phelps, L., & Ensor, A. (1987). The comparison of performance by sex of deaf children on the WISC–R. *Psychology in the Schools, 24*(3), 209–214.

Phelps, L., Leguori, S., Nisewaner, K., & Parker, M. (1993). Practical interpretations of the WISC–III with language-disordered children. *Journal of Psychoeducational Assessment, Monograph Series, Advances in Psychoeducational Assessment, Wechsler Intelligence Scale for Children: Third edition,* 71–76.

Piotrowski, R. J., & Siegel, D. J. (1984). Interpreting WISC–R profiles: Reliability of subtest composites. *Journal of Psychoeducational Assessment, 2,* 183–190.

Plante, T. G., Goldfarb, L. P., & Wadley, V. (1993). Are stress and coping associated with aptitude and achievement testing performance among children? A preliminary investigation. *Journal of School Psychology, 31,* 259–266.

Plas, J. M. (1992). The development of systems thinking: A historical perspective. In

M. J. Fine & C. Carlson (Eds.), *The handbook of family-school intervention: A systems perspective* (pp. 45–56). Boston: Allyn & Bacon.

Platt, J. E., Campbell, M., Green, W. H., & Grega, D. M. (1984). Cognitive effects of lithium carbonate and haloperidol in treatment-resistant aggressive children. *Archives of General Psychiatry, 19,* 171–178.

Plomin, R. (1989). Environment and genes. *American Psychologist, 44,* 105–111.

Pope, K. S. (1989). Malpractice suits, licensing actions, and ethics cases: Frequencies, causes, and costs. *Independent Practitioner, 9,* 22–26.

Pope, K. S. (1990). Ethical and malpractice issues in hospital practice. *American Psychologist, 45,* 1066–1070.

Pope, K. S. (1991). Ethical and legal issues in clinical practice. In M. Hersen, A. E. Kazdin, & A. S. Bellack (Eds.), *The clinical psychology handbook* (2nd ed., pp. 115–127). New York: Pergamon Press.

Pope, K. S., Tabachnick, B. G., & Keith-Spiegel, P. (1987). Ethics of practice: The beliefs and behaviors of psychologists as therapists. *American Psychologist, 42,* 993–1006.

Post, K. R., & Mitchell, H. R. (1993). The WISC–III: A reality check. *Journal of School Psychology, 31,* 541–545.

Powell, D. H. (1987). *Teenagers, when to worry and what to do.* New York: Doubleday.

Prifitera, A., & Dersh, J. (1993). Base rates of WISC–III diagnostic subtest patterns among normal, learning-disabled, and ADHD samples. *Journal of Psychoeducational Assessment, Monograph series, Advances in Psychoeducational Assessment, Wechsler Intelligence Scale for Children: Third edition,* 43–55.

Pryzwansky, W. B., & Hanania, J. S. (1986). Applying problem solving approaches to school psychological reports. *Journal of School Psychology, 24,* 133–141.

Quereshi, M. Y. (1968). Intelligence test scores as a function of sex of experimenter and sex of subject. *Journal of Psychology, 69,* 277–284.

Quinn, P. O., & Rapoport, J. L. (1975). One year follow-up of hyperactive boys treated with imipramine or methylphenidate. *American Journal of Psychiatry, 132,* 241–245.

Ramos, M. C., & Die, A. H. (1986). The WAIS–R Picture Arrangement subtest: What do scores indicate? *Journal of General Psychology, 113*(3), 251–256.

Rapoport, J. L. (1983). The use of drugs: Trends in research. In M. Rutter (Ed.), *Developmental neuropsychiatry* (pp. 385–403). New York: Guilford Press.

Rapoport, J. L. (1983). The use of drugs: Trends in research. In M. Rutter (Ed.), *Developmental neuropsychiatry* (pp. 385–403). New York: Guilford Press.

Rapoport, J. L., & Mikkelsen, E. J. (1978). Antidepressants. In J. S. Werry (Ed.), *Pediatric psychopharmacology: The use of behavior modifying drugs in children* (pp. 208–233). New York: Bruner/Mazel.

Rapport, M. D., DuPaul, G. J., Stoner, G., & Jones, J. T. (1986). Comparing classroom and clinic measures of attention deficit disorder: Differential, idiosyncratic, and dose-response effects of methylphenidate. *Journal of Consulting and Clinical Psychology, 54,* 334–341.

Redlich, F. C., & Pope, K. S. (1980). Ethics of mental health training. *Journal of Nervous and Mental Disease, 168,* 709–714.

Reiff, H. B., & Gerber, P. J. (1990). Cognitive correlates of social perception in students with learning disabilities. *Journal of Learning Disabilities, 23,* 260–262.

Reilly, T. F., Wheeler, L. J., & Etlinger, L. E. (1985). Intelligence versus academic achievement: A comparison of juvenile delinquents and special education classifications. *Criminal Justice and Behavior, 12*(2), 193–208.

Reitan, R. M. (1979). *Manual for administration of neuropsychological test batteries for adults and children.* Tucson, AZ: Reitan Neuropsychological Laboratories, Inc.

Reitan, R. M., & Davison, L. A. (1974). *Clinical neuropsychology: Current status and applications.* Washington, DC: V. H. Winston & Sons.

Reitan, R. M., & Wolfson, D. (1992). *Neuropsychological evaluation of older children.* Tucson, AZ: Neuropsychology Press.

Reitan, R. M., & Wolfson, D. (1993). *The Halstead-Reitan neuropsychological test battery: Theory and clinical interpretation.* Tucson, AZ: Neuropsychology Press.

Reitan, R. M., & Wolfson, D. (1994). *Neuropsychological evaluation of young children.* Tucson, AZ: Neuropsychology Press.

Report Writer: Children's intellectual and achievement tests [Computer software]. (1993). Odessa, FL: Psychological Assessment Resources.

Reschly, D. J. (1978). WISC–R factor structures among Anglos, blacks, Chicanos, and Native-American Papagos. *Journal of Consulting and Clinical Psychology, 46,* 417–422.

Reschly, D. J., & Reschly, J. E. (1979). Validity of WISC–R factor scores in predicting achievement and attention for four sociocultural groups. *Journal of School Psychology, 17,* 355–361.

Reschly, D. J., & Sabers, D. (1979). Analysis of test bias in four groups with the regression definition. *Journal of Educational Measurement, 16,* 1–9.

Rescorla, L., Parker, R., & Stolley, P. (1991). Ability, achievement, and adjustment in homeless children. *American Journal of Orthopsychiatry, 61*(2), 210–220.

Reynolds, C. R. (1980, September). Patterns of intellectual abilities among blacks and whites matched for "g." Paper presented at the annual meeting of the American Psychological Association, Montreal.

Reynolds, C. R. (1982). The problem of bias in psychological assessment. In C. R. Reynolds & T. B. Gutkin (Eds.), *A handbook for school psychology* (pp. 178–208). New York: John Wiley & Sons.

Reynolds, C. R., & Gutkin, T. B. (1980). A regression analysis of test bias on the WISC–R for Anglos and Chicanos referred for psychological services. *Journal of Abnormal Child Psychology, 8,* 237–243.

Reynolds, C. R., & Harding, R. E. (1983). Outcome in two large sample studies of factorial similarity under six methods of comparison. *Educational and Psychological Measurement, 43,* 723–728.

Reynolds, C. R., & Kaiser, S. M. (1990). Test bias in psychological assessment. In T. B. Gutkin & C. R. Reynolds (Eds.), *The handbook of school psychology* (2nd ed., pp. 487–525). New York: John Wiley & Sons.

Reynolds, C. R., & Kaufman, A. S. (1985). Clinical assessment of children's intelligence with the Wechsler scales. In B. B. Wolman (Ed.), *Handbook of intelligence* (pp. 601–661). New York: John Wiley & Sons.

Rogers, C. (1961). *On becoming a person.* Boston: Houghton Mifflin.

Roid, G. H., Prifitera, A., & Weiss, L. G. (1993). Replication of the WISC–III factor structure in an independent sample. *Journal of Psychoeducational Assessment, Monograph Series, Advances in Psychoeducational Assessment, Wechsler Intelligence Scale for Children: Third edition,* 6–21.

Ross, A. O. (1981). *Child behavior therapy: Principles, procedures and empirical basis.* New York: Wiley.

Rourke, B. P. (1981). Neuropsychological assessment of children with learning disabilities. In S. B. Filskov & T. J. Boll (Eds.), *Handbook of clinical neuropsychology* (pp. 453–478). New York: Wiley.

Rourke, B. P. (1983). Reading and spelling disabilities: A developmental neuropsychological perspective. In U. Kirk (Ed.), *Neuropsychology of language, reading, and spelling* (pp. 209–234). New York: Academic Press.

Rourke, B. P., Bakker, D. J., Fisk, J. L., & Strang, J. D. (1983). *Child neuropsychology.* New York: Guilford Press.

Rucker, C. (1967). Report writing in school psychology: A critical investigation. *Journal of School Psychology, 5,* 101–108.

Rudel, R. G., & Denckla, M. B. (1974). Relationship of forward and backward digit repetitions to neurological impairment in children with learning disabilities. *Neuropsychologica, 12,* 109–118.

Rugel, R. P. (1974). WISC subtest scores of disabled readers: A review with respect to Bannatyne's recategorization. *Journal of Learning Disabilities, 7,* 48–55.

Ryan, N. D., Puig-Antich, J., Cooper, T., Rabinovich, H., Ambrosini, P., Davies, M., King, J., Torrer, D., & Fried, J. (1986). Imipramine in adolescent major depression: Plasma level and clinical response. *Acta Psychiatrica Scandinavica, 73,* 275–288.

Saccuzzo, D. P, & Lewandowski, D. G. (1976). The WISC as a diagnostic tool. *Journal of Clinical Psychology, 32,* 115–124.

Safer, D. J., & Krager, J. M. (1983). Trends in medication treatment of hyperactive school children. *Clinical Pediatrics, 22,* 500–504.

Saigh, P. (1981). The effects of positive examiner verbal comments on the total WISC–R performance of institutionalized EMR students. *Journal of School Psychology, 19,* 86–91.

Saigh, P., & Payne, D. (1976). The influence of examiner verbal comments on WISC performances of EMR students. *Journal of School Psychology, 14,* 342–345.

Salvagno, M., & Teglasi, H. (1987). Teacher perceptions of different types of information in psychological reports. *Journal of School Psychology, 25,* 415–424.

Salvia, J., & Ysseldyke, J. E. (1988). *Assessment in special and remedial education* (4th ed.). Boston: Houghton Mifflin.

Salzman, C. (1990). Benzodiazepine dependency: Summary of the APA task force on benzodizepines. *Psychopharmacology Bulletin, 26,* 61–62.

Sandler, A. D., Watson, T. E., & Levine, M. D. (1992). *Journal of Developmental and Behavioral Pediatrics, 13*(3), 202–207.

Sandoval, J. (1979). The WISC–R and internal evidence of test bias with minority groups. *Journal of Consulting and Clinical Psychology, 47,* 919–927.

Sandoval, J., & Millie, M. (1980). Accuracy judgments of WISC–R item difficulties for minority groups. *Journal of Consulting and Clinical Psychology, 48,* 249–253.

Sandoval, J., Sassenrath, J., & Penaloza, M. (1988). Similarity of WISC–R and WAIS–R scores at age 16. *Psychology in the Schools, 25,* 373–379.

Saneda, R. M., & Serafica, F. C. (1991). Plans and the control of behavior in boys with and without learning disabilities. *Journal of Clinical Child Psychology, 20*(4), 386–391.

Sattler, J. M. (1974). *Assessment of children's intelligence* (revised reprint). Philadelphia: Saunders.

Sattler, J. M. (1982). *Assessment of children's intelligence and special abilities* (2nd ed.). Boston: Allyn & Bacon.

Sattler, J. M. (1990). *Assessment of children* (3rd ed., revised reprint). San Diego: Jerome M. Sattler.

Sattler, J. M. (1992). *Assessment of children: WISC-III and WPPSI-R supplement.* San Diego: Jerome M. Sattler.

Sattler, J. M., & Atkinson, L. (1993). Item equivalence across scales: The WPPSI–R and WISC–III. *Psychological Assessment, 5,* 203–206.

Sattler, J. M., & Gwynne, J. (1982). White examiners generally do not impede the intelligence test performance of black children: To debunk a myth. *Journal of Consulting and Clinical Psychology, 50,* 196–208.

Sattler, J. M., Hillix, W., & Neher, L. (1970). Halo effect in examiner scoring of intelligence test responses. *Journal of Consulting and Clinical Psychology, 34,* 172–176.

Satz, P., Orsini, D. L., Saslow, E., & Henry, R. (1985). The pathological left-handedness syndrome. *Brain and Cognition, 4,* 27–46.

Schiff, M. M., Kaufman, A. S., & Kaufman, N. L. (1981). Scatter analysis of WISC–R profiles for learning disabled children with superior intelligence. *Journal of Learning Disabilities, 14,* 400–404.

Schlosser, B., & Moreland, K. L. (Eds.). (1993). *Taming technology: Issues, strategies and resources for the mental health practitioner.* Phoenix, AZ: Division of Independent Practice of the American Psychological Association.

Schofield, N. J., & Ashman, A. F. (1986). The relationship between digit span and cognitive processing across ability groups. *Intelligence, 10*(1), 59–73.

Schooler, N. R., & Kane, J. M. (1982). Research diagnoses for tardive dyskinesia. *Archives of General Psychiatry, 38,* 486–487.

Schwean, V. L., Saklofske, D. H., Yackulic, R. A., & Quinn, D. (1993). WISC–III performance of ADHD children. *Journal of Psychoeducational Assessment, Monograph Series, Advances in Psychoeducational Assessment, Wechsler Intelligence Scale for Children: Third edition,* 56–70.

Segal, H. G., Westen, D., Lohr, N. E., & Silk, K. R. (1993). Clinical assessment of object relations and social cognition using stories told to the Picture Arrangement subtest of the WAIS–R. *Journal of Personality Assessment, 61*(1), 58–80.

Shapiro, A. K., & Shapiro, E. (1989). Tic disorders. In H. I. Kaplan & B. J. Sadock (Eds.), *Comprehensive textbook of psychiatry/V* (Vol. 2, 5th ed., pp. 1865–1878). Baltimore: Williams & Wilkins.

Share, D. L., Silva, P. A., & Adler, C. J. (1987). Factors associated with reading plus spelling retardation and specific spelling retardation. *Developmental Medicine and Child Neurology, 29*(1), 72–84.

Shaw, S. R., Swerdlik, M. E., & Laurent, J. (1993). Review of the WISC–III. *Journal of Psychological Assessment, Monograph Series, Advances in Psychoeducational Assessment, Wechsler Intelligence Scale for Children: Third edition,* 151–160.

Shea, S. (1990). Contemporary psychiatric interviewing: Integration of DSM–III–R, psychodynamic concerns, and mental status. In G. Goldstein & M. Hersen (Eds.), *Handbook of psychological assessment* (2nd ed., pp. 283–307). New York: Pergamon Press.

Shiffrin, R. M., & Schneider, W. (1977). Controlled and automatic human information processing II: Perceptual learning, automatic attending, and a general theory. *Psychological Review, 84*(2).

Sifneos, P. E. (1987). *Short-term dynamic psychotherapy: Evaluation and techniques* (2nd ed.). New York: Plenum Press.

Silber, T. J. (1987). Adolescent marijuana use: Screening and ethics. *Adolescence, 22,* 1–6.

Silverstein, A. B. (1973). Factor structure of the Wechsler Intelligence Scale for Children for three ethnic groups. *Journal of Educational Psychology, 65,* 408–410.

Sipps, G. J., Berry, W., & Lynch, E. M. (1987). WAIS–R and social intelligence: A test of established assumptions that uses the CPI. *Journal of Clinical Psychology, 43,* 499–504.

Slate, J. R., & Chick, D. (1989). WISC–R examiner errors: Cause for concern. *Psychology in the Schools, 26,* 78–84.

Slate, J. R., & Hunnicutt, L. C., Jr. (1988). Examiner errors on the Wechsler scales. *Journal of Psychoeducational Assessment, 6,* 280–288.

Slate, J. R., & Jones, C. H. (1989). Can teaching of the WISC–R be improved? Quasi-experimental exploration. *Professional Psychology: Research and Practice, 20,* 408–410.

Slate, J. R., & Jones, C. H. (1990). Student error in administering the WISC–R: Identifying problem areas. *Measurement and Evaluation in Counseling and Development, 23,* 137–140.

Slate, J. R., Jones, C. H., Coulter, C., & Covert, T. L. (1992). Practitioners' administration and scoring of the WISC–R: Evidence that we do err. *Journal of School Psychology, 30,* 77–82.

Slate, J. R., Jones, C. H., & Covert, T. L. (1992). Rethinking the instructional design for teaching the WISC–R: The effects of practice administrations. *College Student Journal, 26,* 285–289.

Slate, J. R., Jones, C. H., & Murray, R. A. (1991). Teaching administration and scoring of the Wechsler Adult Intelligence Scale-Revised: An empirical evaluation of practice administrations. *Professional Psychology: Research and Practice, 22,* 375–379.

Sloves, R. E., Docherty, E. M., Jr., & Schneider, K. C. (1979). A scientific problem-solving model of psychological assessment. *Professional Psychology, 10,* 28–35.

Smith, C. R. (1985). Learning disabilities: Past and present. *Journal of Learning Disabilities, 18,* 513–518.

Smith, M. D., Coleman, J. M., Dokecki, P. R., & Davis, E. E. (1977a). Intellectual and academic characteristics of school-verified learning disabled children. *Exceptional Child, 43*(3), 352–357.

Smith, M. D., Coleman, J. M., Dokecki, P. R., & Davis, E. E. (1977b). Recategorized WISC–R scores of learning disabled children. *Journal of Learning Disabilities, 10*(7), 437–443.

Sorensen, T., & Snow, B. (1991). How children tell: The process of disclosure in child sexual abuse. *Child Welfare, 70,* 3–15.

Spearman, C. E. (1904). "General intelligence," objectively determined and measured. *American Journal of Psychology, 15,* 201–293.

Spearman, C. E. (1923). *The nature of intelligence and the principles of cognition.* London: Macmillan.

Spearman, C. E. (1927). *The abilities of man.* London: Macmillan.

Spelberg, H. C. (1987). Problem-solving strategies on the block-design task. *Perceptual and Motor Skills, 65*(1), 99–104.

Stankov, L., & Horn, J. L. (1980). Human abilities revealed through auditory tests. *Journal of Educational Psychology, 72,* 21–44.

Stanton, M. D. (1981). An integrated structural-strategic approach to family therapy. *Journal of Marital and Family Therapy, 7,* 427–439.

State of Rhode Island & Providence Plantations, Department of Elementary and Secondary Education. (August, 1992). *Regulations of the Board of Regents for elementary and secondary education governing the special education of students with disabilities.* Providence, RI: Author.

Sternberg, R. J. (Ed.). (1985a). *Human abilities: An information processing approach.* New York: Freeman.

Sternberg, R. J. (1985b). *Beyond IQ: A triarchic theory of human intelligence.* New York: Cambridge University Press.

Sternberg, R. J. (1986). Identifying the gifted through IQ: Why a little bit of knowledge is a dangerous thing. *Roeper Review, 8,* 143–147.

Sternberg, R. J. (Ed.). (1988). *The nature of creativity: Contemporary psychological perspectives.* New York: Cambridge University Press.

Sternberg, R. J. (1993). Rocky's back again: A review of the WISC–III. *Journal of Psychological Assessment, Monograph Series, Advances in Psychoeducational Assessment, Wechsler Intelligence Scale for Children: Third edition,* 161–164.

Sternberg, S. (1966). High-speed scanning in human memory. *Science, 153,* 652–654.

Steyaert, J. P., & Snyder, J. F. (1985). Seating arrangement and state anxiety as related to performance on Digit Span and Digit Symbol of the *Wechsler Adult Intelligence Scale. Psychological Reports, 57,* 807–812.

Strang, H. R., Bridgeman, B., & Carrico, M. F. (1974). Effects of "game" versus "test" task definition for third grade children on three subtests of the Wechsler Intelligence Scale for Children. *Journal of Educational Measurement, 11,* 125–128.

Strupp, H. H., & Binder, J. L. (1984). *Psychotherapy in a new key: A guide to time-limited dynamic psychotherapy.* New York: Basic Books.

Sturgis, D., Verstegen, J., Randolph, D., & Garvin, R. (1980). Professional psychology internships. *Professional Psychology, 11,* 567–573.

Sweet, R., & Ringness, T. (1971). Variations in the test performance of referred boys of differing racial and socioeconomic backgrounds as a function of feedback or monetary reinforcement. *Journal of School Psychology, 9,* 399–409.

Tabachnick, B. G. (1979). Test scatter on the WISC–R. *Journal of Learning Disabilities, 12,* 626–628.

Talley, J. L. (1986). Memory in learning disabled children: Digit Span and the Rey Auditory Verbal Learning Test. *Archives of Clinical Neuropsychology, 1*(4), 315–322.

Taylor, H. G. (1988). Learning disabilities. In E. J. Mash & L. G. Terdal (Eds.), *Behavioral assessment of childhood disorders* (2nd ed., pp. 402–450). New York: Guilford Press.

Taylor, H. G. (1989). Learning disabilities. In E. J. Mash, & R. A. Barkley (Eds.), *Treatment of childhood disorders* (pp. 347–382). New York: Guilford Press.

Taylor, R. L., & Ziegler, E. W. (1987). Comparison of the first principal factor on the WISC–R across ethnic groups. *Educational and Psychological Measurement, 47,* 691–694.

Tellegen, A., & Briggs, P. F. (1967). Old wine in new skins: Grouping Wechsler subtests into new scales. *Journal of Consulting Psychology, 31*(5), 499–506.

Teeter, P. A., & Smith, P. L. (1993). WISC–III and WJ–R predictive and discriminant validity for students with severe emotional disturbance. *Journal of Psychoeducational Assessment, Monograph series, Advances in Psychoeducational Assessment, Wechsler Intelligence Scale for Children: Third edition,* 114–124.

Telzrow, C. F. (1989). Neuropsychological applications of educational and psychological tests. In C. R. Reynolds & E. Fletcher-Janzen (Eds.), *Handbook of clinical child neuropsychology* (pp. 227–245). New York: Plenum Press.

Terrel, F., Taylor, J., & Terrell, S. (1978). Effects of type of social reinforcer on the intelligence test performance of lower class black children. *Journal of Consulting and Clinical Psychology, 46,* 1538–1539.

The Psychological Corporation. (1992a). *Wechsler Individual Achievement Test.* San Antonio, TX: Author.

The Psychological Corporation. (1992b). *Scoring Assistant for the Wechsler Scales* [Computer software]. San Antonio, TX: Author.

The Psychological Corporation. (1994). *WISC–III Writer: The interpretive software system* [Computer software]. San Antonio, TX: Author.

Thompson, R. J., Jr. (1980). The diagnostic utility of the WISC–R measures with children referred to a developmental evaluation center. *Journal of Consulting and Clinical Psychology, 48,* 440–447.

Thorndike, R. L. (1992, March). *Intelligence tests: What we have and what we should have.* Paper presented at the meeting of the National Association of School Psychologists, Nashville, TN.

Thurstone, L. L. (1938). Primary mental abilities. *Psychometric Monographs, No. 1.* Chicago: University of Chicago Press.

Thurstone, L. L. (1947). *Multiple factor analysis.* Chicago: University of Chicago Press.

Treffinger, D. J., & Renzulli, J. S. (1986). Giftedness as potential for creative productivity: Transcending IQ scores. *Roeper Review, 8,* 150–154.

Tuttle, K. S. C., & Smith, III, R. B. (1993). Ten important things to keep in mind when buying assessment software. In B. Schlosser & K. Moreland (Eds.), *Taming technology: Issues, strategies and resources for the mental health practitioner* (pp. 90–92). Phoenix, AZ: Division of Independent Practice of the American Psychological Association.

Udin, H., Olswanger, G., & Vogler, R. E. (1974). Evidence for a spatial gradient of avoidance behavior in humans. *Perceptual and Motor Skills, 39,* 275–278.

U.S. Office of Education. (1968). *First annual report, National Advisory Committee on Handicapped Children.* Washington, DC: U.S. Department of Health, Education and Welfare.

U.S. Public Law 94-142 (The Education for All Handicapped Children Act). (1977, December 29). *Federal Register,* pp. 65082–65085.

Vance, H. B. (1978). Analysis of cognitive abilities for mentally retarded children on the WISC–R. *Psychological Record, 28,* 391–397.

Vance, F. H., Blaha, J., Wallbrown, H., & Engin, A. (1975). The hierarchical factor structure of the Wechsler Intelligence Scale for Children-Revised. *Journal of Psychology, 89,* 223–235.

Vance, H. B., & Fuller, G. B. (1983). Discriminant function analysis of LD/BD children's scores on the WISC–R. *Journal of Clinical Psychology, 39*(5), 749–753.

Vance, H. B., & Singer, M. G. (1979). Recategorization of the WISC–R subtest scaled scores for learning disabled children. *Journal of Learning Disabilities, 12,* 487–491.

Vance, H. B., & Wallbrown, F. H. (1977). Hierarchical factor structure of the WISC–R for referred children and adolescents. *Psychological Reports, 41,* 699–702.

Vance, H. B., & Wallbrown, F. H. (1978). The structure of intelligence for black children: A hierarchical approach. *Psychological Record, 28,* 31–39.

Vance, H. B., Wallbrown, F. H., & Freemont, T. S. (1978). The abilities of retarded students: Further evidence concerning the stimulus trace factor. *Journal of Psychology, 100,* 77–82.

Van der Kolk, B. (Ed.). (1987). *Psychological trauma.* Washington, DC: American Psychiatric Press.

Van Hagen, J., & Kaufman, A. S. (1975). Factor analysis of the WISC–R for a group of mentally retarded children and adolescents. *Journal of Consulting and Clinical Psychology, 43,* 661–667.

Vernon, P. A. (Ed.). (1987). *Speed of information processing and intelligence.* Norwood, NJ: Ablex.

Vernon, P. A. (1990). The use of biological measures to estimate behavioral intelligence. *Educational Psychologist, 25,* 293–304.

Vernon, P. A., & Kantor, L. (1986). Reaction time correlations with intelligence test scores obtained under either timed or untimed conditions. *Intelligence, 10,* 315–330.

Vernon, P. A., & Mori, M. (1992). Intelligence, reaction times, and peripheral nerve conduction velocity. *Intelligence, 16,* 273–288.

Wade, T. C., & Baker, T. B. (1977). Opinions and use of psychological tests: A survey of clinical psychologists. *American Psychologist, 32,* 874–882.

Wapner, J. G., & Connor, K. (1986). The role of defensiveness in cognitive impulsivity. *Child Development, 57,* 1370–1374.

Warren, S., & Brown, W. (1972). Examiner scoring errors on individual tests. *Psychology in the Schools, 10,* 118–122.

Wechsler, D. (1939). *Measurement of adult intelligence.* Baltimore: Williams & Wilkins.

Wechsler, D. (1946). *The Wechsler-Bellevue Intelligence Scale, Form II.* New York: The Psychological Corporation.

Wechsler, D. (1949). *Manual for the Wechsler Intelligence Scale for Children.* New York: The Psychological Corporation.

Wechsler, D. (1955). *Manual for the Wechsler Adult Intelligence Scale.* New York: The Psychological Corporation.

Wechsler, D. (1958). *The measurement and appraisal of adult intelligence* (4th ed.). Baltimore: Williams & Wilkins.

Wechsler, D. (1967). *Manual for the Wechsler Preschool and Primary Scale of Intelligence.* San Antonio, TX: The Psychological Corporation.

Wechsler, D. (1974). *Manual for the Wechsler Intelligence Scale for Children-Revised.* San Antonio, TX: The Psychological Corporation.

Wechsler, D. (1989). *Manual for the Wechsler Preschool and Primary Scale of Intelligence-Revised.* San Antonio, TX: The Psychological Corporation.

Wechsler, D. (1991). *Manual for the Wechsler Intelligence Scale for Children-Third edition.* San Antonio, TX: The Psychological Corporation.

Weinberg, R. A. (1989). Intelligence and IQ: Landmark issues and great debates. *American Psychologist, 44,* 98–104.

Weiner, J. (1985). Teachers' comprehension of psychological reports. *Psychology in the Schools, 22,* 60–64.

Weiner, J. (1987). Factors affecting educators' comprehension of psychological reports. *Psychology in the Schools, 24,* 116–126.

Weise, M. J., Bush, B. R., Newman, R. M., Benes, K. M., & Witt, J. C. (1986). A rose by any other name: The influence of jargon on teacher perceptions of psychological reports. *Journal of Psychoeducational Assessment, 4,* 291–298.

Weiss, D. J. (1985). Adaptive testing by computer. *Journal of Consulting and Clinical Psychology, 53,* 774–789.

Weiss, L. G., Prifitera, A., & Roid, G. (1993). The WISC–III and the fairness of predicting achievement across ethnic and gender groups. *Journal of Psychoeducational Assessment, Monograph series, Advances in Psychoeducational Assessment, Wechsler Intelligence Scale for Children: Third edition,* 35–42.

Weist, M. D., Finney, J. W., & Ollendick, T. H. (1992). Cognitive biases in child behavior therapy. *The Behavior Therapist, 15,* 249–252.

Weller, R. A., & Weller, E. B. (1986). Tricyclic antidepressants in prepubertal depressed children: Review of the literature. *Hillside Journal of Clinical Psychiatry, 8,* 46–55.

Wheeler, P. T., Adams, G. R., & Nielsen, E. C. (1987). Effect of a child's physical attractiveness on verbal scoring of the *Wechsler Intelligence Scale for Children (Revised)* and personality attributions. *Journal of General Psychology, 114,* 109–116.

Whipple, S. C., Parker, E. S., & Noble, E. P. (1988). An atypical neurocognitive profile in alcoholic fathers and their sons. *Journal of Studies on Alcohol, 49*(3), 240–244.

Wielkowicz, R. M. (1990). Interpreting low scores on the WISC–R third factor: It's more than distractibility. *Psychological Assessment: A Journal of Consulting and Clinical Psychology, 2,* 91–97.

Wigfield, A., & Eccles, J. S. (1989). Test anxiety in elementary and secondary school students. *Educational Psychologist, 24,* 159–183.

Wilkinson, G. S. (1993). *The wide range achievement test administration manual* [WRAT-3]. Wilmington, DE: Wide Range.

Williams, J., Zolten, A. J., Rickert, V. I., Spence, G. T., & Ashcraft, E. W. (1993). Use of nonverbal tests to screen for writing dysfluency in school-age children. *Perceptual and Motor Skills, 76*(3, Pt 1), 803–809.

Wilson, H., & Staton, R. D. (1984). Neuropsychological changes in children associated with tricyclic antidepressant therapy. *International Journal of Neuroscience, 24,* 307–312.

Wilson, L. R., & Cone, T. (1984). The regression equation method of determining academic discrepancy. *Journal of School Psychology, 22,* 95–110.

Witmer, J. M., Bornstein, A. V., & Dunham, R. M. (1971). The effects of verbal approval and disapproval upon the performance of third and fourth grade children on four subtests of the Wechsler Intelligence Scale for Children. *Journal of School Psychology, 9,* 347–356.

Woodcock, R. W. (1987). *Woodcock Reading Mastery Tests, Revised, Examiner's manual.* Circle Pines, MN: American Guidance Service.

Woodcock, R. W. (1990). Theoretical foundations of the WJ–R measures of cognitive ability. *Journal of Psychoeducational Assessment, 8,* 231–258.

Woodcock, R. W., & Johnson, M. B. (1977). *Woodcock-Johnson Psycho-Educational Battery-Revised.* Allen, TX: DLM.

Wright, B. D., & Stone, M. H. (1979). *Best test design.* Chicago: MESA Press.

Zachary, R. A. (1990). Wechsler's intelligence scales: Theoretical and practical considerations. *Journal of Psychoeducational Assessment, 8,* 276–289.

Zarske, J. A., & Moore, C. L. (1982). Recategorized WISC–R scores of learning disabled Navajo Indian children. *Psychology in the Schools, 19,* 156–159.

Zarske, J. A., Moore, C. L., & Peterson, J. D. (1981). WISC–R factor structures for diagnosed learning disabled Navajo and Papago children. *Psychology in the Schools, 18,* 402–407.

Zimet, S. G., Zimet, G. D., Farley, G. K., & Adler, S. S. (1994). Comparisons of intellectual performance among children with psychiatric disorders. *Journal of Clinical Psychology, 50,* 131–137.

Zimmerman, I. L., & Woo-Sam, J. M. (1985). Clinical applications. In B. B. Wolman (Ed.), *The handbook of intelligence* (pp. 873–898). New York: John Wiley & Sons.

Zingale, S. A., & Smith, M. D. (1978). WISC–R patterns for learning disabled children at three SES levels. *Psychology in the Schools, 15,* 199–204.

Zins, J. E., & Barnett, D. W. (1983). Report writing: Legislative, ethical, and professional challenges. *Journal of School Psychology, 21,* 219–227.

AUTHOR INDEX

SUBJECT INDEX

A

ACID/S profile, 250–256, 301–302, 321
ADHD, 252–254, 260, 355
American Psychological Association, 7
antianxiety drugs, 363–365
antidepressant drugs, 359–362
antimanic drugs, 362–363
antipsychotic drugs, 356–359
applications of the WISC–III, 36
aspects of the test situation, 129–133
assessment, steps in, 77–78

B

Bannatyne, 256–262, 322
battery, xi
behavioral observation, 135–140
belief/s, ix, x, 381, 382
bias and the Wechsler Scales, 339–349
    bias in construct validity, 342–345
    bias in content validity, 341–342
    bias in predictive or criterion-related
        validity, 345–347
    test bias and the WISC–III, 347–349
biological measures, 5–6
boldface, 294
brief term psychotherapy, 106–108

C

Changes in Performance Subtests, 33–36
Changes in Verbal Subtests, 30–32
characteristics of the examinee and his or her
    role, 127–129
characteristics of the examiner and her or his
    role, 121–126
child abuse, 383–389
Child Test Behavior Observation Form, 135

child psychopharmacology, 351–352
computers and the WISC–III, 367–372
conceptual model, 103
concluding comment, 365–366, 381–390
confidentiality, 16–17
consent, 17
context/s, ix, 15, 292, 381
continuum, 98
creativity, 389
critical thinking, 289–290

D

design features of psychological reports,
    293–295
development of the WISC–III, 2–28
differences between individual subtest scores,
    69–70
differences between IQ and Index scores,
    66–67
differences between a single subtest scaled
    score and an average of subtest score,
    67–69
dual relationships, 17

E

ethical and professional issues regarding
    computer-assisted assessment, 368–370
*Ethical Principles of Psychology and Code of
    Conduct,* 7
Ethics and the WISC–III, 7–19
extrapyramidal syndromes, 357–358

F

factor analysis, 55–60, 245–250
fluid-crystallized model, 262–268, 323, 302–303,
    323